ETHICAL CHALLENGES I[
PSYCHOLOGY AND CYBERP

Our technologies are progressively developing into algorithmic devices that seamlessly interface with digital personhood. This text discusses the ways in which technology is increasingly becoming a part of personhood and the resulting ethical issues. It extends upon the framework for a brain-based cyberpsychology outlined by the author's earlier book *Cyberpsychology and the Brain: The Interaction of Neuroscience and Affective Computing* (Cambridge, 2017). Using this framework, Thomas D. Parsons investigates the ethical issues involved in cyberpsychology research and praxes, which emerge in algorithmically coupled people and technologies. The ethical implications of these ideas are important as we consider the cognitive enhancements that can be afforded by our technologies. If people are intimately linked to their technologies, then removing or damaging the technology could be tantamount to a personal attack. On the other hand, algorithmic devices may threaten autonomy and privacy. This book reviews these and other issues.

THOMAS D. PARSONS is Director of the NetDragon Digital Research Centre and the Computational Neuropsychology and Simulation (CNS) Lab at University of North Texas (UNT). He is full Professor at UNT and a clinical neuropsychologist. In addition to his patents for eHarmony.com's Matching System, he has invented and validated several virtual environments.

ETHICAL CHALLENGES IN DIGITAL PSYCHOLOGY AND CYBERPSYCHOLOGY

THOMAS D. PARSONS

University of North Texas

CAMBRIDGE
UNIVERSITY PRESS

University Printing House, Cambridge CB2 8BS, United Kingdom

One Liberty Plaza, 20th Floor, New York, NY 10006, USA

477 Williamstown Road, Port Melbourne, VIC 3207, Australia

314–321, 3rd Floor, Plot 3, Splendor Forum, Jasola District Centre,
New Delhi – 110025, India

79 Anson Road, #06–04/06, Singapore 079906

Cambridge University Press is part of the University of Cambridge.

It furthers the University's mission by disseminating knowledge in the pursuit of
education, learning, and research at the highest international levels of excellence.

www.cambridge.org
Information on this title: www.cambridge.org/9781108428781
DOI: 10.1017/9781108553384

© Cambridge University Press 2019

First published 2019

Printed in the United Kingdom by TJ International Ltd. Padstow Cornwall

A catalogue record for this publication is available from the British Library.

Library of Congress Cataloging-in-Publication Data
NAMES: Parsons, Thomas D., author.
TITLE: Ethical challenges in digital psychology and cyberpsychology / Thomas D. Parsons,
University of North Texas.
DESCRIPTION: Cambridge, United Kingdom ; New York, NY : Cambridge University Press,
2019. | Includes bibliographical references and index.
IDENTIFIERS: LCCN 2019010901 | ISBN 9781108428781 (hardback : alk. paper)
SUBJECTS: LCSH: Psychologists – Professional ethics. | Psychology – Moral and ethical
aspects. | Internet in psychotherapy. | Virtual reality therapy.
CLASSIFICATION: LCC BF76.4 .P37 2019 | DDC 150–dc23
LC record available at https://lccn.loc.gov/2019010901

ISBN 978-1-108-42878-1 Hardback
ISBN 978-1-108-45103-1 Paperback

I dedicate this book to my virtuous wife, Valerie. "O ye gods, Render me worthy of this noble wife!" (Shakespeare's Julius Caesar*). She believes in me, and so I continue.*

Contents

Figures

Tables

Preface

Our habit of off-loading as much as possible of our cognitive tasks into the environment itself – extruding our minds (that is, our mental projects and activities) into the surrounding world, where a host of peripheral devices we construct can store, process and re-represent our meanings, streamlining, enhancing, and protecting the processes of transformation that are our thinking. This widespread practice of off-loading releases us from the limitations of our animal brains.

Dennett (1996, pp. 134–135)

My iPhone is not my tool, or at least it is not wholly my tool. Parts of it have become parts of me. This is the thesis of the extended mind: when parts of the environment are coupled to the brain in the right way, they become parts of the mind.

Chalmers (2011, p. x)

There is a relatively seamless interaction between brain and algorithm such that a person perceives of the algorithm as being a bona fide extension of a person's mind.

Reiner & Nagel (2017, p. 110)

While cyberpsychology (also known as digital psychology) is often approached as a study of persons using technologies as tools, technologies are increasingly becoming extensions of persons. As can be seen in the quotes above, our technologies are progressively developing into algorithmic devices that seamlessly interface with digital personhood. Advances in cyberpsychology stimuli, measures, platforms, and outcomes often result from studies aimed at investigating the impact technologies have on social, cognitive, and affective processes. As a developing field, cyberpsychology texts have historically emphasized general psychological phenomena associated with or impacted by emerging technologies. Often these texts will reflect subject matter found in computer science, communication theory, graphic and industrial design disciplines, and the social sciences. An unfortunate limitation of these texts is that they rarely discuss the ways in which technologies are increasingly part of personhood or the ethical issues that result. Along with rapid developments in cyberpsychology, there is an increasing need for scientists and practitioners to grapple with the ethical implications of cyberpsychology tools, discoveries, and the algorithmic devices that act as technologies of the extended mind.

The ethical implications of these ideas are important as we consider the cognitive enhancements that can be afforded by our technologies. If persons are intimately linked to their technologies, then removing or damaging the technology could be tantamount to a bodily attack. If certain kinds of cognitive processes involve technologies (ranging from smart-phones for navigation to deep brain stimulation for alleviating neurological disorders), then removing these technologies could be as devastating as a brain lesion. While this is a rather positive view of technologies, there are also ethical conflicts due to threats to autonomy and privacy. These threats may come from algorithms developed by companies interested in manip-ulating persons who are coupled with technologies extending their minds (Reiner & Nagel, 2017; Nagel et al., 2016). These and other ethical issues are reviewed in this book.

This book is the second volume of a planned trilogy. While this book is separate from my book *Cyberpsychology and the Brain: The Interaction of Neuroscience and Affective Computing* (Parsons, 2017; Cambridge University Press), the two are complementary. In the first volume, I proposed a framework for integrating neuroscience and cyberpsychology for the study of social, cognitive, and affective processes and the neural systems that support them. Given this brain-based cyberpsychology approach, cyberpsychology can be understood as a branch of psychology that studies (1) the neurocognitive, affective, and social aspects of humans interacting with technology and (2) affective computing aspects of humans interacting with devices/systems that incorporate computation. As such, a cyberpsychologist working from a brain-based cyberpsychological frame-work studies both the ways in which persons make use of devices and the neurocognitive processes, motivations, intentions, behavioral outcomes, and effects of online and offline use of technology. Four themes emerged from the brain-based cyberpsychology framework: (1) dual process models (automatic and controlled processing) can inform cyberpsychological research; (2) affective (i.e., emotions), cognitive, and social neurosciences offer insights into cyberpsychology; (3) large-scale brain networks and frontal subcortical circuits are involved in human–technology interactions; and (4) technologies can extend mental processes. Using this framework, this second volume investigates the ethical issues involved in cyberpsychology research and praxes, which emerge in algorithmically coupled persons and technologies.

Scope and Audience

This book was written for psychologists who have an interest in ethical issues found in digital psychology and cyberpsychology. Throughout there was an attempt to proffer ethical considerations using examples of persons coupled with advanced technologies. It is important to note that the first few chapters of this book (i.e., Chapters 1–4) are aimed at developing a framework for considering cyberpsychology ethics in terms of human–technology interfaces. This book aims to consider ethical issues of interest to cyberpsychologists related to autonomy (i.e., free will or agency); beneficence (i.e., mercy, kindness, and charity); nonmaleficence (i.e., do no harm); justice (i.e., fair distribution of benefits and burdens); and so forth. Given the growing realization that cyberpsychology (today and even more so in the future) is more than just a study of the impact of technologies on the person's psyche, this book aims to also consider ethical challenges that emerge in our increasingly digital and algorithmic existence.

Moreover, this book can be used as a teaching tool for graduate students in digital psychology and cyberpsychology. It could serve as one of the primary texts for courses on ethical concerns found in digital psychology and cyberpsychology. Alternatively, it could serve as an ancillary text for ethical issues in various psychology courses. Importantly, this text allows the instructor to have a single reference for locating most of the primary ethical concerns facing cyberpsychologists. This is significant because such issues are currently only found in various articles and book chapters. Furthermore, the ethical issues of some cyberpsychology areas found in this book have not been fully examined in the literature. This book critically examines the ethical aspects of cyberpsychology data for assessing a person's cognitive and affective processing of information, memories, truthfulness, culpability, and the probability of future ethical behaviors. Furthermore, the contents of this book consider the personal and societal consequences of the use of various technologies. With each topic considered, the book aims to enhance readers' understandings of ethical quandaries and to help them think critically about the ways in which cyberpsychologists may go about addressing them.

Preface

Organization of This Book

To provide a framework for ethical considerations in a digital age of increasing integration with our technologies, this book is divided into four parts.

Part I introduces ethical approaches in general and a framework for ethical considerations for technologies of the extended mind. While some areas receive brief discussion for the sake of completeness and continuity, other areas, such as ethical implications of a brain-based cyberpsychology, receive greater attention.

- Chapter 1, "Cyberpsychology Theory and Praxes: Ethical and Methodological Considerations," sets the stage for the rest of the book and attempts to place the discussion of Cyberpsychology ethics in line with my previously proposed brain-based cyberpsychology framework for integrating neuroscience and cyberpsychology for the study of social, cognitive, and affective processes and the neural systems that support them (see Parsons, 2017).

- Following Chapter 1, which introduces components of this framework, Chapter 2, "Ethical Approaches to Cyberpsychology," provides the reader with an overview of principlist (e.g., autonomy, beneficence, nonmaleficence, and justice) and traditional normative ethical approaches (e.g., deontological, teleological utilitarianism, social contracts, and virtue ethics). In addition to the traditional normative ethical perspectives, this chapter considers the recently developed metaphysical "information ethics" theory of Luciano Floridi. While Floridi developed his theory of information ethics to complement deontological, utilitarian, contractual, and virtue ethics, information ethics is unlike more traditional ethical theories because it was developed with reference to the Information Age and its connection to digital information (Floridi, 1999).

- Chapter 3, "Digital and Extended Selves in Cyberspace," offers a consideration of the continuity of persons with their technologies. Here there is a discussion of Clark and Chalmers's (1998) hypothesis of the extended mind and the algorithmic devices that can be considered technologies of the extended mind. To a large extent, this chapter is key in that it lays out the framework for an ethics of brain-based cyberpsychology. Following the extended mind thesis, there is a strong prima facie case for ethical concerns accompanying various means of enhancing cognitive performance.

- Chapter 4, "Neuroethics and the Future of Cyberpsychology," concludes Part I with a discussion of the ways in which the ethical framework can be applied to neuroethical considerations. While some approaches to technologies emphasize ethical principles, neuroethics focuses on the neural substrates subserving cognitive processes. In Chapter 4, emphasis is placed on combing these approaches via an argument that mental processes include not only brains but also technologies and even environmental social structures. This allows for the ethical concerns of cyberpsychologists, educational neuroscientists, and neuroethicists to extend far more widely than has previously been recognized. Given the extended mind thesis, a number of ethical concerns about using technologies can be seen to be neuroethical issues. In making decisions about how cyberpsychologists structure research environments and employ technologies, decisions can be made about the ways in which technologies of the extended mind are employed, and such decisions must be informed by neuroethical thinking.

In Part II, "Ethical Cyberpsychology Research and Interventions with Special Populations," there is a discussion of ethical considerations when working with both at-risk populations (e.g., pediatric, geriatric) and clinical populations. In this section, the framework found in Part I is applied to the ethical concerns that may arise when performing research studies and interventions with sensitive populations. Moreover, there is a consideration of the increasing automations found in smart technologies that extend cognitive processes. There is a tradeoff between the personalization that comes with algorithmic devices and the protection of autonomy and privacy.

- In Chapter 5, "Cyberlearning and Ethical Considerations for Using Technology with Children," there is an introduction to cyberlearning, educational neuroscience, and the ethical issues involved in research and interventions with children. Given the growth of smart classrooms and technologies for children, there is an increasing need for ethical approaches that take into account technologies of the student's extended mind. On the techno-optimistic side, computational algorithms allow for a personalized educational approach that could maximize learning for each student as well as provide information that can be generalized to large populations via collaborative knowledgebases (big data and informatics). On the other, more techno-pessimistic, side, there are concerns about automated changes that remove the control found in many current approaches.

- Chapter 6, "Cyberpsychology, Aging, and Gerontechnology," looks specifically at ethical issues in gerontechnological research and practice. Herein, there is a discussion of the ways in which ethical principles can be extended to develop an approach to ethics that emphasizes an extended mind perspective found in Part I. Given the extended mind thesis, there is a robust prima facie rationale for ethical issues related to various smart homes and related smart technologies. The extended mind thesis allows the gerontechnologist to consider ethical concerns related to smart technologies that integrate with the older adults that use them. In making decisions about how gerontologists and designers structure smart home environments and employ gerontechnologies, decisions can be made about the ways in which gerontechnologies of the extended mind are employed, and such decisions must be informed by ethical thinking.

- In Chapter 7, "Problematic Internet Use, Online Gambling, Smartphones, and Video Games," we move into the concerns that arise in the problematic uses of the algorithmic devices. The Internet is increasingly discussed as a new type of cognitive ecology that provides almost constant access to digital information that increasingly extends our cognitive processes. As a result, there is a need to take care not to overpathologize behaviors. Instead, it may be better to consider these behaviors as on a spectrum (i.e., cyber-spectrum disorders). This chapter also discusses the importance of the ethical design of technologies that may lead to legitimate cases of problematic uses of the Internet, as technologies such as online gambling, smartphones, and video games are often designed in ways to reward use.

- Finally, Chapter 8, "Telepsychology and the Ethical Delivery of e-Therapy," looks at several guidelines and considerations for mental health provision in the digital era. The chapter also includes discussions of the importance of proper use of technology media, reflections on pertinent legal and ethical issues, approaches to maintaining secure electronic communications, and strategies for maintaining boundaries. There is an emphasis on considerations needed before clinicians start using technologies in clinical practice and research. Mental health service providers in the digital age need to be mindful of privacy standards, confidentiality, and security. This chapter also reviews these issues related to using technologies of the extended mind for both therapeutic aids to poor health and neurocognitive enhancement of healthy individuals.

In Part III, "Ethical Issues in Social Media and Internet Research," the book turns a light onto ethical concerns in social media research. This is certainly an area of major concern for most cyberpsychologists. In fact, some may go so far as to assert that the primary area of interest for the cyberpsychologist is research into the ways in which persons connect, act, and interact on the Internet and within online social networks. Part III is divided into three sections.

- Part III starts with Chapter 9, "Social Media Ethics Section 1: Facebook, Twitter, and Google – Oh My!," wherein the reader is presented with an exploration of the ethical scandals plaguing the technology giants (e.g., Facebook, Google, and Twitter), which lead to General Data Protection Regulations. Internet service providers such as Facebook, Google, and Twitter are expected more and more to act as good citizens, by bringing their goals in line with societal needs and supporting the rights of their users. These expectations reflect the ethical principles that should guide the actions of Internet service providers in mature information societies. In this chapter, there is consideration of some of the ethical issues found in social media in general, as well as ethical practices of these large technology firms specifically.
- Chapter 10, "Social Media Ethics Section 2: Ethical Research with Social Media," presents discussions of a range of topics where ethical questions for research using social media occur: recruitment, privacy, and anonymity; consent; terms of service; and data usage. In general, the user should be able to limit the sharing of personal information. According to the restricted access/limited control theory, informational privacy does not occur without restrictions on the dissemination of personal information and without some control (as warranted by the particular situation). This chapter also considers various perspectives on whether a user's personal information should be considered as private or as publicly available. The use of the World Wide Web has given rise to worldwide sociocultural transformations that include the extension of each user's cognitive and affective processes. As a result, this chapter also looks at the boundaries between physically internalized cognitive processes and extended cognitive processes in the virtual world that are as tenable as the related distinctions between private and public domains of user data. Given this cyberization, ethical guidelines essential for social media research need to be reexamined.

• Finally, in Chapter 11, "Social Media Ethics Section 3: Digital Citizenship," there is a consideration of the ways in which the new Internet ecology affects ethical considerations about relationships. Part of the discussion is related to issues of being able to connect. This leads to a reflection on the digital divide and various differences in access (e.g., differences related to age, gender, ethnicity, economy, disability). While a younger-aged person in a developed country may find that advanced technologies result in digital selves with extended cognition, an older-aged person on the other side of the digital divide may experience fewer changes to self and community. The chapter also reflects on Luciano Floridi's thoughts about the ethical issues found in the digital divide and their relation to the nature of the information society. The applications of "information ethics" to the digital divide are apparent in Floridi's information ethics. Moreover, Floridi's information ethics include ethical arguments against unjustifiable closures or reductions (in quantity, quality, or value) to the infosphere. Also, in this chapter, the reader will find a discussion of Internet dating and online relations. Of particular note are the ethical concerns from practices of some online dating platforms and their claims. Next there is a consideration of ethical issues for those who have connected. How are we to relate once connected? Here there is a discussion of issues related to cyberbullying and hacking.

In Part IV, "Applied Ethical Considerations," there is an exploration of virtual reality (VR) and video games. Each of these areas deserves its own chapter. Neither fit within earlier parts of the book. Moreover, the use of both VR and video games is increasing dramatically and there is little sign that this rapid increase will cease.

• In Chapter 12, "Virtual Reality Ethics," there is an emphasis on describing some of the ethical concerns that may arise from research, clinical applications, and even personal use of VR and related technologies. Throughout the chapter there are attempts to offer straightforward recommendations for optimal outcomes and minimal risks. It aims to consider the ethical considerations found in the literature, as well as the ethical implications for a brain-based cyberpsychology in the digital era. The chapter begins with a brief overview of VR for use in cyberpsychology. This introduction includes a discussion of models of presence that reflect findings from the human neurosciences. This is followed by an examination of the risks in VR research, as well as recommendations for conducting VR. Finally, the chapter concludes with an exploration of the uses of the virtual environment for investigating ethical dilemmas.

- In Chapter 13, "Video Games, Video Gamers, and the Ethics of Video Game Design," there is an exploration of both the ethical aspects of video games and the ways in which ethical dilemmas are represented in video games. From an ethical perspective, a common approach to assessing the moral worth and impacts of video games is to consider the content of the video games and the relations between playing a video game with that content and behavior in the real world. These video game contents are judged by the contamination thesis: If video game contents are harmful, surely we are obliged to prevent them from spilling over from the virtual world into the real world? Following this thesis, assessment of the morality of decisions and actions in video games are carried out relative to the imagined decisions and actions taking place in the real world. Also, in this chapter, attempts have been made to consider video games in light of some of the main approaches to moral philosophy, as found in Kantian deontological ethics, utilitarianism, and virtue ethics. Finally, there is a discussion of the ways in which video game avatars can be understood as technologies of the extended mind. As such, the relations that develop between the game player and the extended avatar can develop to a point that they are coupled in complex feedback (including feed-forward and feed-around) loops among brain, controllers, and the digital world in which the player's avatar experiences the video game.

Acknowledgments

First, I want to express my appreciation to David Repetto and the rest of the talented editorial staff at Cambridge University Press for their thoroughness and good nature throughout the production of this book.

Thanks also to my students and fellow colleagues. Of note is one of my students who went on to become member of the Computer Science faculty at University of Texas, Timothy (Fred) McMahan. In addition to being an amazing thinker, programmer, and collaborator, he has become a close friend. I should also mention my appreciation for colleagues from my time as a research scientist and faculty member at the Institute for Creative Technologies at the University of Southern California (USC). One of my favorite collaborators at USC was Patrick Kenny. We spent countless hours in Marina del Rey and Venice Beach discussing neuroscience, artificial intelligence, and what it means to be a person in this ever increasingly digital world. During the writing of this book, I spent valuable time with Patrick in Malibu, California. In one drive up the coast with him, I found direction for this book and owe the overall gestalt to him. We also saw dolphins! Thank you Patrick for sharing your amazing brain and for being such a special friend. Another great collaborator and friend is Brendan Rooney at University College Dublin. During travels around England, Wales, and, of course, Ireland, we discussed every possible topic. We also spent time (in what used to be called Parsonstown, Ireland) in a castle! Bren's positive outlook, Irish charm, and enthusiasm for social cognition in media are infectious. I learned a great deal from him about how cognitive and emotional processes interact in the context of media, arts, and entertainment. Thank you Bren. One more collaborator and friend stands out, Tyler Duffield at Oregon Health & Science University. Each week Ty takes time out of his busy schedule as a professor and neuropsychologist to talk with me about computational neuropsychology. Those talks are always a highlight of my week and I look forward to our continued discussions and collaborative projects. To all of these special colleagues and friends, thank you for your thoughtful considerations of the topics found in this book and for your encouragement.

I wish to acknowledge the significant thinkers who have impacted my thoughts about ethics and cyberpsychology. When I was working on my first graduate degree (in Philosophy of Religion), two of my professors, Dr. Al Dueck and Dr. Nancey Murphy, tutored me in the virtue ethics of the Scottish moral philosopher Alasdair MacIntyre. I remember reading MacIntyre's (1985) landmark study in moral theory, *After Virtue*, with Al Dueck and fellow student Neil Stafford. To this day, I feel most impacted by MacIntyre's allegory of a postapocalyptic scenario that no longer had advanced scientific knowledge. MacIntyre was alluding to Walter M. Miller, Jr.'s (1959/1997) science-fiction novel *A Canticle for Leibowitz* to develop his allegory. I read both books again as I prepared the current book. In the allegory, MacIntyre asks the reader to consider what the sciences would look like following reassembly from the fragments of scientific knowledge that endured after the apocalypse. This impact of this simple allegory has endured in my mind. While it is intriguing, I am not sure that it resonates as well with the rapid advances in our increasingly digital existence. Today, we are increasingly integrated with our technologies and they act as extensions of persons. So, while I do appreciate MacIntyre's allegory, I am less and less convinced by the implications (the needed return to Aristotelian virtue theory) in today's digital world.

That said, there are other aspects of MacIntyre that we discussed that need mention. MacIntyre contends that there are three paradigmatic character-types of modernity: "the Rich Aesthete, the Manager, and the Therapist" (1985, p. 29). We would talk for hours about these proposed character-types of modernity, virtue ethics, communitarianism, and the implications of MacIntyre's writing for modernity. Each of them (MacIntyre, Dueck, Murphy, and Stafford) had a robust impact on my thinking and development.

Interestingly enough, as I was researching some of MacIntyre's thoughts on "the Rich Aesthete, the Manager, and the Therapist," I came across Richard Rorty's (1991a, 1991b, 1998) philosophical papers and was immediately fascinated by his dismissal of modern epistemology. While my book on ethics and cyberpsychology is quite different from one Rorty would have written, I find his pragmatism attractive and still see merit in his arguments against universally valid answers to moral questions. With Rorty, I believe that MacIntyre is correct in viewing contemporary moral discourse as a perplexing and inconsistent mixture of concepts. Also with Rorty, however, I disagree with MacIntyre's notion that Aristotelian ways of thinking can be revived to make our moral discourse coherent. Instead (again like Rorty), I feel that ethical discourse in the digital era may be made more coherent via a removal of the last vestiges of those ways of thinking. Finally, Rorty is open to a culture dominated by "the Rich Aesthete, the Manager, and the Therapist" as long as everyone gets to choose whether they will be an aesthete, manager, or therapist.

MacIntyre's allegory of a postapocalyptic world after the loss of scientific knowledge suggests that the traditional normative ethical approaches found in deontological and utilitarian approaches are confusing and inconsistent. This idea led me to Luciano Floridi's (1999, 2008a, 2008b, 2013) information ethics theory. While Floridi developed his theory of information ethics to complement deontological, utilitarian, contractual, and virtue ethics, information ethics is unlike more traditional ethical theories because it was developed with reference to the Information Age and its connection to digital information (Floridi, 1999). I agree with Floridi's perspective that traditional approaches are too anthropocentric and too focused on the impact of an agent's actions on others. Moreover, in my attempts to align this book with my earlier book *Cyberpsychology and the Brain*, Floridi's ideas are helpful in that they move beyond traditional theories and consider the ways in which an agent's actions impact the biological, social, and informational environments.

I also want to mention that the work of Andy Clark and David Chalmers (1998) on extended cognition has provided a framework for extending cognitive processes via an active externalism that has helped me to conceptualize technology and neurobiology in terms of a "coupled system." Moreover, Peter Reiner's (Fitz & Reiner, 2016; Nagel & Reiner, 2018; Reiner & Nagel, 2017) development of these ideas in terms of algorithmic devices that can act as technologies of the extended mind greatly enhanced my thinking about neuroethics.

I offer a special word of thanks to my family. I continue to be indebted to my wife, Valerie. We have been together now for more years (decades even) than we were apart. She has faith in me and makes it possible to make it through the dark nights that at times plague my soul. When she smiles, everything is brighter. She has supported and encouraged me through the writing of each of my five books. Thank you Valerie for all the years together, for your friendship, and for our children Tommy and Sophie.

PART I

Introduction

CHAPTER I

Cyberpsychology Theory and Praxes: Ethical and Methodological Considerations

1.1   Cyberpsychology: Ethics in the Digital Age

Cyberpsychology is a developing branch of psychology with increasing importance as new technologies develop and proliferate in our everyday lives. As a discipline, cyberpsychology overlaps with media psychology, digital psychology, affective computing, and human–computer interaction. While cyberpsychology is a relatively new discipline, it is developing at an alarming rate and has several recent full-length texts (Attrill, 2015; Attrill & Fullwood, 2016; Connolly et al., 2016; Hadlington, 2017; Norman, 2017; Parsons, 2017; Power & Kirwan, 2013). The rapid proliferation of technological progress in an ever increasingly connected world suggests that cyberpsychology will continue to grow. Technological advances surround us and we regularly connect or disconnect from others via multifarious digital venues. While cyberpsychology has called attention to the stimulating potential that these new technologies (and the research behind them) have to offer, less emphasis has been placed on the moral and ethical issues that may result from the widespread use of the Internet, smartphones, virtual/augmented reality, social media, and various other digital technologies. This book offers a first attempt at discussing some of the ethical issues inherent in cyberpsychology research and practice.

Ethical considerations in cyberpsychology require us to acknowledge that cyberpsychology is a subdiscipline of psychology. This is important because psychology developed as a laboratory-based science and cyberpsychology grew out of this scientific psychology. The importance of science for psychology is evident in our codes of ethics, standards, and accreditation criteria (American Psychological Association, 2002, 2013a, 2017; Association of State and Provincial Psychology Boards, 2005). As psychology has developed as a science, it is increasingly calling on neuroscience to observe scientifically the various biological and chemical processes that make the brain and nervous system function. Just as psychological science

3

continues to develop in line with findings from the neurosciences, cyberpsychology stimuli, measures, and platforms are enhancing our awareness of
the impact technologies have on the human brain's structure and function
(see Parsons, 2017). Along with rapid technological developments, there is
an increased need to grapple with the ethical implications of cyberpsychology tools and discoveries. Although several reviews have been written to
synthesize the growing literature on neuroscience and ethics in general
(Clausen & Levy, 2015; Farah, 2012; Illes, 2017; Racine & Aspler, 2017),
there is a dearth of discussion related to the ethical implications of cyberpsychology research, theory, and praxes.

    Ethical issues abound in cyberpsychology and continue to increase in
importance as technologies develop. Take a moment to consider how close
our relations are with our technologies. For some of us, this relationship
allows us to connect with others (smartphones, social media). For others,
technologies allow for rapid access to information (education, research
using the Internet, navigating our environments). There is also the important role that our technologies play in entertainment (e.g., video games).
There are also those who rely on neuroenhancing technologies (e.g.,
cochlear implants, deep brain stimulation, and other neurotechnologies)
for maintaining health and quality of life. Technology affects our brains
and cognitive processes. In fact, some have gone so far as to assert that
technologies act as part of us – we are coupled with technologies in such
a way that they extend who we are and our cognitive processes (Clark &
Chalmers, 1998; Dennett, 1996). For example, Daniel Dennett (1996) has
argued that human intellectual superiority over animals is due to our habit
of offloading our cognitive tasks onto peripheral devices that can be used to
store, process, and re-represent our meanings. Likewise, Andy Clark and
David Chalmers (1998) present us with an "extended mind" theory, in
which cognitive processes go beyond the wetware of the brain to software
and hardware used by the brain. The extended mind is an extended
cognitive system that includes both brain-based cognitive processes and
technologies such as smartphones and the Internet that perform functions
that would otherwise be accomplished via the action of internal brain-
based cognitive processes (see Chapter 3, "Digital and Extended Selves in
Cyberspace").

    These ideas have important ethical implications that increase in impor-
tance as we consider the cognitive enhancements afforded by our technologies. In this book, there is a discussion of the intimate like between
persons and their technologies. This intimate human–technology coupling
means that removing or damaging the technology could be equivalent to

a bodily assault. If particular varieties of cognitive processes involve technologies (ranging from using one's smartphone for navigation to implanting electrodes for deep brain stimulation to alleviate neurological dysfunctions), then taking away or damaging these technologies could be as debilitating as a brain lesion. In addition to the positive benefits of human–technology couplings, there are also ethical conflicts that may arise. These ethical conflicts may include threats to autonomy and privacy that occur from algorithms developed by companies interested in manipulating persons who are coupled with technologies of a person's extended mind (Reiner & Nagel, 2017; Nagel, Hrincu, & Reiner, 2016). These and other ethical issues will be reviewed in this book.

In addition to analyses of the ethical aspects of a brain-based cyberpsychology, discussions in this book include a wider sociocultural discourse. Digital media and associated technologies have the potential to change, both positively and negatively, not only our understandings of humanity in general but also our specific and contextualized notions of personhood, free will, conscious experience, authenticity, and relatedness to others. Hence, technological advances have the potential to transform our *Lebensformen* (i.e., forms of life; Wittgenstein, 1953/2009). To better understand the wider sociocultural discourse, this chapter starts with an investigation of philosophical approaches to technology. This analysis leads to a general discussion of ethical implications for a brain-based cyberpsychology of the extended mind.

1.2 Cyberpsychology Ethics and the Philosophy of Technology

While attitudes toward technology reflect a complex array of positions, the continuum appears to be anchored on either end with two distinctive viewpoints, techno-optimism and techno-pessimism (Winston & Edelbach, 2011). On one end, is the techno-pessimist who focuses on the negative aspects of technology. The techno-pessimist is skeptical of technological solutions and questions the social benefits afforded by technology. For example, a techno-pessimist may see technologies of the extended mind as threats to our autonomy and privacy. On the other end of the continuum, one finds the techno-optimist who tends to focus on the benefits of technology. For the techno-optimist, potential problems of technology will be resolved by technological solutions. Where one falls on the continuum will, to some extent, impact the ways in which one views various ethical issues found in cyberpsychology (see Figure 1.1).

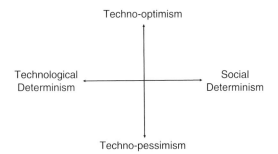

Figure 1.1   Continuum of techno-optimism and techno-pessimism

From a philosophy of technology perspective, cyberpsychology could be discussed in terms of demarcations between two historical phases of technological analyses: (1) classical hermeneutical critiques from the mid-twentieth century that expressed techno-pessimistic concerns about the technologically determined negative impacts of modern technologies on the human condition (Ellul, 1964; Heidegger, 1954; Marcus, 1968; Mumford, 1964; Ortega y Gasset, 1941) or (2) the more recent "empirical turn," wherein cyberpsychology may be viewed from an empirically informed approach to technologies as artifacts or things that are socially determined via local use (Achterhuis, 2001; Brey, 2010; Verbeek, 2011).

1.2.1   Hermeneutical Separation of Persons and Technology

Advocates of the classical hermeneutical approach present technology as a technologically determined metanarrative, wherein technology represents an autonomous, deterministic, and dehumanizing dynamism beyond humanity's abilities to control it. The hermeneutical approach to technological interpretation emphasizes meaning-making and the impacts of technological determinism on what it means to be a person. For example, the French philosopher Jacques Ellul (1964) has argued that "technique" (i.e., technology) is developing at a rate that reflects an inherent and inevitable progress that is increasingly outside of human control. By technique, he means the totality of technological methods that have been rationally devised and that have absolute efficiency (relative to developmental stage) in each area of human activity. Hence, Ellul views technique as something that is beyond control and it has become autonomous. Furthermore, Ellul viewed modern technology as irreversibly shaping the way persons carry out activities of daily living. For Martin Heidegger (1954), technology was not to be considered as a manipulable tool but as a way of "being in the world" that deeply impacts the ways in which persons relate to the world. Max Weber (1903/1958) went so far as to compare technology to an "iron cage" (stahlhartes Gehäuse) that locks persons into modes of being and/or patterns of behavior (see also Maley, 2004). Scholars in this classical hermeneutical frame draw attention to technology's role in bringing about humanity's decline by narrowing experience of things as they are. Heidegger (1954) argues that persons view nature, and increasingly human beings, as raw material for technical operations. Hence, in the classical hermeneutical approach, technology represents an existential threat to us as persons. Ethical considerations of technology from this approach will likely view technologies as destructive to personhood.

1.2.2   *Empirical Turn from Technology to Technologies*

The empirical turn (Achterhuis, 2001; Brey, 2010; Verbeek, 2011) in philosophy marks a shift from a metanarrative of "Technology" (capital "T") to local narratives for each of the "technologies" (lowercase "t") found in situated networks (each with their own socially determined culture, values, and various exigencies). Following the empirical turn, much of the contemporary discussion among philosophers of technology reflects a view that technologies are more ambivalent than deterministic and autonomous (Feenberg, 1995, 1999; Ihde, 1990, 1993; Latour, 1993, 1994; Verbeek, 2005, 2012). While there remains an understanding that technologies can have positive and/or negative impacts on persons, societies, and environments, philosophers of technology in the empirical turn examine each technology empirically and individually. Hence, for contemporary philosophy of technology after the empirical turn, the emphasis is on localized "technologies" rather than a totalizing metanarrative of "Technology." As such, each technology should be viewed within the cultures, values, and varied exigencies relative to the locales that the technologies are deployed. Contemporary philosophers of technology replace their predecessors' technological determinism – with its sweeping claims gleaned from general examples about the effects of media, science, and artistic expression on society as a whole – with a more nuanced approach that focuses on specific instances and artifacts rather than those broad extrapolations.

1.2.3   *The Continuity of Persons and Technology*

In current discourse on the ethical implications of technology, one finds evidence of both the classical hermeneutical concerns of harmful effects (e.g., depersonalization, isolation) and the logical outworking of the empirical turn, wherein emphases are placed on the continuity of persons and technology with the rest of nature. Social media technologies (e.g., Internet, Twitter, texting, smartphones) have the potential to extend our cognitive processes beyond the wetware of our brains. According to the extended mind theory, cognitive processes are understood as going beyond wetware (i.e., the brain) to software and hardware algorithmically coupled with the brain (Clark & Chalmers, 1998; Nagel, Hrincu, & Reiner, 2016; Reiner & Nagel, 2017). In this perspective, human cognition is processed in a system coupled with the environment (Clark, 2008; Clark & Chalmers, 1998). The extended mind theory describes extended cognitive systems that include both brain-based cognitive processes and external objects (e.g., technologies such as smartphones and the Internet) that perform functions that would otherwise be accomplished via the action of internal brain-based cognitive processes (see Chapter 3, "Digital and Extended Selves in Cyberspace"). Clark and Chalmers employ a "parity principle," which states:

> If, as we confront some task, a part of the world functions as a process which, were it to go on in the head, we would have no hesitation in recognizing as part of the cognitive process, then that part of the world is (so we claim) part of the cognitive process. (Clark & Chalmers, 1998, p. 8)

To illustrate the parity principle, Clark and Chalmers employ a *Gedankenerfahrung* (i.e., thought experiment) using fictional characters, Inga and Otto, who must navigate to the Museum of Modern Art (MOMA) on Fifty-Third Street in New York City (see Figure 1.2). Inga is able to recall the directions from her internal brain-based memory processes. For Otto, things are different because his Alzheimer's disease limits his ability to recall the directions from sole use of his internal brain-based memory processes. Otto must also rely on directions found in a notebook that serves as an external aid to his internal brain-based memory processes. This thought experiment elucidates the information-processing loops that extend beyond the neural realm to include elements of our social and technological environments.

The extension of mental processes outside of the brain (e.g., technologies of the extended mind) means that mental processes cannot be fully reduced to brain processes. Take, for example, the potential of smartphones connected to the Internet to extend our brain-based memory. Mobile technologies connected to the Internet allow for novel investigations into the interactions of persons as they engage with a global

Hypothesis of the Extended Mind

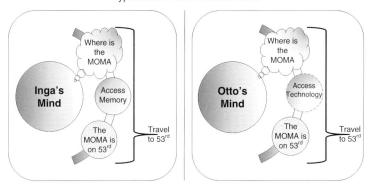

Figure 1.2 Parity principle to support the hypothesis of the extended mind. The fictional characters Inga and Otto must navigate to the Museum of Modern Art (MOMA) on Fifty-Third Street in New York City

workspace and connected knowledgebases. Moreover, mobile access to the Internet may allow for interactive possibilities: a paradigm shift in how we see ourselves and the ways in which we understand the nature of our cognitive and epistemic capabilities (Parsons, 2017). An additional advantage of the extended mind approach is that it moves the discussion beyond the split in the empirical turn from the classical hermeneutical. Levy (2007b) points out that the extended mind thesis alters the focus of neuroethics away from the question of *whether* (capital "T" Technology found in classical hermeneutical discussions) we ought to allow interventions into the mind and toward the question of which interventions (small "t" technologies found in the empirical turn) ought to be allowed and under what conditions.

1.3   Wittgenstein and Technology Games: A Hermeneutical and Empirical Rapprochement

When we turn to ethical aspects of a brain-based cyberpsychology and technologically extended digital selves, digital communities, and increasingly digital *Lebensformen* (i.e., forms of life), it is important to balance the valuations from the classical hermeneutical approach with the empirical turn in philosophy of technology (Coeckelbergh, 2015, 2017). Hence, an ethical cyberpsychology will be as concerned with our continuity with technologies (object-oriented ontology in the empirical turn) as it is with how we relate to (and are impacted by) technologies. How might this balance between personal meaning and technology use be obtained? One approach is stimulated by the philosophical methods that Ludwig Wittgenstein developed in his later works (Wittgenstein, 1953/2009, 1969). Of specific interest is his contention that meaning (hermeneutics) relates to technology use in various situations (empirical turn).

1.3.1   Language Games

Wittgenstein uses the term "language game" to emphasize the fact that the use of language is part of an activity (i.e., a form of life). Hence, meanings of words and the conditions in which they are used are interrelated in a way that comes before the empirical separation between the world (the circumstances), the use of words, and the meaning (hermeneutics) of the words spoken. Therefore, when clarifying the meaning of words found in ethical descriptions of technology, Wittgenstein advises us to ask questions such as:

> How did we learn the meaning of this word ("good" for instance)? From what sort of examples? In what language-games? Then it will be easier for you to see that the words must have a family of meanings. (Wittgenstein, 1953/2009, § 77)

The idea that one does not typically distinguish between the words one uses, their meanings, and the reality they refer to can be extended to our understandings about the positive and negative impacts of technology use in the lives of the people that use them. For Wittgenstein (1953/2009, 1969), the meaning of something (e.g., a technology) is found in the ways in which it is used. While he maintained that philosophy was a kind of analysis (empirical), he tended to distance himself from logical positivist notions (only statements that are empirically verifiable are meaningful) by emphasizing the importance of meaning over empirical verification. In Wittgenstein, one finds that the use of language is related to various activities: giving orders, describing things, and acting in a play. Meaning is derived from use and depends on contexts. Language must be understood in its use and is interwoven with forms of life and language games, with each having their own rules. Language use is a constituent of "language games" that make up a community's "form of life."

Ethical decisions in cyberpsychology are examples of language games. The rules that shape a language game and give it meaning may differ from one technology to another. Ethical use of technology depends on how one does things with technologies in a particular activity (i.e., language games and form of life). Human meaning emerges out of the unique uses given to specific words in a communal context. The meaning of a proposition about technology is found in the set of ethics governing the use of the expression in practice. These ethical rules are merely useful for the particular applications in which a community applies them or not (Dueck & Parsons, 2004). An example might be to assume that the human self could be spoken of as a digital self that follows ethical rules interacting within a social network.

1.3.2 Wittgenstein's Metaphor of the Toolbox

Wittgenstein's approach offers an opportunity for reenvisioning cyberpsychology as technology-in-use (i.e., as a tool) and as a lived technology. Wittgenstein argued that language can be understood as a tool (or technology):

> Think of the tools in a toolbox: there is a hammer, pliers, a saw, a screwdriver, a rule, a glue-pot, glue, nails and screws. – The functions of words are as diverse as the functions of these objects. (And in both cases there are similarities.) (Wittgenstein 1953/2009, §11, p. 9e)

Coeckelbergh (2018) applies Wittgenstein's view of language to technology via a reconceptualization of Wittgenstein's metaphor of the toolbox. This approach uses Wittgenstein's concepts of language games and form of life to develop the idea of "technology games" for a use-oriented, holistic, transcendental, social, and historical approach to technology that balances the empirical turn with normatively sensitivity. Specifically, the ways in which technologies are used is shaped by the games and forms of life that are already in place "before" they are used. Hence, social and cultural grammars of the technologies employed already exist in the particular activities and ways things are done with the technologies. From a Wittgensteinian perspective, there are already language games found in the use of each technology. Moreover, the technologies used are part of those games. The use of technologies is shaped by the games. The use and meaningfulness of technologies require that these technology games and *Lebensformen* (forms of life) involve concrete uses of technology in praxes.

1.3.3 Wittgenstein and the Extended Mind

Wittgenstein (1947/1980a, 1947/1980b) suggests that we attend carefully to the ways in which we actually apprehend another's mind in action. It is not at all clear that mental processes are limited to internal brain properties. Instead, much of our cognition unfolds within the extended coupling of our brains with our environments and shared social processes. In line with Wittgenstein's proposals, ethical aspects of cyberpsychology are not viewed as theoretically demarcated concepts. Instead, cyberpsychology ethics are understood to be features of mental processes (both brain-based and technologically extended) and subsequent behaviors. This approach to an ethical cyberpsychology opens pathways for investigations into the various ways in which ethical issues can appear in cyberpsychology research, theory, and praxes. Hence, ethical issues in cyberpsychology are not necessarily understood as limited to the brain of an individual but, rather, that they are often clearly visible in our technologically extended digital selves and everyday activities (see Chapter 3, "Digital and Extended Selves in Cyberspace"). There is reason to think that Wittgenstein would have been open to the extended mind thesis. In *Culture and Value*, Wittgenstein (1977/1998, p. 24e) wrote: "I really do think with my pen, for my head often knows nothing of what my hand is writing." Wittgenstein's arguments have significant methodological implications for cyberpsychology ethics, specifically that in situ analyses can be used to advance understanding of how ethical issues appear in our use of technologies.

1.4   Groundwork for Ethics and Brain-Based Cyberpsychology

In this book, examples from various areas of cyberpsychology are proffered to generate descriptive accounts of the ethical tendencies in brain-based cyberpsychological research by pointing to modes of evaluative behavior and the specific conditions for meaning-making that prevail in these circumstances. It is important to note that the aim is to bring to the fore those virtues generally taken for granted when communicating that which we believe to be important and valuable. The literature on the human brain and its neural mechanisms as they relate to the Internet (Montag & Reuter, 2017), social media (Meshi, Tamir, & Heekeren, 2015), virtual reality (Parsons, 2015a; Parsons & Phillips, 2016; Parsons, Gaggiolo, & Riva, 2017), and related technologies is continuing to increase (Kane & Parsons, 2017; Parsons, 2016, 2017). Moreover, review of the literature suggests that advances in cyberpsychology stimuli, measures, and platforms highlight the impact technologies have on the human brain's structure and function. As a result, there is an increased need for considerations of the ethical repercussions of cyberpsychology tools and discoveries.

In an effort to include brain science research in the cyberpsychology domain, I previously proposed a framework for integrating neuroscience and cyberpsychology for the study of social, cognitive, and affective processes and the neural systems that support them (see Parsons, 2017). Cyberpsychology viewed from this perspective can be understood as a brain-based cyberpsychology that includes theory and praxes of (1) the neurocognitive, affective, and social aspects of humans interacting with technology and (2) the affective computing aspects of humans interacting with devices/systems that incorporate computation. When working from a brain-based cyberpsychological framework, the cyberpsychologist will consider the neurocognitive processes, motivations, intentions, behavioral outcomes, and effects of online and offline use of technology. Four themes emerged from the brain-based cyberpsychology framework:

1) Dual-process models (automatic and controlled processing) can inform cyberpsychological research
2) Affective (i.e., emotions), cognitive, and social neurosciences offer insights into cyberpsychology
3) Large-scale brain networks and frontal subcortical circuits are involved in human–technology interactions
4) Technologies can extend mental processes.

Ethical decision-making using digital technologies involves the mental processes by which an individual or group using technology (1) is morally aware of an issue's ethical dimensions; (2) makes moral judgments; and (3) establishes moral intent (i.e., motivation).

Evidence from neuroimaging studies suggests that the neural mechanisms involved in recognizing the moral dimensions of an issue and those involved in making moral judgments are distinct from those involved in other types of cognition. However, findings from studies of moral intentions (motivation) appear to be less clear. In the following, there will be a discussion of findings from research in these three areas (moral awareness; judgments; intentions) and a suggestion that the simulation (stimulus presentation, data logging) and modeling found in cyberpsychology will allow for increased understandings in these areas. Furthermore, there will be an explication of the ways in which cyberpsychology may clear up some of the ambiguity in study outcomes.

Building on the four themes identified in my earlier book *Cyberpsychology and the Brain* (Parsons, 2017), the current book aims to investigate the ethical implications of a brain-based cyberpsychology:

1) Ethical decision-making entails dual-process models (automatic and controlled processing)
2) Affective (i.e., emotions) processes play a significant role in ethical decision-making
3) Distinct neural mechanisms appear to be involved in normative approaches to morality and ethical decision-making
4) Technologies of the extended mind inform neuroethical analyses.

Based on these themes, implications can be drawn for ethical practice of a brain-based cyberpsychology. As mentioned earlier in this chapter, it is important to emphasize that "brain-based" does not mean that cognitive processes are reduced to neural firings in the brain. Instead, brains and technologies can become coupled via algorithms and feedback loops to extend cognitive processes. This changes the ethical discussion to the positive and negative implications of technologies of the extended mind.

One emerging area in support of the four themes I introduced in *Cyberpsychology and the Brain* is neuroethics. Roskies (2002) distinguished two branches of neuroethics: (1) ethics of neuroscience – neuroethics as applied ethical reflection on the practices and technologies found in the neurosciences; and (2) neuroscience of ethics – what neurosciences can reveal about the nature of morality and morally relevant topics. Neuroethical research findings offer increasing support for emerging themes that characterize ethical decision-making. First, ethical decision-making entails more than just conscious reasoning; it has automatic, intuitive, and unconscious dimensions as well. Furthermore, emotional processes are apparent in ethical decision-making. This is especially true for certain types of moral dilemmas. Given the first two points, it is not surprising that the neural correlates underpinning ethical decision-making appear to be distinct from those underlying other forms of cognitive processing. Finally, these findings have normative implications for our understandings of technologies of the extended mind.

1.4.1 *Automatic and Controlled Processes in Ethical Decision-Making*

A first theme emerging from my earlier efforts to develop a brain-based cyberpsychology (Parsons, 2017) is that dual-process models (automatic and controlled processing) can inform cyberpsychological research. Likewise, a theme found in neuroethics research is that ethical decision-making also involves the brain's controlled and automatic processes. While controlled processes require specific brain nodes for controlled attention, other brain areas are activated automatically without the necessity for conscious control (Schneider & Shiffrin, 1977; Shiffrin & Schneider, 1977). Controlled processes (e.g., inhibiting a prepotent response during the Stroop task) are associated with conscious awareness, effort, intention, and the capacity for inhibition. Automatic processes (e.g., overlearned responses like reading) are not necessarily in conscious awareness and occur spontaneously.

Examples of controlled and automatic processing abound in cyberpsychology literature: social browsing and social searching on Facebook (Wise, Alhabash, & Park, 2010); risky behavior via social media (Branley & Covey, 2018); problematic Internet use (D'Hondt & Maurage, 2017; Schiebener & Brand, 2017); privacy concern and information disclosure (Aivazpour, Valecha, & Rao, 2017); assessments of social status on social media sites (Slagter van Tryon & Bishop, 2012); effects of distracting ads on automatic responses and controlled processing of online news stories (Kononova, 2013); video games (Boyle et al., 2013); and virtual reality environments (Parsons, Courtney, & Dawson, 2013).

Matthew Lieberman (2007) at UCLA has proposed that neuroimaging studies offer support for these dual processes, with some brain nodes and networks constituting a controlled "reflective" system and others making up an automatic "reflexive" system. Neuroscience researchers have maintained that moral judgment is primarily an automatic (reflexive) process (Haidt, 2001; Hauser, 2006a). Reynolds (2006) suggested a dual-process approach to ethical decision-making process, in which automatic reflexive pattern matching of everyday stimuli activate unconscious brain processes. When faced with ethical situations (like being tempted or bribed), an automatic pattern matching takes place, wherein the brain organizes data into neural patterns, and compares them against base patterns of ethical situations. The automatic (X-System) processing is performed in an iterative and cyclic progression of stimulus structuring and stimulus logging until the presented ethical situation matches an existing ethical representation stored in memory. Following the match, the current ethical situation is represented as an ethical schema that is processed as automatic normative evaluations that prompt the individual to act reflexively in response to the situation. There are situations, however, in which this automatic and reflexive cycle does not result in a match. In such situation, a higher-order, conscious, and controlled reflective process (active judgment involving the C-System) is initialized to consciously deliberate on the ethical situation, refine schemas, and apply relevant moral decision-making.

The dual-process approach to ethical decision-making proposed by Reynolds (2006) comports well with evidence from neuroethics research using moral dilemmas. Two key moral dilemmas are the switch (bystander) and footbridge cases (see Figure 1.3). In the switch case, the participant can initiate a switch that will save five people by redirecting a runaway trolley away from the five people and onto one (killing that individual). For the footbridge case, the participant can save five people further down a track by shoving one person off a footbridge into the path of a runaway trolley. Cushman, Young, and Hauser (2006) presented participants with pairs of different versions of the Trolley Dilemma. Each version was based on one of three normative standards used to assess moral harm: (1) the action principle: acts resulting in harm are worse morally than the harm (of the same amount) resulting from omission; (2) the intention principle (doctrine of the double effect): acting as a means to an end such that intentionally inflicting harm is worse than unintended harm of the same amount); and (3) the contact principle: physical contact with a victim that results in harm is perceived to be worse morally than harm that did not include physical contact. Results revealed that approximately 80 percent of participants maintaining the action principle were able to justify adequately their decision to shove one person onto train tracks to save the lives of others. Contrariwise, only 30 percent of participants provided sufficient justification for their judgments when maintaining the intention principle. Furthermore, 22 percent of the participants who agreed with the intention

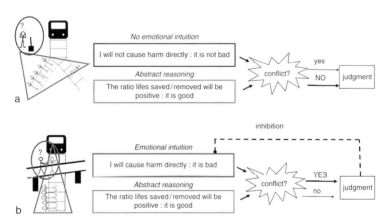

Figure 1.3 Schematic representation of dual processes model of moral judgments about (a) the Trolley Dilemma and (b) the Footbridge Dilemma (from Buon, Seara-Cardoso, & Viding, 2016; reprinted with permission from the publisher)

principle reported uncertainty about justifying their perspective. In a follow-up study that focused on the intention principle, Hauser and colleagues (2007) found very similar results. Findings revealed that (1) moral judgments patterns were consistent with the principle of double effect (permissibility of harm for the greater good if the harm is merely a foreseen side effect); and (2) a majority of participants failing to offer justifications that accounted for their judgments.

From the dual-process perspective, the resolution of these moral dilemmas involves automatic affective responses and controlled cognitive responses. Each performs an essential role in moral decision-making (see also Greene et al., 2008). Automatic affective processes are responses generated in the medial prefrontal cortex and the amygdala to drive nonutilitarian processes and reflect prohibition of harm (Greene et al., 2004). Controlled cognitive evaluations performed in the dorsolateral prefrontal cortex drive utilitarian cost/benefit analyses associated with an action. Neuroethical research has found that damage to the ventromedial prefrontal cortex results in moral decisions promoting harmful behavior to promote a greater good (Ciaramelli et al., 2007; Koenigs et al., 2007). While judgments of correct acts when reading Trolley Dilemmas involve controlled cognitive processes, the decision to apply direct physical force activates automatic affective responses.

1.4.2 Affective Processes Involved in Ethical Decision-Making

A second theme from my book *Cyberpsychology and the Brain* (Parsons, 2017) is that a brain-based cyberpsychology will include the coupling of neurocognitive and affective processes. Both cortical (e.g., insula) and subcortical nuclei (e.g., amygdala, hypothalamus, hippocampus, brainstem) play important roles in the formation of emotions and affective decision-making (Koziol & Budding, 2009; Parvizi, 2009). While a strong top-down (cortical → subcortical) cognitive perspective can be found historically in cyberpsychology, the rise of affective computing (Picard, 1997) and affective neuroscience (Panksepp, 1998, 2004) emphasize the increasing importance of bottom-up (subcortical → cortical) affective and motivational state-control perspectives. This addition to cyberpsychology accentuates the importance of human affect and emotional experience for human learning and decision-making.

In normally functioning persons, the automatic processing (i.e., covert biases) of stimuli (including environmental and contextual factors) related to previous emotional experience of analogous conditions influences decision-making (Bechara & Damasio, 2005). The role of emotions in shaping moral judgments can be seen in the case of Phineas Gage who was injured by a tamping iron (13 pounds; approximately 42 inches long and 2 inches in diameter; see Figure 1.4) that shot directly through his left cheek bone, prefrontal cortex, and anterior dorsal skull (Harlow, 1848; see also Fleischman, 2002; MacMillan, 2000). Hannah Damasio and colleagues (1994) applied volumetric analysis using clues from the remains of Gage's skull and found that Gage's lesion likely involved bilateral anterior orbito-frontal cortex, polar and anterior mesial frontal cortices, and the rostral portion of the anterior cingulate gyrus, with underlying white matter involvement more extensive in the left hemisphere than the right. After his brain injury, Gage appeared to be normal with respect to his motoric functions, intelligence, language, and memory. On returning to his pre-injury work, however, he went from being an efficient and capable foreman to someone who exhibited a range of emotional and behavioral problems. In addition to being undependable at work, he displayed a lack of moral sensibility (Hauser, 2006b), with profane outbursts, disrespect for others, and an overall lack of self-control.

Antonio Damasio (1994) has developed the somatic marker hypothesis from clinical cases (e.g., Phineas Gage and persons like him) of persons with documented deficits in moral behavior following brain injuries. The somatic marker hypothesis asserts that persons possess an internal value biasing mechanism that causes a person to experience bodily (i.e., somatic) feelings that automatically bias a person to be predisposed to act in a certain way prior to any controlled rational processes. Increasing evidence from neuroimaging supports the notion that ethical decision-making includes both intuitive and affective processes (Barsky, Kaplan, & Beal, 2011; Moll et al., 2002; Moll et al., 2005). Brain areas that are thought to play a role in affective processing include the medial orbitofrontal cortex, amygdala, and anterior cingulate cortex. These affective processing areas have been found to have increased activation when persons encounter morally relevant stimuli (Blair, 2007; Decety, Michalska, & Kinzler, 2011; Greene et al., 2001, 2004; Phan et al., 2002; Sanfey & Chang, 2008). Moreover, affective processing appears to play a role in formulating moral judgment. Moll, Eslinger, and de Oliveira-Souza (2001) found that brain regions related to affective processing appear to have greater activation when persons make judgments regarding moral dilemmas (or morally relevant stimuli).

Cyberpsychological research has used functional neuroimaging studies to investigate the impact of exposure to violent video games on the functioning of specific neural structures. When Weber, Ritterfeld, and

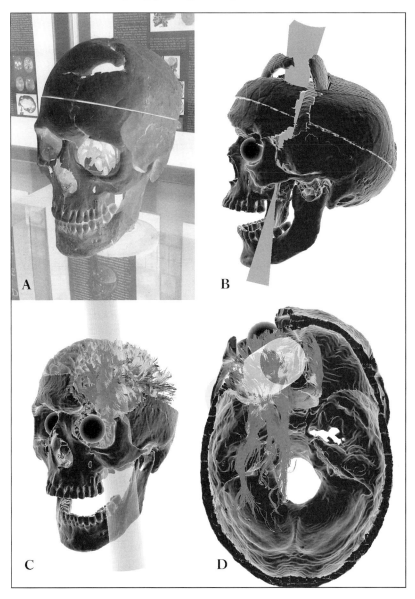

Figure 1.4 Modeling the path of the tamping iron through the Gage skull and its effects on white matter structure: (a) the skull of Phineas Gage on display at the Warren Anatomical Museum at Harvard Medical School; (b) computed topography (CT) image volumes; (c) a rendering of the Gage skull with the best-fit rod trajectory and example fiber pathways in the left hemisphere intersected by the rod; and (d) a view of the interior of the Gage skull showing the extent of fiber pathways intersected by the tamping iron. Moreover, the inverse view from Van Horn and colleagues (2012) was used (reprinted with permission from the publisher)

Mathiak (2006) assessed the brain activity of thirteen adult males as they played a violent video game (i.e., *Tactical Ops: Assault on Terror*), they found reduced neural activity in the anterior cingulate cortex and the amygdala when participants performed aggressive acts in the game. Moreover, video game–based violent activities resulted in decreased activity in the rostral anterior cingulate cortex and increased activity in the dorsal anterior cingulate cortex. In another study of the impacts of acute exposure to violent videogames, Wang and colleagues (2009) found differential engagement of neural circuitry in response to a violent video game as compared to a nonviolent video game. The results of these studies suggest differential engagement of frontolimbic circuitry in response to short-term exposure to a violent video game as compared to a nonviolent video game. Another functional neuroimaging study found increased activation of the dorsal anterior cingulate cortex and reduced activation of the amygdala during play of a first-person shooting game (Mathiak & Weber 2006). Moreover, in another neuroimaging study with tailored violent video game stimuli, King and colleagues (2006) found activation in the ventromedial prefrontal cortex and the amygdala. Findings from these studies reveal brain activations in brain areas implicated in emotional processing of stimuli. In some cases, violent video game stimuli were suggestive of suppressed affective information processing. While these findings are relative to acute effects, repeated suppression of affective information processing could ultimately lead to desensitization to morally salient issues.

1.4.3   Specific Neural Mechanisms Appear to Be Involved in Ethical Decision-Making

A third theme from my book *Cyberpsychology and the Brain* (Parsons, 2017) is that a brain-based cyberpsychology will emphasize neural underpinnings of human–technology interactions. In terms of ethical issues, neuroethics research has revealed that normative ethical approaches appear to have underlying neural correlates. Deontological (see Chapter 2) ethical reasoning and care-based approaches appear to have support from dedicated brain regions (Fiddick, Spampinato, & Grafman, 2005; Blair et al., 2006). Fiddick and colleagues (2005) performed an event-related functional neuroimaging study (twelve males and twelve females) of participants' reasoning about conditional deontic rules (rules regulating a person's behavior). They utilized two different types of rules: social contracts and nonsocial, precautionary rules. While the rules and task demands were matched in logical structure, reasoning about social contracts and precautions activated a different collection of brain areas. For social contracts, the activated brain areas included dorsomedial prefrontal cortex, ventrolateral prefrontal cortex, angular gyrus, and orbitofrontal cortex. The brain areas that were differentially activated by precautions included the insula, lentiform nucleus, posterior cingulate, anterior cingulate, and postcentral gyrus. Reasoning about prescriptive rules resulted in activations of the dorsomedial prefrontal cortex.

In addition to normative utilitarian approaches, utilitarian (i.e., consequentialist – see Chapter 2) judgments appear to be related to brain regions implicated in abstract reasoning and cognitive control. Greene and colleagues (2004) exposed participants to what they termed the "crying baby dilemma," in which participants were instructed to visualize themselves and other civilians hiding from enemy militants who were searching to kill them. While hiding, the participant's baby begins to cry loudly enough to reveal their hiding place. Neuroimaging was performed as participants performed a utilitarian judgment of the appropriateness of smothering their child to death to save those hiding (utilitarian judgment). Results revealed that those who considered the utilitarian option as "appropriate" had greater activation in brain areas associated with cognitive control and abstract reasoning. In this study, brain areas that have been implicated in cognition rather than affective processes appear to have mediated the judgment process. Support for cognitive brain networks underpinning utilitarian judgments can be found in longer reaction times to serious moral dilemma demanding a judgment based on utilitarian considerations (Greene et al., 2008). Moreover, the relation between affective processing and a preference for utilitarian judgments is reinforced by clinical studies relating damage to affect-relevant brain areas to a consequentialist (i.e., utilitarian) approach to solving ethical dilemmas (Greene, 2007; Moll & de Oliveira-Souza, 2007). Adult-onset focal bilateral lesions to the ventromedial prefrontal cortex (brain region implicated in affective processing) results in increased endorsement of utilitarian responses to personal moral dilemmas (Koenigs et al., 2007).

1.4.4 Technologies of the Extended Mind Inform Neuroethical Analyses

An additional component for our understanding of a brain-based cyberpsychology is the notion that technology is an extension of our cognitive processes (see Parsons, 2017). As mentioned above, a number of cyberpsychology technologies (e.g., the Internet, Twitter, texting, smartphones) have the potential to extend our cognitive processes beyond the wetware of our brains.

To better understand the circumstances under which a device qualifies as a technology of the extended mind, it is helpful to explore what is meant by the word "mind." While a fully nuanced account of the term "mind" is beyond the scope of this chapter, a few words of clarification will be helpful to situate the notion of technology of the extended mind in context. Although the term mind is used in this discussion, it is not with the intent of slipping into some version of substance dualism (i.e., there is brain-stuff and mind-stuff). Instead, a specific distinction is made between brain and mind, in which the brain is understood as a thing while the mind is understood as a concept. The aim here is to keep from mixing these ontological levels in a way that so often ends in muddling the relation between brain and mind. A way of considering this issue is to consider the mind as representing the full set of cognitive resources that the person deploys in the service of thinking. Thinking can be understood as reflective, algorithmic, and autonomous (Stanovich, 2009a, 2009b). This approach comports well with the extended mind hypothesis because the idea of a "full set of cognitive resources" allows for additional contributions (in addition to the brain) to conceptions of mental processing.

The extension of mental processes outside of the brain (e.g., technologies of the extended mind) means that mental processes cannot be fully reduced to brain processes. Take, for example, the potential of smartphones connected to the Internet to extend our brain-based memory. The coupling of the brain and the smartphone not only enhances the user's cognitive capacities but also moves the technologies beyond memory assistants to powerful mobile computation devices. In fact, mobile technologies connected to the Internet allow for novel investigations into the interactions of persons as they engage with a global workspace and connected knowledgebases. Moreover, mobile access to the Internet may allow for interactive possibilities: a paradigm shift in how we see ourselves and the ways in which we understand the nature of our cognitive and epistemic capabilities (Parsons, 2017).

1.5   Neuroethical Implications for a Brain-Based Cyberpsychology

Neuroscience findings have the potential to shape ethical discussions among cyberpsychologists. This has import for my contention that greater inclusion of brain science research is needed in the cyberpsychology domain. In this chapter, we have discussed four themes that have emerged from the brain-based cyberpsychology framework: (1) dual-process models (automatic and controlled processing) can inform cyberpsychological research; (2) affective (i.e., emotions), cognitive, and social neurosciences offer insights into cyberpsychology; (3) large-scale brain networks and frontal subcortical circuits are involved in human–technology interactions; and (4) technologies can extend mental processes.

One emerging area in support of these four themes is neuroethics. As mentioned, Roskies (2002) distinguished two branches of neuroethics: (1) ethics of neuroscience – neuroethics as applied ethical reflection on the practices and technologies found in the neurosciences; and (2) neuroscience of ethics – what neurosciences can reveal about the nature of morality and morally relevant topics. Research from neuroethical studies offers increasing support for emerging themes that characterize ethical decision-making. Ethical decision-making entails more than just controlled conscious processes. In fact, ethical decision-making can also involve automatic, intuitive, and unconscious dimensions. Emotional processes are also apparent in ethical decision-making studies like those found in certain types of moral dilemmas. Moreover, the neural correlates underpinning ethical decision-making appear to be distinct from those underlying other forms of cognitive processing. These findings have normative implications for our understandings of technologies of the extended mind. Here, neuroethical studies can facilitate the co-evolution of descriptive and normative theories for cyberpsychology in a symbiotic manner.

In support of my framework for a brain-based cyberpsychology, neuroethics research has shown that moral decision-making is neither completely cognitive (i.e., cold rational processing) nor exclusively affective (i.e., hot emotional processing). This is an important issue for normative approaches that have traditionally considered ethical decision-making as a cold cognitive process devoid of affect (moods and emotions). Research into the neural underpinnings of ethical decision-making offers cyberpsychologists a resource for investigating the neurobiologically support for various ethical perspectives. Moreover, neuroethics research may generate questions beyond "rationalist" approaches to ethical decision-making.

1.6   Conclusions

While cyberpsychology has called attention to the stimulating potential that these new technologies (and the research behind them) have to offer, less emphasis has been placed on the moral and ethical issues that may result from the widespread use of the Internet, smartphones, virtual/augmented reality, social media, and various other digital technologies.

This chapter discussed themes emerging from brain science research in the cyberpsychology domain that will be useful for developing an ethical approach to cyberpsychology that will remain relevant in the face of rapid advances in the neurosciences. Specifically, this chapter emphasized that (1) dual-process models (automatic and controlled processing) can inform cyberpsychological research; 2) affective (i.e., emotions), cognitive, and social neurosciences offer insights into cyberpsychology; 3) large-scale brain networks and frontal subcortical circuits are involved in human–technology interactions; and (4) technologies can extend mental processes.

Using these themes, the following chapters (particularly in Part I) will develop an ethical approach to cyberpsychology research that takes seriously the underlying neural correlates of moral decision-making. This chapter also sets the stage for this book's attempts to place the groundwork for these themes and their implications for future cyberpsychology research and praxes. These themes provide cyberpsychologists with starting points from which they can examine (and in some cases reexamine) assumptions underlying current approaches to cyberpsychology ethics training. In the next chapter ("Ethical Approaches to Cyberpsychology"), we review some of the moral principles and ethical perspectives that are commonly used in cyberpsychology. In addition to the principlist approach developed initially by Beauchamp and Childress (1978), the chapter will discuss some of the leading classical ethical approaches (e.g., deontological, consequential, and virtue ethics) found in the Western tradition.

CHAPTER 2

Ethical Approaches to Cyberpsychology

2.1 Introduction

While most cyberpsychologists are not philosophers and few have extensive experience as ethicists, cyberpsychologists often deal with moral issues and dilemmas. These range from the daily awareness of distributive justice, as they consider the imbalanced allocation of technologies in society, to discussing and balancing the complex issues involved in research. These situations are often challenging and some quite perplexing. Ethical perspectives in cyberpsychology, whether professional or philosophical, can be understood in terms of normative inquiries into applied ethics issues in cyberpsychology research and praxes. For normative theories, the focus is on analyzing and recommending moral systems. Such normative ethical approaches can be juxtaposed against descriptive studies that aim to be nonevaluative in their approach. Descriptive studies focus on describing particular moral systems and reporting the ways in which members of various groups (e.g., cultures) view various moral issues. While descriptive analyses provide information about what "is" the case, normative ethics assess what "ought" to be the case. Ethicists who approach cyberpsychology from the standpoint of descriptive ethics may describe sociological aspects of a particular moral issue (e.g., social impact of a given technology on a particular community). One example may be to describe concerns about the "digital divide" (see Chapter 11) in terms of its impact on various sociodemographic groups. For the normative ethical perspective, the question may be about the fairness of some having access to technology while others do not.

In general, the cyberpsychologist's training in ethical issues typically involves a handful of courses (or perhaps only one course) emphasizing specific developments and the four principles developed initially by Beauchamp and Childress (2001). The content usually involves a discussion of the Nuremburg Code (Allied Control Council, 1949), the

World Medical Association's (1964) *Declaration of Helsinki*, and the Belmont Report (OHRP, 1979). From the Belmont Report (i.e., *The Belmont Report: Ethical Principles and Guidelines for the Protection of Human Subjects Research*), we find three principles that provide the foundation for many current ethical guidelines for behavioral research: respect for persons, beneficence, and justice. While there is some terminological variation used in these guidelines and codes, they include the following ethical principles (see Table 2.1): autonomy (i.e., free will or agency); beneficence (i.e., mercy, kindness, and charity); nonmaleficence (i.e., do no harm); and justice (i.e., fair distribution of benefits and burdens).

The American Psychological Association has modified these principles into five principles found in the *American Psychological Association Ethical Principles of Psychologists and Code of Conduct* (American Psychological Association, 2002, 2010): (1) beneficence and nonmaleficence: continually consider costs and benefits; protect from harm; produce optimal good; (2) fidelity and responsibility: professionalism; be continually aware of one's responsibility to society; (3) integrity: be conscientiously truthful; (4) justice: continuously treat persons in a fair manner; and (5) respect for people's rights and dignity: protect persons' rights (privacy and confidentiality).

While this principlist approach is ubiquitous in research involving human subjects and has become almost universally acceptable for developing professional ethics and codes for various disciplines, developments in the contexts and nature of research in the digital age (especially with the

Table 2.1 *Examples of ethical issues pertaining to cyberpsychology research and practice*

Ethical Principle	Latin Mottos	Moral Issues	Treatment Considerations
Autonomy	*Voluntas aegroti suprema lex* (Patient's will is the supreme law)	free will or agency	Informed consent; competence to consent
Beneficence	*Salus aegroti suprema lex* (Patient safety is the supreme law)	mercy, kindness, and charity	Benefits: Effectiveness
Nonmaleficence	*Primum nil nocere* (First, do no harm)	do no harm	Risks: Side effects
Justice	*Iustitia* (Justice)	fair distribution of benefits and burdens	Rationing and prioritizing

growth of the Internet) have resulted in new ethical questions. The result is a host of questions that these regulations and guidelines do not answer in the context of cyberpsychology. Moreover, they obscure judgments about which consequences are best. When these principles are in conflict, the cyberpsychologist may have difficulty deciding which principle should govern moral decision-making.

In an article on ethical concerns that may arise from research and personal use of virtual reality and related technologies, Madary and Metzinger (2016) contend that following codes of ethical conduct should not be considered a substitute for the researcher's ethical reasoning: scientists must understand that following a code of ethics is not the same as being ethical. A domain-specific ethics code, however consistent, developed, and fine-grained future versions of it may be, can never function as a substitute for ethical reasoning itself (p. 12). Furthermore, they assert that ethical decision-making must consider consistently the contextual and implementational details that cannot be captured in ethical codes of conduct. They recommend that cyberpsychologists conceive of ethical codes as an aid to enduring ethical considerations in applied research areas. Principles function predominantly as checklists that name issues worth remembering when bearing in mind a moral concern. Moreover, principles tend to obfuscate moral decision-making by their failure to be guidelines and by their unmethodical use of moral theory (Clouser & Gert, 1990). Following this line of reasoning, this book does not aim to offer a new code of conduct for cyberpsychology. Instead, it attempts to offer a framework for ethical decision-making that takes seriously work from technologies of the extended mind (see Chapter 3 of this book) using neuroethics (see Chapter 4 of this book).

Part of this framework is the importance of both cognitive and affective processes. Principlist approaches and codes of conduct emphasize controlled cognitive calculations over the often automatic and affective processes often found in valuations and ethical decision-making (see Bechara, & Damasio, 2005; Greene et al., 2001; Naqvi, Shiv, & Bechara, 2006). While principlist approaches focus on cognitive processing alone, findings from neuroscience and neuroimaging tell a different story. For example, Joshua Greene and colleagues (2001, 2004) used neuroimaging (fMRI) to explore the cognitive and affective components of moral decision-making as they took part in a Trolley Dilemma. The Trolley Dilemma involves the participant pushing one innocent stranger in front of a speeding trolley so that the participant can save five other strangers from being killed. As Greene's participants considered these variations, their brains all showed increased activity in areas (i.e., ventral striatum and insula) that assign emotional value to items and in a brain region (the ventromedial prefrontal cortex) that integrates various decision-making approaches. These findings suggest the need to include emotional valuations in decision-making. The neuroscience of ethics (see neuroethics in Chapter 4) allows ethicists to move beyond quasi-absolutist approaches that emphasize cognitive control over automatic and affective processes in the decision-making process. Likewise, the neuroscience of ethics has import for investigations of the values, beliefs, and motivations of digitally networked selves.

2.2   Ethical Issues in Cyberpsychology

Ethical issues in cyberpsychology involve questions of what morality is and what it requires of us. A host of questions emerge: What is the nature of morality in cyberpsychology? What does it mean to be a "self" and to make ethical decisions in a digital age? How do cyberpsychologists know that their ethical decisions are cogent? What does it mean to be morally responsible in digital contexts? What does new evidence from neuroscience have to say to the fields of human–computer interaction, human factors, media psychology, and cyberpsychology?

This book explores many of these questions from the perspective of defining what it means to be a technologically extended moral agent in a digital world (see Chapter 3). While it would be advantageous to have a straightforward set of principles, as well as a simple and uncontroversial definition of what morality is, there are a number of ethical theories with disparate conceptions of what it means to live morally (see Cahn & Forcehimes, 2017; Rachels & Rachels, 2015). In this chapter, there will be a brief overview of some of the leading classical ethical approaches (e.g., deontological, consequential, and virtue ethics) found in the Western tradition.

2.3   Deontological Judgment and Decision-Making

Immanuel Kant developed a deontological (from the Greek *deon* meaning "duty") approach to ethics that emphasizes the rightness or wrongness of actions regardless of the consequences of said actions. Hence, moral principles were not founded on contingencies but on actions defined by their inherent rightness or wrongness. The moral value of an action is the reason behind the action instead of the outcome that follows the action (this contrasts with consequentialism; discussed in Section 2.4). For Kant, the human capacity to act dutifully from principle is the only act that is good in and of itself. The basis for action is the categorical imperative, which comes in two formulations: (1) formula of universal law and (2) formula of humanity as an end in itself. The first formulation of the categorical imperative involves universal law: "Act only according to that maxim by which you can at the same time will that it should become a universal law" (Kant, 1785/1998, p. 422). Hence, an agent may consider an action to be right if and only if said agent is prepared to be so acted on should positions of the parties be reversed. Inherent in the categorical imperative is that the agent act in a manner that treats others as ends in and of themselves and not as means to an end. Moreover, the agent must follow firm rules irrespective of the circumstances or situational factors. Kant also developed a second formulation of the categorical imperative, formula of humanity as end in itself, in which: "Act so that you use humanity, in your own person as well as in that of another, always also as an end and never only as a means" (Kant, 1785/1998, p. 429). In other words, the second formulation of the categorical imperative is stating that it is unethical for one individual to use another person. Instead, the ethical interaction with another must respect them as rational persons.

Kant rejected determinism and assumed that the agent possesses the free will needed for moral judgment and decision-making. The rejection of causal determinism was necessary for the dutiful application of rules. Given that an agent's reason is not causally constrained, it is considered free and it can be applied practically in various situations. In Kant's (1785/1998) *Groundwork of the Metaphysics of Morals*, he discussed the synonymy of reason and free will as determined by moral law. According to Kant, the will is best understood in terms of practical reason and actions may be derived from the laws of reason. The practical is understood as that which is possible through the exercise of freedom and is expressed in action via personality and practical reason in a manner that validates the agent's autonomous nature. Moreover, this combination reconciles the will to choices of right and wrong by associating freedom of choice for either rightness or wrongness. It is important to note that the theorizing of David Hume contrasts with Kant's thesis in that Hume (1739/1978) believed that reason could not provide motivation for moral action: "Reason is wholly inactive, and can never be the source of so active a principle as conscience, or a sense of morals" (p. 455). However, Kant believed that, while physical laws are applicable to appearances, the agent's will is intangible and devoid of empirical evidence for its existence. Moreover, while there is possibility that an agent's will is not free (regardless of claims that it is), agents continue to act on the belief that they have free will. In *The Critique of Pure Reason*, Kant (1781/1998) argues that an agent's actions can be considered to be either moral or immoral. Judgments about an agent's actions are based on reason. They are not subject to the moral judgment of an absolute deity. Instead, agents are autonomous and may choose whether or not to follow practical reason or moral law.

Kant's categorical imperative has been deemed inadequate because, even if it affords a definitive measure for establishing the dutifulness of a specific course of action, it does not generalize to situations with two or more conflicting duties. A. C. Ewing (1965) has posed the limitation this way:

> In cases where two laws conflict it is hard to see how we can rationally decide between them except by considering the goodness or badness of the consequences. However important it is to tell the truth and however evil to lie, there are surely cases where much greater evils can still be averted by a lie, and is lying wrong then? (p. 58)

If there are duties such as maintaining promises and telling the truth, then agents are immobilized when confronted with situations in which they are required either to maintain a promise and lie or to speak the truth and break a promise. Kant's version of deontological ethics does not afford us with a system for resolving such conflicts.

2.3.1   *Evaluating a Hacktivist Scenario Using Kantianism*

Richard is an activist and computer programming mastermind who believes that software should be freely distributed in a manner that allows users to freely utilize, explore, distribute, and change that software. Richard argues that access to computers (hardware and software) and anything that might teach you about the way the world works should be completely free. He is so dedicated to his convictions that he quits his job at Massachusetts Institute of Technology (MIT) and drafts a manifest that outlines his belief that software should be freely available to everyone who can use it. Using his programming abilities and influence, he develops free versions of proprietary software and gives it away as much as he can and as often as he can.

Was Richard's action to undermine companies' proprietary rights morally justifiable?

2.3.2   *Kantian Analysis*

Computer scientists will probably view the hacktivist Richard in the above scenario to be strikingly similar to a former programmer at the MIT Artificial Intelligence Laboratory, Richard Stallman. He left MIT in the early 1980s due to the ways in which he believed they restricted his freedom to create and share his ideas. He penned *The GNU Manifesto* to describe his beliefs and a Unix-compatible software system he had written called GNU (i.e., GNU's Not Unix). Stallman put his beliefs forward in *The GNU Manifesto*, in which he presents a Kantian argument:

> I consider that the golden rule requires that if I like a program I must share it with other people who like it. Software sellers want to divide the users and conquer them, making each user agree not to share with others. I refuse to break solidarity with other users in this way. I cannot in good conscience sign a nondisclosure agreement or a software license agreement. For years I worked within the Artificial Intelligence Lab to resist such tendencies and other inhospitalities, but eventually they had gone too far: I could not remain in an institution where such things are done for me against my will. So that I can continue to use computers without dishonor, I have decided to put together a sufficient body of free software so that I will be able to get along without any software that is not free. I have resigned from the AI lab to deny MIT any legal excuse to prevent me from giving GNU away. (Stallman, 1990, p. 154).

Stallman's arguments in *The GNU Manifesto* are Kantian because he believes that extracting money from users is damaging as it restricts the ways in which the software programs can be used. As a result, the amount of wealth that humanity derives from the program is reduced. By that, he meant that a few get wealthy at the expense of the wealth of knowledge that could be shared by all. Since Stallman sees these practices as resulting in harmful limitation of knowledge, he deems it wrong. From a Kantian perspective, this reflects a rule to hoard that is not universalizable. Instead, as a good Kantian, Stallman would prefer a Hacker Ethic:

> Access to computers – and anything which might teach you about the way the world works – should be unlimited and total. Always yield to the Hands-On Imperative. (Levy, 1984, p. 40)

The Hacker Ethic is a version of Kant's Categorical Imperative – always act so as to promote knowledge, particularly of computers, for one and all. For hackers, this was a maxim of behavior that they hoped would be universalized.

2.4 Teleological Utilitarianism: Consequential Ethical Judgments for Decision-Making

While deontological approaches emphasize the duty (*deon*) of an agent to act in a prescribed manner, teleological theories weigh the utilitarian outcomes or ends (*telos*) to evaluate an agent's actions. For the utilitarian, the telos (Greek for "end") determines the ways in which an agent should always act. The utilitarian goal is to produce the greatest teleological benefit (i.e., good over bad) for all agents impacted by an agent's action. Hence, the choice about the rightness or wrongness of an action is held to a standard of optimizing consequences for all agents impacted by the agent's action. Of course, there may be disagreement over whether the outcome is right or wrong. Two classical utilitarians, Jeremy Bentham (1789) and John Stuart Mill (1861), argued for the utilitarian principle of utility (i.e., Greatest Happiness Principle) in terms of pleasure and pain resulting from an agent's actions. Utilitarianism can be used to rank the cost/benefit of social alternatives according to their goodness. Furthermore, an agent's happiness was argued to be a consequence (Richter, 2010). Today, consequentialists tend to agree that the optimal outcome is happiness and the appropriateness of an action's consequences can be found in the degree to which happiness was produced for those agents impacted by an action. Hence, the consequences following an agent's action are to be considered as right or wrong relative to the judgments that measure an action's quality. For the consequentialist, alternative actions may be considered within the context of either/or decision-making, wherein it appears to the agent that only one or two actions may be considered moral. It is important to note that such an approach does not take into account the practical impossibility that an agent has epistemic access to all potential consequences of any given action.

Given that an agent (decision-maker) cannot know all the consequences that may result from a given action, it is necessary that agents reflect on intentions behind their decided actions. In deciding, the agent should weigh the probability of diverse consequences that could happen as a result. This accentuates the responsibility of the agent who considers the rightness of the consequences. Any moral judgment should be made relative to the consequences. In the process, the agent (as decision-maker) faces the difficulty of sorting through all the potential consequences to determine whether the action offers the optimally desired outcome. In praxes, there are two approaches available to the agent that may direct actions taken. These include act and rule consequentialism. For act consequentialism, the nature of the act is considered moral (i.e., ethical) if and only if the action results in an optimal amount of good for those involved relative to any available alternative. For rule consequentialism, an act is right if it conforms to a rule that is itself part of a set of rules whose acceptance would result in the greatest good. For example, performing an action would be morally wrong if it is prohibited by a code of rules that are accepted absolutely by everyone who would be impacted by the action's consequences.

2.4.1   Utilitarianism and the Trolley Dilemma

A limitation of utilitarianism is that it is deficient when applied to questions of social or individual justice. Given that the classical utilitarian approach aims to maximize the total amount of a particular "utility" (e.g., happiness or preferences) over an entire social network, it seeks the array that realizes maximum utility. Such an arrangement, however, may result in a distribution of costs and benefits that violates commonsensical notions of justice. For example, the Trolley Dilemma, introduced by Philippa Foot (1978) and developed by Judith Jarvis Thomson, places the reader in the role of a trolley driver whose brakes are not working. The trolley driver must choose to turn the trolley at a track spur, which would kill one person, or continue on course and kill five:

> Suppose you are the driver of a trolley. The trolley rounds a bend, and there come into view ahead five track workmen, who have been repairing the track. The track goes through a bit of a valley at that point, and the sides are steep, so you must stop the trolley if you are to avoid running the five men down. You step on the brakes, but alas they don't work. Now you suddenly see a spur of track leading off to the right. You can turn the trolley onto it, and thus save the five men on the straight track ahead. Unfortunately, . . . there is one track workman on that spur of track. He can no more get off the track in time than the five can, so you will kill him if you turn the trolley onto him. (Thomson, 1985, 1395)

The Trolley Dilemma aims to find out whether it is morally permissible to turn the trolley onto the track spur and slay one person in order to save five. Are we to consider the trolley driver as responsible for choosing to kill one person rather than five or should we absolve the driver from responsibility since the driver did not cause the situation?

2.4.2   Evaluating a Scenario Using Act Utilitarianism

Fred is the sole passenger in an autonomous self-driving vehicle. While traveling down a main road, ten people suddenly appear ahead, in the direct path of the car. The autonomous self-driving vehicle was programmed to always perform a cost/benefit analysis that minimizes casualties. As a result, Fred's autonomous self-driving vehicle chooses to swerve off to the side of road where it impacted a barrier, killing Fred but leaving the ten pedestrians unharmed.

Fred is dead. Was the action of the autonomous self-driving vehicle morally justifiable?

2.4.3   Utilitarian Analysis

Autonomous self-driving vehicle scenarios convert the classic utilitarian Trolley Dilemma into a chillingly real-life scenario. Jean-François Bonnefon (University of Toulouse in France), Azim Shariff (University of Oregon), and Iyad Rahwan (Media Lab at MIT) (Bonnefon, Shariff, & Rahwan, 2016) used online Amazon Mechanical Turk surveys to query participants about autonomous self-driving vehicles in ethical quandaries. Results from the series of surveys revealed that participants approve of autonomous self-driving vehicles programmed to choose to sacrifice passengers to save others. However, it is very interesting to note that the respondents typically preferred the option to not ride in such an autonomous self-driving vehicle. Moreover, the respondents reported that they would not support regulations mandating that persons choose altruistic self-sacrifice. In fact, they reported that mandatory regulations for self-sacrifice would decrease their willingness to purchase an autonomous self-driving vehicle.

2.4.4   Brain and Dual-Process Theory for Understanding Trolley Dilemmas

Returning to the Trolley Dilemma, Joshua Greene and colleagues (2001) found that there are differences in brain activations for personal and impersonal moral decisions. For Greene and colleagues (2008), a dual-process theory can be used to describe the processes involved in resolving such dilemmas. In a dual-process perspective, both controlled cognitive responses and automatic affective responses perform essential roles in moral decision-making: (1) controlled cognitive evaluations (dorsolateral prefrontal cortex) drive utilitarian judgments and weigh the costs and benefits associated with an action and (2) automatic affective processes drive nonutilitarian processes and reflect prohibition of harm, in which negative affective responses are generated in the medial prefrontal cortex and the amygdala (Greene et al., 2001, 2004). While judgments of correct acts in response to Trolley Dilemmas tend to involve controlled cognitive processes, the decision to apply direct physical force triggers automatic affective responses (Greene, 2007; Greene et al., 2008).

2.5 Rawls's Theory of Justice

A further limitation for utilitarianism is that the utilitarian calculus is exclusively concerned with the total quantity of happiness produced. From a purely utilitarian calculus, unequal distribution of a given amount of utility is preferred over an equivalent distribution of a lesser amount of utility. A utilitarian system wherein the satisfaction of all desires is to be maximized may result in violations of our intuitive precepts of natural justice. As such, John Rawls (1971) has argued for the rejection of most forms of utilitarianism. For Rawls, it is better to develop a moral theory with justice at its foundation. He contends that a reasonable person operating behind a "veil of ignorance" would choose the principles of "equal liberty" and "difference" as the basis for social justice. By the "Principle of Equal Liberty", he meant that each person in a society has an equal right to the most widespread liberties compatible with parallel liberties for all. According to his second principle, the "Difference Principle", any societal inequalities (e.g., social, economic) should result from an arrangement that delivers the optimal benefit to the least advantaged persons, and is related to positions open to everyone.

2.5.1 Evaluating a Database Scenario Using Social Contract Theory

Mark, the owner of a large social networking company, logs all the personal information and activities of each member of the service, as well as their connections to other users. Using this information, he is able to construct profiles of the customers. For example, a user of Mark's social networking service who endorses liking certain activities and items is likely to be interested in purchasing these items or spending money on certain activities. Mark sells these profiles to companies. The members of Mark's social networking service begin receiving many unsolicited advertisements in their email inboxes and on their browser screens. Some of the members of Mark's social networking service are pleased to receive these advertisements and make use of them to order products. Others are annoyed by the increase in the amount of spam they are receiving.

2.5.2 Rawlsian Analysis

In analyzing this scenario using social contract theory, it is important to consider the rights of the rational agents involved. In this case, the rational agents are Mark, members of Mark's social networking service, and the online companies. The morality of Mark's actions is relative to the question of whether we believe that he abused the privacy rights of his customers. If someone uses Mark's social networking service, both the customer and Mark have information about the experience. An important question here is, to what extent are their rights to this information equal? If both Mark and the social media site user have equal rights to this information, then we may conclude that there is nothing wrong with Mark selling this information to a company. However, it may be the case that the persons using Mark's social networking site have the right to expect interactions to be confidential. If so, we may conclude that Mark was unethical in selling this information without gaining the customer's permission.

A limitation of contract-based theories is that they give the foundation for only a minimalist morality. Agents are constrained to act morally only when there is an explicit or formal contract. While there are multifarious situations that require moral decision-making in the absence of formal contracts or explicit laws, agents still tend to act, in at least some of these situations, as if moral obligations existed.

2.6   Virtue Ethics

Aristotle developed a view that contrasts with both duty and consequence. For Aristotle, ethical understandings were not to be understood in terms of rightness and wrongness. Instead, morality is understood in terms of the agent's character traits displayed in action. An agent's possession and exercise of virtues determine the agent's ethical decision-making. The virtue ethics approach conceptualizes a virtuous agent as one possessing ideal character traits that are the consequence of natural tendencies. Virtual ethics may be understood in contrast to deontological and consequentialist approaches. From a virtue ethics perspective, there is little emphasis on universal duties that constrain actions. Instead, the virtue ethicist considers the wider implications related to one's actions. For Aristotle, agents are considered to be naturally suited to do right regardless of automatic development of inclinations to do "good." Virtuous agents seek to act rightly and desire to act virtuously. The emphasis is on the "integrity" of the moral agent seeking to be a good person. It is important to note that virtue ethics emphasizes both intellectual and moral virtue within each agent. Intellectual virtues are believed to be the result of proper education and represent the excellences (i.e., abilities to understand, reason, and judge well). For Aristotle, virtue is to be understood in terms of practical wisdom formulated by the development of character. Moreover, the virtue of eudaimonism (from the Greek "eudaimonia" or happiness) is expressed in every action aiming at some good. Such goods are considered as ends and all things that are ends in themselves achieve some good. Hence, ends are the greatest goods of all (i.e., happiness, fulfillment, and contentment).

While the West has an Aristotelian virtue ethics, the East also has a virtue ethics in classical Confucian thought. Aristotle's eudaimonia (i.e., happiness) is similar to the dao (i.e., the way) of Confucius. Both ground their ethical views in a concept of human nature. Likewise, Aristotelian practical virtues (i.e., virtues of character) such as practical wisdom are comparable to the general Confucian virtue, ren. Furthermore, both emphasize a doctrine of the mean using archery metaphors. Several scholars have considered the similarities between the Confucian and Western species of virtue ethics (see Angle & Slote, 2013; Ivanhoe, 2013; Van Norden, 2003; Wai-Ying, 2001; Yu, 2013). Yu (2013) identifies two perspectives of the mean in both Aristotelian and Confucian ethics: (1) the mean lies in the middle of excess and deficiency and (2) the mean represents that which is right or appropriate. According to Yu, the archery metaphor unifies these two perspectives, in that success is understood in terms of hitting the proper target. Furthermore, the unity of the virtues shows up in both Aristotle's practical wisdom and Confucius's learning about the rites and judgments of appropriateness. Slingerland (2011) contends that early Confucianism perspectives on morality and ethical education anticipate findings in modern Western cognitive sciences.

In the twentieth century, three philosophers – Elizabeth Anscombe (1958), Bernard Williams (1985), and Alasdair MacIntyre (1985) – have each, in their own way, argued for a return to Aristotelian virtue ethics. Regardless of whether the emphasis was on personal selection, a broad understanding of ethics, or unifying practices that generate virtues, the overarching theme was a discontent with the then-current state of modern moral philosophy. The first of the three is Elizabeth Anscombe (1958), who published a manuscript entitled *Modern Moral Philosophy* that altered the ways in which one considers normative theories. Anscombe critiqued the modern preoccupation with a law conception of ethics that emphasizes duty (e.g., Kant's deontology and Mill's utilitarianism). She argued that these approaches to ethics relied on universal principles that result in an inflexible moral code. Moreover, these inflexible rules are based on a notion of duty (and lawgiver) that has greatly diminished import for modern, secular society. For Anscombe, a return to Aristotelian concepts (e.g., character, virtue, and flourishing) was needed. Moreover, she stressed the significance of affective processes (i.e., emotions) for moral psychology. The second philosopher is Bernard Williams (1985), who emphasized the "good life" and drew a distinction between morality and ethics. For Williams, morality is characterized by concepts such as duty and obligation (and blame). Furthermore, Williams takes ethics to be a broader idea and discards the thin and limiting idea of morality. For Williams, ethics includes several affects (i.e., emotions) that are disallowed by morality as extraneous. Moreover, for Williams, ethical concerns are broader, including social networks, family, and society. The third philosopher is Alasdair MacIntyre (1985), whose work catalyzed increased interest in virtue ethics. MacIntyre aims to proffer an interpretation of virtue that comprises several historical accounts and understandings of the virtues. He concludes that the various instantiations are attributable to diverse praxes that produce dissimilar conceptions of the virtues. It is important to note that, for MacIntyre, each account of virtue involves a preceding account of social and moral structures to be comprehended. Hence, understanding Homeric virtue requires that one observe its communal role in previous societies (e.g., Greek society). For MacIntyre, virtues are implemented within communal praxes that are comprehensive social procedures that pursue goods internal to activities. As such, the virtues are teleological (there is an end goal or telos) and allow for the achievement of goods.

2.6.1   Virtuous Decision-Making

Jack reads about the thousands of people in developing countries with low Internet penetration. He is saddened by the continued digital divide. He sends $1,000 of his hard-earned money to an information infrastructure project in a developing country. Jill receives the same news, but she does not have the same feelings of sadness. Nevertheless, out of a sense of duty, she sends $1,000 of her hard-earned money to the same information infrastructure project.

Who, if anyone, in this case is more moral?

2.6.2   Analysis from Virtue Ethics

From a virtue perspective, most would say that Jack is because he has internalized his moral convictions and does the right thing of his own accord without having to ruminate on and grapple over the circumstances. In a word, Jack has achieved particular moral qualities (i.e., virtues) that perform as behavioral dispositions that result in characteristic acts of moral virtuousness. Jack is a morally good person because of his good character that allows him to naturally do the right thing.

Floridi and Sanders (2005) argued virtue ethics has limited application to discussions of technology because its philosophical anthropology cannot deliver, by itself, an ethics that is satisfactory for a globalized world in general and for the information society in particular. However, others have maintained that Internet culture actually tends to be more homogeneous rather than heterogeneous (Cooper, 2004). In fact, Stamatellos (2011a, 2011b) contends that the homogeneity of cyberspace offers a common social exchange and constitution among Internet users. For Stamatellos, the web may be understood as a cyberpolis and the Internet as the cyberagora of the information society. In the same way that citizens in the ancient Greek polis used the agora to exchange goods and ideas, the "netizens" of the cyberagora interconnect in a network of cultural homogeneity. Online global interaction has a host of ethical issues (privacy, security, equality of access) that should be considered in the aspect of cultural homogeneity. For Stamatellos, Internet cultural homogeneity actually supports virtue ethics and netizenship of the Internet as a new global polis.

2.7   Comparison of Ethical Theories

Deontological (Kantian), teleological (act and rule utilitarianism), social contract (Rawlsian theory of justice), and virtue ethics approaches all assume an objective moral good (see Figure 2.1). Furthermore, each takes other persons into deliberation when delineating what makes an action morally correct.

While act utilitarianism contemplates an action's consequences and calculates the total modification in utility to establish whether an action is right or wrong, rule utilitarianism (as well as Kantianism and Rawlsian social contracts) are rule-based. Each rule-based theory has different methods for determining whether a moral rule is veridical. While the rule utilitarian calculates the long-term consequences of everyone adhering to the rule would be for the total good, Kantians rely on the categorical imperative and Rawlsians consider whether rational people would approve of the rule for the mutual benefit of all. Virtue ethics focuses on the agent instead of the act itself or the consequences of the action (see Table 2.2).

Table 2.2 *Comparison of ethical theories*

Ethical Theory	Emphasis	Advantages	Disadvantages
Deontology	Dutifulness	Rational provision of universal moral rules that treats each person as a moral equal	Cannot resolve conflicting rules and duties. Undervalues the significance of happiness and social utility
Teleological utilitarianism	Consequences	Promotes happiness and utility	Calculation of consequences disregards issues of justice for the marginal populace
Contract	Rights	Framed in the language of rights and offers a motivation for morality	Certain acts have numerous characterizations. Problems of conflicting rights. Proposes only a minimal morality
Virtue	Character	Encourages moral development and moral education	Depends on homogeneous community standards for morality

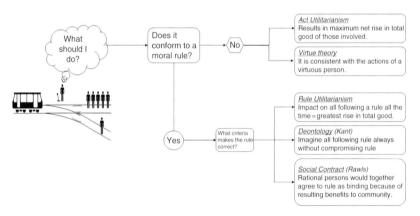

Figure 2.1   Comparison of the ethical approaches to the Trolley Dilemma

2.8   Floridi's Information Ethics

In addition to the traditional normative ethical perspectives, it is worth considering the recently developed metaphysical "information ethics" theory of Luciano Floridi (1999, 2008a, 2008b, 2013). While Floridi developed his theory of information ethics to complement deontological, utilitarian, contractual, and virtue ethics, information ethics is unlike more traditional ethical theories because it was developed with reference to the Information Age and its connection to digital information (Floridi, 1999, 2008a). As mentioned above, Floridi and Sanders (2005) have argued that traditional normative ethical theories have limited application to a globally networked information society. Floridi argues that traditional approaches are too anthropocentric and too focused on the impact of an agent's actions on others. Moreover, he believes that traditional theories do not offer adequate attention to the ways in which an agent's actions effect the biological, social, and informational environments. Floridi prefers a more ecological macroethics that he has termed Information Ethics.

The notable metaphysical claim in Floridi's (2006a) information ethics is that the totality of all that exists does so in the "infosphere" as an informational object or process (see Figure 2.2). Moreover, altering the characteristic data structures of informational objects and processes in the infosphere can result in significant damaged or destruction. Floridi refers to this damage or destruction as "entropy" that acts as an evil that should be avoided or minimized. Floridi's information ethics is also notable for its assertion that everything in the infosphere has at least a minimum value (or Spinozian right) that should be respected. With the construal of every existing entity to be "informational" and consisting of at least a minimal moral worth, Floridi's information ethics can complement traditional normative ethical theories.

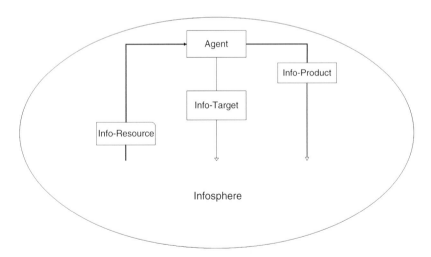

Figure 2.2   Floridi's information ethics and the infosphere

Floridi's information ethics considers everything that exists to be "informational" objects or processes. The information ethics position proposes "that there is something even more elemental than life, namely being – that is, the existence and flourishing of all entities and their global environment – and something more fundamental than suffering, namely entropy. The latter is most emphatically not the physicists' concept of thermodynamic entropy" (Floridi, 2006b, p. 25). Moreover, for Floridi's information ethics, being/information has an inherent value that is validated by understanding the Spinozian right of each informational entity to persist in its own condition. These entities will be described as informational objects (i.e., data clusters) and any existing entity will be a separate, self-contained, data cluster containing:

(i)   The appropriate data structures, which constitute the nature of the entity in question, that is, the state of the object, its unique identity, and its attributes; and

(ii) a collection of operations, functions, or procedures, which are activated by various interactions or stimuli (that is, messages received from other objects or changes within itself) and correspondingly define how the object behaves or reacts to them. (Floridi, 2006b, p. 25)

At Floridi's level of abstraction, informational systems are more than simply living systems. Instead, information systems are elevated agents of any action described informationally. Furthermore, Floridi contends that moral good and evil can be established even in the absence of biologically sentient participants (Floridi & Sanders, 2001, 2004). Hence, Floridi's information ethics framework moves beyond a biocentric focus to an ontocentric one that includes nonbiologic entities (e.g., data entities) that can act as objects of moral discourse.

In Floridi's (2014) book, *The Fourth Revolution*, the metaphysical approach to information ethics is apparent in his claims that the ultimate nature of reality consists of information. Moreover, he asserts that everyone lives in the "infosphere" as "inforgs" (i.e., information organisms):

Minimally, infosphere denotes the whole informational environment constituted by all informational entities, their properties, interactions, processes, and mutual relations . . . . Maximally, infosphere is a concept that can also be used as synonymous with reality, once we interpret the latter informationally. In this case, the suggestion is that what is real is informational and what is informational is real. (p. 41)

2.9   Searle's Critique: What a Computer Cannot Know

In a piece for the *New York Review of Books*, John Searle (2014) calls into question the central claims advanced by Floridi's information ethics. Of particular concern for Searle is the distinction between an epistemic sense (having to do with knowledge) and an ontological sense (having to do with existence). While the epistemic sense draws distinctions between types of claims (beliefs, assertions, assumptions, etc.) and evaluates the epistemic objectivity (e.g., epistemic fact that Rembrandt lived in Amsterdam) versus epistemic subjectivity (subjective opinion that Rembrandt was the greatest Dutch painter that ever lived), Searle contends that beneath this episte-mological distinction between types of claims there is an ontological distinction between modes of existence. While some entities exist without dependence on being experienced (brute facts like mountains and mole-cules), other entities exist only insofar as they are experienced (qualia: pain or itch). For Searle, it is irrelevant whether a machine registers an itch because it not really an itch until it is consciously experienced (in which case it is viewed to be ontologically subjective). A related distinction is between observer independent (brute facts like mountains that exist regardless of our attitudes) and observer dependent (money, government, and marriage) and exist only insofar as people have certain attitudes toward them. While most elements of human civilization (e.g., money, marriage) are observer relative in their ontology because they are created by con-sciousness, the consciousness that creates them is not observer relative. Searle asserts that the distinction between the observer independent sense of information (psychologically real) and the observer relative sense of information (no psychological reality at all) effectively undermines Floridi's concept that we are all living in the infosphere because almost all of the information in the infosphere is observer relative. While con-sciousness in humans (and animals) has intrinsic information, there is no intrinsic information in maps, computers, mountains, or molecules. Moreover, according to Searle, the sense in which they contain informa-tion is in fact relative to conscious minds processing them. The application of these distinctions to Floridi's metaphysical information ethics results in a realization that the information in question is observer relative. Floridi's assertion that "reality" appropriately understood is made up entirely of information falls short in that information exists relative to consciousness.

Searle's biological naturalism is classically illustrated in his Chinese Room Argument. Searle (1980) asks the reader to imagine a monolingual

English speaker who has been locked in a room and given a large batch of Chinese writing, a batch of Chinese script, and a set of rules in English for correlating the batch of Chinese script with the batch of Chinese writing. The rules that correlate one set of formal symbols (i.e., syntactic) with another set of formal symbols allows the monolingual English speaker to identify the symbols entirely by their shapes (see Figure 2.3). An additional batch of Chinese symbols and more instructions in English allow the monolingual English speaker to correlate elements of this third batch with elements of the Chinese scripts and the Chinese writings. Moreover, they instruct the monolingual English speaker to return certain sorts of shapes when presented with certain sorts of Chinese symbols. Those giving the monolingual English speaker the symbols call the large batch of Chinese writing a "script" (i.e., data structure with natural language processing applications), the batch of Chinese script is called a "story," and the set of rules in English are called "questions." The symbols returned by the monolingual English speaker are called "answers to the questions"; the set of rules in English are called "the program." The monolingual English speaker knows none of this. Nevertheless, after a great deal of practice, the monolingual English speaker becomes so efficient at following the instructions that it appears as if the monolingual English speaker's responses are indistinguishable from those of Chinese speakers. Moreover, just observing the answers delivered by the mono-lingual English speaker does not allow observers to know that the mono-lingual English speaker does not know a word of Chinese. Searle's argument is that the production of answers via the manipulation of uninterpreted formal symbols by the monolingual English speaker is the same as a computer running a translation program. In terms of moral agency, there is more to ethical decision-making and actions than simply bringing about good or harm by exceeding (or failing to exceed) a predetermined threshold. Instead, moral agency requires an understand-ing of the nature of the good or harm in question and that the agent's own choice and action brought about the good or harm.

Searle's argument is that Floridi's ontocentric view that data entities can act as objects of moral discourse is flawed unless the computations carried out are done so by conscious human beings. The computations found in Floridi's information ethics are implemented in actual pieces of machinery that are observer relative. According to Searle, the brute physical state transitions in a piece of electronic machinery can only be considered computations relative to some consciousness that can computationally interpret the processes. While it can be stated as an epistemically objective

SEARLE'S CHINESE ROOM

Assume that you are part of a programme designed to reproduce naturally spoken Chinese, about which you know absolutely nothing. You are located in a room in China, which has an input window through which you receive Chinese characters (ideograms conveying questions from the Chinese people outside your room). You then have a complex manual in which you look up instructions on what ideograms form the most appropriate answers to questions written in ideograms. By carefully (and blindly) following the instruction manual, you assemble responses in ideograms that you produce from the output window of your room. If the instruction manual is comprehensive enough, it is possible that Chinese speakers outside the room would be convinced that they are talking to another Chinese-speaking human being inside the room. But do you literally *understand* Chinese? Or are you merely *simulating* the ability to understand Chinese?

Figure 2.3   Chinese Room Argument (from Cavanna, 2018; reprinted with permission from the publisher)

fact that I am composing this manuscript using a word processing program, it is not the case that the word processing program, though implemented electronically, is not an electrical phenomenon. Instead, it exists relative to an observer. Searle's account of consciousness (biological naturalism) is in stark contrast to Floridi's perspective that all the elements of the universe, including persons, are information. The problem for Floridi is how to balance his ontocentric information ethics perspective with atomic physics and evolutionary biology. If Searle is correct, and he appears to be, then all the information found in the universe is either intrinsic or observer relative. Furthermore, both depend on human or animal consciousness. Following Searle, consciousness should be viewed as the basis of information instead of information being the basis of consciousness.

2.10   Extend Mind and the Chinese Room

Searle and his "Chinese Room" are a problem for Floridi to the extent that cognition occurs solely within the brain. For the Chinese Room Argument to hold, one must maintain the assumption that cognitive processes end at the boundaries of skin and skull. However, the thesis advanced by Clark and Chalmers (1998) challenges the supposition that cognition can take place only in a brain. The extended mind view addresses what Searle has referred to as the "systems reply" to the Chinese Room Argument:

> While it is true that the individual person who is locked in the room does not understand the story, the fact is that he is merely part of a whole system, and the system does understand the story. The person has a large ledger in front of him in which are written the rules, he has a lot of scratch paper and pencils for doing calculations, he has "data banks" of sets of Chinese symbols. Now, understanding is not being ascribed to the mere individual; rather it is being ascribed to this whole system of which he is a part. (Searle, 1980, p. 419)

Taking the extended mind approach into consideration, there is an apparent similarity between Searle's monolingual English speaker (and his Chinese room) and Otto (and his notebook). If one accepts that Otto's notebook is an extension of his cognitive processes, then it follows that that the manual used by the monolingual English speaker is an extension of cognitive processes.

While Searle's Chinese room can be a problem for Floridi's Information Ethics, potential assistance may be found in the addition of algorithmic computational processes found in the feedback loops of the extended mind (see Figure 2.4). These algorithms consist of the rules, strategies, and procedures that a person can retrieve from memory to aid problem-solving. Moreover, these algorithms allow for additional contributions (in addition to the brain) to conceptions of mental processing. We do not rely only on our brains to perform activities of daily living. Instead, most of us are extending out cognitive processes with the algorithmic

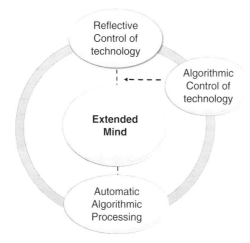

Figure 2.4   Coupling algorithms and the extended mind

devices that we keep close at hand (Fitz & Reiner 2016; Nagel, Hrincu, & Reiner, 2016; Nagel & Reiner, 2018; Reiner & Nagel, 2017).

2.11   Conclusions

Cyberpsychologists often deal with moral issues and dilemmas that range from sociocultural inequities of technological distribution to balancing complex aspects of research. Ethical perspectives in cyberpsychology can be understood in terms of normative and descriptive inquiries into applied ethics issues in cyberpsychology research and praxes. While the cyberpsychologist's training in ethical issues typically emphasizes specific developments and the four principles developed initially by Beauchamp and Childress, developments in the contexts and nature of research in the digital age (especially with the growth of the Internet) have resulted in new ethical questions. The result is a host of questions that these regulations and guidelines do not answer in the context of cyberpsychology. Moreover, they obscure judgments about which consequences are best. When these principles are in conflict, the cyberpsychologist may have difficulty deciding which principle should govern decision-making.

While it would be advantageous to have a straightforward set of principles, there are a number of ethical theories with disparate conceptions of what it means to live morally. In this chapter, there was a brief overview of some of the leading classical ethical approaches (e.g., deontological, consequential, and virtue ethics) found in the Western tradition. Although previous discussion of ethics and technology found in the literature have largely pursued application of leading classical ethical approaches found in the Western tradition to ethical judgments and decision-making, technologies are rapidly becoming more intimately related to our cognitive and emotional processes. As a result, there is a need to start considering ethical aspects of cyberpsychology research that takes seriously the increasing integration of "cyber" with psychology. Floridi's theory of information ethics can be helpful here because it was developed with reference to the Information Age and its connection to digital information. Floridi contends that informational systems are more than simply living systems. Instead, information systems are elevated agents of any action described informationally. Moreover, moral good and evil can be established even in the absence of biologically sentient participants. The information ethics framework moves beyond a biocentric focus to an ontocentric one that includes nonbiologic entities (e.g., data entities) that can act as objects of moral discourse.

As discussed in this chapter, Searle disagrees with Floridi and argues consciousness plays a role in reflective interpretation of information that poses challenges to the purely ontocentric perspective found in Floridi's metaphysical information ethics. Searle's critique leaves the cyberpsychologist with a problem. What does the cyberpsychologist do when faced with the reality that our research involves symbiotic relations between our biological human subjects and novel technologies? Moreover, we need to develop an ethical approach to cyberpsychology that is relevant to our increasingly digital world.

In the next chapter ("Digital and Extended Selves in Cyberspace"), the focus will be on extending our understandings of human conscious processing of information using an extended cognition (also known as "extended mind") approach. According to the extended mind approach, cognitive processes consist of complex feedback (including feedforward and feedaround) loops among brain, body, and the external world (see Clark, 2008; Clark & Chalmers, 1998). Following the extended mind approach, a cyberpsychologist may consider cognitive processes as going beyond wetware (i.e., one's brain) to software and hardware used by one's brain. Moreover, cognition can be viewed as something being processed by a system that is coupled with the environment (Clark, 2008; Clark & Chalmers, 1998). The cyberpsychologist can answer ethical questions using an extended mind approach in which our interactions with technologies like smartphones and the Internet form an extended cognitive system that performs functions that would otherwise be accomplished via the action of internal brain-based cognitive processes. The extension of mental processes outside of the brain (e.g., technologies of the extended mind) means that mental processes cannot be fully reduced to brain processes. According to Andy Clark (2003), we are naturally born cyborgs. So, the addition of neuroethical formulations (see Chapter 4) to a brain-based cyberpsychology perhaps takes us closer to a need for cyborg ethics. In Chapter 4, there will be a discussion of neuroethical approaches to a brain-based cyberpsychology. This will involve a consideration of recent progress in the neurosciences that raises a host of ethical issues concerning the applications of technology and their implications for individuals and society. The resulting neuroethics extends classical ethical approaches and the ways in which we think about ourselves as persons, moral agents, and spiritual beings (Farah, 2005).

CHAPTER 3

Digital and Extended Selves in Cyberspace

3.1   The Continuity of Persons and Technology

Social media technologies (e.g., Internet, Twitter, texting, smartphones) have the potential to extend our cognitive, affective, and social processes beyond the wetware of our brains. An important component for our understanding of the cognitive, affective, and social processes found in cyberpsychology is the notion that technology is an extension of our cognitive processes (Parsons, 2015a, 2017). It is becoming increasingly apparent that the technologies used in cyberpsychology research have the potential to extend a person's cognitive processes beyond the embodied cognition of their forebears (Parsons, Gaggioli, & Riva, 2017). Take your smartphone, for example. Whether you are called on to remember information, compare new information to old, calculate, navigate, or translate, your smartphone can provide you with access to an abundance of information and guidance. Some of this information is accessible publicly via Internet sites that can inform you of everything from the addresses and menus at restaurants in an area to answers arising from debates during dinner conversations. Other information may include more personal information, such as your contacts, emails, text messages, posts, calendar appointments, and even logs of your activities (purchases, articles and books read, films viewed, number of steps taken on a given day, calories, and so forth).

In today's massively interconnected world of persons, machines, and algorithms, some important questions emerge: Is this information part of my mind or is it part of the smartphone? When I use such technologies to help me remember information, compare new information to old, calculate, navigate, or translate is it me doing the thinking or is it the technologies? Perhaps it is an interaction between the two? Does this human–technology interaction form part of an extended mental loop that allows for augmented mental processing inside my skull? If so, what are the ethical implications? If technology extends my mind into the external world, should I apply the same ethical considerations that govern my everyday life to anything that results in my extended mind loop?

3.2   Extended Cognition

A relatively recent development in the philosophy of mind and cognitive science known as "extended mind" (also known as "extended cognition") represents modes of human cognizing as consisting in complex feedback (including feedforward and feed-around) loops among brain, body, and the external world (see Clark, 2008; Clark & Chalmers, 1998; see also Menary, 2010). The catalyst for this theory was a collaborative paper by Andy Clark and David Chalmers (1998) that presented us with an extended mind theory. Following the extended mind approach, a cyberpsychologist may consider cognitive processes as going beyond wetware (i.e., one's brain) to software and hardware used by one's brain. Moreover, cognition can be viewed as something being processed by a system that is coupled with the environment (Clark, 2008; Clark & Chalmers, 1998). The cyberpsychologist can answer the questions raised above using an extended mind approach in which our interactions with technologies like smartphones and the Internet form an extended cognitive system that perform functions that would otherwise be accomplished via the action of internal brain-based cognitive processes.

3.2.1   Parity Principle

The questions mentioned in the previous section are asking about whether we should apply a parity-stance to our ethical considerations of the internal and external mind. Clark and Chalmers answer yes and employ a "parity principle" as follows:

> If, as we confront some task, a part of the world functions as a process which, were it to go on in the head, we would have no hesitation in recognizing as part of the cognitive process, then that part of the world is (so we claim) part of the cognitive process. (Clark & Chalmers, 1998, p. 8)

Early examples of the parity principle can be found in Clark and Chalmers's *Gedankenerfahrung* (i.e., thought experiment), wherein fictional characters Inga and Otto must navigate to a museum on Fifty-Third Street in New York City. While Inga can simply consult her internal brain-based memory processes to recall the proper directions to the museum, Otto has Alzheimer's disease and has limited recall of directions. As a result, Otto must also rely on directions found in a notebook that function as an external supporter for his internal brain-based memory processes. Both Inga and Otto arrive at the museum safely, regardless of the fact that, for Inga, the memory was based on her internal brain-based memory processes and, for Otto, his external notebook. This thought experiment illuminates the information-processing loops that extend outside the neural realm to include elements of our social and technological environments. According to Clark and Chalmers, there are four "trust and glue" criteria for objects that may act as candidate extenders of cognition:

1. **Constancy**.
   Otto's notebook is readily available when he wants it.
2. **Facility**.
   Otto's effort and time to recover information from the notebook are negligible.
3. **Trust**.
   Otto's trust of information written in his notebook is automatic.
4. **Prior endorsement**.
   Otto has, in the past, endorsed information found in the notebook. This is apparent in the fact that he recorded the information in the notebook for future use.

It is important to note that none of the criterion listed is required to hold unconditionally. Take the first criterion of "constancy." The thesis does not necessitate that Otto's notebook be available under every circumstance. Instead, the notebook should be available when Otto finds it helpful. Moreover, "facility" reflects a close coupling of the external aid to its user.

3.2.2   *New Technologies Exemplifying the Extended Mind Thesis*

More recently, Chalmers (2011) and Clark (2010a, 2010b) have updated the technologies that are, in certain situations, accurately described as part of one's mental apparatus. Examples of new technologies exemplifying the extended mind thesis include smartphones (e.g., Apple's iPhone; Samsung Galaxy series), smart watches, iPads, tablets, the Internet, Google Glass, and many others. In a foreword to Andy Clark's (2008) *Supersizing the Mind*, David Chalmers explains his iPhone as follows:

> A month ago, I bought an iPhone. The iPhone has already taken over some of the central functions of my brain. It has replaced part of my memory,

storing phone numbers and addresses that I once would have taxed my brain with. It harbors my desires: I call up a memo with the names of my favorite dishes when I need to order at a local restaurant. I use it to calculate, when I need to figure out bills and tips. It is a tremendous resource in an argument, with Google ever present to help settle disputes. I make plans with it, using its calendar to help determine what I can and can't do in the coming months. I even daydream on the iPhone, idly calling up words and images when my concentration slips. (Chalmers, 2008, p. 1)

These smart technologies may, under some circumstances, realize a user's cognitive states and beliefs external to the physical boundaries of one's body (Clark, 2003). This extension of mental processes outside of the brain requires that mental processes not be fully reduced to brain processes. Smartphones connected to the Internet can extend our brain-based memory and allow for novel investigations into the interactions of persons as they engage with a global workspace and connected knowledgebases. In fact, mobile technologies may allow for interactive possibilities that shift the ways in which we understand ourselves and the nature of our cognitive and epistemic capabilities (Parsons, 2017).

In addition to smartphones, the idea of extended cognitive processes can be applied to the specific sociotechnical context of the Web (Smart, 2012). A "Web-extended mind" is the idea that the Internet can serve as an instrument for realizing human mental states and processes. Take, for example, our everyday enhancements of our cognitive performance using various technologies (e.g., tablets and iPads). We can store our memories using technologies. For example, Otto may not be able to remember what the average temperature is on Mars. He can, with the use of his technologies, recall that while there are various in situ temperatures that have been reported, a commonly reported value is –63 degrees Celsius (–81 degrees Fahrenheit; 210 Kelvin) . The potential for Internet-based extension of our cognitive processes is even more apparent with the advent of mobile Internet technologies. While early iterations of the Internet required that we be plugged in (i.e., wired), later iterations only required that we be near a router. With the influx and expansion of tablets and iPads in our everyday lives, the Internet's vast information base is just a click or utterance away. The technological assets of Internet-enabled tablets and iPads offer several improvements to deliberations on externalization. While the early metaphors emphasized external memory storage, today's Internet-enabled iPads and tablets extend beyond memory assistants to robust mobile computation devices. In fact, Internet-enabled mobile technologies allow cyberpsychologists to investigate the interactions of persons as they participate with a global workspace and connected knowledgebases.

Furthermore, access to the Internet may allow for interactive possibilities that shift the ways in which we see learning and our understanding of cognitive and epistemic competences.

3.3   Brains, Minds, and Technology

3.3.1   Cartesian Dualism

Under what circumstances does a device qualify as a technology of the extended mind? To answer this question we need to explore what is meant by the word "mind." While a fully nuanced elucidation of the term "mind" is beyond the scope of this chapter, a few words of clarification will contextualize our understanding of technology of the extended mind. Advances in neuroscience in general and brain imaging specifically have shown us time and time again that there are neural correlates for mental processes (mind events). Hence, a specific distinction can be made between brain and mind. The distinction herein is not meant to suggest Cartesian dualism (i.e., there is brain-stuff and mind-stuff). René Descartes (1641) argued *sum res cogitans* (i.e., "I am thinking substance") to separate mind and matter, which thereby expelled mind from nature. This view of mind and world considers the mind and its cognitions as completely sequestered from the external world that we endeavor to experience.

3.3.2   Problems for Descartes' Mind as a Thinking Thing

Descartes' idea that the mind is a thinking thing has been critiqued and found wanting. David Hume (1748) argued that introspection about ourselves results in an assemblage of ideas but not in a mind that has the ideas. Instead, we just end up with a stream of impressions without a persisting and substantial self (no personal identity). Likewise, Kant (1781/1998) contended that the mind is a not a substance. Instead, he concluded that the mind is just a unifying factor that acts as a reasonable opening to experience. Ludwig Wittgenstein (1958) argues the issue as follows:

> It is misleading then to talk of thinking as of a "mental activity." We may say that thinking is essentially the activity of operating with signs. This activity is performed by the hand, when we think by writing; by the mouth and larynx, when we think by speaking; and if we think by imagining signs or pictures, I can give you no agent that thinks. If then you say that in such cases the mind thinks, I would only draw your attention to the fact that you are using a metaphor. (p. 6)

In addition to rational arguments against the mind as a thing, there are a host of problems for dualism found in the sciences: clinical neuropsychology (Why does cognition change after brain damage?); physics (How does the immaterial mind causally interact with the material brain?; conservation of energy); biological development (If we begin as material beings, when is the nonphysical mind-stuff added?); and neuroscience (How is it that we are able to neuroimage cognitive processes and how is it that brain stimulation changes cognition?). Following Wittgenstein and the neuroscience, the aim herein is to keep from mixing these ontological levels in a way that so often ends in muddling the relation between brain and mind. A specific distinction can be made between brain and mind, in which the brain is understood as a thing while the mind is understood as a concept.

3.3.3   Unmixing Ontological Levels

For those interested in advancing scientific cyberpsychology, this dualistic conception of mind is not very palatable as it is at odds with most of the clinical neurosciences (Bhugra & Ventriglio, 2017; Casey et al., 2013; Damasio, 1994; Insel et al., 2010; Ventriglio & Bhugra, 2015), as well as the cognitive neurosciences (Churchland, 1986, 1988, 1994, 2002; Churchland & Churchland, 2002; Crick, 1994; Crick & Koch, 2003; Dehaene & Naccache, 2001; Dennett, 1991; Dum, Levinthal, & Strick, 2016; Edelman, 2004; Koch, 2004; Lamme, 2006; Tononi, 2008; Tononi & Koch, 2008; Zeki, 2002). Some may want to argue that an immaterial mind is needed because it is the special stuff that makes it possible for us to have consciousness and qualia to think and act freely. The dualist may want to ask, "How does my brain generate mental states?" This is an important question and one that neuroscientists of consciousness are seeking to answer. However, adding an immaterial mind to fill the gaps just leads to the rejoinder "How does my mind generate mental states?" The mystery continues when we replace brain with mind as the basis of these capacities. As a result, there is no explanatory advantage in the dualist argument for mind as a thinking thing. Ockham's razor can be used here to shave off the immaterial thinking substance, because we ought not to multiply entities beyond what is necessary. A specific distinction can be made between brain and mind, in which the brain is understood as a thing while the mind is understood as a concept. As mentioned, the aim here is to keep from mixing these ontological levels in a way that so often ends in unnecessary muddling of the relation between brain and mind. Our perception of the external world is essential for our activities of daily living. Successful interaction with the external environment is contingent on the brain's sensory processing and can be interrupted by damage both to sensory cortices and to other brain areas. Brain-based cyberpsychologists are increasingly able to explore the ways in which the causal interplay between different brain regions and our technologies impact sensory processing and participant behaviors and decisions.

3.3.4   Brains in Vats

What are cyberpsychologists interested in the interface between humans and technologies to do? One popular *Gedankenerfahrung* is the brain-in -a-vat thought experiment in which a disembodied brain is placed in a life-sustaining vat and stimulated by a supercomputer to produce the same phenomenal content and/or subjective experiences that the brain would have when it was embodied (Putnam, 1982). The brain-in-a-vat thought experiment functions as a methodological device to demonstrate the neural correlates of conscious mental experiences. Thomas Metzinger (2003) describes this as follows:

> [T]here is a minimally sufficient neural correlate for the content of con-sciousness at any given point in time. If all properties of this local neural correlate are fixed, the properties of subjective experience are fixed as well. Of course, the outside world could at the same time undergo considerable changes. For instance, a disembodied but appropriately stimulated brain in a vat could – *phenomenologically* – enjoy exactly the same kind of conscious experience you do right now while reading this book. (p. 547)

This popular thought experiment depicts the intuition that mental pro-cesses (i.e., cognition and consciousness) are contingent on the wetware (i.e., the brain) between our ears. As can be seen in the brain-in-a-vat scenario, you are asked to imagine that your own brain has been detached from your skull and relocated to a vat of nutrient fluids and that your brain is being simulated by a supercomputer to produce phenomenological experiences. In this situation, it is at times argued that your brain has no way of knowing whether it is still in your skull or in a vat. For all we know, this is our current situation.

The extended mind approach views thinking as dependent on both the ongoing work of the brain and/or the extraorganismic environment. Clark (2008) describes the extended mind approach as follows:

> According to EXTENDED, the actual local operations that realize certain forms of human cognizing include inextricable tangles of feedback,

feedforward, and feed-around loops: loops that promiscuously criss-cross the boundaries of brain, body, and world. The local mechanisms of mind, if this is correct, are not all in the head. Cognition leaks out into body and world. (p. xxviii)

Consider Otto in a vat. According to the extended mind approach, a functional parity exists between Otto in a vat and embodied Otto. The functional role played by the notebook (and the rest of the external world) is the same role played by the vat and supercomputer connected to Otto's envatted brain. Some have attempted to make this distinction more clear via the hypothesis of extended cognition (Bernecker, 2014; Palermos, 2014; Pöyhönen, 2014). According to the extended cognition approach, when portions of the environment come to be "properly coupled" to an agent's brain, they can be deemed constitutive parts of the whole cognitive mechanism.

3.4 Dual-Process Approach: Automatic and Controlled Processes

How does the extended mind perform the cognitive operations via external technologies? One approach presented by Parsons (2017) in *Cyberpsychology and the Brain* is a dual-process model (automatic and controlled processing) approach for cyberpsychological research. Decision-making involves the brain's controlled and automatic processes. Controlled processes are cognitive processes that are associated with conscious awareness and require effortful control and intention, as well as capacity for inhibition. On the other hand, automatic processes such as reading are not necessarily in conscious awareness and occur spontaneously (see Table 3.1).

Dual-process approaches consider the mind (ontologically understood as a concept not a thing) or cognitive processes as involving (at least) two quite different systems. Keith Frankish and Jonathan Evans (2009) explain the dual-process approach as follows:

> Dual-process theories hold that human thought processes are subserved by two distinct mechanisms, one fast, automatic and non-conscious, the other slow, controlled and conscious, which operate largely independently and compete for behavioral control. In their boldest form, they claim that humans have, in effect, two separate minds. (p. v)

An example of dual processing can be found in learning to drive. When you first learned to drive, you had to rely on your controlled processing to

Table 3.1 *Dual processes theories: automatic and controlled processes (from Satpute & Lieberman, 2006; reprinted with permission from the publisher)*

X-System	C-System
Parallel processing	Serial processing
Fast operating	Slow operating
Slow learning	Fast learning
Nonreflective consciousness	Reflective consciousness
Phylogenetically older	Phylogenetically newer
Representation of symmetric relations	Representation of asymmetric relations
Representation of common cases	Representation of special cases
	Representation of abstract concepts (e.g., negation, time)

consciously attend to operating the steering wheel, the accelerator (if a manual transmission, you also had to attend to shifting gears), and the brakes. Furthermore, you had to consciously attend to the road, traffic signals, and other people (in and out of cars). When learning to drive, the demands for your attention required even greater controlled processing when other cars and pedestrians were near, when traffic signals change, and when others are in the car. After time, however, you get to the point where you are an experienced driver and many aspects of driving become automated. While driving, you can navigate, react to changes in traffic conditions, and even carry on a conversation without consciously processing many of the automated processes. That said, there are occasions when traffic conditions change dramatically, forcing you to focus your attention once more using controlled cognitive processes.

Again, there are specific neural correlates for both automatic and controlled processes (compare Table 3.1 and Figure 3.1). Neuroimaging studies offer support for specific brain areas involved in these dual processes. While there are particular brain nodes and networks comprising a controlled system, there are other brain nodes and networks making up an automatic system (Goel et al., 2000; Goel & Dolan, 2003; Lieberman, 2007; Satpute & Lieberman, 2006; Spunt & Lieberman, 2014). Mathew Lieberman (2007), at UCLA, have put forward an allocation of neural processes that generally corresponds to automatic and controlled processing (see Figure 3.1).

In their framework, brain regions for automatic processing are referred to as the reflexive X-System (for the "x" in reflexive). Moreover, brain regions involved in controlled processing are called the reflective C-System (for the "c" in reflection). Using the driving example, while driving to work, your

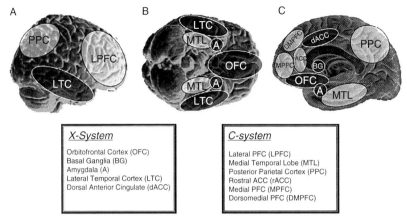

Figure 3.1 Sets of brain areas (i.e., neural correlates) of the reflexive X-System (automatic processing) and reflective C-System (controlled processing) presented on a canonical brain rendering from (a) lateral, (b) ventral, and (c) medial views. It is important to note that the subcortical structures (hippocampus, nucleus accumbens, and amygdala) are displayed on the cortical surface for ease of presentation. Moreover, the inverse view from Satpute & Lieberman (2006) is used (reprinted with permission from the publisher)

mind is on something your friend said to you instead of the task of driving. Out of nowhere, the car in front of you slams on its brakes and you must consciously return your focus to operating your car to keep from hitting the vehicle in front of you. From a neurocognitive perspective, this experience can be understood as back-and-forth procession between your cortex and basal ganglia. Your cortex is being used to consciously process whatever it was your friend had said to you, when you are suddenly aware of danger. The subcortical processing of the basal ganglia (i.e., striatum) and amygdal structures recognize a changed context that biases the frontal cortex to consider the threat, choose an alternative response, and implement that alternative.

3.4.1   *Automatic Processes and Extended Cognition*

According to Daniel Dennett (1996), our remarkable evolutionary success is less a factor of our large frontal lobes and more our capacity for extending our cognitive processes into the environment with which we interact. Hence, our enhanced intelligence is due to

> our habit of off-loading as much as possible of our cognitive tasks into the environment itself – extruding our minds (that is, our mental projects and

activities) into the surrounding world, where a host of peripheral devices we
construct can store, process and re-represent our meanings, streamlining,
enhancing, and protecting the processes of transformation that are our
thinking. This widespread practice of off-loading releases us from the
limitations of our animal brains. (pp. 134–135)

As mentioned in Section 3.2.1, the parity principle is a key component of
the extended mind thesis. Basically, this principle states that, if an external
process in our everyday world functions in a way that we regard as
a cognitive process when it is done with our internal brains, then the
external process should count as a cognitive process just like an internal
one. Hence, if using the calculator app on my smartphone helps me do
controlled mathematical operations faster than I can do with my algorithmic mind, then it should be part of my cognitive processing. Likewise, if an
Internet browsing app on my smartphone can offer intellectual stimulation
more rapidly than associations in my automatic processes, these smartphone applications should be counted as aspects of my cognitive architecture. Chalmers (2011) describes it this way:

> The dispositional beliefs, cognitive processes, perceptual mechanisms, and
> moods considered above all extend beyond the borders of consciousness,
> and it is plausible that it is precisely the nonconscious part of them that is
> extended. I think there is no principled reason why the physical basis of
> consciousness could not be extended in a similar way. It is probably so
> extended in some possible worlds: one could imagine that some of the
> neural correlates of consciousness are replaced by a module on one's belt,
> for example. (p. xiv)

For the cyberpsychologist, our automatic (unconscious) processes can be
thought to include embodied and extended processes. One could argue
that processes that result in conscious results could be included as an aspect
of automatic processes. Returning to the smartphone application example,
I could use my smartphone to connect myself with a cloud-based database
that substantially augments my memory capacity by procuring information at will with my smartphone. Also, with a smartphone, I can connect
with social media applications that could enhance my capacity for infer-
ential judgments and problem-solving.

3.4.2   Frontal Subcortical Circuits for Continuous Reciprocal Causation

How might this all work given the frontal subcortical circuits (see Figure 3.2)
that connect areas of the brain that are involved in automatic and controlled

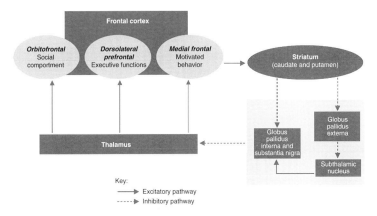

Figure 3.2 Frontal subcortical circuits (after McAllister, 2011; reprinted with permission from the publisher)

processing? Moreover, there are significant roles for posterior parietal and inferotemporal cortical areas via open connections to these circuits. For some time now, a corticocentric myopia has underappreciated the important contributions of subcortical regions to cognitive processing and behaviors (Parvizi, 2009). Cognitive and computational neuroscience increasingly portray the human cortex as a multilevel prediction engine. An important issue for dual-processing approaches is, how do subcortical contributions and affective processes (emotions) correspond with these emerging understandings? Mark Miller and Andy Clark (2018) argue that emotional and subcortical processing are not additional mechanisms operating alongside the multilevel predictive core. Instead, emotion and subcortical processing are apparently intertwined with the development of multilevel predictions that establish our perceptions and select our actions.

Frontal subcortical circuits present an added approach to comprehending neurocognitive processes and they take seriously the role of affective processes through behavior and movement (see chap. 2 in Parsons, 2017). Each frontal subcortical circuit is cortically anchored and includes behaviorally important circuits that start in the dorsolateral prefrontal, orbitofrontal, and superior medial frontal cortices. Each frontal subcortical circuit shares comparable topography and physiology. Furthermore, the frontal subcortical circuits include the same associated structures, which are assembled in parallel (mostly separated from each other) with anatomical locations that are conserved as they pass through the striatum (i.e., caudate and putamen), globus pallidus, substantia nigra, and thalamus (see Figure 3.2).

It is important to note that each frontal subcortical circuit has a direct pathway and indirect pathway. The direct pathway (glutamatergic) results in sustained activation of the cortical component and releases glutamate to the corresponding areas of the striatum, which typically involves the caudate nucleus. The indirect pathway (GABA-ergic) for each frontal subcortical circuit balances the direct pathway and deviates from the direct pathway when striatal efferents project to the globus pallidus externa. While the direct pathway disinhibits the thalamus, the indirect pathway inhibits it. The influences of direct and indirect pathways govern the control of thalamocortical connections and the cognitive, motoric, or behavioral outputs of the frontal subcortical circuits. The frontal subcortical circuits have been found to play roles in motor control, executive functions (dorsolateral prefrontal; dlPFC), motivation (superior medial frontal – i.e., anterior cingulate), and affect (medial orbitofrontal; OFC).

3.5   A Tri-Process Theory: Automatic, Controlled, and Algorithmic

A problem for a corticocentric view is that it entails the supposition of a well-defined separation between a higher "cognitive brain" and a subordinate "emotional brain" and the notion of a one-way influence from higher brain areas (top-down) to lower brain areas but not the other way around (bottom-up). The rapid advances in neuroscience are increasingly calling into question dichotomous views of neural processing (Cromwell & Panksepp, 2011; Miller & Clark, 2018). A way of considering how extended cognition might work, given that frontal subcortical circuits connect areas of the brain that are involved in automatic and controlled processing, is to expand on the dual-process model by subdividing controlled processing into reflective and algorithmic thinking.

3.5.1   Stanovich's Tripartite Model of Cognitive Processing

Stanovich (2009a, 2009b) developed a tripartite model of cognitive processing that includes autonomous (automatic) processing that is generally rapid and nonconscious use of heuristics. He distinguished two forms of controlled processing (slow and effortful) by developing two subdivisions: (1) reflective processing characterizes the goals of cognitive processing, goal-relevant beliefs, and optimizing choices of action; and (2) algorithmic computational processing that includes "mindware" that consists of the

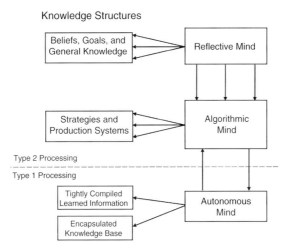

Figure 3.3 Stanovich's (2011) tripartite framework (reprinted with permission from the publisher)

rules, strategies, and procedures that a person can retrieve from memory to aid problem-solving (see Figure 3.3).

The algorithmic mind is notable for its ability to override the (less accurate) heuristic responses generated automatically by the autonomous processor (see Figure 3.4). Using the tripartite model, we can consider the mind as representing the broad array of cognitive resources that one deploys in the service of autonomous (automatic processing), reflective (controlled processes), and algorithmic thinking (Stanovich 2009a, 2009b, 2010; Stanovich, West, & Toplak, 2011).

According to Stanovich's tripartite model (2009a, 2009b, 2010), algorithmic processes are associated with computational efficiency and can be measured with standard intelligence tests. Reflective processes, on the other hand, are associated with critical and rational thought that may not be well measured by many standard intelligence tests. From a cyberpsychological perspective, the tripartite model could be understood using an example from social media use (see Figure 3.4). Let us say that, while you are working hard to meet an important deadline that is quickly approaching, you hear the chime from your smartphone prompting your autonomous processor to automatically reach for your phone and view the update. The autonomous processor is unreflective and furnishes an effortless response: "Grab the smartphone now!" However, you are up against a deadline and know that, if you check your social media notification, you

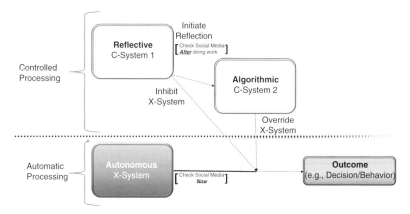

Figure 3.4 Functioning of tripartite framework. Autonomous (automatic) processing is generally rapid and involves nonconscious use of heuristics. Two forms of
controlled processing (slow and effortful) are distinguished by developing two
subdivisions: (1) reflective processing optimizing choices of action and (2) algorithmic mindware for computational processing and overriding the heuristic responses
of the autonomous processor

could be there for hours. Here, your reflective processor could inhibit the
autonomous processor and reassess your current situation: "Might suspend-
ing the desire to check my social media account to allow me to complete my
work be a better answer?" Finally, the algorithmic processor calculates the
final response after weighing the benefit of delayed gratification. Following
the completion of these computations, the algorithmic mind may override
the automatic processor if the valuation of completing one's work is greater
than the immediate gratification of viewing my social media. It is important
to note that the algorithmic processor is separate from the reflective processor in that it uses computational capacity instead of reflection to inhibit the
automatic response from the autonomous processor.

Corgnet, Hernán Gonzalez, and Mateo (2015) applied the tripartite model
to assess the impact of cyberloafing on the job performance of 264 under-
graduates. They conceptualized cyberloafing as searching the Internet or
checking one's Facebook page when the participant is supposed to be
working on a task. The desire to check one's Facebook page could result
in a response by the autonomous processer (automatic) to seek immediate
gratification. Refraining from cyberloafing hinges on the reflective processor's capacity to inhibit this automatic response and remain focused on the
work task. They set up this reflective strategy so that it would lead to delayed
gratification in the form of increased task earnings that could be collected at

the end of the experiment. They hypothesized that, while there would be little relationship between measures of algorithmic processes (measured by the Scholastic Aptitude Test) and cyberloafing, there would be a negative relationship between cyberloafing and assessments of the reflective processes (as measured by the Cognitive Reflection Test – designed specifically to capture cognitive impulsiveness). They found that cyberloafing behaviors (time participants browsed the Internet for nonwork purposes) were not explained by traditional measures of rational thinking (algorithmic processing). This suggests the need for novel measures of reflective processing.

3.5.2 Somatic Markers

A limitation of the tripartite view is that it misses the affective component in judgment and decision-making. It does talk about an autonomous processor that automatically compels action and a reflective processor that can inhibit the autonomous processor so that the algorithmic processor can calculate the final response after weighing the benefit of delayed gratification. What needs more development is this process of valuation and weighing of benefits. This valuation appears to be consistent with the somatic marker hypothesis (Bechara & Damasio, 2005), in which the experience of an emotion (e.g., gut feeling, hunch) results in a somatic marker that weights outcomes to bias future choices of action. Hence, the somatic marker is thought to play a role in decision-making via its biasing of available response selections. When persons are faced with decisions, they experience somatic sensations in advance of real consequences of possible different alternatives. Neuroimaging studies of persons performing risky decision tasks have revealed activation in the orbitofrontal cortex (Ernst et al., 2002; Windmann et al., 2006), which appears to be significant for signaling the anticipated rewards/punishments of an action and for adaptive learning. Furthermore, studies have shown that damage to the ventromedial prefrontal cortex and the amygdala prevents the use of somatic (affective) signals for advantageous decision-making (Bechara et al., 1996). In summary, decision-making models may be enhanced by a somatic marker theory. This will be especially true as we move to ethical decision-making in our uses of technology.

3.6 Technologies of the Extended Mind

The addition of algorithmic computational processing comports well with the extended mind hypothesis because these algorithms consist of the rules, strategies, and procedures that a person can retrieve from memory to aid problem-solving, which allows for additional contributions (in addition to the brain) to conceptions of mental processing. The extension of mental processes outside of the brain means that mental processes cannot be fully reduced to brain processes (Levy, 2007a). Peter Reiner and Saskia Nagel (2017), at the University of British Columbia, point out that we do not rely only on our brains to perform activities of daily living. Instead, most of us are extending our cognitive processes with the algorithmic devices that we keep close at hand. Reiner and colleagues have termed these algorithmic devices as technologies of the extended mind (Fitz & Reiner 2016; Nagel, Hrincu, & Reiner, 2016; Nagel & Reiner, 2018; Reiner & Nagel, 2017). They point out that not every algorithmic function carried out by technologies external to the brain qualifies them as a technology of the extended mind (TEM; an abbreviation used by Reiner and colleagues). Instead, they contend that there is a comparatively continuous interface between brain and algorithm such that the person experiences the algorithmic device as an extension of the person's mind:

> It is not the case that every algorithmic function carried out by devices external to the brain qualifies them as a TEM, but rather that there is a relatively seamless interaction between brain and algorithm such that a person perceives of the algorithm as being a bona fide extension of a person's mind. This raises the bar for inclusion into the category of algorithms that might be considered TEMs. It is also the case that algorithmic functions that do not qualify as TEMs today may do so at some future point in time and vice versa. (Reiner & Nagel, 2017, p. 110)

To illustrate their point, they ask us to imagine a new driver for Uber (i.e., a company that allows nonprofessionals to act as chauffeurs using their own automobiles) who uses a global positioning system (GPS) to navigate New York City. While the driver's GPS is carrying out computational work that is external to his brain, they argue that it is not yet a technology of the extended mind. In fact, they contend, it will not be a technology of the extended mind until the algorithmic calculations and the driver's reliance on them are seamlessly integrated with the driver's cognitive processes. The examples and discussions found in the work of Reiner and colleagues are important because they move beyond the parity principle (found in the work of Clark and Chalmers) to specify the features needed for a technology to be an extension of a person's mind. They emphasize algorithms as key aspects of technologies of the extended mind.

In Figure 3.5, there is a framework for understanding technologies of the extended mind. What sorts of devices can be considered technologies of the

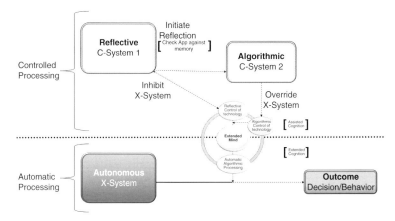

Figure 3.5 Framework for understanding technologies of the extended mind

extended mind? Not every algorithmic function performed by devices (external to the brain) should be understood as a technology of the extended mind. Instead, it is preferable to conceptualize technologies of the extended mind as a fairly continuous interface between brain and algorithm in which the person perceives the algorithm as being an actual extension of her or his mind.

As can be seen in Figure 3.5, there is an addition of automatic algorithmic processes from the technologies to the autonomous (automatic), reflective, and algorithmic processing of the tripartite model. For the technologies of the extended mind framework, the algorithmic processes of the technology can, over time, become an automated and algorithmic coupling of brain and technology. When the user first starts operating a new device, there is a period in which the user relies on controlled cognitive processes to inhibit and override automatic processes initiated by the device (see reflective and algorithmic control of technology in Figure 3.5). After using the technology for a period of time, the operations become overlearned and more or less automatic.

We can extend the idea of a driver using a GPS as a technology of the extended mind with an updated version of Inga's trip to the museum. In this updated scenario, Inga has reached the museum and is given a museum app for her smartphone that is integrated with a GPS. Inga is informed that she can search for exhibits by entering them into the mobile app that will show her the best route to exhibits. Once she arrives at a destination, the augmented reality–enabled mobile app can be used interactively by Inga to learn about the exhibit. This application is particularly helpful because it allows Inga not get lost, as many of the exhibits lead her to visit parts of the museum with which she was unfamiliar. Inga is somewhat skeptical about the mobile app as she is not very familiar with such technologies. In fact, Inga tends to be a bit of a luddite and rarely uses her smartphone for anything other than conversing. As a result, Inga remains alert (see controlled/reflective processing in Figure 3.5) to her environment so that she can be sure that she makes it to the museum exhibits without problem.

After some time, Inga begins to trust the smartphone application and only occasionally stops herself from automatically following the application's guidance (see inhibition and override of technology using reflective and algorithmic control of technology in Figure 3.5). Is Inga's mobile app and GPS functioning as a technology of the extended mind? While it is undoubtedly performing computations that are external to Inga's brain, the GPS in Inga's smartphone application is probably better considered to be cognitive assistance. Why is this the case? The answer is that neither the algorithmic calculations from the device nor Inga's use of them are automated with Inga's cognitive processes (see algorithmic control of technology in Figure 3.5). Now consider a different scenario in which Inga has experienced the exhibits several times over the course of a month. Even though she now has slightly more knowledge of the museum, she always uses the GPS in her smartphone application to navigate through the museum. The smartphone application has not failed her in its directions to exhibits or its information (e.g., artist, history, subtleties of the work) about the art at each exhibit. At this point, when she enters an exhibit into the smartphone application's search interface and the route is presented on the smartphone screen, she automatically follows it to the destination suggested by her smartphone and readily receives information about the art. The smartphone application is beginning to function as a technology of the extended mind because Inga has integrated its algorithmic processes into the working of her mind.

What are the potential ethical implications of Inga using a technology that extends her cognitive processes beyond her brain? One concern may be found with the GPS application for the museum on Inga's smartphone. Recall that Inga's initial use of the GPS application involved vigilant attention (see reflective control of technology in Figure 3.5) to both the application and the environment to make sure that she could trust the functioning of the application and not get lost. Here, the smartphone application is not functioning as a technology of the extended mind because, while it is performing computations that are external to Inga's brain, the GPS in Inga's smartphone is probably better considered as cognitive assistance (see algorithmic control of technology in Figure 3.5).

What if we changed the scenario a bit? Inga has been using the smartphone application for a few weeks and the connection between Inga and the mobile app has extended to the point that Inga has assimilated its algorithmic processing into the working of her mind (see automatic algorithmic processing by technology in Figure 3.5) while traveling both inside the museum and around her neighborhood. This includes traveling to and from work, as well as to and from the locations of various extracurricular activities. Inga is an art appraiser and she uses the application as she works on an assignment in the museum that requires that she travel to a new area of the museum to appraise some new items. Before lunch, she follows the smartphone's GPS to the appraisal area. On her way, she hears alerts from the phone as she passes a sign advertising the museum's constellation of eateries; and alerts chime again when the museum's eateries are just up ahead.

Here, the situation has changed as the algorithms have learned Inga's preferences and are attempting to influence her actions. Moreover, the algorithm from the mobile GPS application may increase its level of suggestion by "asking" Inga whether she would like to take a moment to get something to eat. While Inga may recognize that she needs to complete her assignment (continue to the appraisal area), she reasons that little harm would come from stopping to get something to eat. Here, one finds a clear effect of the technology on Inga that was influential enough to cause an alteration of her plan to complete her assignment. Most likely, Inga's employer and colleagues (as well as ethicists) would view this as undue influence. While the influence is relatively trivial, this scenario reflects a violation of autonomy.

This violation becomes much more pronounced when one considers the fact that the very same algorithm that has become an extension of Inga's mind is also an extension of the mind of the corporate entity that designed the smartphone application. Perhaps the corporate entity was paid by vendors at the museum's café for directing Inga to them. Such potential conflicts of interest muddy the ethical waters when attempting to ascertain the extent to which a technology of the extended mind has resulted in a violation of autonomy.

3.7 Conclusions

Given that technologies of the extended mind are those algorithmic devices that have a relatively seamless interaction between brain and algorithm,

Nagel and Reiner (2018) ask the ethical question, "What should our minds become when they are composed of a blend of brain and external resources?" (pp. 1–2). While Nagel and Reiner do not see an easy answer to this question, they do believe that it is important to have ethical safeguards in place when designing the extensions of our minds. Using a virtue ethics approach to technologies of the extended mind, they suggest that we consider how skillfully one is engaging with this choice. Moreover, is a given application helping us to alleviate suffering or to enhance good and virtue? Hence, what are the consequences of using a particular application and to what extent does it replace or enhance a user's biological brain functions?

The challenges of applying neuroscientific findings to technologies are numerous but attempts will be made in Chapter 4 (and throughout this book) to provide an ethical approach to cyberpsychology research and practice. Moreover, attempts have been made to present a framework for approaching ethical issues in the use of technologies. In Chapter 2 there was a discussion of the ways in which ethical approaches can be used for cyberpsychologists interested in current and emerging technologies. In Chapter 4, there will be an attempt to build on the extended cognition issues discussed in the present chapter to develop a brain-based cyberpsychology approach that uses neuroethics.

Neuroethics and the Future of Cyberpsychology

4.1   Introduction

Cyberpsychological research suggests that we are increasingly merging with our technology (Parsons, 2017; see also Chapter 3). Director of engineering at Google and chancellor of Singularity University, Ray Kurzweil (2010) has gone so far as predicting that, by the 2020s, we will have reverse-engineered the entire brain. Predictions abound related to the potential impact of nanobots on our consciousness, but we are still a long way from transhumanist imaginations about upgrading our brains with implantable computer chips. Despite the media hype about technologies that offer "limitless" possibilities, neuroenhancements typically result in only modest improvements (Farah, 2015a). While Kurzweil's predictions are specula-tive, and the media hype is apparent, there is increasing evidence of technology's accelerating pace. We have entered a transitional period in which our cognitive processers are merging with our technologies. As a result, we are gaining the advantage of what Peter Reiner and Saskia Nagel (2017) have dubbed technologies of the extended mind.

Advances in the human neurosciences and cyberpsychology have stirred interest in the potential for brain-based cyberpsychological investigations (Parsons, 2015a, 2017). Cyberpsychologists have a progressively fertile research field as their participants increasingly rely on technologies from the start of their days when they awaken, then continuing throughout their day, and finally concluding as they drift off to sleep. This is the experience of many of the adult population worldwide (expected to be 2.87 billion in 2020; Statista, 2017) who own a smartphone. It is important to note that these machines are more than just phones; the operations that they perform are remarkably varied, including information storage, calcu-lation, communication, navigation, and the ability to search the compre-hensive storehouses of knowledge. As a result, researchers have added learning to technologies to neuroeducation (Battro & Fischer, 2012;

Parsons, Lin, & Cockerham, 2019; Valentine & Kurczek, 2016), virtual reality to clinical neuropsychological assessments (Kane & Parsons, 2017; Parsons, 2015a, 2016); neuromodulation to pain (Giordano, 2008; Pourmand et al., 2018; Trost & Parsons, 2014); and psychotherapeutic interventions to persons struggling with mental health issues (Bohil, Alicea, & Biocca, 2011). These technologies are extending our cognitive abilities (see Chapter 3) and we are becoming proto-cyborgs (Clark, 2003).

4.2   Neuroscience of Social Media

There have also been developments in social neuroscience (Pan & Hamilton, 2018; Parsons, Gaggioli, & Riva, 2017) that have led to an emerging focus on the neuroscience of social media (Meshi, Tamir, & Heekeren, 2015). In a review of the emerging neuroscience of social media, Meshi, Tamir, and Heekeren (2015) consider an important area of cyberpsychology research – the developing global phenomenon of online social media (around 2 billion users throughout the world consistently using social networking sites). Their review has potential for brain-based cyberpsychologists interested in making use of social media sites to acquire new understanding of social cognitive processes and the neural systems that support them (see Figure 4.1). Social behaviors depend to a large extent on three brain networks: (1) the *mentalizing network* is a set of brain areas

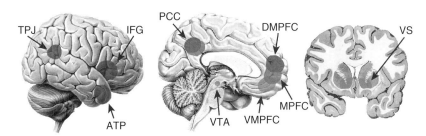

Trends in Cognitive Sciences

Figure 4.1 Proposed brain networks involved in social media use. Neuroimaging of social cognition with offline protocols has disclosed brain networks that may be involved in social media use: (a) the *mentalizing network*: dorsomedial prefrontal cortex (DMPFC), temporoparietal junction (TPJ), anterior temporal lobe (ATL), inferior frontal gyrus (IFG), and the posterior cingulate cortex/precuneus (PCC); (b) the *self-referential cognition network*: medial prefrontal cortex (MPFC) and PCC; and (c) the *reward network*: ventromedial prefrontal cortex (VMPFC), ventral striatum (VS), and ventral tegmental area (VTA) (from Meshi, Tamir, & Heekeren, 2015; reprinted with permission from the publisher)

involved in social cognition (dorsomedial prefrontal cortex, temporoparietal junction, anterior temporal lobe, inferior frontal gyrus, and the posterior cingulate cortex/precuneus; (2) the *self-referential cognition network* (medial prefrontal cortex and posterior cingulate cortex); and (3) the *social reward network* (ventromedial prefrontal cortex, ventral striatum, and ventral tegmental area).

They also outline social motives that drive people to use social media and propose neural systems supporting social media use. The mentalizing network may be involved when I think about how persons in my network will respond to a post I made. It is also involved when I think about how a specific person in my social media network may react on reading my feedback related to a post. Moreover, the mentalizing network could activate when I think about my friend's motivations for posting information online. The next brain network involved in social media is the self-referential cognition network. I may think about myself and then broadcast those thoughts online, which may provoke further self-referential thought. I may receive feedback that results in reflected self-appraisals. Moreover, social comparison requires us to think about our own behavior in relation to other social media users. A third brain network involved in social media is the social reward network. This network may be activated when I receive positive feedback in the form of a "like" or "friend" request. Reading my friends' posts may elicit reward activity because receiving information elicits curiosity. These rewards activate my brain reward system and compel me to return to Facebook for more.

These are just a few examples of areas that are increasingly being considered in terms of dynamic interactions that can be instantiated using emerging technologies. Moral implications for these advances in technologies, and their applications for research with humans, are increasingly apparent. Before cyberpsychologists undertake research with social media, they should take note of potential privacy and ethical concerns regarding this data (Barchard & Williams, 2008; Kosinski, et al., 2015). Even if a cyberpsychologist obtains consent from one participant to use their Facebook data, that does not mean that the cyberpsychologist has permission to download information from other users who did not give consent. If I have consented to be part of a study on Facebook posts and I choose to post a status update that a friend comments on, a cyberpsychologist running the study may have access to my friend's identity and her post and that may be a breach of my friend's privacy. These ethical issues and the brain networks involved in online social networking behaviors are important for cyberpsychology research.

4.3   The Brain and Ethical Decision-Making: Social Neuroscience

Social neuroscientists are increasingly able to identify neural correlates of social cognitive processes. In addition to studies investigating brain activations related to behavioral tasks that elicit emotional arousal, studies are also exploring ethical decision-making in the human brain. While multiple brain regions are often involved in the same social cognitive processes, there are certain brain regions that activate for several cognitive processes (Greene, 2015; Lieberman, 2007). As a result, attempts to extract cyberpsychological conclusions from the specific brain activations may lead to overinterpretation of the results (Lieberman, 2007). Table 4.1 offers a synopsis of brain areas related with significant aspects of ethical decision-making (Robertson, Voegtlin, & Maak, 2017).

As can be seen in Table 4.1, there are several brain regions involved in our ability to understand others, ourselves, and social interacts. These brain and social cognition relations are important for ethical decision-making and moral behaviors. The capacity for reflecting on and regulating oneself as a moral person involves consideration of one's own experiences to make sure that one is able to pursue or evade analogous experiences in the future (Lieberman, 2007). Ethical decision-making also involves one's experience of other minds. This is called the theory of mind (ToM) and it is important for understanding the moral beliefs and intentions of others (Frith & Singer, 2008). This capacity can be understood as taking an intentional stance (belief that we are interacting with another; Dennett, 1987) or mentalizing (observerving and interpreting one's interactions with others; Kliemann & Adolphs, 2018). These abilities allow us to experience empathy for another person's experiences (Frith & Singer, 2008) and interact socially via our understandings of trust, fairness, and cooperation (Tabibnia & Lieberman, 2007). Finally, moral judgments and decisions are an amalgamation of the above-mentioned social cognitive capacities (Robertson, Voegtlin, & Maak, 2017; Yoder & Decety, 2018).

The brain networks and neural systems that are involved in social decision-making depend on the coordination of multiple neurocognitive systems (Figure 4.2) that buttress domain-general processes (e.g., perspective-taking, understanding of mental state, as well as stimulus valuation and response selection [Yoder & Decety, 2018]).

As can be seen in Figure 4.2 (from Yoder & Decety, 2018), the *salience network* (reciprocal connections between the amygdala, anterior insula,

Table 4.1 *Ethical decision-making and the brain (adapted from Robertson, Voegtlin, & Maak, 2017; reprinted with permission from the publisher)*

Concepts related to ethical decision-making	Brain structure involved	Functions associated with brain structure and brain chemistry	Relevance for ethical decision-making	Example references
Self-reflection and self-regulation	Several areas of the prefrontal cortex (PFC) (e.g., medial PFC, ventromedial PFC, lateral PFC)	PFC is associated with cognitive tasks, personality expression, and the orchestration of thoughts and actions in accordance with internal goals; it fulfills an executive function in differentiating between conflicting thoughts (such as good or bad) Medial PFC is associated with reflecting on one's experiences and is active in self-judgment tasks; the ventromedial PFC is involved in autobiographical and episodic memory retrieval; the lateral PFC is associated with focusing on goals and inhibiting one's beliefs when necessary for making rational decisions; lateral and ventrolateral PFC are associated with emotional self-control	Shows the relevance of emotions in ethical decision-making Understanding oneself helps reflection on one's ethical behavior and finding the balance between emotional and cognitive reactions when making ethical decisions Highlights the possibility of self-regulation in the form of impulse control and the reappraisal of emotional events	Damasio (1994), Dimoka (2012), Greene (2015) Johnson et al. (2002), Lieberman (2007)
	Dorsal anterior cingulate cortex (ACC) Amygdala	ACC is relevant for affective, cognitive, and motor control phenomena; also involved in controlling, avoiding, or regulating painful emotions Amygdala is involved in perceiving and processing emotions, and in automatic affective processes	Past and current experiences and positive or negative emotional stimulation trigger intuitive ethical behavior	
Theory of mind (ToM)	Anterior paracingulate cortex Posterior superior temporal sulcus (STS)	ACC is relevant for affective, cognitive, and motor control phenomena; also involved in controlling, avoiding, or regulating painful emotions STS is attributed to multisensory processing capabilities (e.g., voices, speech, and language recognition); involved in social perceptions	Cognitive-rational understanding of others' motives and reasons helps to engage in deliberative ethical reasoning	Bagozzi et al. (2013), Bzdok et al. (2012), Dimoka (2012), Rilling et al. (2004b), Young et al. (2007)

Table 4.1 (cont.)

Concepts related to ethical decision-making	Brain structure involved	Functions associated with brain structure and brain chemistry	Relevance for ethical decision-making	Example references
	Temporoparietal junction (TPJ) Dorsomedial prefrontal cortex (PFC)	TPJ is involved in information processing and perception; integrates information from the external environment and from within the body; important for self/other distinctions Dorsomedial PFC is associated with mentalizing and encoding the psychological traits of others	ToM is a necessary precondition for ideal role-taking processes	
Concepts related to ethical decision-making	Brain structure involved	Functions associated with brain structure and brain chemistry	Relevance for ethical decision-making	Example references
Empathy	Anterior cingulate cortex (ACC) Anterior insula Ventromedial PFC	ACC is relevant for affective, cognitive and motor control phenomena; also involved in controlling, avoiding, or regulating painful emotions Insula plays a major role in representing and integrating emotions; involved in sensation, affect, cognition Ventromedial PFC is relevant for encoding the emotional value of sensory stimuli; also important for adherence to social norms	Emphasizes the importance of recognizing other persons' feelings and emotional states for ethical decision-making Affective emotional reaction to others' harm or unethical treatment triggers ethical sensitivity and awareness	Bagozzi et al. (2013), Bernhardt and Singer (2012), Bzdok et al. (2012), Dimoka (2012), Singer et al. (2004)
Social interaction (including trust, justice, cooperation)	Several areas of the prefrontal cortex PFC (e.g., ventromedial PFC, medial PFC, dorsomedial PFC)	PFC has been associated with cognitive tasks, personality expression and the orchestration of thoughts and actions in accordance with internal goals; it fulfills an executive function in differentiating between conflicting thoughts (like good or bad)	Social lubricants like trust and fairness perceptions influence the propensity to engage in ethical or unethical behavior Shows the importance of trust and justice	Combines the above-mentioned mental abilities to make ethical decisions and behave ethically

Moral judgment	Insula	Insula is associated with sensitivity to norm violations, care and justice cognition	perceptions for successful social interactions and highlights stimulus–response settings that trigger trusting responses and facilitate cooperation	Fumagalli and Priori (2012), Greene et al. (2001), Moll et al. (2002, 2005), Young et al. (2007)
	Amygdala	Amygdala is involved in perceiving and processing emotions, and in automatic affective processes		
	Caudate nucleus	Caudate nucleus is important for feelings of reward		
	Ventromedial prefrontal cortex (PFC)	Ventromedial PFC is activated during moral judgment; it is associated with encoding the emotional value of sensory stimuli, emotional processing and adherence to social norms	Combines the above-mentioned mental abilities to make ethical decisions and behave ethically	
	Dorsolateral prefrontal cortex (PFC)	Dorsolateral PFC is involved in problem-solving, cognitive control, cost-benefit analysis; it is associated with utilitarian moral judgments and deciding on appropriate punishment		
	Anterior cingulate cortex (ACC)	ACC is relevant for affective, cognitive and motor control phenomena and is associated with mediating the conflict between emotional and rational components of moral reasoning		
Moral judgment	Posterior superior temporal sulcus (STS)	STS is associated with multisensory processing capabilities and is activated in moral dilemmas, social cognition, and ethical decision-making		
	Temporoparietal junction (TPJ)	TPJ is attributed to moral intuition and involved in belief attribution during moral judgment		
	Insula	Insula is associated with moral processing, sensitivity to norm violations, care, and justice cognition		
	Amygdala	Amygdala is activated in processing moral emotions and, consequently, during evaluation of moral judgment		

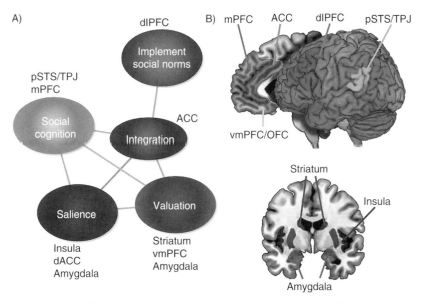

Figure 4.2 Cognitive architecture and brain regions underlying social decision-making and morality. Schematic diagram of (a) neurocognitive processes involved in decision-making and (b) related cortical and subcortical areas (from Yoder & Decety, 2018; reprinted with permission from the publisher)

and dorsal anterior cingulate cortex) organizes extensive changes in neural recruitment in response to motivationally pertinent cues. *Valuation* is performed via brain areas (ventral striatum, amygdala, ventromedial prefrontal cortex, and orbitofrontal cortex) that inform and preserve stimulus–value relations, which are vital for reward learning. *Social cognition* involves specific brain areas (posterior superior temporal sulcus, temporoparietal junction, and medial prefrontal cortex) underlying mental state understanding. *Integration* is performed via an integrative hub (anterior cingulate cortex) that receives inputs from these assorted regions and computes the anticipated reward value of alternative actions. Finally, *social norm implementation* involves the dynamic contributions of the dorsolateral prefrontal cortex to cognitive control and prompting goal-direct behaviors. Hence, the dorsolateral prefrontal cortex is vital for ethical execution of social norms.

4.4 Neuroethics

Exploration into moral cognition has revealed the neural networks and computations involved in judging intentionality and detriment, as well as how those systems interact to generate judgments of responsibility (Krueger & Hoffman, 2016; Yoder & Decety, 2018). Moreover, the emerging field of neuroethics draws from interdisciplinary research into ethical musings about the nature of the brain and the ways in which decisions are processed in and by the brain. The discipline of neuroethics is often understood as twofold, with both the neuroscience of ethics and the ethics of neuroscience as two domains of inquiry (Roskies, 2002; Levy, 2007a). Herein, the main concern is the neuroscience of ethics and investigations of the digital self, values, beliefs, and motivations. Although neuroethics builds on the more established approaches of closely related areas (e.g., medical ethics, bioethics, and the ethics of genetics), it emphasizes ethical quandaries that are uniquely relevant to advances in the cognitive, affective, clinical, and social neurosciences (Farah, 2012; Glannon, 2006).

4.4.1   *From Bioethics to Neuroethics*

Judy Illes of Stanford and Stephanie J. Bird at Massachusetts Institute of Technology (2006) trace the development of neuroethics from prefrontal lobotomies in the late nineteenth and early twentieth century to today's neurotechnologies (see Figure 4.3). They draw on the history of bioethics and ethics in neuroscience to discuss the ways in which our fast-paced technological advances call for a modern neuroethics that can reflect on the theoretical, empirical, practical, and policy issues facing us today.

As Illes and Bird illustrate in Figure 4.3, modern ethical challenges span back from prefrontal lobotomies that were introduced to treat mentally ill patients in the late nineteenth and early twentieth century; next to human experimentation that occurred during the 1930s and 1940s that ultimately led to the Nuremberg trials; and then on to the 1960s and the establishment of two main professional neuroscience organizations. This led to the creation of committees and roundtables dedicated to social issues in the 1970s and 1980s. Also important were the disclosures of the Tuskegee studies and other human subject research violations that led to the publication of the Belmont Report. The 1980s were notable for the Office of Technology Assessment that surveyed the potential impact of neuroscience. In 1993, UNESCO founded the International Bioethics Committee (IBC). In 1996, the IBC fashioned an independent report on the ethical implications of neuroscience advances. In 2002, the Dana Foundation hosted a meeting called 'Neuroethics: Mapping the Field' in San Francisco (CA, USA). Furthermore, the Society for Neuroscience

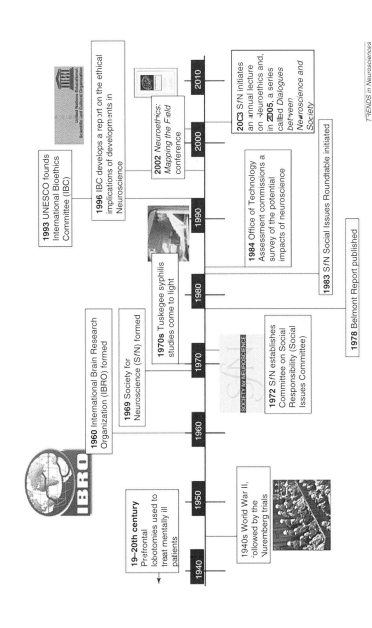

Figure 4.3 Neuroethical milestones in the history of neuroscience (from Illes & Bird, 2006; reprinted with permission from the publisher)

19–20th century Prefrontal lobotomies used to treat mentally ill patients

1940s World War II, followed by the Nuremberg trials

1960 International Brain Research Organization (IBRO) formed

1969 Society for Neuroscience (SfN) formed

1970s Tuskegee syphilis studies come to light

1972 SfN establishes Committee on Social Responsibility (Social Issues Committee)

1978 Belmont Report published

1983 SfN Social Issues Roundtable initiated

1984 Office of Technology Assessment commissions a survey of the potential impacts of neuroscience

1993 UNESCO founds International Bioethics Committee (IBC)

1996 IBC develops a report on the ethical implications of developments in Neuroscience

2002 *Neuroethics: Mapping the Field* conference

2003 SfN initiates an annual lecture on neuroethics and, in 2005, a series called *Dialogues between Neuroscience and Society*

SOCIETY for NEUROSCIENCE

TRENDS in Neurosciences

established an annual lecture on Neuroethics in 2003 and a "Dialogues between Neuroscience and Society" series in 2005. The areas that neuroethics cover is expanding and there are a number of developing research areas for cyberpsychologists (Parsons, 2017; Wiederhold, 2015), such as technologies of the extended mind (Heersmink, 2017; Heersmink & Carter, 2017; Levy, 2007a, 2007b, 2011; Reiner & Nagel, 2017); neuroeducation and educational technologies (Hardiman et al., 2012; Heersmink & Knight, 2018; Howard-Jones & Fenton, 2012; Parsons, 2019; Semetsky, 2009); gerontechnologies (Robillard et al., 2013; Samet & Stern, 2011); neuroimaging (Fins, 2008; Illes, Kirschen, & Gabrieli, 2003); brain stimulation (Clausen, 2010; Kadosh et al., 2012); as well as the neurological basis of ethical thought and behavior (Yoder & Decety, 2018). The terrains covered by neuroethics are enlarging continuously.

4.4.2   Neuroethics in an Era of Brain Projects

The National Institutes of Health has introduced an initiative called Brain Research through Advancing Innovative Neurotechnologies (BRAIN; http://braininitiative.nih.gov/) that aims to investigate the ways in which dynamic patterns of neural activity are transformed into cognition, emotion, perception, and action in health and disease (Greely, Ramos, & Grady, 2016). The goal is to establish a comprehensive and mechanistic understanding of mental processes. This research initiative aims to explore the brain-based processing of thoughts, feelings, perceptions, learning, deciding, and acting. Technological capabilities and tool development in contemporary neuroscience are progressing rapidly. New directions in science are more the product of the inauguration of novel tools than of new concepts (Evers, 2017). The BRAIN initiative embodies this belief and aims to deliver powerful new tools and technologies that fall into two main classes: (1) technologies for monitoring neural circuit activity and (2) technologies that enable the modulation of neural circuits (Ramos et al., 2018). As can be expected, the ethical issues attached to the medical and nonmedical use of neurotechnologies are profound.

4.4.3   A Neuroethics Toolbox

Martha Farah (2015b) presents an ethics toolbox for neurotechnologies. She suggests that neuroethics tends to use a combination of principlist, deontological, and consequential ethical approaches to answer ethical quandaries. As discussed in Chapter 2, Thomas Beauchamp and James

Childress (2013) developed a list of specific principles that investigators can use to guide research and practice: respect for autonomy (right to control one's own life), beneficence (duty to help others), nonmaleficence (duty to "do no harm"), and justice (duties to society – equity and obeying the law). Farah also mentions ethical principles that reflect ethical intuitions in particular contexts: repugnance (Would an act be repugnant?), natural is good (preference for us as we naturally are compared to technologically enhanced versions of ourselves), and the therapy/enhancement distinction (illness and health are distinct states).

4.4.3.1   Deontological Neuroethics

In Chapter 2, there was a discussion of deontological ethics, which portrays our sense that persons should be treated as an end in themselves and not as a means to something else. We can see deontological ethics in our protection of human subjects in cyberpsychology research. Cyberpsychologists act deontologically when they insist that informed consent be used so that they do not violate a study participant's right to autonomy. Farah also points to issues of personhood in bioethics, in which persons have rights and duties that are found in principles of deontological ethics. For example, if an artificial intelligence achieves conscious awareness, then we may decide that it has personhood and making it serve us may be unethical. This example calls for us to examine the question "What is a person?" For the deontologist following Kant, personhood would be related to the cognitive capacities and resources for thinking and acting ethically. For others, the criteria may be broadened to include rationality and conscious self-awareness. Another Kantian idea is to give persons dignity by distinguishing them from objects. From Kant's perspective, while an object can be justly swapped for another object when they are valued to be of equal price, persons have a "worth beyond value." Some neuroethicists use the Kantian concept of dignity to discuss neurotechnological enhancements (Clewis, 2017; Dees, 2007).

4.4.3.2   Consequential Neuroethics

Farah also argues that neuroethicists use consequentialist reasoning when adjudicating the rightness and wrongness of a given decision. Also discussed in Chapter 2, consequentialism is the ethical framework that judges acts as right or wrong depending on the expected value of its outcomes. Cyberpsychologists often discuss "risk/benefit ratios" in Internal Review Board applications. For example, a cyberpsychologist attempting to validate a remote scalpel-wielding robot for lifesaving operations would not sanction its use with actual humans without first submitting it to focused validation studies with nonhuman manikins, even though it seems right to use it right away based on a simple calculation of aggregate benefits (saving lives in remote areas without surgeons) and costs (butchering patients).

When it comes to neurotechnologies, Bentham's original hedonistic consequentialism is updated to a preference consequentialism, in which we act to maximally satisfy our more well-thought-out preferences. Others prefer a perfectionist consequentialism, in which we aim to maximize achievement of our human potential. If technologies allow us to fully flourish, then the addition of them to our lives and persons is justified. Relative to our potentially self-aware artificial intelligence example mentioned above, the consequentialist calculus has been applied to notions of sentience. While we typically think of humans as highly sentient (animals may be less sentient), a self-aware and conscious artificial intelligence would also appear to be sentient.

4.4.3.3 Problems for Deontological and Consequentialist Approaches to Neuroethics

While neuroethicists have attempted to reconcile the two approaches, this tends to result in less than satisfactory resolutions to ethical dilemmas. This may be due to the fact that taking a consequentialist approach is appropriate for understanding controlled cognitive evaluations; nonconsequentialist approaches may better describe automatic affective responding. In addition to comporting well with the dual-process approaches found in psychology, this comports well with our understandings of brain processes. As mentioned in Chapter 2, Greene and colleagues' (2001, 2004) work with the Trolley Dilemma revealed brain activations in the dorsolateral prefrontal cortex for controlled cognitive evaluations that drive consequentialist judgments and weigh the costs and benefits associated with an action. Greene also found brain activations in the medial prefrontal cortex and the amygdala for automatic affective processes that drive nonconsequentialist processes and reflect prohibition of harm, in which negative affective responses are generated. While judgments of correct acts in response to Trolley Dilemmas tend to involve controlled cognitive processes, the decision to apply direct physical force triggers automatic affective responses (Greene, 2007; Greene et al., 2008).

The neuroethics toolbox offered by Farah cannot be applied algorithmically to reach definitive solutions. Instead, the neuroethics toolbox can be seen as a set of approaches that can be used to identify and underscore morally pertinent reflections on given situations. Deontological and consequentialist approaches are only two of the tools that one should have in one's neuroethical toolbox. Moreover, the neuroethical toolbox should be expanded to include various ethical approaches to enable ethical deliberation. Neuroethical perspectives in cyberpsychology can be understood in terms of normative and descriptive inquiries into applied ethics issues in cyberpsychology research and praxes. While the cyberpsychologist may at sometimes prefer to apply a neuroethical approach that emphasizes specific developments (Illes & Bird, 2006) and/or the four principles developed initially by Beauchamp and Childress (1978), developments in the contexts and nature of research in the digital age (especially with the growth of the Internet) have resulted in new neuroethical questions. The result is a host of questions that these regulations and guidelines do not answer in the context of cyberpsychology. Moreover, they obscure judgments about which consequences are best. When these principles are in conflict, the cyberpsychologist may have difficulty deciding which principle should govern decision-making.

4.5   Neuroethics of the Extended Mind

In Chapter 3, "Digital and Extended Selves in Cyberspace," we discussed the potential of technologies (this would include the neurotechnologies found in neuroethics) for extending our understandings of human cognition using an extended cognition (also known as the "extended mind") approach. Following the extended mind approach, a cyberpsychologist may consider cognitive processes as going beyond wetware (i.e., one's brain) to software and hardware used by one's brain. Moreover, cognition can be viewed as something being processed by a system that is coupled with the environment. The cyberpsychologist can answer neuroethical questions using an extended mind approach in which our interactions with technologies form an extended cognitive system that performs functions that would otherwise be accomplished via the action of internal brain-based cognitive processes.

Deliberations on neuroethical issues for technologies of the extended mind are not new (see, for example, Heersmink, 2017; Heersmink & Carter, 2017; Levy, 2007a, 2007b, 2011; Nagel, Hrincu, & Reiner, 2016; Reiner & Nagel, 2017). They were introduced in Neil Levy's (2007a) paper that contended for the significant possibilities of the extended mind hypothesis for neuroethics:

> Neuroethics focuses ethical thought on the physical substrate subserving cognition, but if we accept that this substrate includes not only brains, but

also material culture, and even social structures, we see that neuroethical concern should extend far more widely than has previously been recognized. In light of the extended mind thesis, a great many questions that are not usually seen as falling within its purview – questions about social policy, about technology, about food and even about entertainment – can be seen to be neuroethical issues. (p. 10)

Specifically, Levy argues that, if a cognitive process that happens in the external world would readily be classified as part of the cognitive toolkit when it goes on inside my head, then it is, at least for that point in time, part of the cognitive process (see Chapter 3 for discussion of the parity principle). The extended mind hypothesis can be extended to an ethical parity principle for neuroethics.

In Levy's (2007b) book *Neuroethics: Challenges for the 21st Century*, he posits two neuroethical aspects of the parity principle that can be used for discussion of moral concerns about neurological modification and enhancement: strong (extended cognition) and weak (embedded cognition) ethical parity (see Table 4.2). According to the "strong" version of the ethical parity principle (strong EPP), the mind extends into the external environment, meaning that modifications of external props (used for thinking) are *ceteris paribus* ethically on par with changes in the brain. Some may prefer an embedded mind perspective. According to this perspective, while environmental objects may be crucial to the performance of some cognitive processes (e.g., Otto's use of his notebook), it does not follow that such objects are thereby part of the processes that comprise that ability (Rupert, 2004). For persons preferring this perspective, Levy offers a "weak" version of the ethical parity principle (weak EPP). According to Levy's weak version, alterations of external props are *ceteris paribus* on par ethically with changes in the brain to the exact degree to which one's purposes for concluding that alterations in the brain are dissatisfactory. This also applies to changes of the environment in which it is embedded.

Support for Levy's ethical parity principle is drawn from Clark and Chalmers's (1998) view that "in some cases interfering with someone's environment will have the same moral significance as interfering with their person" (p. 18).

4.5.1   Technologies of the Extended Mind

A decade after Levy's neuroethical parity principle for extended cognition, the world has changed a great deal. The iPhone was introduced in 2007

Table 4.2 *Two versions of Levy's neuroethical parity principle*

Level	Theoretical Principle	Praxes	Example
Strong EPP *Extended cognition*	• Adjustments of external props (iPhones) used for cognitive processes have *ceteris paribus* ethical parity with changes in the brain • If we accept cognitive parity (mind extends into external environment) • Then we should accept ethical parity	• Ethical use of interventions into the cognitive environment ought to be consistent with our ethical responses to interventions into the brain	• If replacing Otto's notebook with an iPhone raises no ethical questions at all • Then we ought not to regard analogous interventions into the brain as ethically problematic
Weak EPP *Embedded cognition*	• Adjustments of external props have *ceteris paribus* ethical parity with a change in the brain . . . • To the exact extent to which one's explanations for deciding that brain changes are problematic can be transferred to changes of the environment in which it is embedded	• Asks us to examine the rational reasons we find some alterations of the mind (narrowly construed) ethically impermissible or problematic	• If it is unproblematic to give someone access to an iPhone that would enhance their memory • Then a relevant difference is needed between giving them an iPhone and giving them drugs to enhance memory, before we can condemn the latter

Note: EPP = ethical parity principle.

and, in the decade that followed its introduction (and Levy's initial thesis), the number of smartphone users has skyrocketed (see Figure 4.4).

As can be seen in Figure 4.4, the first generation of iPhones in 2007 sold almost 1.4 million units worldwide. Since then, sales of the iPhone have seen a strong increase, reaching 150 million units by 2013. By the time we get to 2017, sales of the iPhone in a single year were almost 217 million. This is only part of the story as other vendors also have huge sales. Looking around, it seems apparent that technologies of the extended mind are here to stay.

Interestingly enough, ten years after Levy's ethical parity principle and the introduction of the iPhone, Peter Reiner and Saskia Nagel (2017)

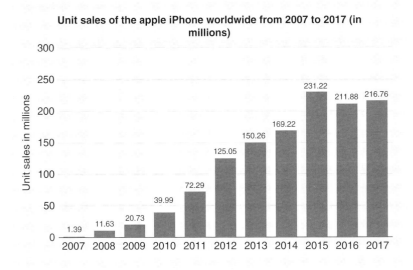

Figure 4.4 Number of iPhones sold from 2007 to 2014 (in millions) (Statista, 2017)

present an update to these ideas in their article "Technologies of the extended mind: Defining the issues."

Reiner and Nagel (2017; see also Nagel, Hrincu, & Reiner, 2016) present three issues that have particular import for further discussion: (1) threats to autonomy from manipulations of technologies of a person's extended mind; (2) threats to privacy by examinations technologies of a person's extended mind; and (3) cognitive enhancements via technologies extending a person's mind (see Table 4.3).

Threats to my autonomy occur when the algorithms in the technologies extending my cognition unduly influence my decision-making. My decisions are guided frequently by contributions from others (e.g., my students; peers; friends, and family) and/or the books and materials that I read, as well as my physical environment. This has prompted some to update traditional notions of autonomy (Beauchamp and Childress, 2001) to a relational autonomy (Christman, 2004; Mackenzie, 2010; Nedelsky, 1989). In the same way that establishing what influences are due and undue in the context of others can be a difficult task, so too can it be difficult to determine the influence of technologies that extend a user's mind. It is worth considering Reiner and Nagel's (2017) description of three general features of algorithms that could impact the degree to which a technology's influences may be deemed to be autonomy violations: (1) the algorithm's

Table 4.3 Three neuroethical issues for technologies of the extended mind

Principle	Algorithm	Example	Violation
Autonomy *Individual should not be unduly influenced when making decisions*	1) algorithm's persuasiveness in decision-making 2) the gravity of the decision 3) algorithm's ability to identify preferences	• Imagine that I have been using a GPS app for weeks and its algorithmic output influences my decisions while I am driving • GPS app gathers a good deal of information about my daily activities and preferences • While driving, GPS app calls attention to a billboard and alerts me to the fact that a bakery is just up ahead • Although I am trying to manage my intake of sugar, I decide to stop at the bakery and have a donut	• GPS program has clearly influenced me • I altered my second-order desires about food intake • Some would call this an undue influence (even though it is a trivial infraction)
Privacy *Individual's thoughts are private in that only that individual has "privileged access" to them*	The same algorithm that is an extension of my mind is also an extension of the mind of the corporate entity that designed the GPS app	• The GPS app is designed to send information about my daily activities and preferences to the corporate entity that designed it	• GPS program has clearly invaded my privacy • My information can be used by the company and released to others
Cognitive Enhancements *Attempts to bolster cognitive function with technology*	The algorithm that extends my mind can also challenge the sense of who we are as humans	• Instead of calling attention to the billboard, the GPS app might consult a database that indicates I frequently shop at an organic grocery store • Instead of suggesting that I get something sweet, the GPS app now suggests that I may wish to get a piece of organic blueberry pie • The GPS app also monitors my activity levels during the day – reminds me that I went for a 5K run this morning and can probably afford the calories	• Once again, the GPS app has influenced me to alter my second-order desires about my food intake • The suggestions are aligned with my overall desire to eat organic food, and they include at least a rough calculation on calories burned earlier in the day

persuasiveness in decision-making; (2) the gravity of the decision; and (3) the algorithm's ability to identify the user's preferences (see also Nagel, Hrincu, & Reiner, 2016).

In terms of persuasiveness of technologies, violations to autonomy may be apparent when my decision-making is influenced (Verbeek, 2006, 2009). If I am still able to participate thoughtfully in decision-making and can reflect on the situation, then the impact of the technology will not be considered to be a violation of my autonomy because there is no impediment to my self-regulation. For their next factor, the gravity (i.e., seriousness) of the decision is relative to the level of potential harm or benefit I may experience as a result of a given decision. Hence, the lower the assumed potential costs or benefits, the lower the apparent seriousness of the decision. Finally, their third factor, the ability to learn about my preferences, is important. If a technology simply executes a set of preprogrammed directives, then there is less concern. On the other hand, if the technology can monitor and learn from my behaviors and preferences, then there is increased possibility that an autonomy infraction may occur.

4.6   Cognitive Enhancement

Another area of concern for neuroethics is the use of advanced technologies to enhance cognitive abilities (Farah et al., 2004; Lalancette & Campbell, 2012; Parens, 2000). Developments in scientific knowledge are promising for the enhancement of cognitive performance, memory, and/or or productivity through new applications of neuropharmaceuticals and/or possible technological advances (Forlini, Gauthier, & Racine, 2013). Cognitive enhancement refers to the capability of achieving psychological enhancements beyond what is needed to maintain or restore good health, such as modifications to memory and/or executive functions (Farah et al. 2004; Juengst, 1998). As a result, the widespread use of cognitive enhancers has led some to conclude that cognitive enhancement is now a socially accepted practice (Berg et al., 2009; Farah et al. 2004; Singh & Kelleher, 2010), and there are increasing calls for discussions of the ethical issues surrounding the use of biomedical techniques to enhance cognition (Gaucher, Payot, & Racine, 2013).

4.7   Conclusions

The challenges of applying neuroscientific findings to technologies of the extended mind are numerous but have a common denominator: the

framework supporting a brain-based cyberpsychology has to be well
defined and explicit. Herein, there has been a discussion of the ways in
which such frameworks can be extended to develop a brain-based cyberpsychology approach to ethics that emphasizes the advances in cognitive,
affective, and social neuroscience.

Extending the framework, to some extent, involves the recognition that
our mental states are constituted by our neurocognitive and affective states
and a shifting collection of external resources and scaffolding. Our understanding of what constitutes a person is partially a function of the person's
environment, inasmuch as the person's capacities are dependent on features of her context. Moreover, a person's identity is largely a product of
social relations to others. Hence, persons are as much a product of their
environments as of features of themselves from the skin in (i.e., the brain).
The implications for neuroethical approaches to a brain-based cyberlearning extend to the technologies extending minds.

Following the extended mind thesis, there is a strong prima facie case for
ethical concerns accompanying various means of enhancing cognitive
performance. While some approaches to technologies emphasize ethical
principles, neuroethics focuses on the neural substrates subserving cognitive processes. Herein, the emphasis has been on combining these
approaches via an argument that mental processes include not only brains
but also technologies and even environmental social structures. This allows
for the ethical concerns of cyberpsychologists, educational neuroscientists,
and neuroethicists to extend far more widely than has previously been
recognized. Given the extended mind thesis, a number of ethical concerns
about using technologies can be seen to be neuroethical issues. In making
decisions about how cyberpsychologists structure research environments
and employ technologies, decisions can be made about the ways in which
technologies of the extended mind are employed, and such decisions must
be informed by neuroethical thinking.

PART II

Ethical Cyberpsychology Research and Interventions with Special Populations

CHAPTER 5

Cyberlearning and Ethical Considerations for Using Technology with Children

5.1 Introduction

Cyberlearning is a recent blending of cyberpsychology with learning technologies that is increasing in importance as new technologies proliferate our classrooms. Cyberlearning involves the convergence of psychology, education, learning technologies, computer science, engineering, and information science. There is a growing national interest in directing the integration of technology into educational theories and praxes. This is expressly the case with the use of information and networking technologies. Cyberlearning programs have been developed by the National Science Foundation to fund exploratory and synergistic research projects that emphasize learning technologies for learners of all ages in science, technology, engineering, and mathematics. A similar rate of advances is apparent in the growing number of laboratories around the world that are interested in the interaction between neuroscience and education (Stein & Fischer, 2011).

Technological advances inhere education and educators regularly connect or disconnect from others via assorted digital venues. Although the recent surge of interest in cyberlearning has resulted in greater attention to the potential of new technologies (and the research behind them), less emphasis has been placed on the moral and ethical issues that may result from the widespread use of the brain-based cyberlearning technologies. This chapter aims to discuss some of the ethical issues inherent in brain-based cyberlearning research and practice. Brain-based learning technologies have the potential for both positive and negative change of not only understandings of humanity in general but also specific and contextualized notions of personhood, free will, conscious experience, authenticity, and relatedness to others.

5.2 Ethical Research with Children

Ethical research with children is of great significance to cyberpsychologists who work with children and families. Researchers must take extra care when applying ethical approaches to work with children and young people (Alderson & Morrow, 2004; Holt, 2004). Discussions about research ethics with children often emphasize two main issues: informed consent and protection of research responders. Of course, both of these issues are particularly problematic for research with children. The issue of informed consent is often one of the most discussed. Should cyberpsychologists solicit children's participation in research by obtaining parental/legal guardian consent only or should we also approach children for their consent? Traditional approaches to research with children seek consent from the child's caregiver and children's consent is sought less regularly. That said, some psychologists have argued that children should be invited to be research participants (Woodhead & Faulkner, 2000). Furthermore, researchers are increasingly recognizing children as capable of taking part in decisions related to their well-being (Hordyk, 2017; Jenks, 2000).

Protection of children as they take part in research is another important issue. It is necessary that research with children and young people be ethical, sensitive, respectful, and protected. It is also important that children and young people have the same rights of withdrawal from research projects and should have the same rights related to the research data they provide. Children should also have the same degree of confidentiality and privacy that adults experience, with the added provision that researchers will need to handle issues of disclosure related to harm as and when they arise. Unfortunately, little has been written specifically to guide the ethical considerations of cyberpsychologists interested in research with children.

5.3   Ethics in Educational Technology

Although most educational technologists are not philosophers, they often deal with moral issues and dilemmas that range from the imbalanced allocation of technologies in schools to ethical research with learning technologies. Moreover, a UNICEF report by Livingstone, Byrne, and Carr (2016) estimates that one in three Internet users are children (i.e., more than 2 billion children). As a result, children are increasingly having their personal information logged and their digital footprints captured. The information logged and stored in school district intranets and on the Internet is emerging into big datasets that may substantially influence their opportunities as well as their "digital" and "offline" identities. Moreover, the technologies used by children are increasingly adaptive and can be personalized to the child.

What makes these ethical issues even more challenging is the fact that training in ethical issues is often limited to a course (or just parts of courses) emphasizing codes of conduct and ethical principles (e.g., those developed initially by Beauchamp and Childress, 2013). Typically, the content includes the Nuremburg Code (Allied Control Council, 1949), the World Medical Association's (1964) *Declaration of Helsinki*, and the Belmont Report (OHRP, 1979). The Belmont Report (i.e., *Ethical Principles and Guidelines for the Protection of Human Subjects Research*) provides three principles that offer the foundation for many existing ethical guidelines for behavioral research: respect for persons, beneficence, and justice (OHRP, 1979). While there is some terminological variation used in these guidelines and codes, they include the following ethical principles (see Chapter 2 of this book): autonomy (i.e., free will or agency); beneficence (i.e., mercy, kindness, and charity); nonmaleficence (i.e., do no harm); and justice (i.e., fair distribution of benefits and burdens).

It is important to note that the Association for Educational Communications and Technology (AECT) has made attempts to define ethical research and practice: "Educational technology is the study and ethical practice of facilitating learning and improving performance by creating, using, and managing appropriate technological processes and resources" (Januszewski & Molenda, 2007, p. 1). Moreover, the AECT journal *TechTrends* has a column on assorted facets of normative and applied ethics in educational technology (Yeaman, 2016). Michael Spector (2005), at the University of North Texas, even went so far as to suggest an Educratic Oath for educators that included the following principles:

1) Restraining from acts that impair learning/instruction
2) Encouraging acts that improve learning/instruction
3) Acting in an evidence-based manner
4) Disseminating instruction principles
5) Respecting individual rights.

Unfortunately, the Educratic Oath was not widely accepted. As a result, Spector (2015, 2016; Spector et al., 2013) moved from principles alone to a framework with three interacting dimensions (values, principles, and people) that are relative to context (e.g., school, home, community, etc.) and technology (see Figure 5.1).

While Spector's principlist Educratic Oath and interrelated dimensions have merit, the growing interface among the neuroscience, education, and learning technologies calls for a brain science–informed look at ethical issues in neuroeducational research and cyberlearing. Paul Howard-Jones and Kate Fenton (2012) have argued that many ethical issues cannot be addressed satisfactorily using the principles and guidance available in the

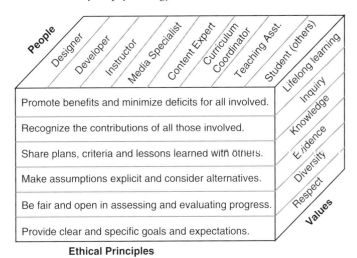

Figure 5.1   Spector's ethical framework for educational technologies (from Spector, 2005; reprinted with permission from the publisher)

neuroscience or educational literatures alone, or by employing these in simple combination. The addition of educational technologies into a brain-based cyberlearning approach to ethics calls for an even greater level of inclusion of advances found in cognitive, affective, and social neurosciences that have the potential to revolutionize educational assessments (Parsons, 2015a, 2017; Parsons, Gaggiolo, & Riva, 2017) and training using technology-rich environments (Immordino-Yang & Singh, 2011).

5.4   Brain-Based Cyberlearning and Educational Technologies

Recently, there has been a surge in research relating the human brain's neural mechanisms to the Internet (Montag & Reuter, 2017), social media (Meshi, Tamir, & Heekeren, 2015), virtual reality (Bohil, Alicea, & Biocca, 2011; Parsons et al., 2009; Parsons, Gaggiolo, & Riva, 2017), and related technologies (Kane & Parsons, 2017; Parsons, 2016, 2017). In my 2017 book *Cyberpsychology and the Brain* (see Chapter 1 of this book for a review), I proposed a framework for combining neuroscience and cyberpsychology for the study of social, cognitive, and affective processes and the neural systems that support them. Following this brain-based cyberpsychology approach, a cyberlearning approach that draws from the neurosciences can be understood as (1) the neurocognitive, affective, and social aspects of students interacting with technology and (2) affective computing aspects of students interacting with devices/systems that incorporate computation. As such, a brain-based cyberlearning approach will be interested in both the ways in which educators and students make use of devices and the neurocognitive processes, motivations, intentions, behavioral outcomes, and effects of online and offline use of technology.

5.4.1 Key Neuroeducational Themes for a Brain-Based Cyberlearning

Key themes are emerging from the neurosciences that can be applied to a brain-based cyberlearning. First of all, there is developing research that corroborates the long-standing perspective of educationalists that reasoning and learning involve both cognitive and affective processes that occur in social and cultural contexts (Fischer & Bidell, 2006; Frith & Frith, 2007; Mitchell, 2008). Howard-Jones and colleagues (2016) have argued that educational neuroscience is more than just a way to improve, explain, or analyze teaching. Instead, educational neuroscience endeavors to elucidate the ways in which students learn and how learning affects the brain. From there, educational neuroscience findings can be applied in the classroom. Educational neuroscience can be defined as an interdisciplinary field that involves many perspectives and areas of expertise (e.g., psychology, neuroscience, and education) that can be translated and integrated (Figure 5.2). To address this question, Feiler and Stabio (2018) performed a systematic and comprehensive literature review and thematically analyzed all reported definitions and mission statements with three major themes emerging.

5.4.2 Social Neuroscience and Cyberlearning

Social and affective neuroscientific evidence links students' bodies and cognitions in processes of emotion. Moreover, social neuroscientific evidence links students' self-perceptions to the understanding of others (Immordino-Yang, 2008; Uddin et al., 2007). The exchanges between students and others lead to social extensions of their cognitive processes. Likewise, the relations among students, smart classrooms, and cyberlearning technologies assist in extending their cognitive processes. Although students and educators act in accord with subjective objectives and concerns that mature over time as they interrelate socially, the values, judgments, and calculations made with technologies represent the data, algorithms, and system constraints that were programmed by their developers

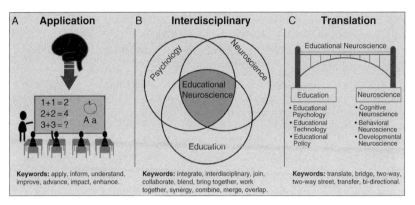

Figure 5.2 Three major themes are found within the field of educational neu-roscience: (a) neuroscience findings applied in the classroom; (b) interdisciplinary collaboration (education, psychology, neuroscience); and (c) an integration of technical languages between education and neuroscience (from Feiler & Stabio, 2018; reprinted with permission from the publisher)

(Immordino-Yang & Singh, 2011). Given that the strictures administering these calculations are often determined outside of interactions with the student (either previously or throughout postprocessing), there are appre-hensions about the possible ethical implications of using these technologies.

5.4.3   Example Approaches to Educational Neuroscience

Neville and colleagues (2013) conducted a study that offers an example of the interdisciplinary collaboration found in educational neuroscience and exem-plifies current approaches to assessment and intervention. They used an eight-week training program aimed at enhancing the selective attention of preschool students (see Figure 5.3). As can be seen in Figure 5.3, Neville and colleagues perform a pretest then apply a selective attention intervention, which is followed by a postassessment.

While such educational neuroscience approaches are enhancing traditional approaches, ethical concerns arise with computer automated approaches found in cyberlearning environments. On the techno-optimistic side, computational algorithms allow for a personalized educational approach that could maximize learning for each student as well as provide information that can be generalized to large populations via collaborative knowledgebases (big data and infor-matics). On the other, more techno-pessimistic side, there are concerns about automated changes that remove the control found in many current approaches.

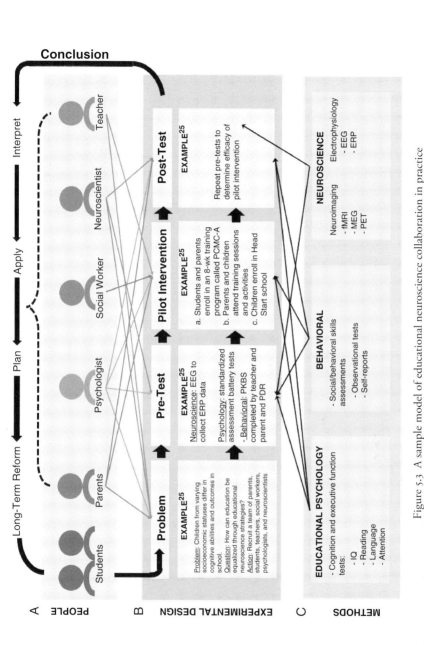

Figure 5.3 A sample model of educational neuroscience collaboration in practice

Note: EEG = Electroencephalography; ERP = Event Related Potential; fMRI = Functional Magnetic Resonance Imaging; IQ = Intelligence Quotient; MEG = Magnetoencephalography; PET = Positron Emission Tomography.

What happens to the educational neuroscience assessment and intervention when algorithms decide when and how to intervene on a student's cognitive processes? What ethical considerations and guidelines will be in place to make sure that the student's autonomy and privacy are maintained?

Progress in cyberlearning technologies has intensified our cognizance of the influence technologies have on the structure and function of the student's brain. Along with these advances is an enlarged need to contend with the ethical implications of cyberlearning tools and findings. Even though more than a few reviews have been published that bring together the expanding neuroethics (see Chapter 4 of this book) literature in general (Clausen & Levy, 2015; Farah, 2012; Heersmink, 2017; Heersmink & Carter, 2017; Illes, 2017; Levy, 2007a, 2007b, 2011; Nagel, Hrincu, & Reiner, 2016; Racine & Aspler, 2017; Reiner & Nagel, 2017), there is much less published on the ethical implications of brain-based cyberlearning research, theory, and praxes. A brain-based cyberlearning framework can be developed from the neurosciences, education, and technologies of the extended mind. Educational theories and praxes are being transformed by the neurosciences. The ethical issues confronting a quickly emerging brain-based cyberlearning fall under at least two distinct types: (1) those received from other areas of ethics (e.g., neuroethics; Lalancette & Campbell, 2012) and (2) those that are exclusive to or engendered by the field of cyberlearning and other more general areas of concern to mind, brain, and educational technologies (Stein & Fischer, 2011).

5.5   Technologies of the Student's Extended Mind

An additional component for our understanding of cognitive, affective, and social processes for cyberlearning is the notion that technology is an extension of our cognitive processes (Parsons, 2015a, 2017). It is becoming increasingly apparent that the educational technologies used in schools have the potential to extend a child's cognitive processes beyond the embodied cognition of their forebears (Parsons, Gaggioli, & Riva, 2017). As discussed in Chapter 3, the extended mind theory views cognitive processes as going beyond wetware (i.e., child's brain) to educational software and hardware used by the child's brain. This perspective allows for an understanding of the child's cognition as processed in a system coupled with the child's environment.

5.5.1   Parity Principle

The extended cognitive system includes both brain-based cognitive processes and external objects (e.g., technologies such as tablets, iPads, smartphones) that serve to accomplish functions that would otherwise be attained via the action of brain-based cognitive processes acting internally to the student (Clark, 2008; Clark & Chalmers, 1998). Proponents of extended cognition make use of a "parity principle" that states:

> If, as we confront some task, a part of the world functions as a process which, were it to go on in the head, we would have no hesitation in recognizing as part of the cognitive process, then that part of the world is (so we claim) part of the cognitive process. (Clark & Chalmers, 1998, p. 8)

From the parity principle, one can argue that, if a process that happens in the classroom (external world) would readily be classified as part of the cognitive toolkit when it goes on in the student's head, then it is, at least for that point in time, part of the cognitive process.

5.5.2   Functional Parity

Richard Heersmink and Simon Knight (2018) discuss a functional parity in terms of technologies (i.e., artifacts) that complement existing brain functions instead of replicating what the brain already does (see also Sutton, 2010). They consider the relation between technology and the student's brain in terms of cognitive integration, in which the student's cognitive systems and technologies are integrated into wider systems that perform cognitive tasks multi-dimensionally (see also Heersmink, 2015) According to Heersmink and Knight (2018, pp. 4–5), these dimensions include the following:

> Information flow describes the information trajectories between the embodied brain and external artifacts. This may be one-way, where information flows from an artifact to an agent (e.g., when navigating with a map). This may be two-way, where information is first offloaded onto an artifact and then later used to perform some cognitive task (e.g., when writing an appointment in your diary and looking it up at some later point). Information flow can also be reciprocal, where there are many interdependent cycles of offloading and intake (e.g., when making a calculation with pen and paper or writing an article).
>
> Accessibility describes the level of availability of the artifact. Some artifacts are easily available (e.g., one's smartphone), whereas others are not (e.g., a library book in Alaska). Reliable access to external information is essential for how and how often a cognitive task unfolds (Clark & Chalmers, 1998).
>
> Durability describes how often we interact and couple with an artifact Wilson and Clark (2009) propose a trichotomy between one-offs (e.g., using a shopping list), repeated (e.g., using a map), and permanent (e.g., using a smartphone) relationships to cognitive artifacts.

Trust describes how much trust an agent puts into the information the artifact provides. When we trust information, we think it is true. When we do not trust information, we think it is false, or we are not sure whether it is true. Trust is important, as information we do not trust we typically do not use (Clark & Chalmers, 1998).

Procedural transparency describes the degree of transparency-in-use. The easier it is to use and interact with an artifact, the more procedurally transparent it is. For example, to be able to use a computer, a user must learn how to use a mouse, keyboard, and (touch)screen. This is difficult at first, but becomes easier and more fluent after frequent use, as one's perceptual-motor processes become proceduralized such that one does not have to think about how to use the artifacts.

Informational transparency describes the ease with which information can be interpreted. Some information is opaque, which means we cannot interpret it. Certain scientific symbols or formulas, for example, are for most people opaque as they do not know their meaning. Other information is transparent. One's native language is often fully transparent.

Personalization describes how much the artifact is personalized (Sterelny, 2010). Some artifacts are not personalized and are thus interchangeable (e.g., a tourist map of Sydney), whereas other artifacts are highly personalized (e.g., a notebook). Personalization often streamlines a cognitive task and thus makes performing the task easier.

For Heersmink and Knight (2018), these dimensions are on a spectrum and together make up a multidimensional space in which both embedded and extended cognitive systems can be located with particular dimensional configurations (see also Smart, Clowes, & Heersmink, 2017). On one side of the continuum, we find shallow integration, in which the technology (i.e., artifact) only assists an internal cognitive system. On the other side of the continuum, there is dense integration, wherein the technology (i.e., artifact) is part of an extended cognitive system.

5.5.3   Web-Extended Mind

Paul Smart (2012) has applied the idea of extended cognitive processes to the specific sociotechnical context of the Web (see also Smart, Clowes, & Heersmink, 2017; Smart & Shadbolt, 2018). The "Web-extended mind" was introduced in Chapter 3 and considers the Internet to be a mechanism that realizes human mental states and processes. As mentioned in Chapter 3, examples can be found in the ways in which students regularly enhance their cognitive performance with various technologies (e.g., tablets and iPads). Students are able to store their memories using technologies. While a student may not be able to remember what the average daytime temperature is on Mars, her technologies can aid her recall that a commonly reported temperature is –63 degrees Celsius (–81 degrees Fahrenheit; 210 Kelvin).

Though the Internet was initially constrained by wires, advanced iterations only had to be close to a router. These days, with the increasing availability of tablets and iPads in the classroom, the immense amount of information on the Internet is easily accessible by the student. The quantity of tablets and smartphones found in schools is rapidly moving to the point where billions of students will have access. Furthermore, the technological resources of tablets and iPads present numerous enhancements to discussions of externalization. While initial metaphors highlighted external memory storage, the iPads and tablets connected to the Internet today extend well beyond memory assistants to robust mobile computation devices. In fact, mobile technologies connected to the Internet offer educators and cyberlearning researchers the opportunity to investigate the interactions of students as they participate with a global workspace and connected knowledgebases. Additionally, Internet access may enable a major shift in how we see student learning and the ways in which we understand the nature of students' cognitive and epistemic abilities.

5.6 When Does a Device Qualify as an Extender of Cognition

It is important to consider the circumstances under which a device qualifies as a technology of the student's extended mind. As mentioned in Chapter 3, it is helpful to explore what is meant by the word "mind." As discussed in earlier chapters, the notion of technology of the extended mind can be applied here to delineate what a technology of the student's mind would be. As discussed in Part I of this book, the term mind (used liberally in this book) is not to be confused with some version of substance dualism (i.e., there is brain-stuff and mind-stuff). Instead, a specific distinction was made in Part I of this book between brain as a thing while the mind is understood as a concept. The aim is to keep from mixing these ontological levels in a way that so often ends in muddling the relation between brain and mind. A way of considering this issue is to consider the mind as representing the full set of cognitive resources that the student deploys in the service of thinking. Thinking can be understood as reflective, algorithmic, and autonomous thinking (Stanovich, 2009a, 2009b). This approach comports well with the extended mind hypothesis because the idea of a "full set of cognitive resources" allows for additional contributions (in addition to the brain) to conceptions of mental processing. The extension of mental processes outside of the brain (e.g., technologies of the student's extended mind) means that mental processes cannot be fully reduced to brain processes (Levy, 2007a; Nagel, Hrincu, & Reiner, 2016; Reiner & Nagel, 2017).

What sorts of devices can be considered technologies of the student's extended mind? When answering this question, it is important to note that not every algorithmic function completed by technologies (external to the student's brain) should be understood as a technology of the student's extended mind. Instead, it is preferable to theorize a technology of the student's extended mind as a rather continuous interface between brain and algorithm in which the student perceives the algorithm as a real extension of her mind. Consider, for example, an updated version of context-based learning games like the ones developed by the MIT Media Lab in the early 2000s (Klopfer et al., 2005; Mystery at the Museum, 2003). In *Mystery at the Museum*, the student takes part in an indoor augmented reality simulation that is enacted through the Boston Museum of Science. The contextual story contains a robbery that happened in a science museum and the students are told to catch the burglar by playacting the character of a biologist, technologist, or detective so that they can determine what was taken and what procedures were used throughout the burglary. *Mystery at the Museum* was executed using Wi-Fi for short-range data acquisition and communication. For our updated version, we could have the students use a smartphone application synchronized with the smartphone's Global Positioning System (GPS).

Imagine a twelve-year-old girl named Sophie who has been taught how to enter exhibits into the search engine of a smartphone application that will show her the best route to destinations for the context-based learning game quest. Once she arrives at the destination, the augmented reality–enabled smartphone can be used interactively by Sophie to learn about science and to solve the mysteries of the fictional burglary. This smartphone application is specifically accommodating because it allows Sophie to not get lost, as many of the game destinations lead her to visit parts of the museum with which she was unacquainted. Sophie has heard stories from her classmates that they are doing work on the museum in some areas and she cannot be sure that the smartphone application for the museum always leads to the right place. As a result, Sophie remains alert to her environment so that she can be sure that she makes it to quest destinations in the museum without a problem.

Is this smartphone application functioning as a technology of the student's extended mind? While it is certainly working out the pathways that are external to Sophie's brain, the smartphone application is probably better considered as offering cognitive assistance because neither the algorithmic calculations nor Sophie's use of them are coupled with Sophie's cognitive processes. What if we change the scenario a bit to allow more time and use of the smartphone application? Let us say that Sophie has now taken part in the context-based learning game several times over the course of a month. Even though she now has somewhat greater acquaintance with the museum, she always uses the smartphone application and GPS to navigate through the museum, and it has not failed her. At this point, when she enters an exhibit into the smartphone application's search interface and the route is presented on the screen, she routinely abides by the directions and follows them to the destination suggested by her smartphone. The smartphone application is beginning to function as a technology of the student's extended mind because Sophie has integrated its algorithmic output into the working of her mind.

5.7 Neuroethical Issues for Technologies Extending the Student's Mind

What are the potential ethical implications of Sophie using a technology that extends her cognitive processes beyond her brain? As discussed in Chapter 4, neuroethics is one place to look for brain-based ethics. Neuroethicists consider the ethical implications of the brain's interfacing with technologies. Also discussed in Chapter 4 was Neil Levy's (2007a) paper that argued for the substantial implications of the extended mind hypothesis for neuroethics. From a neuroethical perspective, Levy argues that the parity principle (if a cognitive process that happens in the classroom would readily be classified as part of the cognitive toolkit when it goes on in the student's head, then it is, at least for that point in time, part of the cognitive process) introduced in Chapter 3 of this book can be extended to an ethical parity principle for neuroethics. As mentioned in earlier chapters, Reiner and Nagel (2017; see also Nagel, Hrincu, & Reiner, 2016) extend beyond the parity principle with an emphasis on algorithms and algorithmic devices. They point out that not every algorithmic function carried out by technologies external to the brain qualifies them as a technology of the extended mind. Instead, they contend that there is a comparatively continuous interface between brain and algorithm such that the person experiences the algorithmic device as an extension of the person's mind. They present three issues that have particular import for further discussion: (1) threats to autonomy from manipulations of technologies of a person's extended mind; (2) threats to privacy by examinations technologies of a person's extended mind; and (3) cognitive enhancements via technologies extending a person's mind. In the following, there is a discussion of Reiner and Nagel's article as it applies to technologies extending the student's mind.

5.7.1   Autonomy and Privacy

A fundamental feature of Reiner and Nagel's first issue, autonomy, is that the autonomous student should not be unduly influenced when making decisions. It is important to note that decisions made by students are guided frequently by the contribution of others (e.g., teachers, peers, caregivers) and/or the books and materials that they read, as well as their physical environment (e.g., classroom, playground). Reiner and Nagel (2017) describe three features of algorithms that could impact the degree to which influences are considered to be autonomy violations (see Chapter 4 of this book):

1) The algorithm's persuasiveness in decision-making
2) The gravity of the decision
3) The algorithm's ability to identify the student's preferences.

The persuasiveness of technologies can result in autonomy violations when decision-making is influenced (Verbeek 2006, 2009). If Sophie continues to be able to make thoughtful decisions and can reflect on the situation, then there is less probability of the technology violating her autonomy because she is still able to self-regulate. The gravity (i.e., seriousness) of a decision made by Sophie while using the smartphone application is moderated by the extent to which Sophie may be harmed or benefited. Consequently, the lesser the presumed possible harm or benefits, the lower the apparent seriousness of the decision. The ability to learn about Sophie's preferences is important. If a technology simply executes a set of preprogrammed directives, then there is less concern. On the other hand, if the technology can monitor and learn from Sophie's behaviors and preferences, then there is the increased possibility that an autonomy infraction may occur.

Given these factors, an extension of the smartphone application example (see Section 5.6) can be offered to illustrate the relevant issues for Sophie. Remember that when Sophie first started using the smartphone application she paid close attention to both the application and the environment to make sure that she could trust the application and not get lost. At this point, the smartphone application is not functioning as a technology of Sophie's extended mind because, while it is performing computations that are external to Sophie's brain, the museum application in Sophie's smartphone is probably better considered as offering her cognitive assistance. After Sophie uses the smartphone application for a few weeks, and the relationship between Sophie and the smartphone application has grown more intimate, she now integrates its algorithmic output into the working of her mind while traveling both inside the museum and around her neighborhood (e.g., to and from school, as well as to and from the locations of various extracurricular activities). Sophie is continuing her training in the museum and, while working on an assignment that requires that she travel to an exhibit, she hears alerts from the tablet as she passes a sign advertising the museum's constellation of eateries (on the first floor, right across from the museum's store); and alerts chime again when the museum's eateries are just up ahead.

Here, the situation has changed as the algorithms have learned Sophie's preferences and are attempting to influence her actions. Moreover, the algorithm from the smartphone application may increase its level of suggestion by "asking" Sophie whether she would like to take a moment to get something to eat, or perhaps shop in the museum's store (right across from the museum's eateries). While Sophie may recognize that she needs to complete her assignment (continue her quest to solve the fictional burglary mysteries), she reasons that little harm would come from stopping to get something to eat and perusing the gift shop. Here, one finds a clear effect of the technology on Sophie that was influential enough to cause an alteration of her second-order desires to complete her assignment. Most likely, parents and teachers (as well as ethicists) would view this as undue influence. While the influence is relatively trivial, this scenario reflects a violation of autonomy.

As mentioned in Chapter 4, such autonomy violations become even more obvious when one considers the fact that the very same algorithm that has become an extension of Sophie's mind is also an extension of the mind of the corporate entity that designed the smartphone application. Here, we may have a violation of Sophie's privacy and autonomy. Perhaps the corporate entity was paid by vendors at the café and the store to collect Sophie's personal information and then direct Sophie to them. Such potential conflicts of interest muddy the ethical waters when attempting to ascertain the extent to which a technology of the student's extended mind has resulted in a violation of autonomy.

Also, in terms of privacy, it is important to note that Sophie's extended memory, like the smartphone application, notes on her smartphone, and Internet-based applications such as Google Calendar, can be accessed by others. It is important to educate students like Sophie to use technologies in the best possible way and to make them aware that their extended minds might be accessed by others (Reiner & Nagel, 2017). In fact, it may be a good idea that this education be added as part of primary, secondary, and university curricula.

5.7.2   Cognitive Enhancement

The use of advanced technologies to enhance cognitive abilities can be an issue of concern for cyberlearning (Farah et al., 2004; Lalancette & Campbell, 2012; Parens, 2000). Cognitive enhancement involves augmentations beyond what is needed to sustain or reinstate good health, such as modifications to memory and/or executive functions (Farah et al., 2004; Juengst, 1998). Technological advances (neuropharmaceuticals, devices) are promising to enhance students' cognitive performance, memory, and/or productivity (Forlini, Gauthier, & Racine, 2013). Students are consuming prescription drugs more and more to cognitively enhance their academic performance (Howard-Jones, 2010; Maher, 2008; Poulin, 2001; Wilens et al., 2008). The so called "smart pills" are nootropics (i.e., neuropharmaceuticals) that were originally established to treat neurodevelopmental and other brain-based disorders. These nootropics have started making their way into schools because healthy (typically developing) students believe that they can use them to enhance memory (piracetam), wakefulness (modafinil), and attention (methylphenidate/Ritalin).

The increasingly prevalent use of cognitive enhancers has led some to construe cognitive enhancement as socially accepted practices (Berg et al., 2009; Farah et al. 2004; Singh & Kelleher, 2010). That said, there are calls for deliberations on the ethical issues inherent in the use of biomedical techniques to enhance cognition (Gaucher, Payot, & Racine, 2013). Singh and Kelleher (2010) have recommended that professional medical associations develop policy statements that reflect on neuroenhancement in primary care. A report published by the Academy of Medical Sciences in the United Kingdom, considered issues related to cognitive enhancers and suggested concerns related to:

– Possible side effects of cognitive enhancers, including long-term effects such as changes in personality

– Devaluation of nonenhanced (i.e., normal) achievement and the inherent worth of effort and motivation in learning
– Inequality in access in situations where acquisition of cognitive enhancers is cost-prohibitive
– Pressure to use cognitive enhancers and the exacerbation of an already overcompetitive culture.

Likewise, the American Academy of Neurology recently developed and published a position statement regarding the ethics of pediatric enhancement within the patient–parent–physician relationship (Graf et al., 2013). Physicians were cautioned to not prescribe cognitive enhancers to children or adolescents. The decision was based on the fiduciary responsibility of physicians toward their pediatric patients.

5.8 Educating and Assessing Extended Cognitive Systems

Richard Heersmink and Simon Knight (2018) discuss the ways in which extended cognitive systems should be educated and assessed. They build on Ben Kotzee's (2018) argument that educators should teach children to participate in responsible practices of technology use. To do this, educators will need to reverse-engineer the cognitive integration, show the steps that integration has developed over, and raise the educator's approaches toward those technologies. Heersmink and Knight (2018) also draw on Mike Wheeler's (2011) reflection on the role of technology in education from an extended mind perspective; he urges us to focus on the education of coupled assemblages between the student and technologies of the extended mind. He asserts that this emphasis is completely consistent with the objective of providing the student's brain with the competences necessary for efficient involvements in such assemblages. For Wheeler, it is important that we aim to educate extended cognitive systems and permit students to utilize technology when they carry out exams.

5.9 Conclusions

Ethical issues in learning technologies are readily apparent in classroom and research. Efforts have been made by the AECT to define ethical research and practice. Furthermore, attempts have been made to present a framework for approaching ethical issues in the use of educational technologies (Spector, 2016). Herein, there has been a discussion of the ways in which such frameworks can be extended to develop a brain-based cyberlearning approach to ethics that emphasizes the advances in cognitive, affective, and social neuroscience. Although there are numerous challenges involved in applying neuroscientific findings to learning technologies, this chapter provides some thoughts on the potential of technologies of students' extended minds for brain-based cyberlearning.

This extended framework involves to some extent the recognition that students' cognitive processes are constituted by their neurocognitive and affective states, as well as a shifting collection of external resources and scaffolding. Our interpretation of what constitutes personhood is in part a function of the student's environment, inasmuch as the student's abilities are reliant on aspects of her context. Additionally, a student's identity is mostly an artifact of social relations to others. For this reason, students are as much a product of their environments as of features of themselves from the skin in (i.e., the brain). The consequences for neuroethical approaches to a brain-based cyberlearning spread to the technologies extending students' cognitive processes.

Given the extended mind thesis put forth herein, there is a robust prima facie rationale for ethical issues related to various cognitive enhancements. Whereas some approaches to learning technologies stress ethical principles, neuroethics emphasizes the neural substrates subserving cognitive processes. In this chapter, the focus has been on integrating these approaches via an argument that mental processes include not only brains but also learning technologies, and even classroom social structures. As a result, ethical concerns of educational technologists, educational neuroscientists, and neuroethicists can extend far more widely. The extended mind thesis allows the cyberpsychologist to consider ethical concerns related to educational technologies in terms of neuroethical issues. In making decisions about how educators structure classroom environments and employ educational technologies, decisions can be made about the ways in which technologies of the extended mind are employed, and such decisions must be informed by neuroethical thinking.

More work is needed for research and training of educators in the education and assessment of extended cognitive systems. Educators should teach children to participate in responsible practices of technology use. Moreover, educators will need to reverse-engineer the cognitive integration, show the steps that integration has developed over, and raise the educator's approaches toward those technologies. From an extended mind perspective, the role of technology in education should emphasize the education of coupled assemblages between the student and technologies of the extended mind.

CHAPTER 6

Cyberpsychology, Aging, and Gerontechnology

6.1 Introduction

In developed countries, older adult populations are multiplying at a notable rate due to enhanced healthcare, technological access, and enriched living conditions (Bleakley et al., 2015). In fact, there are some projections suggesting that, in the next few decades, a fifth of the US population will be sixty-five years of age or older (Blazer, Maslow, & Eden, 2012; Jacobsen et al., 2011). Even though technologies have become virtually ubiquitous, older Americans continue to trail behind younger cohorts. Cyberpsychological research with older adults has historically been viewed from a "digital divide," with large clefts separating older adult use of technology and the Internet when compared to their younger counterparts (Bidmon, Terlutter, & Röttl, 2014; Carpenter & Buday, 2007, Czaja & Lee, 2007; DiMaggio et al., 2004, Hill, Betts, & Gardner, 2015; Kiel, 2005; Norris, 2001). Part of this discrepancy between age cohorts is that some older adults are apprehensive and/or daunted by the thought of learning to use new technologies or about issues related to security (Braun, 2013; Laguna & Babcock, 1997; Vroman, Arthanat & Lysack, 2015).

Nevertheless, older adults are increasingly reporting that technology has benefits (Mitzner et al., 2010; Wagner, Hassanein, & Head, 2010), including enhancing their abilities to keep in touch and communicate with others (Cotten, Anderson, & McCullough, 2013; Kurniawan, 2008; Sum et al., 2008). Although there has been a good deal of attention in the past to the digital divide, there are increasing numbers of older adults that use technologies to maintain their social networks and make their lives easier. In fact, there is some evidence that portions of the older adult population are beginning to accept technology in a manner similar to younger adults (Jimoh et al., 2012; Olson et al., 2011; Xu et al., 2010). Older adults are increasingly using mobile technologies such as email, social networking,

Table 6.1 *Technology utilization rates by age cohort and technology type*

		Age Cohort	
Data Source	Technology Type	50–64	65 and Older
Pew Research Center (2014)	Internet	2013 = 87%	2015 = 59%
Pew Research Center (2015)	Email	2014 = 91%	2015 = 87%
Pew Research Center (2016)	SMS/text messaging	2015 = 92%	2015 = 92%
Pew Research Center (2016)	Tablets	2015 = 37%	2015 = 32%
Pew Research Center (2016)	E-readers	2015 = 19%	2015 = 19%
Pew Research Center (2016)	Smartphones	2015 = 58% owned	2015 = 30% owned
Pew Research Center (2016)	Cell phones	2015 = 90% owned	2015 = 78% owned

online phone calls, chat/instant messaging, and smartphones. Table 6.1 provides basic utilization rates of each type of technology by age group.

William Chopik (2016) examined the benefits of technology use in 591 older adults using five technology-based behaviors (i.e., email, social networking, online phone calls, chat/instant messaging, smartphone use). Moreover, perceptions of technology usability and benefits were also assessed. Findings revealed that older adults endorsed generally positive attitudes toward technology. Greater use of social technologies was associated with better self-rated health, fewer chronic illnesses, higher subjective well-being, and fewer depressive symptoms. Relations between social technology use and health (physical and psychological) were mediated by reduced loneliness.

6.2   Gerontechnology

Cyberpsychologists interested in the intersection of technology and aging are often interested in the growing specialty area of gerontechnology, which offers promise for decreasing the digital divide. In an early reflection on the discipline, Bouma (1992) defined gerontechnology as "the study of technology and aging for the improvement of the daily functioning of the elderly" (p. 1). According to Bronswijk and colleagues (2009), gerontechnology can be understood as an interdisciplinary field that connects enduring and novel technologies to address the demands of an aging population. The term "gerontechnology" can be understood as a combination of the words "gerontology," which involves the scientific study of aging, and "technology," which involves research into novel techniques, artifacts, and provisions (Harrington & Harrington, 2000). Research activities in gerontechnology explore the neurobiological, psychological, social, and health-related aspects of aging (Bouma et al., 2007). Furthermore, there is an emphasis on the ways in which various limitations to quality of life may be compensated for by particular technologies (Fozard, 2005). There is a growing body of research suggesting that the use of various gerontechnologies (in persons age fifty-five or older) has contributed positively to quality of life. Estimates suggest that Internet use is associated with approximately 20 percent decreases in depression (Ford & Ford, 2009).

6.3   Gerontechnological Values and Principles

Gerontechnologists have long held that technologies used to help aging populations are, like other technologies, ones that should not be viewed as value-neutral (Bouma, 2010; Widdershoven, 1998). Instead, gerontechnologies are value-laden in the goal functions of the technologies and the peripheries in which these functions are realized. Moreover, value assumptions are involved in the assessment of costs, benefits, and/or the risks of failure that potentially accompany various technological advances. Various ethical principles have been proposed for gerontechnology design and implementation. As mentioned in Chapter 2 of this book, the Belmont Report distinguishes four ethical principles that are significant for cyberpsychologists, namely autonomy, beneficence, nonmaleficence, and justice (see Department of Health, Education, and Welfare, 2014). Also mentioned earlier in this book (see Chapter 2), is the reality that ethical principles do not offer comprehensive solutions to all ethical questions found in aging and technology. More accurately, ethical principles can be considered principles with limited applicability. While a principle may be helpful in response to some ethical quandaries, other principles may offer differing recommendations to the same problem in other situations (Rauhala-Hayes, 1997). Outcomes to ethical evaluation in a principlist approach often depend on which principle is given primacy. As a result, such approaches do allow for one to arrive at somewhat disparate solutions. As a result, cyberpsychologists carrying out research into the design and adoption of gerontechnologies will want to carefully analyze and reflect on their ethical decisions to ascertain which principles are in conflict and what potential resolutions could be offered by assigning various weightings to different principles.

6.4   Autonomy, Informed Consent, and Decision-Making – Capacity

An important ingredient in healthy quality of life for older persons is their ability for sustained autonomy and independence. By autonomy, we mean the older adult's fundamental right to make choices independently. In cyberpsychology, autonomy refers to the older adult's ability to offer informed consent. The older adult's ability to give informed consent is relative to the accessibility of relevant information, their capacity to make informed decisions, and their ability to make free choices (Roberts, 2002).

6.4.1 Older Adult Decision-Making

The capacity of older adults for decision-making is contingent on their ability to understand the pertinent information, process that information, personalize the context in which their decision occurs, and their facility in stating their choice (Walaszek, 2009). Hence, gerontechnological interventions are only appropriate when the older adult has been presented with adequate information regarding their choices, the possible consequences, and meaningful choices. So, according to the principle of autonomy, we should not install any devices against the older adult's will. Furthermore, the older adult must be given sufficient information to make decisions concerning the adoption and use of technologies (Rauhala-Hayes, 1997). Another important issue here is that we cannot override the older adult's will by coercion, threats, or restrictions to their freedom. According to Rauhala-Hayes (1997), this necessitates the possession of several cognitive abilities such as the capacity for receiving and understanding information and the ability to thoughtfully consider such information, explain the rationale for a decision, and carry out decisions.

6.4.2 Autonomy Extends to Our Design Choices

For cyberpsychologists, it is important to note that respect for autonomy extends to our design choices. Designing for an older adult's autonomy includes showing respect to older adults and treating them as valued members of society. There is a need for tradeoffs among principles. Batya Friedman and Peter Kahn (2012), at the University of Washington, contend that human values and ethics can be included in designs. One may ask, however, how exactly do ethics and values become implicated in technological designs? Friedman and Kahn offer three approaches from the literature: embodied position (i.e., designer's own values), exogenous position (i.e., societal values), and interactional position (i.e., values of the user of the technology). Embodied, exogenous, and interactional aspects of design are ways designers may become more aware of how values and ethics can be integrated into the technological designs and their uses. Moreover, Friedman and Kahn suggest that engagement in value-sensitive design can be accomplished via twelve human values: human welfare, ownership and property, privacy, freedom from bias, universal usability, trust, autonomy, informed consent, accountability, calmness, identity, and environmental sustainability.

6.4.3   Tradeoffs among Principles and Values

It is important to note that tradeoffs among principles and values are important, including those between autonomy and security. There certainly are points at which the responsibility to carry out decisions in relation to design, adoption, and use of technical devices moves from the designer, to the older adult, and on to caregivers. The ethical question here is who decides when this point is reached? Also, is there a danger that stressing autonomy too much would lead to isolation, loneliness, and depression for the older adult? Hence, principles and values need to be contextualized. Ethical issues related to the adoption and use of gerontechnology often emerge and are resolved within a social, political, and economic context (Widdershoven, 1998).

6.5   Mobile Technologies with Older Adults

As persons age, social connections with relatives and friends become more valued. Older adults are increasingly reporting that technology has benefits (Mitzner et al., 2010; Wagner, Hassanein, & Head, 2010), including enhancing their abilities to keep in touch and communicate with others (Cotten, Anderson, & McCullough, 2013; Kurniawan, 2008; Sum et al., 2008). There are increasing numbers of older adults that use technologies to maintain their social networks. For cyberpsychologists, one area of gerontechnology that holds promise is the use of technologies by older adults. Mobile technologies (e.g., tablet computers, iPads, and e-readers) have been used with older adults to expand their knowledge of a wide range of areas, including news, hobbies, weather, social networking, and even health information. Tablet computers (also known as tablets) provide cyberpsychologists with an opportunity for research into the use of information communication technologies by older adults. Tablets can be attractive to older adults because they are portable and have graphical user interfaces that are easily maneuvered. Moreover, these tablet computers offer older adult users social networking applications, music, videos, online books, and a host of applications. While there is increasing discussion of the possibilities that tablet computers hold for research with older adults, the impacts of these mobile technologies on older adults is addressed in relatively few studies. In one of these studies, Julie Delello and Rochell McWhorter (2017), at the University of Texas, explored the potential of iPad technology for enhancing the lives of older adult participants. Specifically, they were interested in whether iPad use would increase knowledge, as well as strengthen bonds to family and society. The results of their study revealed that iPads can be used to diminish social isolation by linking older adults with online communities, renewing prior relations, and enhancing familial communications.

6.6   Extending the Aging Mind

In Part I of this book, there was an introduction to technologies of the extended mind. This builds off of Clark and Chalmers's (1998) *Gedankenerfahrung* (i.e., thought experiment), wherein fictional characters Inga and Otto want to navigate to a museum on Fifty-Third Street, in New York City. Inga is able to easily refer to her internal brain-based memory processes to remember the appropriate route to the museum; Otto is an aging adult with Alzheimer's disease. As a result, Otto has limited recall of directions to the museum. Thus, Otto must also rely on directions found in a notebook that function as an external supporter for his internal brain-based memory processes. Both Inga and Otto arrive at the museum safely, regardless of the fact that, for Inga, the memory was based on her internal brain-based memory processes and, for Otto, his external notebook. This thought experiment illuminates the information-processing loops that extend outside the neural realm to include elements of our social and technological environments.

The extension of mental processes outside of the older adult's brain (e.g., technologies of the extended aging mind) means that mental processes cannot be fully reduced to brain processes (Levy, 2007a, 2007b; Nagel, Hrincu, & Reiner, 2016; Reiner & Nagel, 2017). We return again to the question of what sorts of devices can be considered technologies of the extended mind – this time for the aging mind. As discussed in Chapter 3, not every algorithmic function performed by devices (external to the brain) should be understood as a technology of the extended mind. Instead, it is preferable to conceptualize technologies of the extended mind as a fairly continuous interface between brain and algorithm in which the person perceives the algorithm as being an actual extension of her or his mind.

6.6.1   Inga Gets a Smartphone with a Memory Application

Let us return to Otto's experience with the notebook he uses to help him navigate to the museum (see Clark & Chalmers, 1998). In a new consideration of the ethical implications of the extended mind and technologies, Adam Carter, Andy Clark, and Orestis Palermos (2018) ask us to reflect on a scenario in which an older adult – perchance to safeguard against the early onset of some form of dementia (e.g., Alzheimer's, Parkinson's) – starts relying on a user-friendly note-taking application on her smartphone for information encoding, storage, and retrieval. For the sake of the example, let us say that Inga has watched Otto deteriorate and now wants to take steps to rely on her smartphone in a manner similar to Otto with his notebook. When Inga learns new information, she records it in the "memory application" on her smartphone. After some time using the application in this way, she gets to the point that, when she needs old information, she automatically and unreflectively accesses the application.

6.6.2   Inga's Smartphone Application Becomes Personalized

Clark and colleagues refine this scenario and make it more robust by including additional capabilities to the smartphone memory application. Every time Inga looks up an entry, the smartphone application now suggests comparable or associated information she might want to consider. The notes that have not been used for a long time are weighted as less important and seem to fade out from the recommended items and the ones that are most regularly put forth are weighted as more important and emerge as top suggestions. This biasing of suggestions based on machine learning algorithms (i.e., artificial intelligence) in the smartphone application is reflective of the tripartite view and somatic marker hypothesis introduced in Chapter 3. The tripartite view (Stanovich, 2009a, 2009b, 2010) includes an autonomous processor that automatically compels action and a reflective processor that can inhibit the autonomous processor so that the algorithmic processor can calculate the final response after weighing the benefit of delayed gratification. This autonomous processor can be extended to the smartphone application to aid in decision-making when Inga experiences disruption of the frontal subcortical circuits (see Chapter 3 of this book) that so often accompanies dementias.

6.6.3   Biosensors and the Somatic Marker Hypothesis

It is possible that the smartphone application could go further by adding information from wearable biosensors that could emulate functions of the somatic marker hypothesis (Bechara & Damasio, 2005; Damasio, 1994). This would allow the smartphone application to add an affective (i.e., emotional valuation or biasing) process of valuation and weighing of benefits. The valuation in the tripartite model appears to be consistent with the somatic marker hypothesis (Bechara & Damasio, 2005), in which the experience of an emotion (e.g., gut feeling, hunch) results in a somatic marker that weights outcomes to bias future choices of action. Hence, the somatic marker is thought to play a role in decision-making via its biasing of available response selections. When persons are faced with decisions, they experience somatic sensations in advance of real consequences of possible different alternatives. Neuroimaging studies of persons perform-ing risky decision tasks have revealed activation in the orbitofrontal cortex (Ernst et al., 2002; Windmann et al., 2006), which appears to be significant for signaling the anticipated rewards/punishments of an action and for adaptive learning. Furthermore, studies have shown that damage to the ventromedial prefrontal cortex and the amygdala prevents the use of somatic (affective) signals for advantageous decision-making (Bechara et al., 1996). In summary, decision-making models may be enhanced by a somatic marker theory. This will be especially true as we move to ethical decision-making in our uses of technology.

6.6.4   Biosensors Integrated with Smartphone Applications

Perhaps Inga could wear a wireless wristband like the Empatica E4, which was developed in Rosalind Picard's Media Lab at Massachusetts Institute of Technology (MIT). The Empatica E4 wristband is a wearable noninva-sive monitoring system that could be used for collecting psychophysiolo-gical data about Inga's arousal (e.g., emotional reactions) states and syncing them with the smartphone application (see Figure 6.1). This system would allow the acquisition of Inga's biosignals, including her heart rate (HR) and skin conductance. Heart rate variability (HRV) and skin conductance have been found to be associated with automatic emotion processes and social cognition (Bradley & Lang, 2000; Critchley, 2002; Quintana et al., 2012).

Inga's noninvasively acquired biosignals would be wirelessly trans-mitted, using Bluetooth wireless communication, for online monitoring,

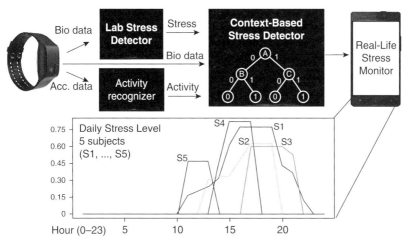

Figure 6.1 Empatica for psychophysiological detection in real-life environments (from Gjoreski et al., 2017; reprinted with permission from the publisher)

data storage, and updating the smartphone memory application. Inga's Empatica wristband uses active noise-cancellation technology to lessen movement artifact and external interference and it provides very clean signals with very few artifacts. Movement artifact is virtually absent. Inga's HRV, which refers to the beat-to-beat alterations in her HR, would be evaluated on the basis of electrocardiogram (ECG) recordings during Inga's everyday activities (see Parsons & Courtney, 2011; Parsons & Reinebold, 2012; Parsons, 2017). The following features would be calculated from recorded ECG signals:

- the mean value of the HR (Mean HR)
- the standard deviation of the RR intervals (time elapsed between two successive R-waves; SDNN)
- the root mean square of successive difference of the RR intervals (RMSSD)
- the ratio of the Low Frequency over the High Frequency (LF/HF).

Moreover, Inga's smartphone application could draw data from wearable biosensors to assess her psychophysiological responses using photoplethysmography, which measures blood volume pulse (BVP), from which HR, HRV, and other cardiovascular features may be derived; motion-based activity using a three-axis accelerometer; electrodermal activity (EDA; used to measure sympathetic nervous system arousal and to derive features related to stress, engagement, and excitement); and infrared thermopile (measure of peripheral skin temperature). Of note is the use of electrodermal metrics. Skin conductance response is inexpensive and relatively easy to use and requires minimal intervention on Inga. Skin conductance response has been linked to measures of arousal, excitement, fear, emotion, and attention, which offers a useful metric for assessing Inga's responses to everyday situations. The data can then be processed and filtered before being sent to the smartphone application for biasing/valuating of decisions. The information from the biosensors (from the wristband) will give the smartphone application real-time information about Inga's emotional responses. The smartphone application can identify various levels of psychophysiological responding.

6.6.5 Affective Computing

While the reader may think that this all sounds a bit too much like science fiction, it is important to note that Rosalind Picard (inventor of Inga's biosensing wristband) coined the phrase (and many view her to be responsible for the discipline) "affective computing" in her book *Affective Computing* (Picard, 1997). Moreover, Picard is understood to be a pioneer of affective computing and she directs the Affective Computing Research Group at the MIT Media Lab. Picard (1997) has described affective computing as a discipline that pulls from computer science, engineering, psychology, and education to investigate how affect impacts interactions between humans and technology. Affective computing is a field of study that aims to design machines that can recognize, interpret, process, and simulate human affects (Parsons, 2017; Schwark, 2015). As a discipline, affective computing has gained popularity rapidly in the last decade because it has apparent potential in the next generation of human–computer interfaces (Calvo et al., 2015). In Picard's work, she endeavors to remove the affective barrier between humans and machines. It is likely that affective computing and cyberpsychological studies of human–computer interactions can be enhanced using the same principles that govern human–human interactions found in social and affective neuroscience (Parsons, 2017).

6.6.6   Affective Computing for Cognitive Assistive Technologies in Aging

Julie Robillard, at the University of British Columbia, and Jess Hoey, at the University of Waterloo, have discussed the potential of affective computing for cognitive assistive technologies in aging (Robillard & Hoey, 2018). They argue that the adoption and effectiveness of cognitive assistive technologies depend on utilizing the subtleties of human emotion. In a recent study aimed at detecting stress in real life with an Empatica (unobtrusive wrist device), Gjoreski and colleagues (2017) developed a method for stress detection that can accurately, continuously, and unobtrusively monitor psychological stress in real life. Their approach included a context-based stress detector that uses the outputs of a stress detector, activity recognizer, and other contexts to provide a decision in twenty-minute intervals. They used fifty-five days of real-life data to show that their method detects (recalls) stress events with a level of 95 percent precision.

Returning to Inga's wearable biosensor, when it is synced with her smartphone application, it can even track her current location and automatically project previous entries related to her decisions and emotional reactions to that location or the type of event Inga is attending. The smartphone application also automatically weights relations between the various categories of information – weighted relations that, relative to the frequency they are being followed and Inga's emotional reactions to them, are more heavily weighted (get stronger) or less heavily weighted (get weaker). This is increasingly available with the advent of the Semantic Web (Berners-Lee, Hendler, & Lassila, 2001; Carter, Clark, & Palermos, 2018). Over time, Inga's reliance on the smartphone application becomes automatic and second nature to her. The smartphone application has, in effect, begun to play the functional role of Inga's automatic processes (e.g., information encoding, storage, and automatic when-needed retrieval, as well as automatic biasing of future decisions).

Kadian Davis and colleagues (2015), at Eindhoven University of Technology in the Netherlands, have used Damasio's (1994) somatic marker hypothesis and biosensors to propose an unobtrusive approach to improving bonding relations between the older adults and their caregivers. Following Damasio's somatic marker hypothesis, they use a wearable device to capture somatic markers (i.e., biosignals such as ECG, blood pressure, and EDA) that correlate with their "Social Hue" application, which offers a bidirectional application that aims to foster social presence. Activity and emotional states are detected via biosensors and transformed into ambient lighting in the older adult's home. This could be useful given that independent living at home is an ever-increasing issue in gerontechnology. The ethical aspects are notable as independence relies on social relations. Moreover, there are several studies that are emerging related to the design of elderly monitoring systems that use pervasive technologies such as sensors and actuators (see, for example, Hossain & Ahmed, 2012; Majumder et al., 2017; Ruyter & Pelgrim, 2007). These technologies can be used for detecting emergencies and notifying caregivers. It is important to note, however, that older adults are a vulnerable group and, at times, they can be easily coerced into giving up control and privacy.

6.7   Smart Homes for Elderly Healthcare

Smart homes integrate environmental and wearable biosensors, actuators, and modern communication and information technologies to allow for constant and remote monitoring of older adults. Moreover, smart homes may potentially enable older adults to stay in their own familiar home environments instead of expensive and limited healthcare facilities. Caregivers and healthcare personnel are able to monitor the older adult's overall health condition in real time. Furthermore, these smart homes allow caregivers and health personnel to give the older adult feedback and support from distant facilities. As can be seen in Figure 6.2, comprehensive smart homes involve the integration of multiple technologies along with a wide range of environmental and biosensors (for a review, see Van Hoof, Demiris, & Wouters, 2017).

As Figure 6.2 reveals, almost every aspect of the older adult can now be monitored. Smart homes and related smart technologies have emerged as potential solutions to some of the pressures found in an overburdened care system for older adults who value their autonomies. Of course, this level of monitoring and manipulation of the older adult's environment also comes with ethical concerns related to the extent to which these technologies are ethically and practically acceptable. Some ethical questions include:

– Does the autonomy found in smart homes lead to a socially isolated older adult?
– To what extent does the older adult understand the nature of the smart homes technologies, and can the gerontechnologist be sure that the older adult is able to consent to their use?

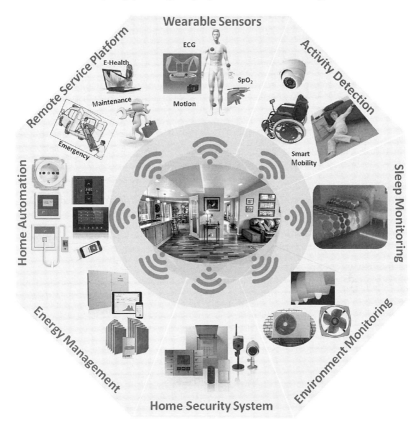

Figure 6.2 Smart homes integrated with automated systems for elderly healthcare (from Majumder et al., 2017; reprinted with permission from the publisher)

– Who should have access to and control the data generated by smart home systems that monitor the older adult's activities, psychophysiological arousal, and decisions?

6.7.1 *Ethical Smart Homes that Support Moral Values and Sociocultural Considerations*

While innovative gerontechnologies can provide support to an older adult, there are ethical issues that need to be addressed to make sure that these smart homes and related technologies support moral values and sociocultural considerations. Important issues include informed consent, privacy, information management, and the older adult's own control of the environment. As adults age and become more vulnerable, it becomes even more important that these ethical concerns be clearly defined. Ad van Berlo (2002) has alliterated a three P's approach to answering ethical questions in smart home technologies: Perspectives (i.e., older people's perspectives about the new technology), Principles (i.e., autonomy, beneficence, nonmaleficence, and justice), and Paradigms (i.e., contextual situations). According to van Berlo, perspectives relate to considerations of the views of all persons involved in proposed actions and the consequences of not taking various actions. As for principles, van Berlo emphasizes the need for gerontechnologists to respect the older adult's autonomy; to do our best for the older adult (beneficence); to not harm the older adult (nonmaleficence); and to seek justice. Finally, paradigms can be used by the gerontechnologist to provide reference situations wherein the appropriateness of a particular solution may be evaluated.

There are, however, others who challenge the approach that views the older adult as independent and self-determining. According to Zwijsen, Niemeijer, and Hertogh (2011), it may be better to take an ethical approach that views the older adult as social and reciprocal. This may shed a different light on the ethical aspects. Take, for example, a multicultural society such as that found in major metropolitan cities of the United States like New York or Los Angeles; older adults come from multifarious backgrounds. As a result, the views and attitudes of these older adults toward aging and care can be vastly different. For example, older immigrants who value collaborative coexistence may have a negative view of independent living. In fact, for them, smart homes could be viewed as antisocial. Hence, the integration of smart homes and related technologies into the older adult's environment should be done with careful consideration of sociocultural considerations and mores.

6.8 Privacy versus Safety

Several gerontechnologists have pointed to the potential of smart homes and monitoring (i.e., surveillance) technologies for infringing on the older adult's autonomy and privacy (Bharucha et al., 2009; Hughes 2008a, 2008b; Hughes et al., 2008; Perry, Beyer, & Holm, 2008; Robinson et al., 2007). For example, Casas and colleagues (2006) have warned that there are psychological ramifications of the "Big Brother" effect from surveillance technologies. Likewise, Robinson and colleagues (2007) surveyed persons with dementia and found that they endorsed concern over surveillance and the identity of a "Big Brother." It is important to note, however, that rights to personal health and/or safety are at times valued above rights to privacy and dignity (Eltis, 2005; Plastow, 2006).

These issues become even more pronounced when considering technologies of the extended aging mind. Smartphone applications and smart homes are increasingly able to personalize their approaches to us via machine learning. Are our thoughts our own in such situations? As pointed out in earlier chapters, smart technologies are designed by persons and corporations that often want to both make lives better and make money while doing so. As soon as a corporate entity attempts to extract information from us, we are, in an important sense, less free and autonomous. In this era of Big Data, governments and corporations have access to huge amounts of personal data. Yet, from an extended mind perspective, privacy can be compromised by laws that suggest the older adult's private life is just in the person's head. Take, for example, warrantless searching of a smartphone. For persons accepting technologies of the extended mind perspective, this is essentially a warrantless infiltration of the older adult's mind.

What if Inga starts to experience the same Alzheimer's symptoms that disrupted Otto? Her Alzheimer's disease progresses to the point that she has limited ability to safely look after herself. As a result, her son decides that her house should be turned into a smart home where her every activity is monitored. Included in this is a monitoring of her emotional valence and decision-making. Inga used the smartphone application for a long enough period that there is now a well-developed database and personalization algorithms related to her interests, activities, and psychophysiological reactions to various stimuli and situations. This information is ported over into the smart home with the most up-to-date Internet of Things (IoT) appliances and applications. This network of devices, home appliances, and other items embedded within sensors, software, electronics, and actuators connects Inga with her personalized cloud space developed over time from her interactions with technologies. As critics have noted, while such an IoT-based smart home offers Inga a host of possibilities for enhancing her life and increases her access to information, the threats to her privacy are huge, as is the possibility of social control and political manipulation (for discussion of IoT concerns, see Howard, 2015). Moreover, Inga's personalized smart home may impact her personal agency, privacy, and autonomy. Instead of viewing the smart home and related technologies as mere tools, perhaps we should view them as active extensions of Inga's agency (see Verbeek, 2011).

Inga has been living in the smart home for some time now and the relationship between Inga and the smart home has grown more intimate – Inga now integrates its algorithmic output into the working of her mind while carrying out her everyday activities. While watching television, she hears suggestions from her smart television that tailors shows and commercials to her preferences and activities. In particular, she is increasingly exposed to content suggesting that Inga upgrade her refrigerator from the basic unit she currently has to a brand-new one with several improvements and amenities. Here, the algorithms have learned Inga's preferences and are attempting to influence her actions. Moreover, the algorithms from the smart home application that monitors her current IoT-enabled refrigerator may increase the level of suggestion by "asking" Inga if she is satisfied with her current refrigerator when she takes a moment to get something to eat. While Inga may recognize that she did not purchase the refrigerator with the extra amenities because it was outside of her budget, she reasons that little harm would come from surfing the Web for deals on an upgraded refrigerator. Here, one finds a clear effect of the technology on Inga that was influential enough to cause an alteration of her second-order desires to stay within her budget. Most likely, Inga's son (as well as ethicists) would view this as undue influence. While the influence is relatively trivial, this scenario reflects a violation of autonomy. This violation becomes much more pronounced when one considers the fact that the very same algorithm that has become an extension of Inga's mind is also an extension of the mind of the corporate entity that designed the smart home and IoT appliances. Perhaps the corporate entity was paid by the company making the refrigerator for directing Inga to them. Such potential conflicts of interest muddy the ethical waters when attempting to ascertain the extent to which a technology of the extended mind has resulted in a violation of autonomy.

6.9   Conclusions

Ethical issues in gerontechnologies are readily apparent in research and practice. Herein, there has been a discussion of the ways in which ethical principles can be extended to develop an approach to ethics that emphasizes an extended mind perspective. Given the extended mind thesis put forth herein, there is a robust prima facie rationale for ethical issues related to various smart homes and related smart technologies. In this chapter, the focus has been on integrating approaches via an argument that mental processes include not only brains but also gerontechnologies and even smart homes and social structures. As a result, ethical concerns of geron-technologists can extend far more widely. The extended mind thesis allows the gerontechnologist to consider ethical concerns related to smart tech-nologies that integrate with the older adults who use them. In making decisions about how gerontologists and designers structure smart home environments and employ gerontechnologies, decisions can be made about the ways in which gerontechnologies of the extended mind are employed, and such decisions must be informed by ethical thinking.

More work is needed for research and training of gerontechnologists in the design and implementation of extended cognitive systems. Gerontechnologists should work with designers, caregivers, health profes-sionals, and older adults themselves to participate in responsible practices of technology use. Moreover, gerontechnologists will need to reverse-engineer the cognitive integration, show the steps that integration has developed over, and raise the gerontechnologist's approaches toward those technologies. From an extended mind perspective, the role of tech-nology for aging adults should emphasize the coupled assemblages between the older adults and technologies of the extended mind.

CHAPTER 7

Problematic Internet Use, Online Gambling, Smartphones, and Video Games

7.1 Introduction

Problematic uses of the Internet, online gambling, smartphones, and video games are all receiving increasing recognition as potential public health burdens (Griffiths et al., 2016; Kuss & Lopez-Fernandez 2016; World Health Organization, 2015). Although there is some disagreement about whether persons that excessively use the Internet are addicted or just use the Internet excessively as a medium to fuel their other addictions, Internet gaming disorder has been categorized in the revised *Diagnostic and Statistical Manual of Mental Disorders* as a condition for further study (American Psychiatric Association, 2013). Furthermore, excessive gaming and Internet use often co-occurs in people with psychiatric conditions (González-Bueso et al., 2018; Ko et al., 2012), including anxiety and depression (Yen et al., 2007), sleep disorders (Lam, 2014), attention deficit/hyperactivity disorder (Ceyhan & Ceyhan, 2008; Yen et al., 2007), obsessive compulsiveness (Jiménez-Murcia et al., 2014; Strittmatter et al., 2015), social problems (Ceyhan & Ceyhan 2008; Ferguson, Coulson, & Barnett, 2011), physical health problems (Kelley & Gruber, 2012), and decreased job productivity and unemployment (Young, 2010).

While there are parallels to other addictions, the American Psychiatric Association prefers the term "Internet Gaming Disorder" over "Internet addiction" because a gaming addict is not necessarily addicted to the Internet but simply uses it as a medium to engage in the chosen behavior. According to Starcevic and Billieux (2017), Internet-related disorders are best conceptualized within a spectrum of related and yet independent disorders. For the purposes of this chapter, cyber-spectrum disorders will be used for all discussions of various forms of problematic use of the Internet, online gambling, smartphones, and/or video games.

7.2 How and Why People Develop Problems with Internet Use, Social Media, and Gaming

The issues surrounding problematic uses of the Internet, online gambling, smartphones, and video games are multifaceted, with several facets coming into play in assorted ways. Growing evidence suggests that Internet addiction is associated with brain structural changes and decreased control of executive functioning. Neuroimaging findings reveal that brain regions associated with executive function (e.g., orbitofrontal cortex) had decreased cortical thickness in Internet-addicted adolescents (Hong et al., 2013). Neuroimaging results have consistently revealed brain regions associated with executive function (e.g., left lateral orbitofrontal cortex, insula cortex, and entorhinal cortex) had decreased cortical thickness in Internet gambling disordered participants. Further, reduced cortical thickness of the left lateral orbitofrontal cortex was associated with impaired cognitive control (for a review, see chapter 7 of Parsons, 2017).

Matthias Brand and colleagues (2016) have developed an Interaction of Person–Affect–Cognition–Execution (I-PACE) model of specific Internet-use disorders. The I-PACE framework is based on previous theoretical considerations and empirical findings. It offers a model for conceptualizing the processes underlying problematic use of the Internet and cyber-addictions. The model emphasizes relations among predisposing neurobiological and psychological factors that impact affective and cognitive responses (e.g., reduced executive functioning) to situational triggers in combination (see Figure 7.1).

Simply put, there are several issues involved in how and why persons develop problematic Internet use, online gambling, excessive use of smartphones, and compulsions to play video games. As can be seen in the I-PACE model, the use of such technologies has specific impacts on cognitive and affective processing. For some people, the effects are more potent given predisposing factors. The use of these technologies has given rise to worldwide sociocultural transformations that include the performance of cognitive and affective processes (Clowes, 2015). The digital and coupled technologies such as the Internet, smartphones, and video games are powerful, convenient, portable, and capable of storing vast amounts of salient data about people's lived experiences on the cloud. Moreover, these technologies take part in the operations of our cognitive (e.g., memory) processes (Clowes, 2015). In fact, our connections to digital information now permeate most aspects of our lives. This has led to the integration of

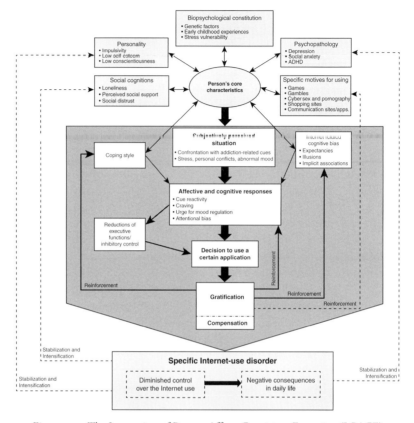

Figure 7.1   The Interaction of Person–Affect–Cognition–Execution (I-PACE)
model on the development and maintenance of a specific Internet-use disorder
(from Brand et al., 2016; reprinted with permission from the publisher)
Note that the emboldened lines with arrows denote the primary pathways of the
addiction process.

these technologies (e.g., Internet, smartphones) into the cognitive tasks we
perform in our activities of daily living.

7.2.1   The Internet Is a New Type of Cognitive Ecology

Paul Smart (2012, 2014, 2018) at the University of Southampton goes so far
as to argue that the Internet is a new type of cognitive ecology that provides
almost constant access to digital information that increasingly extends our
cognitive processes (see also Smart, Heersmink, & Clowes, 2017). As such,
these digital extensions of our cognitive processes are expanding into

Luciano Floridi's (2014) infosphere (see Chapter 2 of this book). According to Floridi, the ultimate nature of reality consists of information. Moreover, he asserts that everyone lives in the "infosphere" as "inforgs" (i.e., information organisms):

> Minimally, infosphere denotes the whole informational environment constituted by all informational entities, their properties, interactions, processes, and mutual relations ... Maximally, infosphere is a concept that can also be used as synonymous with reality, once we interpret the latter informationally. In this case, the suggestion is that what is real is informational and what is informational is real. (p. 41)

The notable metaphysical claim in Floridi's information ethics is that the totality of all that exists does so in the "infosphere" as an informational object or process. Altering the characteristic data structures of informational objects and processes in the infosphere can result in significant damage or destruction. Floridi refers to this damage or destruction as "entropy" that acts as an evil that should be avoided or minimized. Floridi's information ethics is also notable for its assertion that everything in the infosphere has at least a minimum value (or Spinozian right) that should be respected. The construal of every existing entity to be "informational" and consisting of at least a minimal moral worth, Floridi's information ethics can complement traditional normative ethical theories. Hence, our entire existence is increasingly permeated with technologies that can both make our lives better and cause problems. As mentioned in Chapter 1 of this book, technologies impact our brains. Given that we are surrounded by technologies, there is need for considerations of the ethical issues surrounding the impacts of these technologies on our autonomy and privacy.

7.2.2   Caught in the Spider Web of the World Wide Web

As discussed in Chapter 3, technologies extend our cognitive processes. The extension of our cognitive processes to the World Wide Web is analogous to a spider and its web. Richard Menary (2007), at Macquarie University, considers the relations between a spider and its web. He asks us to deliberate on whether a web is part of the spider's system for ensnaring prey or merely a tool that can be used by the spider to fulfill its goals. Menary asks us:

> Do you think that the web is simply a product of the relevant organs of the spider, albeit a product crucial to its ability to catch prey? Or do you think

that the web is a part of the spider's prey-catching system – a system that is not bounded by the body of the spider but includes the web? After all, the spider creates and carefully maintains and manipulates the web and it is through the web that she is able to efficiently catch and consume her prey. (Menary, 2007, p. 1)

Menary is alluding to the work of the evolutionary biologist Sir Richard Dawkins (1982) on the extended phenotype. The idea of the extended phenotype is that the composite set of an organism's observable traits (i.e., phenotype) is not completely held within the organism itself but, in fact, comprises more than a few facets of the external world. Dawkins (1982) contends that "in a very real sense her web is a temporary functional extension of her body, a huge extension of the effective catchment area of her predatory organs" (p. 198).

Menary also pulls from Ruth Millikan to understand the organismic system. The system should not be considered in terms of the body alone. Instead, one needs also to consider the organism's place in, and in relation to, its environment. The organismic system involves "a coordination among parts or subsystems, each of which requires that the other parts or subsystems have normal structure and are functioning normally" (Millikan, 1993, p. 160). The spider's aptitude for trapping prey is an organismic process that should be considered in lieu of the functional operations of the spider and web in operation. This is important, for web and predatory, perceptual, and motor organs each have a role to play in this process and these roles must be coordinated. Menary extends the analogy between the organismic system of the spider and web working in concert to the extended cognition (Carter et al., 2018; Clark & Chalmers, 1998; Menary, 2010) found in externalist theories of mind, wherein cognitive systems extend into the external environment and are comprised of both neural and external components such as smartphones (see Chapter 3 of this book) and even other people.

7.2.3   Implications for Cyber-Spectrum Disorders

Experiencing cyber-addictions and problematic reliance on technologies is similar to finding oneself caught in a spider's web. Given the discussion in Chapter 3 and 4 related to technologies of the extended mind and the ethical implications that algorithmic devices can have for our brain processes, it follows that technologies can become so integrated into our lives that they act like Menary's (2007) spider and its prey-catching web system – a system that is not bounded by the body of the user but includes the web of technologies that make up our increasingly digital existence. The Internet, smartphones, wearable devices, and video games are all aspects of our activities of daily living, and they allow for continuous connections to online information, social media, and computational applications that shape and support the course of our daily activities and relations (Smart, Clowes, & Heersmink, 2017). The conceptualization of digital technologies as extensions of our cognitive processes within an infosphere rather than as tools leads to a reconceptualization of problematic uses of the Internet, online gambling, smartphones, and video games. If the Internet and related technologies are not just tools to be utilized, the theoretical models supporting addictive behaviors may need some fresh consideration.

7.2.4   *Variable-Ratio Schedules*

Social media platforms have a strong impact on users because affirmations from social media (e.g., likes, text chimes, ringtones) from other users occur only sporadically. From a behavioral perspective, this rate of online reinforcement represents a variable-ratio schedule that produces the sort of high steady rate of responding found in gambling and lottery games. How does this reward system become activated for social media users? The answer is that social media platforms (e.g., Facebook) have multiple variable-ratio reinforcement schedules built into them – I could receive a "like," a friend request, a comment on the My Status update, or be tagged in a photo. Any of these situations (among the many other possible) might place me in a state of anticipation. This variable-ratio pattern of reinforcement can be more addicting than receiving affirmation every time because (at least in part) my brain endeavors to predict rewards. In variable-ratio reward schedules, the brain cannot find the pattern and it will promote a behavior until it finds a pattern. In situations where the rewards (e.g., affirmations, chimes) are random, the brain's attempt at pattern recognition may continue compulsively. The activation of the reward network via variable-ratio schedules may help to explain the increasing usage trend that is apparent in recent years. Moreover, variable-ratio schedules may help to explain the increased instances of social media use resulting in cyber-addiction. Excessive social media use can become a serious problem. It may be the case that self-disclosing and subsequent activation of the reward pathways in the brain is linked to the development of cyber-addiction (for more on this, see Parsons, 2017).

7.2.5   The Brain's Reward System

What happens in the person's brain when he or she sees someone "like" their post on a social media site? The answer may involve a part of the ventral striatum that lies in a region in the basal forebrain rostral to the preoptic area of the hypothalamus. Specifically, the reinforcing effect that occurs when a person experiences a "like" reflects activity in the nucleus accumbens. The nucleus accumbens has an important role in the neuro-cognitive processing of reward, pleasure, reinforcement learning, aversion, and motivation. *Dopamine acts in the nucleus accumbens to attach motivational significance to stimuli associated with reward.* Dopaminergic neurons found in the ventral tegmental area (VTA) connect via the mesolimbic pathway and modulate the activity of neurons within the nucleus accumbens that are activated directly or indirectly by drugs such as opiates and amphetamines (see Parsons, 2017).

Video game play has also been found to result in substantial dopamine release in the dopaminergic system as well as addiction (for a review, see Parsons, 2017). Results from neuroimaging studies have revealed that video game play activates the brain's motivational systems. In an early positron emission tomography study, Koepp and colleagues (1998) found large releases of striatal dopamine in participants playing an action video game (note, that there is need for further replication). Furthermore, Hoeft and colleagues (2008) used functional magnetic resonance imaging of participants as they performed a simple computer game. Results revealed brain activation in regions typically associated with reward and addiction: the nucleus accumbens and orbitofrontal cortex. The orbitofrontal cortex is involved in the coding of stimulus–reward value and, along with the ventral striatum (i.e., the nucleus accumbens), is implicated in representing predicted future reward. Ventral striatal reward–related activation in video games has been found when the player's rewards (winning) were coupled to the observed rewards of another player (Kätsyri et al., 2013).

As mentioned (see Figure 7.1), Matthias Brand and colleagues (2016) have developed an I-PACE model of specific Internet-use disorders. The model emphasizes relations among predisposing neurobiological and psychological factors that impact affective and cognitive responses (e.g., reduced executive functioning) to situational triggers in combination. According to Brand and colleagues (2016), conditioning may enhance the neurobiological and psychological associations found in the reinforcement circle of addiction (see Figure 7.2).

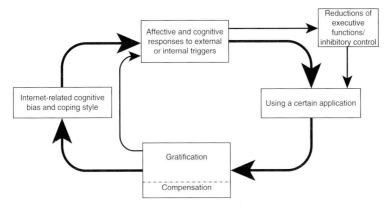

Figure 7.2 The reinforcement circle representing a temporal dynamic of the affective and cognitive contributions to cyber-addictions (from Brand et al., 2016; reprinted with permission from the publisher)
Note that the emboldened lines with arrows denote the primary pathways of the addiction process. It is also important to note that the unemboldened lines with arrows represent the added connections that cultivate within the addiction process.

The Internet, smartphones, and video games are so prevalent in the social environment and have become so integrated into our cognitive systems that they are prime external factors through which our brains relate to and structure external representations. Smartphone GPS, Facebook, Google, and other aspects of the Internet are impacting people's brains and extending cognitive processes (Clowes, 2013). While this can enhance one's life, the pervasive and covert influences can also be disruptive to a user's autonomy. Constant exposure to algorithms and algorithmic devices aimed at manipulating thoughts and behaviors brings with it a host of ethical concerns and dilemmas.

7.3 Positive Computing, Aristotelian Virtue Ethics, and Well-Being

While there certainly are persons who problematically use and overuse the Internet and related technologies (e.g., smartphones, video games), not everyone that actively engages in social media and video games is expressing addictive behaviors. Instead, it is better to consider these behaviors on a spectrum (i.e., cyber-spectrum disorders). Otherwise, we may pathologize what is increasingly normal behavior. If cyberpsychologists interested in cyber-spectrum disorders do not consider the Internet, smartphones, wearable devices, and video games to make up much of the current infosphere, they run the risk of pathologizing everyday behaviors. This sentiment reflects recent conclusions made by Billieux, Thorens, and colleagues (2015) following their study on problematic involvement in online games:

> To conclude, we would like to emphasize the current trend to consider a high commitment to (or a passion for) a wide range of daily or leisure activities such as video game playing as "behavioral addictions" . . . Indeed, in the recently released DSM-5, Internet gaming disorder was proposed as a tentative new psychiatric condition and conceptualized as an addictive disorder. Besides this evolution leading to growing pathologization of everyday behaviors, it also neglects the evidence that excessive behaviors (e.g., playing video games, gambling, eating, shopping) are heterogeneous and multi-determined. (p. 249)

In a paper discussing the overpathologizing of everyday life and behaviors, Billieux, Schimmenti, and colleagues (2015b) argue that the label "behavioral addiction" is often applied incorrectly to conduct that is simply beyond the norm. They give the following as examples: compulsive buying (shopaholics), binge eating (overeating), excessive work involvement (workaholics), hypersexuality, and excessive physical exercise. They point out that the criteria commonly used for identifying behavioral addictions lend themselves to pathologizing excessive involvement in any type of activity as a psychiatric disorder (Billieux, Schimmenti et al., 2015b).

From an ethical perspective, this practice is similar to that found in the work of positive psychologists such as Martin Seligman and Mihaly Csikszentmihalyi (2000) who aimed "to catalyze a change in the focus of psychology from preoccupation only with repairing the worst things in life to also building positive qualities" (Seligman & Csikszentmihalyi, 2000, p. 5). Laura King (2011), at the University of Missouri, is a positive psychologist interested in Aristotle's (350 BCE/1998 CE) virtue ethics and the meaning of happiness. King (2011) points out that a rift in positive psychology has led to bifurcating happiness into hedonic well-being (shallow, fleeting, and subjective) and eudaimonic well-being (deeper and less morally ambiguous). With her colleagues (Biswas-Diener, Kashdan, & King, 2009; Kashdan, Biswas-Diener, & King, 2008), King has suggested that this division of happiness into hedonic and eudaimonic well-being is ill-advised. In addition to eudaimonic well-being lacking a specific definition, hedonic and eudaimonic well-being overlap considerably, conceptually, and empirically. In fact, she points to the lack of evidence for a qualitative difference between the happiness that arises from what positive psychologists call eudaimonic activities and the happiness that emerges otherwise.

An application of positive psychology to the digital era is the emerging dialogue in the cyberpsychology community related to positive computing. In 2012, world-renowned cyberpsychologists from Italy (Giuseppe Riva and Andrea Gaggioli), Spain (Christina Botella, Mariano Alcaniz, and Rosa Baños), and Belgium (Brenda Wiederhold, also in the United States) published a paper on the present and future of positive technologies. In this paper, Botella and colleagues (2012) define positive technology as "the scientific and applied approach for improving the quality of our personal experience with the goal of increasing wellness, and generating strengths and resilience in individuals, organizations, and society" (p. 78). They classify positive technologies according to their objectives. Technologies of Aristotle's hedonic well-being for "the enjoying self" include those devices that aim to produce positive changes in mood states. For example, the group in Spain developed the Engaging Media for Mental Health Applications (EMMA) that used Virtual Emotional Parks that combined mood induction procedures with virtual reality to induce positive emotions (happiness and relaxation). Likewise, Riva's group in Italy developed Relaxation Island, a mood device that uses virtual reality and interactive digital media to enhance users' mood states. There are also technologies of Aristotle's eudaimonic well-being for the "the growing self" that were designed to support individuals in reaching engaging and self-actualizing experiences. For example, the authors developed an application called Emotional Activities Related to Health (EARTH) within the framework of the MARS500 research project that aims to assist astronauts for a future mission to Mars. The EARTH system includes the virtual environments and mood induction procedures to focus on significant events of one's life experiences and also one's future plans.

7.4 Aristotle's Virtue Ethics and Problematic Uses of Digital Technologies

How does Aristotle's virtue ethics relate to the discussion of problematic uses of the Internet, online gambling, smartphones, and video games? First, there is the issue of recognizing that, instead of placing persons into a box of "addicted" or "nonaddicted," it may be better to consider users of technology as falling on a cyber-spectrum of disorder from heavy use to problematic use. Moreover, a "spectrum" implies wide variation in the type and severity of symptoms people experience and allows for theoretical formulations that include all ethnic, racial, and economic groups.

A second consideration for understanding Aristotle's virtue ethics in terms of a cyber-spectrum is that the Internet and related technologies (e.g., smartphones and video games) are increasingly being viewed as a new type of cognitive ecology that provides almost constant access to digital information and results in increased extension of our cognitive processes. The Internet, smartphones, and video games are so prevalent and integrated into our social-cognitive systems that they are prime external factors through which our brains relate to and structure external representations. The use of smartphones, GPS applications, social networking sites, and other aspects of the Internet will increasingly impact people's brains and extend cognitive processes. What may look like behavioral addiction to an octogenarian may look like the norm for that vast majority of millennials. Likewise, what appears to be a persistent use of technologies today probably pales in comparison to the human–computer interfaces that will be experienced by persons a generation from now. So, an important question for pathologizing technology use is whether it actually represents a neurobiological compulsion or simply the logical outworking of a spectrum of technology use in our normal everyday lives.

This leads to a third consideration for Aristotelian virtue, happiness, and leading the good life. Again, while there are studies pointing to problematic findings related to technology use, it can be difficult to see the positive among all the negative conclusions. This is compounded by the fact that much of what is called "addiction" or "problematic" may reflect the over-pathologizing of everyday activities. Examples of this can be seen in Billieux, Philippot, and colleagues' (2015c) discussion of whether too much use of smartphones can be classified as a behavioral addiction (for critical discussions, see Billieux, Schimmenti et al., 2015b; Mihordin, 2012). They concluded that conceptualizing excessive behaviors (e.g., smartphone use) within an addiction model can be a simplification of an individual's psychological functioning, contributing to incomplete clinical significance.

What about someone spending hours and hours on Internet gaming? Does this person have an Internet gaming disorder along the lines of the "addiction model"? Is this person following Aristotle's virtue model and exhibiting superior levels of motivational, affective, cognitive, interpersonal, and social striving as they aim to be the best gamer possible? Recent research emphasizes the need for cyberpsychologists to consider the functions and individual motives that drive online gaming to ascertain whether they are in fact being used excessively. Labels of "dysfunctional" gaming may suggest that the Internet gamer is using an avoidance strategy to keep from facing negative life events, when, in fact, the gamer desires to attain exceptional game performance with achievements that go beyond the norm (e.g., having a commanding avatar or becoming a guild master for a well-respected guild; see Billieux et al., 2013).

Barna Konkolÿ Thege and colleagues (2015), at the University of Calgary, completed a five-year longitudinal study on the natural course and impact of several behaviors that have been considered behavioral addictions in the literature (i.e., exercising, sexual behavior, shopping, online chatting, video gaming, problem eating behaviors). Results revealed that the excessive involvement in these behaviors tends to be rather transient for most individuals. Hence, the oft-labeled "excess" of such behaviors that have been suggestive of addiction in the literature may often reflect context-dependent and transient states with frequent spontaneous recovery.

7.5   Ethical Design

As mentioned in the previous sections, a set of factors that arguably contribute to legitimate cases of problematic uses of the Internet, online gambling, smartphones, and video games is that these technologies are often designed in ways to reward use. What happens when an individual receives a "like" to their posted content on a Facebook page? Typically, this represents a rewarding experience for the person and promotes further social networking. When a person sees a friend "like" their Facebook post, a change happens in that person's brain. This change may reflect activity in the nucleus accumbens, which has an important role in the neurocognitive processing of reward, pleasure, reinforcement learning, aversion, and motivation. Dopamine acts in the nucleus accumbens to attach motivational significance to stimuli associated with reward. Given that social affirmation tends to be a rewarding experience for the vast majority of users, it is not surprising that Facebook affirmations would result in activation of the nucleus accumbens. Moreover, the prefrontal cortex and amygdala share interconnections with the ventral tegmental area and nucleus accumbens and can modulate dopamine transmission and neuronal activity. It is important to note, however, that just because these areas have been found to be associated with Facebook "likes," activation alone is not sufficient for the establishment of an addiction. Nevertheless, brain activations in these areas do raise an interesting possibility that Facebook "likes" and other affirmations (e.g., a chime for an incoming text or email) are powerful stimuli. Internet applications, social media (e.g., Facebook, Twitter), smartphone applications, laptops, PCs, and game consoles all provide us with the reinforcements we are biologically programmed to need and desire. For example, connecting with others socially is a deeply rooted desire in humans and our brains have evolved to release the dopamine reward every time we use these technologies.

7.5.1   Neurobiologically Tuned Algorithms for Manipulating Users

An important issue for the discussion of the ethical aspects of these digital technologies is that many designers realize how brains operate and they are faced with whether or not it is moral to manipulate users with this knowledge. For example, affirmations from social media (e.g., "likes," text chimes, ringtones) from other users occur only sporadically. From a cyberpsychology and behavioral perspective, this rate of online reinforcement represents a variable-ratio schedule that produces the sort of high steady rate of responding found in gambling and lottery games. As introduced in Section 7.2.4, the same variable-ratio reinforcement schedules can be found in social media platforms like Facebook. Receiving a "like," a friend request, a comment on the user's status update, or being tagged in a photo can place the user in a state of anticipation.

7.5.2   Corporate Capitalization on Brain Manipulation and Ethical Egoism

What would happen if corporations that focused on establishing and maintaining user traffic were to discover these neurocognitive findings? They would of course adopt these principles and exploit them to make money. According to Liu and Li (2016), "It is every manufacturer's desire to drive its target customers to form a long-term habit of regularly using its product. Previous studies indicate that the habit of using a certain product can indeed by formed in a systemic manner, once the right sequence is followed" (p. 119). One of the most obvious habit-forming techniques known to programmers is the well-timed push notification and it describes the following sequence. Nir Eyal (2014) actually wrote what is now considered a seminal description of tricks for building habit-forming products. According to the "Hooked Model," it all starts with what Eyal calls the "trigger" and the model is comprised of four sequential but interrelated phases:

1) **Trigger phase**: a trigger (internal and/or external) notifies the user what should be done next and how it should be done (i.e., how to act).

2) **Action phase**: the user acts on the information offered by the trigger.
3) **Reward phase**: the user is rewarded on a variable schedule for acting on the above triggered behavior.
4) **Investment phase**: the increased time and effort of the user making use of the product increases the user's valuation of the product.

The main point is that habits are initiated by a trigger. This means a specific chunk of data explicitly prompts the user to act. Although notifications are not the only kind of trigger, they may be the most prevalent in the "stickiest" products in use. The capacity of notifications to prompt action on them just cost a mere tap on the screen. Smartphone applications are designed to use push notifications for increased pervasiveness (Oulasvirta et al., 2012). Moreover, social media applications such as Facebook are designed to be habit-forming and notifications are a significant aspect of that approach.

This practice is so successful that entire companies have been formed to optimize push notifications. Take, for example, Dopamine Labs (also known as Boundless Mind: www.boundless.ai/), a company that sells neurobiologically tuned algorithms for manipulating users to the application developers. The company provides services to help application developers design addicting applications. Dopamine Labs and its clients are not concerned with whether you develop bad habits or if their technologies lead to problematic uses of the Internet, online gambling, smartphones, and video games. Strangely enough, the company is open to making money off persons who they have helped to addict. They have created an application called Space that reduces the drive to continue a behavior.

While it seems hard to justify the design of manipulative technologies using traditional approaches found in moral philosophy, there may be some support from ethical egoism. The ethical egoist holds that each person ought always to do those acts that will best serve his or her own best self-interest. This is to be differentiated from psychological egoism, which is a theory about how persons do in fact behave. Instead, ethical egoism is a theory about one's moral obligation to seek one's own self-interest. The rightness or wrongness of one's conduct depends on fulfilling one's own self-interest. Adam Smith (1776) promoted an egoistic approach toward morality grounded on the economic benefits that this would convey to society. Smith advocated individual self-interest in a competitive marketplace to engender a state of optimal goodness for society as a whole. According to Smith, competition causes each individual to generate a better product and market it at a lower price than competitors. For example, if a persuasive technologies company plans to outlast the competition, they will need to find ways of making their application better and selling it for less money to get more client companies. The persuasive technologies company gains but so too does the client company. Thus, the persuasive technologies company's self-interest leads to the best overall situation for the industry. For Smith, this was best described as an "invisible hand" that almost numinously guides the economy when we pursue our self-interest. To some extent, Smith's economic argument is more of an argument for utilitarian use of self-interest to attain the good of all.

So, perhaps we should look at the more straightforward brand of egoism found in Ayn Rand's (1964) virtue of selfishness. Rand contends that selfishness is a virtue and altruism a vice. For Rand, altruism erodes one's ability to understand the value of an individual life. Instead of altruism, Rand argued that persons ought to profit from their own actions. Moreover, Rand believed that we have an inalienable right to seek our own happiness and fulfillment, regardless of its effects on others. Hence, a technology designer or company that designs applications should not worry about the impacts on others. Instead, the duty is to the self.

7.5.3   *Technological Design and the Societal Dimension*

There are of course opponents to this perspective. According to Grunwald (2014), technology should not be considered to be detached from the societal dimension. Instead, technological design decisions are morally relevant and ethical considerations should be involved in the design process. Likewise, Von Schomberg (2014) shares this value-laden perspective of technological development and contends that ethics should be included in the design process. Doing so can lead to greater acceptance of designs and technologies. Moreover, ethical reflection on persuasive technologies should take into account the intentions of the persuaders, behavioral and attitudinal aims of the persuasive technology, and methods of persuasion (Berdichevsky & Neuenschwander, 1999; Fogg, 2002).

Jilles Smids (2012) of Eindhoven University of Technology, in the Netherlands, has argued that the most significant ethical question concerning persuasive technologies is the voluntariness of changes they bring about. According to Smids, "voluntary change brought about by a persuasive technology (PT) implies both the absence of controlling influences like manipulation and coercion, and an agent who acts intentional in changing his behavior" (p. 123). Smids aims to differentiate among persuasive technologies that aim at voluntary changes, coercive technologies that aim to control users by application of credible threat, and manipulative technologies that aim to control users by covertly influencing users without the user's awareness or ability to control. For Smids, voluntariness requires that the user be free from external controlling influences. Smids points to autonomy and freedom as fundamental values in Western societies. As such, users of persuasive technologies have a prima facie and foundational right not to be manipulated in ways that violate voluntariness. This is true even in cases where the intentions behind the manipulation and its aims are praiseworthy. According to Smids, the ends of an involuntary persuasive technology simply do not immediately justify their means; additional justification is needed.

Smids looks to Nelson and colleagues' (2011) bioethical analysis of voluntariness in informed consent. Nelson and colleagues argue that an action is voluntary if, and only if, the action is

1) intentional (i.e., agent has intentional control); and
2) unrestricted (i.e., substantially free of controlling influences).

For example, if Tommy decides to get away from social media for a while and closes his smartphone to focus on his schoolwork, he is acting intentionally. If Tommy is prevented from studying by notifications from his smartphone that were initiated by a manipulative technology algorithm aimed at prompting users to check their phone when it has gone idle, then Tommy is subject to a controlling influence.

7.6   Conclusions

As mentioned at the beginning of this chapter, problematic uses of the Internet, online gambling, smartphones, and video games are all receiving increasing recognition as potential public health burdens. Regardless of disagreements about diagnostic categories, Internet gaming disorder has been categorized in the revised *Diagnostic and Statistical Manual of Mental Disorders* as a condition for further study and excessive technology use often co-occurs in people with psychiatric conditions. That said, the issues surrounding problematic uses of the Internet, online gambling, smartphones, and video games are multifaceted, with several facets coming into play in assorted ways.

These issues are compounded by the fact that the Internet is increasingly discussed as a new type of cognitive ecology that provides almost constant access to digital information that increasingly extends our cognitive processes. The Internet, smartphones, and video games are so prevalent in the social environment and they have become so integrated into our cognitive systems that they are prime external factors through which our brains relate to and structure external representations. Smartphone GPS, Facebook, Google, and other aspects of the Internet are impacting people's brains and extending cognitive processes.

The implications for cyber-spectrum disorders include a recognition that the Internet, smartphones, wearable devices, and video games are all aspects of our activities of daily living, and they allow for continuous connections to online information, social media, and computational applications that shape and support the course of our daily activities and relations. By moving from the idea that digital technologies are simply tools to conceiving of them the as extensions of our cognitive processes within an infosphere can influence our discussion of problematic uses of these technologies (e.g., Internet, online gambling, smartphones, and video games). Moreover, this can adjust the way we think about theoretical models supporting addictive behaviors.

If cyberpsychologists interested in cyber-spectrum disorders do not consider the Internet, smartphones, wearable devices, and video games to make up much of the current infosphere, they run the risk of pathologizing everyday behaviors. Instead of pathologizing behaviors, it may be better to consider these behaviors on a spectrum (i.e., cyber-spectrum disorders). That said, there are concerns related to the ethical design of technologies that may lead to legitimate cases of problematic uses of the Internet, online gambling, smartphones, and video games, namely that these technologies are often designed in ways to reward use.

CHAPTER 8

Telepsychology and the Ethical Delivery of e-Therapy

8.1 Introduction

In most aspects of our everyday lives, extraordinary innovations in information and communication technology are taking place. We are now able to visually and verbally communicate with people from around the world (in most parts of the world) at any moment. Communication is the foundation of a fruitful change in psychotherapeutic alliances and it is not surprising that the progress in communication technologies has had an important influence on the profession. These technological advances have not gone unnoticed by mental health professionals, who are showing heightened interest in the potential of technologies to aid in their delivery of services, as well as for managing their practice (Norcross, Hedges, & Prochaska, 2002; Norcross, Pfund, & Prochaska, 2013). Although technological developments bring a good deal of malleability to the field of psychotherapy, there are also ethical challenges that come with them. These ethical issues can frustrate the process, usefulness, and the safety of psychotherapy.

In many parts of the world, there is a notable proliferation of online therapy, professional networking sites for therapists, continuing education, and sites that can help patients find a therapist. The propagation of these online resources makes it increasingly difficult for psychotherapists to have a successful practice completely devoid of the digital interface. For therapists with varying degrees of online presence, there is the potential for intersections with both professional and personal spheres. While a therapist may take steps to insulate their private lives from their clients, it can be the case that their nonprofessional online activities occur in the same online space as their clients'. A range of ethical quandaries may emerge from this shared space. While professional ethical guidelines do offer direction for navigating client–therapist interactions in general, the online arena is a new playing field for many therapists.

A further issue is that therapists often do not receive the training in information technologies necessary to prepare them for ethical challenges (e.g., privacy, electronic security, legal implications) that arise when using these technologies. Moreover, technologies update and change so often that there is a need for ethical approaches that will allow the therapist to keep pace with the changes and anticipate resulting ethical dilemmas. Therapists may struggle with, and may have questions about, how to interpret practice guidelines developed for face-to-face therapy when they are performing therapy online. While there are professional ethical guidelines provided by the American Psychological Association (2013b, 2013c) and the International Society for Mental Health Online (2009), the emergence of new technologies in new locations may involve ethical questions that require greater nuance relative to sociocultural contexts.

In this chapter, there will be a consideration of potential ethical issues that might arise in the context of psychotherapeutic interactions in the digital era. Part of the discussion will include considerations about whether a given client's situation and/or disposition are appropriate for e-therapy and the ways in which therapists may frame e-therapy. This chapter also draws attention to legal issues and ethical issues related to privacy (i.e., confidentiality), electronic security, and boundaries. A goal of this chapter is to aid the clinician in understanding the relevance and applicability of ethical codes and guidelines in the digital era. To do this, situations and circumstances are placed within an extended mind framework, wherein neuroethical considerations can be discussed.

8.2   Telepsychology and e-Therapy: Some Terminology

Online mental health services and e-therapy interactions can come in several shapes and sizes with an accompanying array of terminologies. Before diving into the ethical issues, it may be helpful to first familiarize ourselves with some of the terminologies used. In this section, there is a brief consideration of terms such as telehealth, telepsychology, m-Health, and related concepts. First, there is the umbrella term "telehealth," which relates to telemedicine in the same way that health relates to medicine (Bashshur et al., 2011). Under the umbrella, we find several "tele" areas such as telepsychiatry, telepsychology, teleneuropsychology, and others (see Figure 8.1). Of particular note here are subdisciplines such as tele-mental health and telepsychology. Nickelson (1998) defined tele-mental health as "the use of telecommunications and information technology to provide access to health assessment, intervention, consultation, supervision, education, and information across distance" (p. 527). Various technologies associated with tele-mental health have evolved (Abbott, Klein, & Ciechomski, 2008), so too has its commonly understood definition. More recently, the American Psychological Association (2013b) has added to and clarified this definition in terms of telepsychology as "the preparation, transmission, communication, or related processing of information by electrical, electromagnetic, electromechanical, electrooptical, or electronic means" (p. 792). Moreover, the various technological modalities that comprise telepsychology have been updated to include "telephone, mobile devices, interactive videoconferencing, email, chat, text, and Internet (e.g., self-help websites, blogs, and social media)" (American Psychological Association, 2013b, p. 792). As such, telepsychology has come to refer to the provision of psychological services via electronic communication technologies such as text-based – email, chat rooms, text messaging – and nontext-based – telephone and video teleconferencing (Maheu et al., 2004; Barnett & Kolmes, 2016). Also included are mobile applications and Web-based platforms (American Psychological Association, 2013b). Some of the terms that fall under the umbrella term "telepsychology" include cybertherapy, e-therapy, Internet therapy, and online therapy (see Figure 8.1).

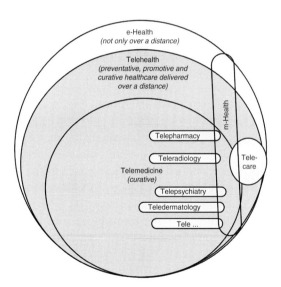

Figure 8.1 Telemedicine, e-health, telehealth, telecare, and m-health. Here, one finds the relations among e-health, telehealth, telemedicine, telecare, and m-health (from Van Dyk, 2014; reprinted with permission from the publisher)

Another distinction that may be helpful is that found between "synchronous" and "asynchronous" communications. In telepsychology, when someone mentions "synchronous" communication, they are most likely referring to forms of media in which two parties (e.g., therapist and client) are communicating with each other in real time. This may be accomplished via video teleconferencing, chatting, or even using the telephone. By "asynchronous" communication, the telepsychologist likely means that the communications are occurring via media wherein the two parties (e.g., therapist and client) can leave messages for each other that can be received and responded to at a later point in time. Examples of this asynchronous communication include emails, voice recordings, and perhaps even online bulletin boards. Some consider "synchronous" and "asynchronous" communications in terms of asynchronous telemonitoring and synchronous intervention. During asynchronous telemonitoring, the patient (or client, depending on the therapeutic orientation) is monitored and feedback delivered via technologies (e.g., email, Internet, cell phone, automated messaging systems, or other equipment) without face-to-face contact. Synchronous interventions are more interactive and involve the therapist's communication in real time, such as face-to-face contact (image and voice) via video teleconferencing (Kern, 2006).

Telepsychologists also distinguish between "standalone" versus "augmented" use of technology in psychotherapy. By "standalone" technology use, the telepsychologist is likely referring to situations where technology is necessary for the e-therapy to occur. Here, the telepsychologist performing e-therapy with a client may have technology as the only form of communication. Typically, video telehealth studies involve standalone video teleconference systems (i.e., video monitor with mounted video camera and telecommunication connection) that are assembled in a therapist's office (Gros et al., 2013). For example, the telepsychologist may never be in the same room as the client during therapy but they may converse via video teleconferencing. On the other hand, a therapist might conduct sessions face-to-face in the same room but augment the session with technologies such as email, phone communication, social networking sites, or other media technologies.

E-health and m-health are terms introduced into the literature that indicate the rapid technological innovations and their wider use in healthcare. Both e-health and m-health have come to be understood as designations for emerging technologies in healthcare (Istepanian & Lacal, 2003; Oh et al., 2005; World Health Organization, 2008). While the term "e-health" is a cousin to other e-words (e.g., e-commerce, e-business, e-solutions) that were introduced by commercial interests in the late

1990s, "m-health" was introduced in 2003 in response to expanding mobile communication technologies. It is important to note that the terms e-health and telehealth are at times used interchangeably. The main difference between the two concepts is that e-health applications, as opposed to telehealth, are not limited to remote healthcare (i.e., healthcare over a distance). A related issue for telehealth is "telecare," which is the nonstop, automated, and remote monitoring of real-time health exigencies over time in order to manage the risks associated with independent living. Given that telehealth is a preventative health application, it falls under telehealth rather than telemedicine.

8.3   Legal Issues Related to Technology Use in Mental Health

Before diving into the ethical issues inherent in using technology to provide mental health services, there are legal issues that need to be discussed. There are two primary regulatory structures that are available for consideration by mental health professionals interested in using technology in their research and practice: (1) the Health Information Portability and Accountability Act (HIPAA, 1996) and (2) the Health Information Technology for Economic and Clinical Health Act (HITECH Act, 2009). The first regulatory framework, HIPAA, maintains that service providers must employ reasonable precautions to ensure that the patient's digital medical privacy is protected. For example, therapists wishing to provide telepsychological assessment and interventions need to follow HIPAA guidelines when assessing the risks involved in the use of various hardware/software and network connections. Furthermore, the HITECH Act may need to be consulted when therapists are responsible for signing business associate agreements for entering data into third-party cloud storage services. Finally, for work with college students, it may also be important to consider the Family Educational Rights and Privacy Act (FERPA) of 1974.

8.4   Ethical Principles Related to Technology Use in Mental Health

There are several practice guidelines that have been developed for various professional organizations. Examples include the American Psychological Association (2013b), the American Telemedicine Association (2009), the American Counseling Association (1999), the International Society for Mental Health Online (2009), and the National Board for Certified

Counselors (1997). Each of these sets of guidelines aims to put forth appropriate standards for the use of technologies for the provision of mental health services. Moreover, each emphasizes the required under-standing of technical aspects such as privacy settings and encryption. There is also the issue of engendering boundary confusion through the use of social media (e.g., "friending" in Facebook, following on Twitter) and unrealistic expectations for email communications. In the following sec-tions, these will be aggregated and summarized.

8.4.1   Balancing Beneficence and Nonmaleficence

Mental health providers may be faced with ethical quandaries when they receive a referral for work with a client who is experiencing difficulties (e.g., depressive symptoms, relational issues). It may be that the client lives in a geographically isolated area that may also have limited access to therapists in their location. For the therapist, this poses a dilemma. If the therapist takes the client on without first having a face-to-face assessment, the therapist may miss potential risk factors that contraindicate distance ther-apy (nonmaleficence). On the other hand, if the therapist refuses to take the client on, they may fall short of an obligation to, always and without exception, favor the well-being and interest of the client (beneficence). Here, we see the tension between the predominant ethical principles of beneficence (the therapist's action taken to cause benefit) and nonmalefi-cence (the therapist's avoidance of an action that could cause harm). Kakli Gupta and colleagues (2016) recommend that the therapist first meets with a client for a face-to-face assessment that includes four criteria to inform whether the client would benefit from therapy via video teleconferencing:

1) client's presenting concerns (i.e., nature and severity)
2) client's access to and comfort with technologies
3) client's access to a private and confidential space
4) client's verbal expressiveness (i.e., client's capacity for a good-enough online communication).

Taken together, these four points can help the therapist navigate between the Scylla and Charybdis of acting to benefit the client without causing harm. Even if the client is comfortable with technologies and has access to both the necessary technologies for the e-therapy and a private space, there may be times when the nature and the severity of the client's presentation contraindicate e-therapy. For example, e-therapy is likely contraindicated for clients who present with severe personality disorder, psychotic disorder, suicidality, and/or who are homicidal (Ragusea & VandeCreek, 2003). Finally, even if all of the above check out, there is still the issue of the client's communication abilities. Video teleconferencing and other forms of e-therapy tend to rely a great deal on verbal expression. As a result, there is a risk of missing communication cues.

8.4.2 *Privacy and Confidentiality*

The practice of e-Therapy and online research has the potential to negatively impact on privacy and confidentiality (Lustgarten, 2015; Lustgarten & Colbow, 2017). This is apparent in the broad range of privacy policies and terms of service found in third-party providers (e.g., Facebook, Twitter, Apple, Google, Microsoft). Potential HIPAA violations and information technology vulnerabilities are apparent in informational notices, client waivers, records of electronic communications, and electronic transfers of client information. It is important to underscore that professional organizations typically place culpability for ethical violations on the service providers (see, for example, American Psychological Association, 2017; Joint Task Force, 2013).

Therapists need to take steps to ensure that their clients are provided with information that adequately explains the limitations of computer technology in the therapeutic process in general and the difficulties of ensuring complete client confidentiality of information transmitted through electronic communications.

A closely related issue is that of securing electronic transmissions of data from interception by third parties, without consent by the user. To safeguard against this, therapists should make sure that they are encrypting the transmission of data (Elhai & Hall, 2015). Likewise, physical electronic devices need to be password-protected to make sure that the client's metadata (phone numbers and email addresses) and confidential information (voicemails and other communications) are protected (Elhai & Hall, 2015). Parsons, McMahan, and Kane (2018) provide practice parameters to mitigate the risk of potential confidentiality breaches. In addition to describing software and hardware configurations that can impact telepsychological platforms, they outline best practices for developers and practicing psychologists to minimize error when using advanced technologies. Throughout, they emphasize the need for developers to provide bench-test results for their software's performance on various devices and minimum specifications (documented in manuals) for the hardware (e.g., computer, monitor, input devices) in the psychologist's practice.

8.4.3   Boundaries

Therapists practicing telepsychology also need to consider the ways in which boundaries may be violated in telepsychology settings. While a good deal of literature exists related to professional guidelines for ethics, legalities, practice, and logistics, less emphasis has been given to therapeutic boundaries in the telepsychology relationship. This is important because telepsychology and e-therapy occur in a shared online space (e.g., Internet, social media, social networking sites) where a client or therapist may choose to "friend" a therapist on Facebook or "follow" each other on Twitter. Moreover, therapists and/or clients may search for information about each other online (Kolmes, 2012; Sabin & Harland, 2017; Zur, 2008). Take Facebook's graph search (Facebook, 2014), for example, which allows users to search for any publicly available data (e.g., comments on public content posted by third parties) about a Facebook member. Such services may be helpful for research but they also bring increased potential for boundary violations (Gamble & Morris, 2014; Sabin & Harland, 2017).

Daniel Lannin and Norman Scott (2013), at Iowa State University, discuss social networking ethics for psychologists in terms of psychologists providing services in rural settings. For years, psychologists in rural areas have needed to balance transparency and disclosure while maintaining boundaries. As Lannin and Scott point out, psychologists practicing in today's digital age need to consider the world as smaller and their clients as more local. As such, it is important that psychologists examine their privacy settings to preclude requests and follows from clients (Lannin & Scott, 2013). Furthermore, therapists should think about employing a policy that outlines expectations for contact on social media.

Katherine Drum and Heather Littleton (2014), at East Carolina University, outline issues and recommendations for therapeutic boundaries in telepsychology. They identified two specific factors that may amplify the potential for harmful boundary crossings and violations: (1) the flexibility of service delivery may encourage more frequent and more casual behaviors and (2) the physical distance may lead some to assume protection from boundary crossings and violations. To safeguard against boundary violations, they offer the following nine best-practice recommendations:

1. Maintain professional hours and respect the timing of sessions
2. Be timely and consistent in feedback and manage excessive communications

3. Preserve a private, consistent, professional, and culturally sensitive setting
4. Ensure the privacy of nonclients and prevent unintentional self-disclosures
5. Make certain that telecommunication technologies used convey professionalism
6. Model appropriate self-boundaries
7. Safeguard the privacy of the therapist's work
8. Use professional language and consider alternative interpretations
9. Maintain competence in the practice of telepsychology.

These recommendations should be helpful for psychologists interested in navigating the new challenges and issues for providing competent and ethical care with e-therapy. Thoughtful consideration of the distinctive boundary issues that can emerge in telepsychology will aid therapists who choose to perform e-therapy.

8.4.4   *Telepsychology and e-Therapy Competencies*

A well-thought-out summary of ethical principles can be found in Lustgarten and Elhai (2018) and their emphasis on five domains (legal and ethical) as well as their implications for research and praxes (see Table 8.1): legal; welfare; privacy and confidentiality; security; and boundaries.

Important resources are found in various professional guidelines and in the table that Lustgarten and Elhai use to describe therapist competencies for each of the five areas, as well as recommendations for the therapist employing novel technologies in research and praxes.

8.4.5   *Considerations for Ethical Decision-Making*

For the therapist confronted with cumulative interest in telepsychology, what precautions should be in place to thwart potential harms? John Torous and Laura Weiss Roberts (2017), at Stanford, suggest a framework for the ethical use of telepsychology and m-Health. In their framework, they outline a series of steps that can be used by the mental health service provider to enhance decision-making approaches for the ethical use of technologies (see Figure 8.2).

For Torous and Roberts, the therapist should start with questioning whether technology use could provide a benefit to the client. While there is a dearth of clinical outcomes data, the therapist can assess clinical benefit

Table 8.1 *Competencies for technology use in practice and research (adapted from Lustgarten & Elhai, 2018; reprinted with permission from the publisher)*

Domains	Competencies	Recommendations
Legal	• Maintain understanding of American Psychological Association guidelines, code, and licensure jurisdiction of use. • Describe the legal protections that patients/participants have when data is created. • Detail what regulations apply to psychological work.	• Consult with a lawyer who specializes in healthcare policy and privacy. • Read HIPAA, HITECH, and FERPA. • Attend technology-oriented workshops and continuing education that focus on legal considerations.
Welfare	• Recognize external threats to patients/participants when technology is employed. • Collaborate in informed consent and decisions to utilize technology. • Develop methods to verify locations of patients/participants.	• Practice and utilize an ethical decision-making approach to technology use. • Conduct a risk assessment with client prior to using technology. • Lock patient and provider devices.
Privacy and Confidentiality	• Maintain understanding of current risks to privacy and confidentiality around technology. • Assess points of ingress (i.e., intrusions to privacy). • Develop understanding of corporate policies that govern data created by third-party platforms.	• Use HIPAA-compliant platforms. • Employ zero-knowledge privacy applications such as Signal Messenger.
Security	• Collaborate with patients/participants to maintain security of devices. • Maintain awareness of threats to secure software and hardware.	• Avoid public Wi-Fi hotspots; otherwise, use a Virtual Private Network (VPN) if using a shared network. • Encrypt hard drives on both computers and smartphones. • Use dice-generated phrase passwords.
Boundaries	• Assess patient/participant risk for boundary violations (bidirectionally). • Describe the appropriateness for or against technology use. • Outline business practices for technology use.	• Review and lock privacy settings to social media websites. • Set up automatic email, phone, and/or other contact methods to support notifications and information to patients/participants. • Preempt and/or write potential rules for technology use in informed consent processes.

relative to the therapeutic relationship. Assuming that there is a potential benefit, the therapist can next consider potential risks to the therapeutic relationship. For cases where the client's presenting problems indicate a high safety risk (e.g., chronic mental health conditions with high risk of relapse or recurrence and potentially limited insight or judgment), the therapist may be concerned about a greater potential for harm to the therapeutic relationship. While some clients may not have the capacity needed for providing informed consent to use the technology, others may have the decisional capacity to consent but a history of limited impulse control. Torous and Roberts suggest a spectrum of vulnerability to harm in the therapeutic relationship that may change over time.

Next, Torous and Roberts consider the ethical tensions in confidentiality between corporations providing technologies and mental health service providers. This necessitates a discussion between the therapist and the client about risks to confidentiality that occur with various social media companies. For example, companies such as Facebook, Apple, Microsoft, and others may collect user data, archive it, share it, and even sell it to other companies. Therapists should encourage clients to review the terms of service for their media applications. Finally, the therapist is guided to both initiate and maintain a continuing dialogue with the client about whether using the technology aligns with treatment goals and expectations.

While the principles and approaches discussed thus far in the chapter are helpful, there is still more that can be said about ethical decision-making in light of new technologies that are increasingly used as part of telepsychology. Such technologies offer great promise for the theory and praxes of cyberpsychology but they also bring new ethical challenges. The need for a more well-developed understanding of persons and ethics in the digital era is especially true in light of advances in the neuroscience, neuroethics, and technologies of the extended mind.

8.5   Extended Mind Thesis for Extending Telepsychology

Much of the discussion thus far in this chapter has involved segmenting the roles in e-therapy into therapist, client, and their use of technologies. While Torous and Roberts discuss the use of technology in terms of the potential impacts it has on the therapist–client relationship, each is partitioned into separate spaces. The prevalence of this perspective may be due to the assumption that the brain is functioning as a self-contained physical symbol system that operates like a computer. From this perspective, distinct pieces of

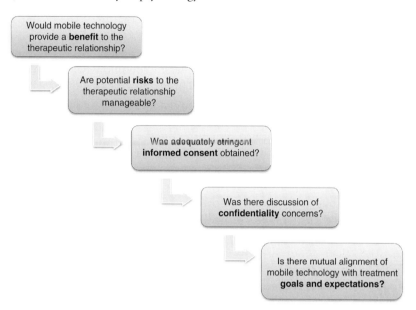

Would mobile technology provide a **benefit** to the therapeutic relationship?

Are potential **risks** to the therapeutic relationship manageable?

Was adequately stringent **informed consent** obtained?

Was there discussion of **confidentiality** concerns?

Is there mutual alignment of mobile technology with treatment **goals and expectations?**

Figure 8.2 Ethical safeguards for the use of mobile technologies in clinical practice (from Torous & Roberts, 2017; reprinted with permission from the publisher)

information are coded as symbols (e.g., "cat," "blue," etc.) in particular memory locations in the brain. These coded symbols can be retrieved and manipulated by a central operating system. This perspective fits well with conceptualizations of the "self" as an active, brain-based intentional agent managing bodily senses and the processing of perceptual information.

A problem for the physical symbol system theory is that, while it can explain the ways in which a client undertakes static tasks such as calculating logical problems, it does not do well in explaining dynamic tasks found in the client's everyday activities, for instance recognizing the therapist's face, multitasking with digital media, or driving. The massive quantity of symbols required for such tasks, as well as their unlimited variability, would cause the central operating system to be hugely cumbersome and sluggish. Furthermore, physical symbol systems involve rigid rules applied to specific symbols. Damage to, or loss of, any of the precise loci where these rules (or symbols) are stored would result in an abrupt failure of important processes. When we look at the brain, we see that this picture does not fit with our brains and their consistent processing even with regular loss of neurons.

In an effort to answer problems raised by the physical symbols system perspective, one solution was to reconceptualize the mental in terms of connectionist neural networks. While symbols are still present in neural networks, they are not coded in discrete brain areas that are manipulated by a central operating system. Instead, they are coded in a distributed fashion and spread throughout a large network of interconnected neurons. Furthermore, we have come to understand the brain not as a single undifferentiated neural network but as a series of interconnected networks that each perform particular functions. This calls into question whether there is a "self" network that acts as a central coordinating network above all the others. However, this simply repeats the concerns found with the physical symbols system theory, wherein one system is required to encompass and operate all of the massive informational outputs of the others. Instead, it is preferable to envisage an assemblage of functional neural networks (each with a rather modest function that interact with each other based on simple rules). Our idea of self (i.e., human consciousness) functions in much the same way. The self can be understood as an assembly of neural networks that are connected in a manner that allows for cognitive and affective processes, as well as behaviors. Hence, the self does not need to be considered as a central processor in our frontal lobes but, rather, as a massively interconnected distribution of functional neural networks.

8.6   Deep Brain Stimulation for Direct Connections to Our Neural Networks

Our technologies can extend the self via direct (and, in some cases, indirect – see Section 8.7) connections to our neural networks. Progress in the neuroscience is illuminating both the malfunctioning connections underlying psychological disorders and the potential of deep brain stimulation for therapeutic change. Today, mental health service providers can benefit from neuroscientific approaches that are supplanting traditional psychological theories that emphasize the mental over the biological in treatment of mental illnesses. For example, autism is now understood to be an irregularity in the connections among neurons that can often be attributed to genetic mutations. Likewise, schizophrenia can now be diagnosed and cared for as a neurodevelopmental disorder. Interestingly, disorders such as depression have received less acceptance as a brain disorder by the public, or even among clinicians. One reason for this slow acceptance that mental disorders like depression are biological in nature is that, unlike traditional neurological illnesses (e.g., post-stroke, Parkinson's disease), where the damage is visible, we have not had the technology necessary for identifying mental disorders like depression in the brain. That said, progress in neuroimaging technologies is enhancing our capabilities for mapping brain functions. Moreover, these technologies allow us to detect glitches in activities of specific brain areas and/or disrupted communications among brain regions that function together as circuits to perform normal mental operations. Malfunctioning neural circuits malfunction may underlie many mental disorders.

Take depression as an example. Persons with depression tend to have decreased energy and low mood levels. While some symptoms such as slower reaction times, difficulties in memory formation, and inhibition make it appear that some brain activity levels appear to be underactive, symptoms like anxiety and sleep disturbances suggest other brain areas are overactive. Neuroimaging of the brain regions that are most impacted in depression reveals imbalances in Brodmann area 25, which functions as a hub for a depression circuit. Brodmann area 25 has direct connections to brain areas that mediate fear and anxiety (the amygdala) and those involved in stress responses (the hypothalamus). These brain regions, in turn, are connected to brain areas involved in memory processing (the hippocampus) and the processing of sensory perceptions and emotions (the insula; see Figure 8.3).

Clients with a smaller than normal Brodmann area 25 and a gene variant that inhibits serotonin processing are at increased risk of depression. It is important to note that researchers have targeted a number of additional brain areas involved in depression. Subsequently, several areas are now being targeted for treating depression.

Helen Mayberg directs the Center for Advanced Circuit Therapeutics at Mount Sinai's Icahn School of Medicine. Mayberg is a neurologist well-known for her work with brain circuits in depression and for her pioneering deep brain stimulation research. She started her work at Toronto and then, with her colleagues at Emory University, she revealed that Brodmann area 25 (subgenual cingulate cortex) is overly active in depression and that symptom improvement after various forms of treatment (medication, psychotherapy) is related to decreased activity in this circuit. Moreover, Mayberg and colleagues (2005; see also Mayberg, 2009) have performed deep brain stimulation on this depression circuit. First, they drill two holes in a patient's skull and slide two low-voltage electrodes deep into the brain until they reach Brodmann brain area 25. Once the electrodes are in place (tip of subcallosal cingulate), they are wired to a battery pack that has been implanted in the patient's chest. Next, the electrodes are activated. Electrical

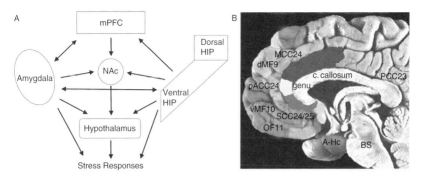

Figure 8.3 Cortico-limbic circuitry implicated in mood regulation and depression: (a) simplified schematic diagram of the cortico-limbic circuitry and the many interactions across the various brain regions; (b) midline sagittal view of the human brain illustrating the location of major PFC regions, with the anterior cingulate cortex highlighted (from Akil et al., 2017; reprinted with permission from the publisher) *Note:* In part (a) not all known connections are depicted. Likewise, not all outputs of each region are depicted. mPFC, medial prefrontal cortex; HIP, hippocampus; NAc, nucleus accumbens. In part (b) blue, MCC24, mid-cingulate cortex; yellow, pACC24, pre-genual anterior cingulate cortex; red, SCC24/25, subcallosal cingulate cortex. Other brain regions noted include dMF9, dorsomedial frontal cortex; vMF10, ventromedial frontal; OF11, orbitofrontal; A-Hc, amygdala-hippocampus in the temporal lobe; BS, brainstem; PCC23, posterior cingulate cortex; c. callosum, corpus callosum.

pulses (stimulation) are continuously delivered to the brain and their level and frequency are customized to the patient. Mayberg and colleagues have demonstrated that direct electrical stimulation near Brodmann area 25 reduces the activity of this node and can result in decreased depression in people who did not respond to standard therapies. As mentioned, in addition to Brodmann area 25, researchers have targeted a number of other brain areas involved in depression. As a result, there are now several areas being targeted for treating depression. Although it is uncertain precisely how deep brain stimulation functions to diminish depression, scientists believe that the pulses act to "reset" the malfunctioning brain area so that it returns to normal functioning. This extended cognitive and affective circuit includes both the wetware-based brain circuit and the hardware-based electrodes and battery. Together, they extend the patient's cognitive and affective processes.

What are the ethical implications of deep brain stimulation? Let us start with the potential side effects. There are risks with deep brain stimulation that are similar to those found with any stereotactic neurosurgical procedures, including intracranial bleeding, hardware-related complications (e.g., dislocation, lead fracture, and infection), and stimulation-induced side effects (relative to stimulation electrode location) such as mania, depression, laughter, penile erection, and aggression. The invasiveness of deep brain stimulation and the potential for subsequent side effects have made it an area of ethical discussion in the neuroethical literature (Clausen, 2010; Schermer, 2011). Furthermore, the financial cost of deep brain stimulation treatment has resulted in discussions about its cost-effectiveness (McIntosh, 2011).

From a principlist approach, these neuroethical considerations can include the principles of nonmaleficence, beneficence, justice, and respect for autonomy, as well as the additional principles of subsidiarity and proportionality (Schermer, 2011). As mentioned, there are a number of risks and benefits associated with deep brain stimulation that must be weighed when aiming to produce the optimal balance of potential benefits and risks while maintaining respect for the patient and the autonomous desires of the patient. The principle of nonmaleficence, *primum nil nocere* ("First, do no harm"), calls for the minimization of the risks and potential side effects (physical and psychological) of deep brain stimulation. Furthermore, it calls for an assessment of the potential impacts of deep brain stimulation on personal identity and the developing brain. We also have the principle of beneficence, *salus aegroti suprema lex* ("patient safety is the supreme law"), which calls for optimizing the effectiveness of the deep brain stimulation treatment both during the surgery and with the subsequent psychosocial care. Additionally, there is the principle of justice, *iustitia* ("equal distribution of treatment") that calls for the optimal rationing and prioritization of deep brain stimulation treatment for patients. Further, there is the principle of autonomy, *voluntas aegroti suprema lex* ("respect the patient's well-informed choice"), which relies on informed and necessary competence to consent. This principle involves additional questions when deep brain stimulation is used with children. The principle of autonomy also entails best-case approaches to managing unrealistic expectations and even desperation in the patient. Finally, the principles of subsidiarity (the "select minimal burden option") and proportionality of risks and benefits are important for ensuring optimal patient selection for deep brain stimulation. Given these considerations, deep brain stimulation should only be used when other less burdensome or risky treatment options have been exhausted.

8.7   m-Health for Indirect Connections to Our Neural Networks

Cybertherapy and m-health applications allow the client to connect with both therapists and technologies to extend their resources for growth and development. One may ask, however, why would we need to hypothesize that, say, a smartphone application is part of our mind rather than merely a tool used by it? Recognition of the widely accepted neuroconnectionist perspective described in Section 8.6 involves recognition that the self is composed of relatively simple, interconnected parts. As a result, internalist approaches to mind that limit cognitive processes to the inside of the skull are less satisfactory. Why not allow the connections to extend cognitive processes to the environment, people, and technologies that surround us? Cybertherapy and m-health technologies can be applied to malfunctioning brain processes. This new perspective can be applied to work on technologies of the extended mind (see Chapter 3 in this book), in which cognitive processes are not limited to the brain but, instead, literally spread into the external world as we interact with others and with technologies. As mentioned in Chapter 3, Daniel Dennett (1996) has pointed to the fact that our remarkable evolutionary success is less a factor of our large frontal lobes but, rather, one of our capacity for extending our cognitive processes into the environment with which we interact. According to Dennett, we have a habit of offloading as much of our cognitive tasks as possible into our surrounding worlds, where a host of peripheral devices can help us store, process, and re-represent our meanings. Moreover, these devices can streamline, enhance, and protect the processes of transformation in our thinking.

The application of extended cognition to our understanding of psychotherapy and mental health services is starting to emerge, as is apparent in works linking extended mind with borderline personality disorder (Bray, 2008); psychopathology (Drayson, 2009; Sneddon, 2002); sexual dysfunction (Merritt, 2013); neurodevelopmental disorder impaction frontostriatal functioning like attention deficit/hyperactivity disorder and autism (Sneddon, 2002); social anxiety disorder (Carter, Gordon, & Palermos, 2016); dispositional affective states (Colombetti & Roberts, 2015); sex offenders (Ward, 2009; Ward & Casey, 2010); and dementia (Clark & Chalmers, 1998; Clark, 2008; Nelson, 2009; Wilson & Lenart, 2015). Others have applied the extended mind approach to psychotherapy (Shennan, 2016) and treating depression (Hoffman, 2016).

Recently, Ginger Hoffman (2016), at Saint Joseph's University (Philadelphia), has argued for the inclusion of the extended mind approach in psychiatric practice. She believes that it could have important impacts on diagnostic decision-making, interventions, and shift research priorities and change the way that psychiatrically affected individuals think of themselves. Arguing from an extended mind perspective, Hoffman

(2016) asks us to consider Iain and Emma – two individuals with depression and diminished feelings of self-worth. Almost every day, Iain feels uncertain about his worth. To counteract these feelings, he checks his internal, brain-based memory of a list he developed years ago that clearly commends his virtues and emphasizes his worth. Emma also consistently feels uncertain about her worth. Instead of a list inside her head, when Emma is feeling low in worth, she looks to an old letter that she wrote years ago. She keeps the letter by her side at all times. The letter clearly commends her virtues and asserts her worth. When Emma consults the letter, she recalls her worth. Hoffman argues that, from an extended mind perspective, both Iain and Emma have mental resources attesting to their worth.

Following Hoffman's argument, it seems apparent that the same idea can be applied to digital technologies that provide ubiquitous Internet connectivity. Smartphone technologies offer to provide global, cost-effective, and evidence-based mental health services on demand and in real time (Aboujaoude, Salame, & Naim, 2015; Firth et al., 2017). Imagine an individual, Valerie, who has been taking part in e-therapy to deal with major life setbacks that have led to depression. In addition to her face-to-face video teleconferencing sessions, she uses a smartphone application between the sessions. Her e-therapy focuses on replacing depressed thoughts with nondepressed (healthy) thoughts, which leads to enhanced feelings of self-worth. Once identified in e-therapy, these healthy thoughts related to her self-worth are recorded and saved into a database. Also included in the database are voice recordings from her e-therapy sessions that are analyzed using speech emotion recognition (El Ayadi, Kamel, & Karray, 2011; Wu, Parsons, Mower, & Narayanan, 2010; Wu, Parsons, & Narayanan, 2010; Zeng et al., 2009). Outside of therapy, Valerie can consult a smartphone application that links to the database with suggestions, inspiration, and support for her self-worth. Her eTherapist uses a back-end system to send short text messages to Valerie via a messaging system, similar to a Short Message Service (SMS). The messaging system is used by the eTherapist to deliver personalized messages of encouragement as well as weekly general educational messages. When Valerie receives the messages, she inputs a rating into the application and it learns what messages work best for her. The application monitors her smartphone usage patterns to identify mood-based metrics – number of incoming/outgoing calls; duration of incoming/outgoing calls; outgoing text messages; application usage (Faurholt-Jepsen et al., 2016; LiKamWa et al., 2013). She wears a wristband that includes physiological sensors (such as heart rate, breathing, skin conduction, physical activity) and allows the application to access them. This allows for identification of her arousal (categorized as emotion states) using physiological signals (Calvo & D'Mello, 2010; Jerritta et al., 2011; Sun et al., 2010). After she has used the system for a period of time, it develops algorithms that automate the messages from the database.

What are the ethical implications of Valerie's e-therapy and smartphone application? Many of the ethical concerns about e-therapy were discussed earlier in this chapter. Moreover, privacy can be protected by making sure that all Internet (including her therapist's back-end system) and smartphone activities (including Valerie's smartphone application) are secured by means of Secure Sockets Layer (SSL) encrypted information. However, the extended cognitive and affective processes found in the smartphone application and its algorithms call for some additional consideration. While the smartphone application could be helpful in reestablishing Valerie's self-worth, it could come at a price for her autonomy. Her use of the smartphone application could develop into an addictive behavior, similar to gambling, that may start to interfere with her everyday life. Although not an official diagnosis, a number of studies have found classic addiction symptomology in persons who overuse smartphones, including distorted perceptions of time spent on the smartphone, preoccupation with the smartphone, withdrawal symptoms, and negative effects on their everyday lives (e.g., Kwon et al., 2013; Lanaj, Johnson, & Barnes, 2014; Lin et al., 2015). One can easily imagine the heightened impacts of a smartphone application with passive and active data analytics that resulted in a personalized algorithm aimed at making Valerie feel better. Moreover, the smartphone application may result in increased susceptibility to other smartphone applications and social media that have been designed to compel users to check for message notifications. These notifications pull Valerie to Facebook, Twitter, and/or YouTube and she finds herself tapping and scrolling for hours. Designers of these applications have developed subtle psychological reinforcements that can be used to make Valerie develop habits. For example, the designers have developed methods for varying the rewards Valerie receives to create "a craving." Moreover, these applications were designed to exploit negative emotions that can act as triggers for various behaviors.

8.8 Therapy versus Enhancement

In Chapter 4, we discussed neuroethics applied to technologies of the extended mind. Often, in neuroethics, the emphasis is on neuroenhancement. A significant distinction that needs to be kept in mind when thinking about neuroethical issues is between therapy and enhancement. This distinction is often helpful in cases that call for discernment between appropriate and inappropriate uses of various technologies. Typically, "therapy" entails treating problematic thoughts, feelings, and/ or behaviors, whereas "enhancement" characteristically entails improving something that is not a problem or enriching something to a status that we might describe as performing better than normal. Following the Bush-era President's Council on Bioethics (2003) and the more recent Presidential Commission for the Study of Bioethical Issues (2014), therapeutic use of technologies involves treating patients with known diseases, disabilities, or impairments, in an effort to restore them to a normal state of health and fitness. The use of technologies for enhancement involves altering the "normal" workings of the human body and cognitive processes, to augment or expand their native capacities and performances.

The move from applying technologies for therapy to using them for enhancement is significant and raises ethical concerns about the provision of mental health services; the meaning of "natural," human dignity, and numerous other fundamental postulations about technological advancement; as well as what it means to be a person. Supporters of simply accepting the transition from therapy to enhancement as the next logical step in our development contend that it is unfeasible to draw a strict line between therapy and enhancement (Bostrom & Savulescu, 2009; Harris, 2010). Justification for this perspective is buttressed by the vague boundaries delineating both of these conceptions (Lin & Allhoff, 2008). Typically, the debate is expressed in moral terms, with those that are more in the bioconservative camp arguing that therapy is morally acceptable and enhancement is morally problematic (Buchanan et al., 2001; Daniels, 2008). Those that are in the more progressive camp propose that, even if we could differentiate between therapy and enhancement, there is no moral difference between them (Bostrom, 2008; Bostrom & Savulescu, 2009; Harris, 2010).

There are, of course, varying levels of both therapeutic interventions and cognitive enhancements. From the therapeutic interventions standpoint, we have discussed a range of technologically extended treatments – from indirect human–computer interfaces (smartphone applications, e-therapy) to direct neurotechnological interfaces using deep brain stimulation. The implications of these therapeutic interventions are discussed in the previous sections. However, there is still a need for a discussion of the ethical issues related to enhancement. As mentioned, enhancements come in varying levels – from indirect external artifacts that can enhance our cognitive abilities to direct interfaces that change our neurochemical processes (nootropics) and/or neurocognitive circuits (brain stimulation).

Advances in neurotechnologies are apparent in the increased use (both therapeutically and for enhancement) of methodologies such as transcranial magnetic stimulation, brain–computer interfaces, brain implants, and genetic engineering (Bostrom & Sandberg, 2006, 2009). Brain–machine interfaces range from indirect interactions based on scalp-level electrical signals to direct interactions between neural tissue and electronic transducers. While direct approaches such as deep brain stimulation (discussed in Section 8.6) are neurosurgical treatments for various neurological (Parkinson's, essential tremor, epilepsy) and psychiatric issues (depression, obsessive compulsive disorder, posttraumatic stress disorder), there are also noninvasive approaches, for instance transcranial magnetic stimulation of targeted brain areas for therapy (depression and other psychopathology; Bermudes, Lanocha, & Janicak, 2017) and cognitive enhancement (Luber & Lisanby, 2014).

Much of the neuroethical discussion in relation to neuroenhancement has been around pharmacological enhancement. In a 2004 overview paper, Martha Farah and colleagues explained that "In contrast to the other neurotechnologies … whose potential use for enhancement is still hypothetical, pharmacological enhancement has already begun" (Farah et al., 2004, p. 421). As a result, much of the neuroethical discussion has focused more on the ethical aspects of psychopharmaceuticals (Lynch, Palmer, & Gall, 2011; Turner & Sahakian 2006). Pharmaceutical enhancement of normal neurocognitive function is readily apparent across the lifespan in our society, from students in elementary school to aging baby boomers. Prescription stimulants are often used as study aids for high school and college students who do not have attention deficit/hyperactivity disorder. Moreover, over-the-counter nutritional supplements are increasingly used as memory aids.

Today, we are increasingly seeing that the arguments related to enhancement via pharmaceuticals apply to other areas such as brain–computer interfaces, transcranial direct current stimulation (tDCS), and related enhancers that can be purchased off-the-shelf. For example, tDCS is a safe, portable, and low-cost approach to noninvasive brain stimulation. Likewise, there are now several consumer-grade brain–computer interfaces that can be used for enhancing mood (two-channel Muse, $200; one-channel Neurosky $100; fourteen-channel Emotiv $800), cognitive processing (fourteen-channel Emotiv $800), athletic performance (Versus

$400), and general brain monitoring (sixteen-channel OpenBCI, $945; fourteen-channel Emotiv $800). In addition to active enhancements with controlled applications, there are now passive enhancements with which we automatically and algorithmically interact. Take, for example, the numerous cognitive extensions in smartphone applications, navigation systems, schedule reminders, social media, notes, automated logging of data, automated calculations, and computing.

Whatever the enhancement, there are apparent concomitant ethical concerns for various constituencies. These include both the academic and the industrial development of enhancers, as well as the mental health service providers who act as gatekeepers to them. Additionally, there are the individuals themselves who must choose whether or not to use neuro-cognitive enhancers. Moreover, there are instances where parents and caregivers must decide whether or not enhancers should be given. As neurocognitive enhancers increase in availability, employers and educators will also need to face ethical dilemmas in the management and evaluation of those who might be unenhanced, enhanced, or over-enhanced. There are also regulatory agencies that may be called on over the considerations of "lifestyle" benefits and the defining of acceptable risks.

There are four broad ethical areas that can be used for shaping delibera-tions on the ethical challenges of neurocognitive enhancement and poten-tial societal responses (see Farah et al., 2004): safety, coercion, distributive justice, and personhood. First is the issue of safety. Neurocognitive enhancements involve complex interventions that may increase the risk of unanticipated problems. For example, neurocognitive enhancements that allow one to have a super-memory could interfere with that person's capacity for understanding the material that was learned. Moreover, super-memory alone does not entail an ability to relate recalled information to new learning or other knowledge. There are also potential hidden costs of neurocognitive enhancement.

A second ethical concern is coercion. As neurocognitive enhancers become increasingly prevalent, there will likely be circumstances in which persons feel pressure to enhance their cognitive abilities. For exam-ple, Sophia may be an ambitious student working at a competitive aca-demic program and aiming for a career in a highly competitive job with equally high demands. Her educators may see benefit in students who are more attentive and open to the materials that are being covered. Likewise, the career Sophia aims toward after graduate school is competitive and the employer wants employees that are consistently performing at optimal attention and minimal forgetfulness. Sophia's situation may involve explicit coercion in that her main professor and her employer both encouraged her to take neurocognitive enhancers. For Sophia, this was compounded by the fact that she wanted to be highly competitive with her peers in both academia and with her coworkers. This involved a level of implicit coercion exerting an incentive for Sophia to use neurocognitive enhancers. Legislation has been introduced in the United States to preclude school personnel from encouraging the use of cognitive enhancers (see Legislative Commissioners' Office, General Statutes of Connecticut, Title 10, Ch. 169, section 10-212b).

A third ethical concern is distributive justice. Like most things in life, neurocognitive enhancers will probably not be fairly distributed. Attentional enhancers (e.g., Ritalin) are often used by normal healthy college students. While some people will be able to afford neurocognitive enhancers, there will undoubtedly be cost barriers to legal neurocognitive enhancement. These barriers add to the disadvantages that are already faced by people of low socioeconomic status. That said, unequal access tends to not be a justification for barring neurocognitive enhancement, any more than it is justification for barring private tutoring or cosmetic surgery.

A final ethical concern is personhood. There are concerns that enhancing a person's neurocognitive functioning via neurocognitive enhancement may impact what we mean by persons. This could be from direct enhancements (e.g., psychopharmaceuticals, transcranial magnetic stimulation, or deep brain stimulation) or indirect enhancements (e.g., smartphone applications, navigation systems, schedule reminders, social media, notes, automated logging of data, automated calculations, or computing) that may interfere with Sophia's identity and capabilities. Sophia's brain realizes her cognitive and affective capabilities, which can be viewed as important for her moral status. At what point in her cognitive enhancement does Sophia lose her personality or, even further, her personhood? These questions intersect with our understanding of what it means for Sophia to be a person, for her to be healthy and whole, for her work to be meaningful, and for the ways in which we value human life in all its instantiations. Considering these issues, we are confronted with the conflicting values of different approaches to these issues. On the one hand, there are some who may view Sophia's neurocognitive enhancement as self-improvement. We often consider self-improvement to be a commendable goal. Typically, Sophia would be encouraged to use innovations (e.g., smartphone applications) that save time and effort. We see this as acceptable because these technologies increase productivity and allow for increased effort to be expended on potentially more worthy goals. On the other hand, Sophia's choice to use neurocognitive enhancers to improve her natural endowments (e.g., for traits such as attention and memory) may strike some as an unfair advantage and/or perhaps even a change in who Sophia is as a person. When Sophia improves her productivity via a neurocognitive enhancer, she might also be undermining the value and dignity of hard work. So, a lot depends on one's worldview (Weltanschauung). For some, Sophia's self-transformation that occurs via neurocognitive interventions can be viewed as self-actualizing. For others, neurocognitive enhancers are a threat to Sophia's personal identity.

8.9   Conclusions

In this chapter, several issues were outlined for mental health provision in the digital era. These guidelines and considerations should be carefully deliberated on when employing new technologies in clinical research and practice. The chapter also included discussions of the importance of the proper use of technology media, reflections on pertinent legal and ethical issues, approaches to maintaining secure electronic communications, and strategies for maintaining boundaries. There was an emphasis on considerations needed before clinicians start using technologies in clinical practice and research. Mental health service providers in the digital age need to be mindful of privacy standards, confidentiality, and security.

This chapter also reviewed the above issues from a technologies of the extended mind perspective. Our technologies can extend the self via direct (deep brain stimulation, pharmaceuticals) and indirect (smartphone applications, navigation systems, schedule reminders, social media, notes, automated logging of data, automated calculations, and computing) connections to our neural networks. Progress in the neurosciences is illuminating both the malfunctioning connections underlying psychological disorders and the potential of direct and indirect brain connections for therapeutic change. Today, mental health service providers can benefit from neuroscientific approaches that are supplanting traditional psychological theories that emphasize the mental over the biological in treatment of mental illnesses. That said, there are concerns related to the therapy versus enhancement divide. Hence, this chapter also considered issues related to using technologies of the extended mind for both therapeutic aids to poor health and neurocognitive enhancement of healthy individuals.

PART III

Ethical Issues in Social Media and Internet Research

CHAPTER 9

Social Media Ethics Section 1: Facebook, Twitter, and Google – Oh My!

9.1 Introduction

On Thursday, July 26, 2018, Facebook experienced the largest single-day drop in value in Wall Street history. On that day, Facebook's market value plummeted by more than $100 billion (down 19 percent). Why did this happen? While part of this reflects declining growth in users and revenue, a good deal of the loss can be attributed to Facebook's years of privacy lapses. Facebook's principal approach to revenue generation violates the ethical principle of privacy. Its core business is gathering extensive data on its users so that they can optimally target those users with advertising. In May 2018, the European Union imposed a stringent new regulatory regime called the General Data Protection Regulation to provide users with enhanced privacy protections and compel Facebook (and other tech companies) to overhaul their practices in collecting data and consent from users. Severe financial penalties will be delivered to those companies who fail to comply. In the United States, a multiagency federal investigation was launched to investigate Facebook's dealing with Cambridge Analytica (a political firm hired by the Trump campaign) that inappropriately accessed the information of 87 million people.

Facebook has experienced more than one ethical scandal leading to this sour day on Wall Street. Like Facebook, other big technology firms, such as Twitter and Google, have been plagued with rising concerns about ethical practices. Internet service providers such as Facebook, Google, and Twitter are more and more expected to act as good citizens, by bringing their goals in line with societal needs and supporting the rights of their users (Madelin, 2011; Taddeo & Floridi, 2016, 2017). These expectations reflect the ethical principles that should guide the actions of Internet service providers in mature information societies (Floridi, 2015). In this chapter, we will consider some of the ethical issues found in social media in general, as well as ethical practices of these large technology firms specifically. While it is acknowledged that there are social networking sites (e.g., LinkedIn, Instagram, Snapchat) other than Facebook, microblogging services (e.g., Tumblr, Plurk) other than Twitter, and search engines (Bing, DuckDuckGo, Yahoo!) other than Google, the focus will be on these three as they tend to dominate (at least in terms of users) the infosphere.

9.2   Social Media

The digital age is marked by an ever-increasing proliferation of social media that involves the exchange of personal information. Concurrently, there has been a notable increase in social networking sites that compel users to develop personal profiles and networks with local and distant others (Boyd & Ellison, 2007) and self-disclose personal information via profile updates, status updates, sharing photos and videos, and commenting on the posts of others (Nosko, Wood, & Molema, 2010). This ever-increasing exchange of personal information on social networking sites also introduces new and mounting concerns about privacy risks and consequences (Fogel & Nehmad, 2009).

9.3   What Is Privacy

Establishing an adequate understanding of what privacy is can be important for discussions of our experiences with social media. Several legal and philosophical attempts to define the concept of privacy have been attempted. Additionally, the concept of privacy can be understood differently, relative to economic and cultural factors (Bellman et al., 2004). H. J. McCloskey (1985) recognizes some of the complexities involved in establishing a clear and coherent account of privacy:

> We demand recognition of our right to privacy, we complain when privacy is invaded, yet we encounter difficulties immediately [when] we seek to explain what we mean by privacy, what is the area, the content of privacy, what is outside that area, what constitutes a loss of privacy, a loss to which we have consented, a justified loss, an unjustified loss. (p. 343)

What then is privacy? In his 1967 book *Privacy and Freedom*, Alan Westin offered a definition that seems relevant even in the digital era: "The claim of individuals, groups or institutions to determine for themselves when, how, and to what extent information about them is communicated to others" (Westin, 1967, p. 7). At its simplest, privacy of personal information may be understood as "the right to control one's own information"

(Gavison, 1980, p. 421). Is it a static or dynamic concept? According to James Moor (2006), privacy is better understood as an evolving concept with contents that are often influenced by the political and technological features of the society's environment.

9.3.1   *Privacy Is Important for Personal Relations*

In terms of ethics, privacy concerns are often at the forefront when social networking sites are involved. Why does privacy matter? Why should the user of a social networking site care about whether mundane personal information and situations are made available? In a seminal paper on privacy, James Rachels (1975) argued that privacy is important because it allows for the selective disclosure of personal information in various developing and continuing personal relations. In the absence of this selective control of personal information, the variety of associations would become smaller; relations would fade. According to Rachels:

> I want now to give an account of the value of privacy based on the idea that there is a close connection between our ability to control who has access to us and to information about us, and our ability to create and maintain different sorts of social relationships with different people. According to this account, privacy is necessary if we are to maintain the variety of social relationships with other people that we want to have and that is why it is important to us. By a "social relationship" I do not mean anything especially unusual or technical; I mean the sort of thing which we usually have in mind when we say of two people that they are friends or that they are husband and wife or that one is the other's employer. (p. 326)

Rachels maintains that we value privacy because it allows us to take part in various kinds of social relationships that are defined (in part) by how much information about ourselves that we share with others. An aspect of distinguishing our close friends from acquaintances is the amount and level of personal information that we share. Our reason for valuing privacy, then, is that it allows us to maintain a level of control in our relations. Rachels's paper has been widely anthologized in computer ethics texts (Ermann, Williams, & Shauf, 1997; Johnson, 2001; Johnson & Nissenbaum, 1995; Quinn, 2009). As such, many consider it as an important starting point for discussions about ethical issues in computer information privacy. In the digital age, we often give up too much control over our personal information. This can result in problems for our relationships.

9.3.2   Privacy in Ubiquitous Social Computing Systems

While Rachels's theory elucidates the significance of privacy in everyday situations (i.e., when little of great importance seems to be at stake), privacy issues become more complicated in ubiquitous social computing systems, as these combine online social interactions with context-aware computing (Sharma, Lomash, & Bawa, 2015). Likewise, Norman Mooradian (2009) aims to reassess and resituate Rachels's information privacy theory in light of these developments. The challenge that digital-age information technology presents to Rachels's articulation of privacy is that this definition of personal information is too narrow. The prevalence of big data that exemplifies information technology today raises questions about the relation between privacy and information that is not intimate or sensitive and that is more and more collected in public. The amplified collection of a person's data will not necessarily impact social relationships because such data lacks contextual factors important to Rachels's general theory.

For Mooradian, social networking sites make explicit a user's social networks and their structures. Moreover, personal information is communicated through these structures. As a result, new information is captured and new risks are posed. While Mooradian has argued that the collection and aggregation of this information does not support Rachels's theory of personal information privacy, he does view it as having application to some aspects of social computing. By that, Mooradian means that Rachels's information privacy theory can be used to highlight privacy issues that arise within social networks and may help direct their design. Take, for example, the friending that occurs in social networking sites. Rachels's theory of personal information privacy can be applied to the creation and maintenance of friendships online. Given that the purpose of social networking sites is to provide new and enabling venues for social interaction, Rachels's personal information theory has relevance for understanding the ways in which privacy is important to the functioning of relationships at these sites.

9.3.3   Restricted Access/Limited Control

In addition to impacts on relationships, privacy violations in the digital era are experienced as even more egregious when there is a lack of transparency from social networking sites about how our personal information will be used. In examining this, Herman Tavani and James Moor (2001) have formulated a "Restricted Access/Limited Control" theory of personal privacy. According to their theory, personal information must, at times, be shared with others, which means that the proper use of personal information should fall somewhere along a spectrum ranging from total privacy to complete disclosure. According to the "restricted access" aspect of the model, the privacy condition holds in situations wherein the user has the ability to protect personal data from some parties while opening up to others (Tavani, 2007). Moor has described this approach to a person's privacy as applicable "in a situation with regard to others if and only if in that situation the individual is normatively protected from intrusion, interference, and information access by others" (Moor, 1997, p. 30). A "situation" is understood as a relationship, activity, or state of affairs where restricted access is reasonably warranted (Moor, 1991; Tavani, 2000).

It is important to note that Moor and Tavani also distinguish between situations that are naturally private (e.g., a prepper living off the information grid) and those that are normatively private, such as the therapist–patient relationship. The distinction between naturally private and normatively private situations allows for differentiations between the conditions required for having privacy and having a right to privacy (Tavani & Moor, 2001. Moreover, the distinction allows for differentiations between privacy losses and privacy violations. In a naturally private situation, privacy can be lost but not violated because there are no conventional, legal, or ethical norms according to which one has a right, or even an expectation, to be protected. In a normatively private situation, personal privacy is protected by conventional norms (e.g., formal laws and informal policies).

9.3.4 *Publicity Principle*

Moor's approach necessitates that the rules for establishing normatively private situations be transparent, public, and open to debate. For example, his "Publicity Principle" asserts that the rules and conditions governing private situations should be "clear and known to persons affected by them" (Moor, 2000, p. 32). Hence, an important aspect of Moor's model for an appropriate privacy policy is openness (i.e., transparency) that allows all parties in the situation or context to be informed and updated about what the rules are at any given point in time. Tavani (2008a) asks us to consider how the publicity principle might be worked into a privacy policy that involves cookies technology.

Cookies are files that Internet sites send to, and retrieve from, the user's computer systems while they surf the Internet and take part in Internet activities. These cookies allow Internet website owners to gather information about users' online browsing preferences as they interact with their sites. What expectations should we have about various websites that we peruse retaining our information? This concern is compounded by the fact that many of the individuals surfing the Internet and interacting on various sites may not realize that they are subject to privacy-related threats posed by these cookies.

According to Tavani, an appropriate policy would need to describe clearly the rules impacting the privacy expectations and requirements for users who interact with Internet websites that use cookies. As a start, the policy would need to inform users that the website they are planning to access uses cookies. Moreover, the users would need to be informed about whether the personal data logged via cookies could be used in subsequent contexts. Following the presentation of information to the user, informed decisions can be made by the user about whether to accept or reject cookies.

9.4   Informed Consent

People also require "limited control" over their personal data so that they can make sure that they can restrict access to it. One avenue for such control is informed consent. While there is a lengthy history of informed consent bioethics, the applications to information technology take on the newer forms of terms of service or end-user license agreements. Faden and Beauchamp (1986) proffered the seminal form of informed consent, effective consent, that is now found in technology situations. The idea of effective consent includes aspects of autonomy (consent decision), competence (capacity for giving consent), disclosure (risks, benefits, terms, conditions, limitations), understanding (by consenter), and voluntariness (by consenter). While traditional human subjects research ethics typically involves face-to-face contact between researcher and participant (allows for questions and answers), technological applications are usually devoid of that contact, which weakens the ability to uphold autonomy, competence, and understanding. Moreover, there are limits to understanding the implications of a disclosure of personal information.

In situations where a person provides personal information to a professional party (e.g., a social networking site), that user should be notified any time that the personal data will be made available to a third party (e.g., a company wanting the data for targeted advertising). Furthermore, the user should be able to limit the sharing of that personal information. According to the restricted access/limited control theory, informational privacy does not occur without restrictions on the dissemination of personal information and without some control (as warranted by the particular situation).

Helen Nissenbaum (2011) has discussed two substantive considerations related to informed consent, or notice-and-consent. First, there is the right to privacy as a right to control information about oneself. This can be seen in the transparency and choice discussions in Section 9.3.3. A second consideration is the compatibility of notice-and-consent with a competitive free market that allows service providers and consumers to trade goods at prices the market determines. An issue here is that personal information is, at times, conceived as part of the price of online exchange. As long as users are informed of a service provider's practices in gathering and using personal information, there is little concern. However, problems arise with the lack of limits to the amount of surreptitious and flagrant data gathering, dissemination, aggregation, analysis, and profiling being done by corporations.

A further issue is that terms of service or end-user license agreements are often made up of thousands of words in text that can be difficult to read. In these situations, the emphasis is on disclosure, which limits the ethical contents (autonomy, competence, and understanding) found in face-to-face informed consenting (Flick, 2013). While this is not adequate for typical informed consent, technology companies continue with this approach because it has become the de facto standard (Flick, 2016). Furthermore, it allows social networking sites who want to perform research to omit words such as "research" from their terms of service.

Catherine Flick (2013, 2016), at De Montfort University, has argued that this sort of informed consent is completely inappropriate for information technology. Instead, she suggests that a theory of waiver of normative expectations may be better suited (see also Manson & O'Neill, 2007). Flick uses Manson and O'Neill's (2007) theory of waiver of normative expectations, in which informed consent is framed as a series of waivers of expected behavioral and social norms. To make an informed decision, the user must be involved in an effective communication framework that allows for simple and straightforward language. The focus is shifted from assessment of the consenter's autonomy to assessing the communication quality related to the norms that are to be waived. Disclosure problems found in excessively long and complicated terms of service can be addressed more directly by the waiver-based approach.

9.5   General Data Protection Regulation

Thus far, there has been a discussion of some of the prime ethical issues for social media companies. Given the many notable concerns related to data protection, privacy, and informed consent, the European Union crafted the General Data Protection Regulation. This is a regulation on data protection and privacy for all individuals within the European Union and the European Economic Area. Included is guidance on the export of personal data outside of these areas. The General Data Protection Regulation, agreed on by the European Parliament and Council in April 2016, replaced the Data Protection Directive 95/46/EC in spring 2018 as the main law regulating the ways in which companies protect personal data. Some of the chief privacy and data protections of the General Data Protection Regulation include consent of users for data processing; anonymization of harvested data to protect privacy; notifications of data breaches; safety precautions for the transfer of data across borders; and requiring that a data protection officer is in place for certain companies to safeguard General Data Protection Regulation adherence. In summary, the General Data Protection Regulation requires companies to follow these basic principles for safeguarding the processing and movement of citizens' personal data.

9.6   Facebook

Facebook is an online social networking service with more than a billion monthly active users (Facebook Inc., 2015). On Facebook, users can maintain personal profile pages, connect with others, and visit other users' pages. Online social networking sites such as Facebook have transformed how we communicate with our family, friends, groups, and communities. Moreover, Facebook has impacted the ways in which users approach many everyday activities. Since April 2018, Facebook has been the most popular social network globally. The formerly most popular social network, Friendster, was surpassed by MySpace, which was itself transcended by Facebook. Facebook does not charge any fees for enabling users to communicate, stay up to date, and keep in touch with friends and family all over the world. Facebook, however, does cost you your privacy.

9.6.1   Cambridge Analytica

The Federal Trade Commission investigation of Facebook was launched to assess whether Facebook violated a 2011 consent decree when it shared data with Cambridge Analytica and other companies. While Cambridge Analytica was once the exemplar for intelligent data-driven electioneering, they are now anathema. How did this happen? In March 2018, multiple media outlets reported on Cambridge Analytica's acquisition and use of personal data about Facebook users. The data reportedly was derived from an application created in 2013 by data scientist Aleksandr Kogan. At the time, Facebook permitted application developers to gather data not only about users of the application but also about their Facebook friends. In March 2018, Facebook broadcast limitations on data harvesting by third parties, together with considerably diminishing the types of data that application developers can access. Also in March 2018, the British High Court granted the Information Commissioner's Office a warrant to search Cambridge Analytica's London offices. The personal data of nearly 87 million Facebook users was attained through the 270,000 Facebook users who used a Facebook app called This Is Your Digital Life. In an interesting turn of events, following the Cambridge Analytica incident, Facebook attempted to reassure users by allowing them to download their data archive from Facebook so that they would have a better knowledge of what information Facebook maintains. Unfortunately for Facebook, the result undermined Facebook's credibility because users found that videos they thought they had deleted were in fact still stored in Facebook's archive.

An additional outcome from the Cambridge Analytica episode was Facebook's disclosure that malicious actors had used the platform's search tools to collect personal information about millions of users. Until April 2018, third parties were able to create a database by simply running a script that entered phone numbers or email addresses into Facebook's search function. Also in April 2018, we found out from Bloomberg that Facebook scans images and links sent between users via Messenger. According to Facebook, the scans are performed so that they can flag content that does not adhere to their platform's standards. While automatically scanning images and links may sound good in theory, some users see this as an additional violation at a time when Facebook's reputation for maintaining user privacy is being questioned. In May 2018, the ultimate outcome from the Cambridge Analytica scandal and related fallout was the company (as well as its parent company) filing for insolvency proceedings and closing operations. Meanwhile, Facebook continues to make assurances to users that they are working diligently to reduce risks.

9.6.2   Evolution of Facebook's Privacy Policies

The Cambridge Analytica incident (as well as the subsequent fallout over Facebook's archive) was not the first privacy concern for Facebook. This is interesting to note because Facebook originally (Facebook's public launch was in 2004) had rather restrictive default privacy settings. The only persons who could view a user profile were those who were members of a user's network. Furthermore, most of each user's profile (detailed personal data and photos) was available for viewing by friends only. Interestingly enough, much of Facebook's early appeal was that it was more private than its competitors (e.g., MySpace user profiles were entirely public). By 2007, however, Facebook's default privacy settings had changed dramatically and all users were able to see the basic profile information (e.g., name and picture) of all other users. Moreover, the amount of personal information (photos and detailed personal data) available to users in a network increased.

In 2007, Facebook faced a major incident following the release of a feature called Beacon that allowed third-party websites to notify a user's Facebook friends that the user was performing an action on their site. For example, Fred is a Facebook user who decided to skip a party with some acquaintances. He does not know these acquaintances (who happen to also be Facebook friends) very well and tells them he is busy. Instead of going to the party, he chooses instead to do some shopping on Amazon, order some food online, stream some new music, and read an online article from a computer science magazine. This personal information is automatically posted for all his Facebook friends to see. Meanwhile, Fred's acquaintances at the party are also his Facebook friends. They see that he is not at the party because he is busy with leisure activities. In addition to being frustrated with Facebook for broadcasting his personal information, Fred had to manually opt out of sharing on each of the third-party sites because there was no option for disabling all sharing through Beacon with one selection. Furthermore, Fred learns that Facebook was recording information about his browsing habits on all Beacon partner sites. As a result, he started seeing ads targeted to him related to the places he had visited and his activities. Fred was not happy with Facebook sharing his personal information without his permission or for Facebook's recording of all his browsing habits. Given the negative response by users, Beacon was eventually removed.

Another incident that caused privacy concerns was Facebook's introduction of its "Places" feature that allowed users to "check in" at real-world locations. In addition to personal check-ins, this feature also allows the user to check in a friend at a location without the friend's permission. Fred almost left Facebook after the last embarrassment with Beacon but he decides to stay. Fred is asked by the same acquaintances as before to meet them for dinner. While he initially accepted, he later hears from his friend Stephanie that she wants him to see a movie with her. He decides to join Stephanie at the theater instead of meeting the acquaintances for dinner. Fred does not realize that Stephanie decides to check him in on Places and when he arrives at the theater Stephanie's check-in is automatically trans- mitted to Fred's contacts. When Fred comes out of the movie and sees a notification that he was "checked in" at the theater (he had his smart- phone off during the movie), he hurriedly removes the notification from his Facebook wall but the damage is done and his Facebook acquaintances unfriend him. Now Fred has to go through the unclear privacy options and disable Places.

A further major change to privacy settings occurred in 2009, with each user's name, picture, and basic information appearing in Google search results. As a result, this personal information could be viewed by the entire Internet. Facebook prompted its users to change their privacy settings to this new, more open default. While users had a choice in whether or not they would adjust these new settings, many chose to merely accept these settings instead of drudge through pages of detailed information. Furthermore, the privacy settings page included a considerable amount of very comprehensive options that proved to be rather unclear for many users. This was compounded by the fact that Facebook often made changes to the available privacy options, which made it difficult for users to stay abreast.

Following an outcry from users who complained that they had been tricked into sharing their personal information, Facebook responded by restoring a small number (most changes remained in effect) of the privacy options. However, this only lasted until 2010, when the default privacy settings were once again tweaked. Since that time, Facebook has evolved the settings to the point that most personal information (with the excep- tion of photos and wall postings) is visible to the entire Internet by default. Moreover, some basic information (e.g., the user's name, picture, and affiliations) is visible to the whole Internet.

As can be seen from the above examples and discussion, Facebook violates privacy in multiple areas. In the next chapter, we will consider an emotion contagion experiment conducted by Facebook on almost 700,000 Facebook users without user permission (Kramer et al., 2014). Some may argue that

Facebook users should have known better than to expect privacy when they accepted Facebook's free service model. Did those users really think that Facebook, which does not charge anything for its services to users, was merely offering a free public service? That said, it seems intuitively clear to many that blaming the user is not the best approach (Flick, 2016). At a minimum, there must be some shared culpability. When a user is on Facebook or adjusts settings, most would agree with D'Arcy and Young (2012) that we expect privacy to be a right or company obligation: "Crucially, these rights and obligations hold regardless of the perceptions that users have of their online interactions" (pp. 535–536). The tech companies will likely want to point to their terms of service. However, that only compounds the issue as research has shown that it would take the average person approximately 244 hours per year to read all of the privacy policies for sites they use (McDonald & Cranor, 2008). This is around 40 minutes per day. It is important to point out that these findings were from a study published more than a decade ago in 2008 when estimates of Internet use reflected 72 minutes per day. Today, the average use is closer to 3 hours per day.

9.7   Twitter

Twitter, like other microblogging services, has enabled a colossal interconnection of social media users (Java et al., 2007). The support of rapid, brief, and "real-time" content sharing among Twitter's millions of users makes it possible for massive quantities of data to be sent and received very rapidly (Zhao & Rosson, 2009). The growth of Twitter and its number of users has been aided by developments in the mobile domain, permitting users to share text, photos, and videos directly from a news source or geographic location (Westerman, Spence, & Van Der Heide, 2014). Social media reports have been used to distribute up-to-the minute communications about protests after a challenged presidential election in Iran (Grossman, 2009), to provide updates and information and raise money following an earthquake in Haiti (Muralidharan et al., 2011), and to share information about a revolution in Egypt (Wilson & Dunn, 2011). Twitter is notable among social media venues for its size-limited messages that are easy to read and allow for links to other web content.

9.7.1   Twitter and Privacy

It is apparent that Facebook has had a difficult time with maintaining user privacy. With all the focus on Facebook, it can be easy to forget about all the other tech companies that collect our personal data. Twitter is of course one of them. Following Facebook's issues with Cambridge Analytica, Twitter has made attempts to enhance the health of its platform. Amid scrutiny of Twitter's role in the distribution of fake news, election interference, and wider data privacy criticisms, it has taken efforts to purge dubious accounts from users' follower metrics and eradicated 143,000 apps for policy violations. These efforts reflect Twitter's desire (like other tech companies) to comply with the General Data Protection Regulation (see Section 9.5). In the face of all these changes and account purges, Twitter lost a million monthly active users and Twitter's stock plunged by 15 percent.

9.7.2 *Metadata*

Why would Twitter need to take these efforts to comply with data protection regulations? Was it, like Facebook, gathering data from your devices (e.g., smartphones, laptops) and from websites you visit that include content from Twitter? The answer is yes. In fact, this tracking can occur irrespective of whether you are logged into Twitter. The reality of the digital era is that our metadata is ubiquitously extended. Everything that a Twitter user tweets, every picture taken, and every status update posted, is logged and available for data mining. This metadata can be used by the authorities to search for and develop profiles on persons. Additionally, Twitter collects your personal contact data from your family, friends, acquaintances, business contacts, and anyone else with your email address or phone number in their contacts. This happens when your contacts upload their contacts to Twitter (note that Facebook does this as well). As a result, Twitter develops a wide-ranging profile of you from your own actions on social media, web browsing, locations visited, and interests.

It is important to note that metadata on Twitter can also be used to precisely identify each and every one of us. In fact, Beatrice Perez, Mirco Musolesi, and Gianluca Stringhini (2018), at University College London and the Alan Turing Institute, have shown that our tweets and related metadata, regardless of how unidentified we might perceive them to be, can be traced back to us with an amazing level of accuracy. Perez and colleagues used Twitter to quantify the distinctiveness of the relation between metadata and user identity. More precisely, they analyzed atomic fields in the metadata and methodically combined them in an effort to classify new tweets as belonging to an account. They used various machine learning algorithms of increasing complexity. Using a supervised machine learning algorithm, they were able to identify any user from a group of 10,000 with approximately 96.7 percent accuracy. When they widened the space of their search and considered the ten most likely candidates, they enhanced the accuracy of the model to 99.22 percent. How are these data scientists able to use metadata from Twitter to identify users? Part of the answer is found in the realization that Twitter holds 144 pieces of metadata on each user, which is publicly accessible through Twitter's application program interface.

9.8   Google

Google is an Internet phenomena. No other search engine can claim the significance that Google can for so many users. Google was adopted quickly and its user base is global in scope. Moreover, there is Google's influence on society in toto. It may be fair to say that no online activity has the same level of embeddedness as Googling. At no financial cost to its millions of users, Google processes more than 40,000 search queries per second. This converts to more than 3.5 billion Google searches per day and 1.2 trillion Google searches every year. Of course, like other "free" Internet services, there is a price to pay in terms of privacy. Google's privacy policy has been updated twenty-eight times since the company's start in 1999. This includes three times in 2017 alone. In 2015, Google made the most changes – five times in a single year. One recent example is Google's response to the European Union's General Data Protection Regulation that entirely alters the ways in which large technology companies handle user data.

Why have so many concerns been raised about Google's access to our personal data? Part of the answer is the amount of data gathered passively, without our explicit knowledge of when or how this is happening. The amount of data that Google has on each user can fill volumes. Google offers users the option of downloading an archive of all the data it stores about the user at www.google.com/takeout. If you are like many users, when you first heard of this, you went to the application and downloaded information related to your calendar, location history, music you listen to, items you purchased, your Google groups, Google hangout sessions, the smartphones you have owned, the pages you shared, and the list goes on and on.

Users can also have a look at just specific areas like all of your Google searches (even the deleted ones), all the applications you use, your location history, and all of your YouTube history. What are some examples of what Google is storing?

- Google search history of the user: https://myactivity.google.com /myactivity
- YouTube history of the user: www.youtube.com/feed/history/ search_history
- Location and timeline of places user visited: www.google.com/maps/ timeline
- Application use by the user: https://security.google.com/settings/secur ity/permissions
- Advertisement profile on the user: www.google.com/settings/ads/

Well, first, there are your Google searches. Google logs your Google search history and your YouTube history across all your devices. In some cases, this means that even if you deleted your search history and smartphone history on one device, Google may still have data stored from other devices. Google also knows where you have visited. Unless you immediately disabled location tracking, Google logs your location every time you turn on your smartphone. The Google timeline shows everywhere that you have been since the first day that you started using Google on your smartphone. The application can see the time of day that you were in the location and the time it took you to arrive at that location from your previous one. Furthermore, Google logs data on every app and extension you use – how often, where, and with whom you use them. Google even has an advertisement profile on each user that is developed from your locations, age, gender, career, hobbies, interests, relationship status, and income.

Another issue of ethical interest for users of Google is the Knowledge Graph, which presents the user with answers to queries instead of links to potential answers. While the Knowledge Graph enhances the user's ability to find information, there is the question of whether we should trust Google as a de facto gatekeeper of our knowledgebases. Conventionally, search engines were understood as gatekeepers leading Internet users to the immense stores of information on the Internet (Tavani, 2011). Katrine Juel Vang (2013), at the University of Southern Denmark, argues that the Knowledge Graph extends Google Search beyond its historical role as a provider of multiple relevant Internet links. Furthermore, Juel Vang argues that the convenient design of the Knowledge Graph will contest the autonomy of the user. This happens when a user presents a general query and Google returns possible points of interest to the search query. Juel Vang sees this added expedient quality in Google Search as arousing mainly two concerns:

1) **The democratic concern.** When achieving an instant response to a query on Google's site, why frequent the remainder of the search results? Thus, Google reasserts and amplifies its already powerful position – now more than ever retaining the traffic of its users.

2) **The epistemological concern.** Making answers to queries instantaneous is bound to have an effect on our information skills. For a long time, Google has been making information retrieval on the Internet still easier. Admittedly, to many users, the retrieval process was already down to assessing the eight to twelve search results on the first page of search results, and, as shown by Pan and colleagues (2007), the ranking position is perhaps the most crucial parameter on which users assess search results in Google. Only now, with the convenient design of the Knowledge Graph, the activity of assessing the results is also rendered increasingly superfluous (Juel Vang, 2013, p. 247).

The Knowledge Graph presents the user with answers in a manner that dramatically reduces the potential of the user visiting sites other than the ones suggested by Google. For Juel Vang, this is problematic. From both an ethical and a democratic perspective, it is implausible that the answers from Google offer a diverse and nuanced knowledge of the information on the Web.

9.9   Normative Ethical Considerations for Social Media

From a normative ethics perspective, we can see various approaches to dealing with the practices of technology giants like Google, Facebook, and Twitter. Utilitarians (consequentialists) concentrate on the consequences of actions; deontologists emphasize the nature of the act, in terms of one's duties and others' rights; and virtue ethicists focus or the moral character of the agent (Johnson, 2001). Hence, the normative ethical perspective views the activities of technology companies and their users relative to principles, rules, or adopting virtuous habits and behaviors. Through contrasting ethical approaches to informational privacy, cyberpsychologists are able to expand understanding into the differences in privacy protection approaches.

9.9.1   Rights-Based Deontological Approaches

Within the deontological tradition, the Kantian individual is considered an autonomous agent who makes moral judgments and decisions founded on rational considerations (Bell & Adam, 2004). This viewpoint allows for rational consideration of the impacts of technology and how ethical issues may be addressed. From a deontological approach, with reference to Kant's formula for humanity and his example of deceit, the user would be viewed as unable literally to agree to the deceit because the deceit hides the actual bargain being offered. Similarly, Facebook's obfuscating of the degree to which the company shares information about users may be vulnerable to the charge that it renders "consent" to privacy practices meaningless.

The European Union tends to take a rather strict deontological approach that "rests upon a conviction that privacy is an inalienable right – one that states must protect, even if at considerable economic and other sorts of costs" (Ess, 2009, p. 55). The European Union's approach to privacy is reflected in comprehensive statutes (e.g., the General Data Protection Regulation) that can be enforced by law to safeguard citizens' personal data in all circumstances. Deontological, or rights-based, approaches believe that the morality of a particular privacy policy is whether that privacy policy respects individual persons and not whether the majority is impacted in a desirable manner by such a privacy policy.

9.9.2   *Interest-Based Utilitarian Approaches*

Interest-based utilitarian approaches advance the view that privacy policies can be judged as morally right or morally wrong simply in virtue of the consequences that would result from having such privacy policies. In the United States, there is a robust anti-regulation approach to Internet privacy (led by Internet companies like Google) that advocates for a utilitarian or "business friendly" approach to data protection (Ess, 2009, p. 55), maintaining that online business practices requiring access to user data provide the greatest good for the greatest number (Ess, 2009). Evidence for a utilitarian ethical approach can also be found in a US market-dominated privacy policy that consists of loosely defined self-regulatory practices (industry norms, codes of conduct, and contracts) among online users, companies, and the US Government (Fernback & Papacharissi, 2007; McStay & Bakir, 2006). Such interest-based approaches can point away from collective safeguarding and point in the direction of individual choice and responsibility. In the European Union model, this takes the form of "opting in" if a user wants personal data collected (here data is protected by default). Contrariwise, in the United States, users must "opt out" if they want their data to be protected (here the default is that the data is unprotected). From an interest-based utilitarian approach, the emphasis is on promoting privacy policies that would produce the greatest good (happiness) for the greatest number of persons.

9.9.3   Virtue Ethics

It can be argued that there are difficulties for both rights-based and interest-based approaches. Utilitarians (interest-based consequentialists) can be so concerned with sponsoring happiness for the majority that they discount the significance of justice and fairness for each person. Equally, deontologists (rights-based Kantians) can be faulted for paying too little attention to the value of happiness and social utility because they are so focused on the moral rights of each person. An alternative can be found in virtue ethics because of the types of choices users are presented with in the digital era (Artz, 1994). A virtue ethics approach emphasizes character formation over action (rights and interest-based) approaches to computer ethics. A number of computer ethicists have argued for virtue ethical approaches to computer ethics because virtue-based principles aid users to make virtuous decisions about how to act on ethical problems presented during use. While there are several approaches to virtue ethics, computer ethicists commonly accentuate the Aristotelian approach (Stamatellos, 2011a).

In a virtue ethics approach to information privacy, self-development is applicable to online communities and social networking, where the act of self-development is a necessary prerequisite and demand by the online users (Stamatellos, 2011b). Siponen and Iivari (2006) recommend that virtue theory should be considered in information sciences and that virtue ethics can guide the application of policies and guidelines. A virtue ethics information privacy act should be safeguarded not only by privacy policies or online rules but also by inspiring the user to be better educated, to self-develop, and to be more self-aware (Grodzinsky, 2001). Persons who are educated in autonomy and self-justice have greater self-awareness and enhanced understandings of their own values and rights.

9.9.4   Floridi's Ontological Approach

Luciano Floridi (1999) has questioned whether it is always possible to apply standard moral theories to certain computer ethics issues. Floridi contends that the concept of privacy is not well developed in the standard macro-ethical theories (e.g., utilitarianism, Kantianism, and virtue ethics) used in computer ethics. For example, he has argued that, since challenges in computer ethics strain the conceptual resources of traditional moral approaches, such approaches cannot be applied straightforwardly to ethical issues in computing.

The suggestion is finally advanced that a person has a right to both exclusive ownership and unique control/use of her private information and that she must be treated differently from a mere packet of information ... We have seen that a person, a free and responsible agent, is after all a packet of information. She is equivalent to an information microenvironment, a constantly elastic and permeable entity with centres and peripheries but with boundaries that are neither sharply drawn nor rigidly fixed in time. (Floridi, 1999, p. 53)

Likewise, for Floridi, privacy is best understood as packets of information that are both part of the user's me-hood and a violation of the information environment wherein the user resides and acts.

Privacy is nothing less than the defence of the personal integrity of a packet of information, the individual; and the invasion of an individual's informational privacy, the unauthorized access, dispersion and misuse of her information is a trespass into her me-hood and a disruption of the information environment that it constitutes. The violation is not a violation of ownership, of personal rights, of instrumental values or of Consequentialist rules, but a violation of the nature of information itself, an offence against the integrity of the me-hood and the efforts made by the individual to construct it as a whole, accurate, autonomous entity independent from, and yet present within, the world. (Floridi, 1999, p. 53)

Here one finds Floridi's foundation for a privacy framework that he has since referred to as the "ontological interpretation of informational privacy" (Floridi, 2005) and as the "ontological theory of informational privacy" (Floridi, 2006). Floridi's approach shifts the locus of a privacy violation away from conditions tied to an agent's personal rights to conditions impacting the information environment, which the agent constitutes.

Tavani (2008b) agrees with much of Floridi's ontological interpretation. That said, he does point to two specific challenges for Floridi's theory of informational privacy. Tavani argues that an adequate privacy theory should be able to:

1) differentiate informational privacy from other kinds of privacy, including psychological privacy
2) distinguish between descriptive and normative aspects of informational privacy in a way that differentiates a (mere) loss of privacy from a violation of privacy. (Tavani, 2008b, p. 155)

While Tavani contends that Floridi's privacy theory does not explicitly address either challenge, he does concede that Floridi's ontological theory presents a novel way of analyzing the impact that digital technologies have had for informational privacy.

9.9.5   James Moor and Just Consequentialism

Tavani prefers James Moor's ethical approach for applying ethical theory to computer ethics. Moor suggests a method that integrates aspects of utilitarian and deontological theories into one comprehensive moral theory. He references comparable approaches proffered by Rawls (1971) and Gert (1998) to include aspects of the two traditional moral theories into one coherent unifying theory. Moor's just consequentialism underscores the consequences of privacy policies within the constraints of justice. His amalgamation of consequentialist and deontological approaches makes just consequentialism a practical approach to the ethical problems of computer and information ethics. Tavani (2011) describes the key elements of Moor's just consequentialism as follows:

1. Deliberate over various policies from an impartial point of view to determine whether they meet the criteria for being ethical policies. A policy is ethical, if it
    a. does not cause any unnecessary harms to individuals and groups, and
    b. supports individual rights, the fulfilling of duties, etc.
2. Select the best policy from the set of just policies arrived at in the deliberation stage by ranking ethical policies in terms of benefits and (justifiable) harms. In doing this, be sure to
    a. weigh carefully between the good consequences and bad consequences in the ethical policies, and
    b. distinguish between disagreements about facts and disagreements about principles and values, when deciding which particular ethical policy should be adopted. (Knowledge about the facts surrounding a particular case should inform the decision-making process.) (Tavani, 2011, pp. 69–70)

It is important to note that Tavani and Moor both emphasize the need for self-development in the appropriate habits of character such as kindness, truthfulness, honesty, trustworthiness, helpfulness, generosity, and justice. As a result, until the correct habits are developed, it may be problematic for a person to effectively carry out the steps in a just-consequentialist model. Moreover, this emphasis on character development and virtual traits reflects aspects of virtue ethics.

9.10   Conclusions

Technology giants have experienced more than one ethical scandal leading to the recent emphasis on General Data Protection Regulation. Big technology firms, such as Facebook, Twitter, and Google, have been plagued with rising concerns about ethical practices, and are more and more expected to act as good citizens, by bringing their goals in line with societal needs and supporting the rights of their users. These expectations reflect the ethical principles that should guide the actions of Internet service providers in mature information societies. In this chapter, we considered some of the ethical issues found in social media in general, as well as the ethical practices of these large technology firms specifically. In the next chapter, ethical principles will be applied to ethical research using social media.

CHAPTER 10

Social Media Ethics Section 2: Ethical Research with Social Media

10.1 Introduction

Large technology corporations (e.g., Facebook, Twitter, Google) have powerful online presences (e.g., search engines, social networks) and they have become significant parts of the daily lives of billions of people around the world. While there is an increasing number of studies focusing on the influence of social media platforms and the potential of these platforms for research in particular, less attention has been paid to ethical considerations. This is unfortunate because these social media platforms proffer several tools that can be used to economically recruit large and diverse samples. Promising aspects of these tools include (1) being able to move beyond relatively small convenience samples from disproportionately Western, educated, industrialized, rich, and democratic (WEIRD) samples (Henrich, Heine, & Norenzayan, 2010) and (2) large knowledgebases with detailed demographic profiles and records of a vast amount of studies (Paulhus & Vazire, 2007).

While social media platforms have made it easier than ever before to observe large numbers of users from diverse samples, new ethical challenges are apparent for online research with human subjects (Barchard & Williams, 2008). This has been illustrated by a lack of privacy safeguards in a publicly released data set that was developed from the Facebook accounts of an entire cohort of college students (Zimmer, 2010). A further example can be found in a study where researchers scraped and then published data on nearly 70,000 users from the dating site OKCupid. While the data was scraped from a public site, there were concerns about publishing research using identifiable data without informed consent (Leetaru, 2016). In perhaps the largest online study performed without informed consent, researchers manipulated the moods of Facebook users in a study on emotional contagion (Kramer, Guillory, & Hancock, 2014).

While there are many more examples of ethical violations that are discussed in this chapter, cyberpsychologists do not have a host of guidelines for ethical online research with human subjects (Kosinski et al., 2015; Solberg, 2010). Part of this issue is the lack of a clear consensus on what is needed. Some scholars express concerns about the lack of guidelines and call for firmer regulations and more concentrated debate around ethical standards (Goel, 2014). Other scholars contend that research involving social media data may not necessitate as exacting ethics and consent procedures as other types of research since data is publicly accessible and studies tend to involve "minimal risk" to participants (Grimmelmann, 2015). This dearth of well-defined guidelines is compounded by the rapid and continual technological advances. Given the lack of consensus around well-defined guidelines, researchers and institutional review board members may under- or overestimate the potential risks for participants. As a result, cyberpsychologists may be discouraged from performing online research or even submitting studies for review (Kosinski et al., 2015).

This chapter reviews some of the opportunities, as well as challenges, presented by social media platforms to researchers. It is important to note that this chapter is not a complete and comprehensive compendium of social media research methods. Furthermore, it does not offer an all-encompassing set of regulations that can be applied to all social media research blindly. As Kelsey Beninger (2017) has argued, ethical considerations in social media research are not ones that can be boiled down to a checklist. Instead, one must consider the whole research methodology: the topic under investigation, the time period in which data is collected, the participants, and the sensitivity of the content. For Beninger, decisions about whether informed consent is necessary from users who have posted content to public sites are relative to the nature of the content under study and the possible consequences disclosure can have for research participants (see also Townsend & Wallace, 2016). Following this line of thought, this chapter presents ethical issues to be considered relative to the particularities of the data being collected, the groups under study, and the potential consequences for participants. Moreover, the contents of this chapter are intended to offer material that will help cyberpsychology researchers develop research studies with a mind toward ethically responsible research. Attempts are made to present a number of practical recommendations for conducting ethical research within these tools. This is important because some of the advantages found in research using social media platforms (e.g., simple access to sizeable amounts of personal data) contain significant ethical concerns that are rarely addressed in practical means. In the following, there is a discussion of some key ethical issues in social media research: recruitment, privacy, anonymity; consent; terms of service; and data usage.

10.2   Is Recruitment Different in Online Research?

Social media platforms enable investigators to recruit potential participants for research in the clinical and social sciences (Gelinas et al., 2017). Using social media platforms, researchers have access to wider segments of the population than may otherwise be accessible. Moreover, researchers are able to target participants on the basis of personal information that may allow for inferences about participant eligibility for specific studies. While there is increasing interest in social media platforms for recruitment, there is little ethical guidance for researchers and/or institutional review boards (Andrews, 2012). This is often confounded by the fact that the few institutional review boards with focused policies on social media recruitment lack consistent agreement about the ways in which the most pressing issues should be identified and/or approached (Gelinas et al., 2017).

Although recruitment for research using social media platforms is directed by norms similar to those that guide more traditional analogue recruitment, social media does provide circumstances in which contexts may differ. Hence, recruitment in online social media can have differences from traditional approaches to recruitment. Elizabeth Buchanan and Charles Ess (2008) point out that the principle of justice found in traditional recruitment is difficult to maintain in recruitment of participants for online research. In traditional recruitment, a key principle is that of justice. According to this principle, recruitment is just when the participants have an equal or fair chance of taking part in the research. Moreover, justice necessitates that the costs and benefits of research be distributed fairly. It is also important to safeguard against unfair targeting of individuals (e.g., the Tuskegee experiments). Hence, there must be some justifiable reason for inclusion and exclusion of participants. Maintaining the principle of justice in recruitment is more easily accomplished in traditional research studies where targeted participant groups are "controlled." Contrariwise, recruitment using social media platforms involves participants who are self-selected based on some attribute. As a result, the traditional approaches to safeguarding justice may not be as applicable because just representation in the participant pool may not be possible. Nevertheless, it is important for the cyberpsychologist to consider ethical obligations for recruiting online.

Gelinas and colleagues (2017) contend that respect for privacy and investigator transparency are the most salient ethical considerations. Respect for privacy is founded on the norms of respect for persons and beneficence. Respect for privacy in the social media recruitment context is significant given the quantity of personal data accessible. While the personal data accessible online has been voluntarily made public, the users did not have research participation in mind when they disclosed their personal information. Instead, they disclosed the personal information because they wanted to connect socially with others. Gelinas and colleagues also argue for the importance of investigator transparency, which is grounded primarily in respect for persons. Transparency requires investigators engaged in social media recruitment to (1) "avoid deception and refrain from fabricating online identities to gain access to these online communities" and (2) "proactively disclose their presence on social media when collecting information for recruitment purposes" (Gelinas et al., 2017, p. 7).

In sum, existing ethical guidelines and practices need some development so that they can be more readily applied to social media data that obscure the lines between public and private spheres. As mentioned, social networking sites contain personal data that was originally intended for a particular audience in the user's online social network. This includes an assortment of intimate and distant ties. As such, the public nature of this data can be questioned. This is the case even if users understand that a wider network of "friends" can see, and interact with, their posted content. Boyd and Crawford (2012) have contended that even data that can be considered truly public (e.g., data posted on a Twitter timeline from a nonprivate account) may not be intended for additional use by those who initially generated the data. The ethical implication here is that it is unclear how social media researchers can be epistemologically warranted (have justified true belief) that users are consenting to their personal data being used and analyzed in ways they cannot predict. Issues of boundary specification are typical of all data produced in social media platforms and spread to comments, likes, and reposting (Quan-Haase & McCay-Peet, 2016).

10.3   Informed Consent

As mentioned in Chapter 9, "Social Media Ethics Section 1: Facebook, Twitter, and Google – Oh My!," informed consent allows participants some control over their personal data so that they can restrict access to it. Seminal work by Faden and Beauchamp (1986) outlined informed consent in terms of effective consent, which is now found in discussions of social media research. While traditional human subjects research ethics typically involves face-to-face contact between researcher and participant, technological applications are usually devoid of that contact. Traditional approaches to informed consent are replaced by terms of service or end-user license agreements. This weakens the social media researcher's ability to uphold autonomy, competence, and understanding. Moreover, there are limits to understanding the implications of a disclosure of personal information.

Helen Nissenbaum (2011) has discussed the compatibility of informed consent (notice-and-consent) with a competitive free market that allows online social media service providers and users to trade goods at prices the market determines. The issue here is that the traditional informed consent may not be practical for social media research because the user's personal data is at times conceived as part of the price of online exchange. While there is little concern when the users are informed of a service provider's practices in gathering and using personal information, problems arise with the lack of limits to the amount of surreptitious and flagrant data gathering, dissemination, aggregation, analysis, and profiling being done by corporations.

While informed consents in traditional face-to-face social science research aim at protecting participants and researchers (autonomy, competence, disclosure, understanding, and voluntariness), terms of service agreements fail to offer similar safeguards. In fact, the online environment is replete with hundreds of pages of license and consent forms. As a result of their length and ubiquity, users have grown accustomed to simply clicking "Agree" without first reading the fine print (Böhme & Köpsell, 2010). Unfortunately, the result is that both the social media users are at risk. Some social media researchers use the design flexibility offered by the online environment to develop consent forms that are practical and easy for the participant.

10.3.1   Is Consenting via "Terms of Use" Enough?

A controversial aspect of social media research ethics is found in ethical concerns surrounding collaborations between academic and corporate researchers. Much of this concern accompanies the publication of large-scale studies by social media companies collaborating with academics (e.g., Kramer, Guillory, & Hancock, 2014). An issue is that users are often not directly informed about studies before or after they have been completed. Jessica Vitak (2017) has argued that social media (e.g., Facebook) research has questionable methods and practices "Due in part to the media's misrepresentations of the methodological processes – and because users felt uncomfortable not knowing what was going on 'behind the scenes' at the company" (p. 634). Results from such studies have increasingly resulted in public outcry about the ethical practices of big data analytics. Moreover, there is increasing desire for deep reflection on the ethics of social media research, the need for greater transparency, the inherent biases of big data, and the impacts of such research on users (Hargittai, 2015; Tufekci, 2015).

10.3.2 Facebook Emotional Contagion Study

In 2014, Facebook, working with academics, took the data from around 3 million English-language posts written by approximately 700,000 (N = 689,003) Facebook users and manipulated the moods of those users. All this was done in an experiment performed without participants being informed. The experimental design consisted of a manipulation of the Facebook News Feed of the uninformed (and without informed consent) users that filtered out particular posts with positive and negative emotion words. In the following period, an analysis of the emotional content in the participants' posts was performed to assess whether exposure to emotional content would impact the participants. Hence, they were interested in how the participants' emotions were altered by observing their subsequent posts. They found that basic emotions were contagious, though the effects were small.

The researchers were likely enthusiastic to publish an article (in a prestigious journal no less) showing that emotional contagion occurs in a computer-mediated setting based purely on textual content. The reactions of the international news media (e.g., Atlantic, Forbes, The Independent, New York Times, Venture Beat) and among scholars (for a detailed collection of responses, see Grimmelmann, 2014) were less than enthusiastic. From an ethical perspective, the typical discussion asked whether the procedures used to authorize research were adequate and whether Facebook users could have been harmed by an experiment aimed at manipulating moods in positive and negative directions. Arthur Caplan and Charles Seife (2014) contended that the study was best viewed as a "violation of the rights of research subjects." Likewise, Nicholas Evans did not feel that what Facebook was doing is unethical by itself: "But in the Facebook study, the independent oversight didn't happen, and as far as we know the debriefing didn't happen. The way the study was conducted was unethical."

On the other hand, the researchers who performed the study believe that the benefits outweighed the costs. The first author of the paper, Adam D. I. Kramer (2014), attempted to vindicate the research in a Facebook post:

> The reason we did this research is because we care about the emotional impact of Facebook and the people that use our product. We felt that it was important to investigate the common worry that seeing friends post positive content leads to people feeling negative or left out. At the same time, we were concerned that exposure to friends' negativity might lead people to avoid visiting Facebook.

From a consequentialist perspective, the rightness or wrongness of this study can be couched in terms of whether the findings were worth all of the anxiety and lack of consent. In fact, Kramer (2014) also noted: "In hindsight, the research benefits of the paper may not have justified all of this anxiety." Perhaps he has a point. However, there is also the issue of whether the study was appropriately handled by Facebook, Cornell University, and the journal. Moreover, there is the issue of whether users' agreements to the terms of service constituted informed consents to participate in an experiment that manipulated their moods in positive and negative directions. Puschmann and Bozdag (2014) offer a description both pro and contra the emotion contagion study (see Table 10.1).

Evan Selinger and Woodrow Hartzog (2016) argue for an additional ethical concern for the Facebook emotional contagion experiment. According to them, it was ethically problematic that the researchers co-opted user information in a manner that (1) violated identity-based norms and (2) exploited the vulnerability of users disclosing on social media when they could not control the ways in which personal data is displayed in this technologically mediated environment:

> At bottom, this aspect of the problem has two inter-related dimensions: 1) it highlights the limits of control users have over their disclosures in some mediated environments, and thereby the limited agency they can exhibit to ensure information is responsibly disclosed; and 2) it concerns companies imposing an undesirable identity – namely, collaborator – upon users as a cost of using information and communication services. (p. 36)

For Selinger and Hartzog (2016), weighing the consequences after the fact misses the point of ethical review. Even if Facebook's emotional contagion experiment benefited our understanding of emotion contagion in online environments, and had no adverse consequences to any user's life, this should have been part of the institutional review board discussion before the study, not afterwards. Moreover, they are concerned that the emotion

Table 10.1 *Pro and contra arguments related to the Facebook emotional contagion study (adapted from Puschmann & Bozdag, 2014; reprinted with permission from the publisher)*

Argument Theme	Pro Experiment	Contra Experiment
Benefits of online experiments for the individual	• Filtering reduces clutter • Users want filtered rather than unfiltered content	• Users are not aware of filtering • Filtering cannot be controlled • Filtering mechanisms are not transparent
Informed consent and its many interpretations	• Accepting terms of service is a form of consent • Opt-in is annoying to users • Opt-in influences user behavior	• Possibility of biased user behavior does not counter informed consent • Users could be informed postexperiment • Consenting to unknown hazards is problematic
The ubiquity of online social experiments	• Experiments are essential to platform improvement • Differ from offline experiments by being unique and novel • Provide opportunities to study human behavior at scale	• Same principles that govern offline experiments can be applied • Experiments should not be conducted at large scale when there is no need • Alternatives should be considered • Users should be able to influence or stop the experiments and provide feedback
Different perceptions of risk in online experiments	• Withholding information does not cause danger • In the long term, benefits will outweigh risks	• If participation is not voluntary, it is manipulative • Persuasion is likely to benefit the persuader at least as much as the persuaded
Benefits of online experimentation for the society	• Online experiments create new opportunities for science and society • Constant scrutiny will have a chilling effect on collaboration between industry and academia	• Exact benefits are unclear • We learn less about human interaction than about media effects • It is not sufficient to equate scientific benefit with social benefit
The unavoidability of online experiments	• Online platforms cannot be improved without experimentation • Incremental improvement is the only way to succeed	• Potential risks also need consideration • Judging risks to be minimal without having considered them is premature

contagion study exploited users' inability to control the ways in which their personal data was presented to others in the technologically mediated environment.

10.4 Public versus Private: What if the Data Is Already Public?

Issues related to public versus private data are apparent in the ethical discussions around social media research. Today, most people have some of their basic information available publicly and at least some of that data is potentially indexed by external search engines. Ulrike Schultze and Richard Mason (2012) discuss the ways in which expectations of privacy can be assessed (see Table 10.2).

For Schultze and Mason (2012), social media research that includes a majority of characteristics found in the "private" column would have a higher level of privacy expectations. Contrariwise, social media research that has more of the characteristics listed under "public" would have lower levels of privacy expectations.

Table 10.2 *Public versus private spaces (from Schultze & Mason, 2012; reprinted with permission from the publisher)*

	Public		Private
Group size	Relatively large	...	Relatively small
Communicative purpose	Nonsensitive; professional, networking for career development	...	Sensitive; personal (e.g., medical, fantasy, fears), support, role-playing
Social status of community	Socially accepted or even revered	...	Socially stigmatized, marginalized, deviant
Intended audience for contribution	Broad; general, global public	...	Restrictive; community of people with shared experience
Community membership policy	Open; minimal member registration requirements, if any	...	Closed; registration and member profile required
Norms and expectations	Open; public communication, perhaps receiving acclaim	...	Trust, confidentiality, privacy, maintain anonymity to most viewers
Content storage and accessibility	Published; stored and made publicly accessible automatically	...	Unpublished; ephemeral conversation not recorded/ stored automatically

10.4.1 Insufficient Anonymization

To some extent, public versus private considerations reflect anonymity and what strategy is best for maintaining ethically responsible research. Is publicly available data by default public? If so, can it be examined by cyberpsychologists for social media research (Boyd & Crawford, 2012; Stewart, 2017)? From a user's perspective, anonymizing their personal data would most likely present the lowest risk in terms of associating study content with a specific user's account. While it is common in social media research to anonymize all data, some social media platforms (e.g., such as Twitter) view anonymizing data to be a violation of the terms and conditions of use.

Even when data is believed to have been sufficiently anonymized, there are cases in which the precautions taken were insufficient. Take, for example, the group of researchers who publicly released a data set in 2008 that was developed from the Facebook accounts of an entire cohort of college students – "Tastes, Ties, and Time" (T3). This project was a National Science Foundation funding award to researchers at Harvard and UCLA. The purpose of the grant-funded project was to model the social network dynamics of a large group of students (N = 1,640) by downloading and analyzing Facebook data from a complete freshman class. The announcement that accompanied the data release indicated the distinctiveness of the data:

> The dataset comprises machine-readable files of virtually all the information posted on approximately 1,700 [Facebook] profiles by an entire cohort of students at an anonymous, northeastern American university. Profiles were sampled at 1-year intervals, beginning in 2006. This first wave covers first-year profiles, and three additional waves of data will be added over time, one for each year of the cohort's college career. Though friendships outside the cohort are not part of the data, this snapshot of an entire class over its 4 years in college, including supplementary information about where students lived on campus, makes it possible to pose diverse questions about the relationships between social networks, online and offline. (Zimmer, 2010, p. 313)

According to Parry (2011), the researchers downloaded data related to each student's gender, home state, academic major, political opinions, friends' network, and romantic preferences. The determination of race and ethnicity was established via photographs and club affiliations. The researchers logged which students appeared in students' photo albums and collected entertainment preferences (e.g., music, books, movies). The T3 project was lauded as a significant advance in the study of the ways in which race and culture influence college relations and how relations and interests develop over time.

Given the potential privacy violations, the T3 team made attempts to protect the identities of the participants by removing students' names and identification numbers from the data set, delaying the release of the participant cultural interests, and requiring other researchers to agree to a "terms and conditions for use" that aimed at eliminating a variety of uses of the data that could compromise student privacy. Additionally, they underwent institutional review for protections of human subjects (Lewis et al., 2008). Unfortunately, Harvard's institutional review board approved a protocol wherein students were not informed that they were subjects in the T3 research project.

In addition to being ethically questionable, it becomes a public scandal when Michael Zimmer (Assistant Professor at the University of Wisconsin Milwaukee's School of Information Studies) identified the school as Harvard. Hence, the precautions failed to offer sufficient privacy protections as the identity of the institution was quickly discovered. In a thorough analysis of the ethical mistakes of the researchers involved in this study, Zimmer (2010) communicated the ways in which the social media researchers failed to protect the users' privacy: the vast quantity of data collected, inappropriate access of accounts (with no consent), unsanctioned secondary use of data, and errors in personal data. Moreover, by making the users' personal data publicly accessible without taking the needed steps to protect individual users, the social media researchers failed to reflect on the potential consequences of their data collection and aggregation.

10.4.2   Not All Data Sets Available Online Are Necessarily Public

It is important to note that, just because a data set is available online, it is not necessarily public. Zeller has questioned whether social media researchers should analyze any data that is available online. What about data that has been released from a hacker and posted online? For example, should a social media researcher use data online that was posted by a hacker who had hacked into an online data service? Emily Dreyfuss (2015) wrote about the hacking of the website Ashley Madison (created to romantically connect married individuals for extramarital affairs) and the posting of personal user information online. The online dating service had around 40 million users in 2015 when the social media service was hacked; data on user accounts was retrieved and personal user data was posted online for all to see and access.

Likewise, James Eng (2014) tells the story of Snapchat being hacked by third-party applications. Snapchat is a social media service that allows for ephemeral and nonretrievable pictures and messages to be posted but only for a limited time before they become inaccessible. While Snapchat users relied on the ephemeral and nonretrievable nature of this data (Bayer et al., 2015), third-party applications made these pictures and messages available. A website called SnapchatDB.info went online and offered a database containing the usernames and phone numbers of 4.6 million Snapchat accounts for download. According to an Australia-based group called Gibson Security, Snapchat's application code has several security vulnerabilities. Gibson Security has posted an online report that explains the ways in which the Snapchat application could be hacked to expose user account information (https://gibsonsec.org/sn apchat/fulldisclosure/). What should social media researchers do with leaked data sets? According to Zeller (2017), social media researchers are responsible for establishing a data set's origins and the nature of consent given by users. In sum, just because data is publicly available online does not mean that it was obtained legally or that it conforms to the standards of scholarly ethical practice.

10.4.3   *Private and Public Determined via Social Norms and Praxes*

That said, there is disagreement among cyberpsychologists and other social media researchers about whether the gathering of publicly available data should be considered as part of regulatory definitions of human subjects research. Moreover, there is lack of agreement on whether consent and institutional review board approval are required (Schultze & Mason, 2012; Solberg, 2010; Wilson, Gosling, & Graham, 2012). Some suggest that the division between private and public is less an issue of accessibility and more one of social norms and praxes (Frankel & Siang, 1999; King, 1996; Schultze & Mason, 2012; Waskul, 1996). Dennis Waskul and Mark Douglass (1996) suggest that these social norms give direction to the discussion of private versus public information. They compare the context of online interaction to an everyday discussion in a park to illustrate their thoughts:

> You are seated on a bench in a public park with a group of close personal friends. Small talk quickly dissipates into issues of a more serious nature. In the course of confiding personal and private issues to your friends, you turn your head to discover someone tape recording the discussion. Outraged, you confront this person, who proceeds to explain some ambiguous research project, and attempts to justify the act by citing the public context of your discussion . . . after all, this is a public park. (p. 132)

Waskul and Douglass (1996) ask whether you would feel outraged that your privacy was unacceptably violated. Would we demand that this researcher inform us of what institution (or agency) sponsored and/or approved this research? Ultimately, would we be at all convinced by arguments about the public accessibility of the information?

10.4.4   Private and Public in Archival Research

For others, the mining of public data is not a violation of social norms. For these researchers, such activities are equivalent to conducting archival research (as in the humanities; e.g., history) that typically does not require the protection of human subjects (Bruckman, 2002; Herring, 1996; Kosinski et al., 2015). Michal Kosinski and colleagues (2015) offer conditions for using private user information that is available publicly without consent:

- It is reasonable to assume that the data was knowingly made public by the individuals
- Data is anonymized after collection and no attempts are made to deanonymize it
- There is no interaction or communication with the individuals in the sample
- No information that can be attributed to a single individual, including demographic profiles and samples of text or other content, is to be published or used to illustrate the results of the study (p. 553).

For Kosinski and colleagues, not meeting any one of their conditions should result in close scrutiny by an institutional review board.

10.4.5   Private and Public in Extended Minds

As introduced in Chapter 3, "Digital and Extended Selves in Cyberspace" (and discussed subsequently in the chapters that followed), the use of the World Wide Web has given rise to worldwide sociocultural transformations that include the extension of each user's cognitive and affective processes (Clowes, 2015). Digital and coupled technologies such as the Internet, smartphones, and social media platforms are powerful, convenient, portable, and capable of storing vast amounts of salient data about people's lived experiences on the cloud. Moreover, these technologies take part in the operations of the user's cognitive (e.g., memory) processes (Clowes, 2015). In fact, our connections to digital information now permeate most aspects of our lives. This has led to the integration of these technologies (e.g., Internet, smartphones) into the cognitive tasks we perform in our activities of daily living. Paul Smart (2012, 2014, 2018) has developed arguments for viewing the Internet as a new type of cognitive ecology that provides almost constant access to digital information and increasingly extends our cognitive processes (see also Smart et al., 2017). As such, these digital extensions of our cognitive processes are expanding into Luciano Floridi's (2014) infosphere (see Chapter 2 of this book). According to Floridi, the ultimate nature of reality consists of information. Moreover, he asserts that everyone lives in the "infosphere" as "inforgs" (i.e., information organisms). The notable metaphysical claim in Floridi's information ethics is that the totality of all that exists does so in the "infosphere" as an informational object or process.

In a paper entitled "Studying cyborgs: re-examining internet studies as human subjects research," Ulrike Schultze and Richard Mason (2012) argue that virtual communities and social networks are increasingly assuming and consuming further facets of people's lives. As a result, the boundaries between physically internalized cognitive processes and extended cognitive processes in the virtual world are as tenable as the related distinctions between private and public domains of user data. Given this cyberization, ethical guidelines essential for social media research need to be reexamined. Schultze and Mason outline a framework to guide social media researchers. Figure 10.1 (two figures in the original article that are here placed side by side as a single figure) reflects the relevant human subjects research for both traditional (left side of figure) activities (face-to-face surveys, interviews, in-person experiments) and downloading personal data (from postings, profiles and the like). They define human subjects in terms of three key decision points summarized in Figure 10.1. Furthermore, the decision tree illustrates the two conditions under which the research is exempt from human subjects review by a research ethics committees. It also illustrates two conditions under which a research ethics committee review should assess human subject protections. On the right-hand side of Figure 10.1, one finds a comparative decision tree that can be used for decisions where technology can be viewed as an extension of the person.

Note that for Schultze and Mason (2012), the human subjects framework for studying cyborgs (decision tree on the right of Figure 10.1) includes three dimensions (entanglement, interaction/intervention, and privacy) that can be considered together prior to deciding on whether the research deals with human subjects. Furthermore, the social media researcher is directed to rate each dimension on a low-to-high scale. The

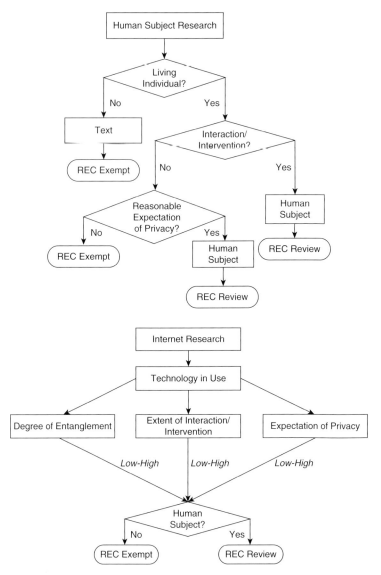

Figure 10.1 Comparative decision trees for both traditional face-to-face human subjects research (decision tree on the left of the figure) with a human subjects framework for studying cyborgs (decision tree on the right of the figure) (adapted from two figures found in Schultze & Mason, 2012; reprinted with permission from the publisher)

resulting framework has the potential to present a more holistic treatment of the social and technical issues surrounding social media research in an age of Internet-extended cognition (cyborgian entanglement).

10.5 Conclusions

In this chapter, there have been discussions of a range of topics where ethical questions for research using social media occur: recruitment, privacy, anonymity; consent; terms of service; and data usage. In general, the user should be able to limit the sharing of personal information. According to the restricted access/limited control theory, informational privacy does not occur without restrictions on the dissemination of personal information and without some control (as warranted by the particular situation).

This chapter also considered various perspectives on whether a user's personal information should be considered as private or as publicly available. In situations where a user's personal information is found on social networking sites, there are questions about whether that user should be notified any time that the personal data is made available to a third party (e.g., a company wanting the data for targeted advertising). For some, the answer is relative to social norms and should be treated the way we treat offline personal information that can be accessed in public. For others, information found in the public domain should be viewed the same way that we view archival research in the humanities (e.g., history). Such studies typically do not require the protection of human subjects. A third perspective can be found in digitally extended selves in cyberspace. The use of the World Wide Web has given rise to worldwide sociocultural transformations that include the extension of each user's cognitive and affective processes. As a result, the boundaries between physically internalized cognitive processes and extended cognitive processes in the virtual world are as tenable as the related distinctions between private and public domains of user data. Given this cyberization, ethical guidelines essential for social media research need to be reexamined.

CHAPTER 11

Social Media Ethics Section 3: Digital Citizenship

11.1 Introduction

The effortlessly available online knowledgebase found in the Internet has essentially succeeded other media in terms of acquiring knowledge for daily life. In this digital age, persons in Western industrialized countries are progressively exhibiting themselves online and communicating with others in disembodied contexts that span time and space. Posting, tweeting, and blogging are popular platforms for communicating thoughts and feelings with varying levels of anonymity. This has brought about a new age of digital citizenship. Like other types of citizenship, this new age includes those who are born into the digital environment and those who immigrate (or at least attempt to) and seek digital citizenship. Access is always an issue, with those who are already digital citizens having varying views on responsibilities to decrease inequity in access. Some are interested in open borders and others are less interested in whether or not others may have access.

Prensky (2001) has argued that there is a digital divide that has resulted in at least two cohorts of Internet users. One way to look at this is in terms of persons who have had access to the Internet and related technologies since a very early age. These "Digital Natives" are technology users that had Internet technologies as part of their development. On the other hand, there are also "Digital Immigrants" who adopted these technologies later in life. Digital Natives are "native speakers" of the digital language of computers, video games, and the Internet. While Digital Immigrants learn and adapt to the digital environment, they always retain, to some degree, their "accent."

In much of this book, there are investigations of various ethical concerns (e.g., privacy, autonomy) that influence individuals as they make use of various technologies. In this chapter, the emphasis broadens to include sociodemographic, sociopolitical institutions, and social sectors. In Section 11.2, "Those Who Cannot Connect: The Digital

Divide," there is an emphasis on the ethical issues related to social equity and information access. In Section 11.3, "Those Seeking to Connect: Online Dating," we turn to ethical aspects of Internet matching companies. In Section 11.4, "Digital Citizenship: Ethics for the Connected," there is a consideration of ethical implications related to digital citizenship.

11.2 Those Who Cannot Connect: The Digital Divide

What are the ethical concerns related to social equity and information access? The benefits of the Internet (access to information, education, entertainment, healthcare, and/or governmental services) and the digital revolution do not empower everyone equally. This creation of social inequalities relative to access has become known as the digital divide (Brown, López, & Lopez, 2016, Mossberger, Tolbert, & Hamilton, 2012; Prensky, 2001). Social inequalities emerge from the contrasting experiences between those who can totally benefit from digital opportunities and those who cannot. As Zillien and Hargittai (2009) have pointed out, "the digital divide is generally regarded as a new form of social inequality, in which different patterns of media usage influence life chances to different degrees depending on the particular activities in which people engage online" (p. 275).

Digital inequalities are apparent among persons, households, organizations, communities, and nations (Dewan & Riggins, 2005). For individuals, these digital disparities often exist among persons with lower incomes and/or education levels, disabilities, ethnic minorities, women, older aged, and those living in rural areas (Campos-Castillo, 2015; Ferro, Helbig, & Gil-Garcia, 2011; Hilbert, 2011; Lengsfeld, 2011; Vicente & Lopez, 2010). Among developing nations, digital divisions are apparent in the inequality of access to digital technologies among developing nations. As O'Hara and Stevens (2006) argue, the disparities among groups involving access to digital technologies are "tied closely to economic inequality." There is a growing emphasis on the importance of digital technologies to cultivate both a nation's economic development (Lee, Gholami, & Tong, 2005; World Bank, 2016) and citizens' quality of life of (Dewan & Riggins, 2005; Kim, Lee, & Menon, 2009). To increase access, some countries have introduced policies aimed at bridging the divide. For example, in the United States, the Clinton administration established the National Information Infrastructure to bridge the divide so that all Americans would have appropriate access to digital technologies.

Since that time, several developed and developing countries have initiated national information infrastructure policies (Bojnec & Fertő, 2012).

11.2.1   Age and the Digital Divide

While many born within the past few decades and raised in Western industrialized countries have experienced the ubiquitous and effortlessly available online knowledgebase found in the Internet since birth, there is not necessarily an equal distribution of access. Prensky's (2001) digital divide discusses at least two Internet user cohorts. The relation of each cohort to technology can be very different. Moreover, each has differing cognitive styles. Persons who have had access to the Internet and related technologies since a very early age are referred to as "Digital Natives" that had Internet technologies as part of their development. That said, there are also "Digital Immigrants" who adopted these technologies later in life. There are digital natives who are "native speakers" of the digital language (e.g., computers, video games and the Internet) and digital immigrants who to some degree retain their "accent" as they learn and adapt to the digital environment. For example, the "digital immigrant accent" is apparent in how they gather their information. The Internet does not tend to be their first choice for information. Another example would be printing out an email or a digitized document in order to edit it. On the other hand, if one is a Digital Native, the use of the Internet and consumption of digitized information are second nature. Even though technologies are increasingly prevalent, older adults continue to trail behind their younger counterparts. As mentioned in Chapter 6 of this book, cyberpsychological research with older adults has historically been viewed from a "digital divide," with large clefts separating older-adult use of technology and the Internet when compared to their younger counterparts. Part of this discrepancy between age cohorts is that some older adults are apprehensive and/or daunted by the thought of learning to use new technologies or about issues related to security.

11.2.2   Race and the Digital Divide

Some scholars contend that there are differences in the ways that historically marginalized and majority groups use digital technologies. While some uses of digital technologies are considered capital-enhancing (e.g., Internet use to improve education, career, and health), others are simply entertaining (e.g., video games, recreational surfing, and online gambling) diversions that offer limited potential for increasing academic or economic capital (DiMaggio & Hargittai, 2001; Hargittai & Hinnant, 2008; van Deursen & van Dijk, 2014). In a review of Internet studies, Daniels (2013) found that race and racism manifest in a number of ways in terms of access and use. Emerging research findings suggest that ethnic and racial differences in the use of digital technologies persist even after one controls for socioeconomic status (Jung, Qiu, & Kim, 2001; Milioni, Doudaki, & Demertzis, 2014).

While racial majorities (i.e., White or Asian American males) use digital technologies for enhancement (e.g., educational, financial), historically marginalized communities may use these technologies primarily for entertainment (DiMaggio et al., 2004; van Deursen & van Dijk, 2014; Zillien & Hargittai, 2009). For example, Zhang (2015) used two "big data" analytic tools to investigate the relation between sociodemographic groupings and usage of (as well as interest in) websites that represented either capital-enhancing (KhanAcademy.org) or entertaining (CartoonNetwork.com) uses of the Internet. Results revealed that Black students are more likely to use websites dedicated to cartoons than education. The authors conclude that varying uses of digital technologies between these groups may reproduce educational and socioeconomic inequalities.

11.2.3   *Gender and the Digital Divide*

There is concern related to the inequalities of access to digital technologies between men and women. Huyer and colleagues (2005) found that women use digital technologies for smaller amounts of times when compared to men. Given the importance of digital technologies for equitable development in both developed and developing nations, this gender gap (fewer women accessing and using digital technologies) reflects a growing concern (Ghadially, 2007; Hilbert, 2011; Mori, 2011). Some have argued that these differences may be exacerbated by situations where women are from sociodemographic groups that have less money, time, and learning opportunities (Ghadially, 2007). For example, Hilbert (2011) found the gender gap in accessibility found in developing nations is related to greater inequalities in education, employment, and health.

What are the causes of differences in digital access? Culture is often pointed to as a reason for the overrepresentation of digital technologies (Allen et al., 2006; Wilson, 2003). The underrepresentation of women may be related to the fact that women are outnumbered by men in science, technology, engineering, and mathematics education (World Bank, 2016).

This may be due to institutional structures that promote gender stereo-typing of school subjects, impact self-confidence, and limited access to computer training (Ahuja, 2002; Forson & Özbilgin, 2003). Furthermore, gender differences are based also on cultural differences (Mujtaba, 2007; Zauchner et al., 2000).

11.2.4   The Digital Divide and Persons with Disabilities

Digital technologies (e.g., the Internet) offer potential opportunities for enhanced accessibility to information and services for people with disabil-ities. However, the use of digital technologies by persons with disabilities tends to be much lower than the use of these technologies by persons in the general population. A consumer experiences report by the UK Office of Communications (Ofcom, 2013) described Internet usage among persons with disabilities as disproportionately lower than that of the general population. In a Pew Research Center report, Fox (2011) stated that the amount of Internet use among Americans with disabilities was 54 percent, which was much lower than the 81 percent usage among adults with no disability. As a result, some prefer to call this the "disability divide" (D'Aubin, 2007). The lower use of digital technologies by persons with disabilities is related to lower socioeconomic status, limited financial resources, and dependence on others (Internet Society, 2012).

11.2.5   Is the Digital Divide an Ethical Issue?

As can be seen in our earlier discussion, the digital divide can be defined in terms of intranational and international divides, economic, as well as dependencia and interdependence theory. From a moral perspective, some point to unequal distributions of information and power (Moss, 2002) and others ethical concerns related to inequitable access to digital technologies. From a moral philosophy approach, however, there is no definitive consensus. For example, not all instances where groups are divided relative to unequal access to goods are ethical problems. Tavani (2011) points out that a skeptic could argue that this is not an ethical issue because there are many divides that are not ethical violations. He gives the example of the divide that exists between those who have Mercedes-Benz automobiles and those who do not results in a "Mercedes-Benz divide," with many people being the have-nots. A response could be that the existing divisions between the "haves" and the "have-nots" for vital resources such as food and healthcare are considered by many ethicists to reflect unjust distribution of primary goods and resources. Travani asks us to consider whether unequal access to digital technologies is more like the Mercedes-Benz divide or divisions related to access to food and healthcare.

While some have understood the digital divide in terms of access, others have argued that the digital divide is more complex than the bifurcation into the "haves" and "have-nots" (Selwyn, 2004). While the "digital divide" once focused on access to computers, there is increasing emphasis on a "second digital divide" between those who have the digital skills for efficient navigation on the information highway and those that get lost in the labyrinth of digital technologies (Ghobadi & Ghobadi, 2015; Hargittai & Hinnant, 2008; Mariën & Prodnik, 2014; Ragnedda, 2017). Hence, the discussion now includes what Benjamin Compaine (2001a, 2001b) calls the "information haves and have-nots." Compaine's definition of the digital divide involves a gap (perceived or actual) between those who have access to current "information tools" and those who do not. Moreover, he suggests that the gap can be understood as existing (or perceived to exist) between those who have the ability to use these technologies and those who do not. Hence, for Compaine, simply having access to digital technologies is not enough. Instead, persons must also possess the knowledge and ability to use these technologies. Given these expanding understandings of the digital divide, scholars are increasingly evaluating the sociocultural context of users of digital technologies in their studies of the digital divide (Kvasny, 2006; Lupton, 2014).

For Maria Canellopoulou-Bottis and Ken Himma (2008), while reducing the digital divide is likely a good thing to do, it is not necessarily a moral obligation. The point they were attempting to make was that failing to do a moral good is not the same as being immoral. For example, risking one's life to save another person is a morally good thing to do but failing to risk one's life to save another is not necessarily being immoral. Hence, one is not morally obligated to risk one's life (though there may be exceptions for some professions – for example, firefighters, police officers, paramedics). Ethicists refer to such acts as "supererogatory," in that the act of risking one's life to save another person is morally good but not a moral obligation. According to Canellopoulou-Bottis and Himma, it is helpful to note that while supererogatory acts are praiseworthy, obligatory acts are more often considered mandatory acts that one should just do. Likewise, while nonperformance of obligatory acts is often considered blameworthy, not performing supererogatory acts typically does not receive denunciation.

The application of the Canellopoulou-Bottis and Himma line of reasoning to ethical considerations related to bridging the digital divide reveals the complexity involved in establishing moral obligation. It is important to note that Himma (2007) himself has argued that there is moral support for bridging the digital divide in just about all classically theistic religions, our ordinary intuitions, and classic ethical theories such as deontology and consequentialism. He presents deontological theories, for example, that "almost universally hold that we have an obligation to help the poor." Take, for example, the principle of beneficence and the prima facie obligation that persons have to help the poor.

11.2.6   Floridi's Information Ethics Approach to the Digital Divide

An argument for moral reasoning in discussions of ethical concerns found in the digital divide can be found in Luciano Floridi's (2001, 2002) information ethics. According to Floridi, the ethical issues found in the digital divide are related to the nature of the information society. Floridi's infosphere presents new cognitive processes found in learning, trading, and cultural activities. He contends that the gaps found in the digital divide are problematic in themselves, as well as their societal roles (e.g., insufficient healthcare, lack of educational equity, and human rights). The applications of "information ethics" to the digital divide is apparent in Floridi's information ethics and ethical arguments against unjustifiable closures or reductions (in quantity, quality, or value) to the infosphere.

In developing his conceptualization of the digital divide, Floridi (2001) has proposed horizontal and vertical digital divides. He postulated that the vertical digital divide is a temporal one that distinguished the current digital/information era from past generations. According to Floridi, the horizontal gap includes persons that are segregated (i.e., separated spatially) and sometimes self-segregated as netizens that are both technologically proficient and technologically active. Hence, the digital divide puts an end to temporal and spatial constrictions but produces new technological limitations between the in-group and the outsiders. Floridi (2001) believes that the time and space barriers disempower, discriminate, and generate dependency. Moreover, he contends that information ethics offers a rejoinder to the emergence of the horizontal digital divide. Floridi (2001, p. 1) argues that a novel ecological model is needed that can be used for developing ethical norms that may bridge the digital divide:

1. Information entropy ought not to be caused in the infosphere
2. Information entropy ought to be prevented in the infosphere
3. Information entropy ought to be removed from the infosphere
4. Information ought to be promoted by extending, improving, enriching, and opening the infosphere, that is, by ensuring information quantity, quality, variety, security, ownership, privacy, pluralism, and access.

Floridi aims to broaden the ethical concerns of the digital divide from the biosphere's biophysical ecosystem to the infosphere's informational ecosystem made up of informational entities. This may make persons aware of the new ethical needs for bridging the digital divide. In Floridi's (2015) edited work *The Online Manifesto: Being Human in a Hyperconnected World*, he points to a group of information ethicists that contend that there is a need "to launch an open debate on the impacts of the computational era on public spaces, politics, and societal expectations toward policymaking in the Digital Agenda" (p. 7). Distinctions between public and private information are being blurred in at least four ways:

1. The blurring of the distinction between reality and virtuality
2. The blurring of the distinctions between human, machine, and nature
3. The reversal from information scarcity to information abundance
4. The shift from the primacy of entities to the primacy of interactions.

Floridi contends that reality in our current digital era should be conceptualized as both physical (biosphere) and digital (infosphere). Moreover, in the digital age, both the physical and the digital can be controlled and exploited. He points out that the high technology societies that brought about the information revolution have fallen short of coping adequately with the ethical impacts of advanced technologies. Preindustrial cultures were able to maintain a nonmaterialistic Weltanschauung that was able to perceive both physical and immaterial (i.e., spiritual) realities as worthy of respect. The introduction of the infosphere to ethical discussions of technologically advanced societies reintroduces value into the nonphysical aspects of our existence in the digital era.

It is important to note that the increasing prevalence of mobile Internet technologies will shrink dramatically the digital divide (Stump, Gong, & Li, 2008). This sentiment is also apparent in popular news sources such as the *New York Times* piece on mobile Internet use and how it shrinks the digital divide (Wortham, 2009) and IBM's report that the fissure between information haves and have-nots will not continue to exist with the arrival of mobile technology (Graham, Hale, & Stephens, 2012).

11.3   Those Seeking to Connect: Online Dating

11.3.1   *Internet Dating and Online Relationships*

Online dating websites are an increasingly prevalent way for many individuals to seek out potential romantic partners. A survey of online dating and relationships by the Pew Internet and American Life Project reported that 38 percent of American adults who are currently single and looking for a partner have used online dating sites or mobile dating apps (Smith & Duggan, 2013). Across demographics, attitudes toward Internet dating are becoming increasingly positive. This has not gone unnoticed by companies seeking to capitalize on the desires of persons to connect. In 1995, the first online dating site, "match.com," was launched. Since that time, Internet dating sites have emerged to address every desire and demographic. In 2007, Internet dating companies like OkCupid and Zoosk began to incorporate social networking and included data on geographical proximity and mutual online acquaintances. According to a 2013 article from *Forbes* magazine, there were more than 2,500 online dating services in the United States and more than 8,000 sites worldwide (Zwilling, 2013). While online dating sites such as Match and eHarmony were developed to appeal to the adult general public, other sites like Christian Mingle, JDate, and Black People Meet are based on shared group identity. Interestingly, individuals in some immigrant communities living in the United States appear to be using online dating sites to enhance networking (Bunt, 2009; Hammer, 2015). Research using online dating sites has consistently found racial group dating preferences (Feliciano, Lee, & Robnett, 2011; Feliciano, Robnett, & Komaie, 2009). Moreover, increased Internet use has changed how individuals interact with members of the same faith and the ways in which they seek potential romantic partners (Brasher, 2004).

A report in the journal *Psychological Science in the Public Interest* critically analyzed online dating sites from the perspective of psychological science. In this review, Eli J. Finkel (Northwestern University), Paul W. Eastwick (Texas A&M University), Benjamin R. Karney (UCLA), Harry T. Reis (University of Rochester), and Susan Sprecher (Illinois State University) analyzed the access, communication, and matching services provided by online dating sites (Finkel et al., 2012). While they conceded that online dating sites offer access to a greater number of possible partners, they question whether or not this is a good thing. For example, it may be that the dramatic increase in available profiles online will lead to commoditization of these potential partners. This, they believe, could result in reduced interest and/or commitment to any one person. Another issue of concern that they point to for these online dating sites is that the communications that occur may result in unrealistic expectations (as well as disappointment) when potential partners meet in real life.

11.3.2   Scientific Matching Algorithms

Perhaps one of the greatest contentions of the authors of the *Psychological Science in the Public Interest* report (Finkel et al., 2012) is the lack of empirical support for claims of Internet matching companies that they had advanced scientific matching algorithms. The authors found little evidence to support claims that these matching algorithms enhance predictions about whether those matched are in fact good matches or whether they will have chemistry with each other. Of course, one of the reasons for this is the proprietary nature of these algorithms. While well-trained PhDs in Psychology and Data Science developed some of these companies, there are commercial (due to proprietary information and intellectual property) and ethical limitations (e.g., consent, privacy; see the discussion of OkCupid in Section 11.3.3) for companies running studies on their users and publishing the results. One way that some groups have attempted to handle this is via patents (e.g., eHarmony: US Patent No. 6,735,568, 2014/0180942; Facebook: US Patent No. 9,609,072; JDate: US Patent No. 5,950,200) but this does not represent actual scientific evidence and/or empirical verification by nonbiased investigators. Others have taken steps to empirically validate their matching systems with large-scale studies of their user base. Several ethical concerns have resulted from these studies because they were performed without the users realizing that they were being experimented on.

   The company eHarmony has come under a great deal of scrutiny given its unsubstantiated claims for superior scientific algorithms. What evidence does eHarmony have for such claims? They often point to the credentials of their researchers, the successful marriages, and the published results. Unfortunately, credentials are not enough. That just means that they should know how to perform rigorous empirical assessments of their algorithms. Unfortunately, they have not done this. There are a handful of publications with unreplicated (and perhaps unreplicable given the lack of transparency related to their algorithms) results (Epstein, 2007; Finkel et al., 2012). In their above-mentioned exhaustive review of Internet dating sites in the journal *Psychological Science in the Public Interest*, Finkel and colleagues (2012) criticized claims made by companies like eHarmony that assert their computerized algorithms will help match users with a "soul mate."

In addition to the academic backlash, eHarmony's scientific claims have been disparaged by the Advertising Standards Authority (ASA). The ASA went so far as to ban eHarmony from making the claim that it has a scientifically proven matching system. According to the ASA, eHarmony's claims are misleading because the company has not proven that its service provided a greater chance of finding lasting love. This is an important note and not one to be taken lightly. Statements such as "scientifically proven" should be held to a higher standard. The company eHarmony has insufficient proof that It has approached that standard.

11.3.3   Ethical Concerns Around OkCupid Experiments with Matching Algorithm

Some efforts have been made by online dating websites to perform experiments on their user base. For example, OkCupid, a free online dating site, performed experiments on their user base (12 million people at the time of the study; Suddath, 2014). Unfortunately, these experiments were performed without first informing their users. OkCupid matches users using mathematical algorithms derived from user answers to questions about their preferences. Three separate experiments were described in the company's blog (Benbunan-Fich, 2017; Rudder, 2014). In two of the studies, OkCupid investigated various aspects of their website interface. For these two OkCupid experiments, an A/B testing approach was used to compare the behavior of a segment of users exposed to the standard site with another segment that viewed a different version. The advantage of the design is that the changes to the user interface are straightforward and this significantly limits deception.

In these two studies, the OkCupid researchers investigated the effectiveness of pictures and text displayed in their user interface. In a "love blind"–day experiment (January 15, 2013), OkCupid removed pictures from all profiles. Throughout the picture-blackout phase, there was a greater amount of communication among "blind" (no pictures available) users. However, the level of communication dropped dramatically after the pictures were made visible once again. In a related experiment, OkCupid researchers manipulated the user interface to display profile pictures with or without profile text. Furthermore, they replaced the typical personality rating scales and looks with a solitary scale aimed at assessing the user's perceptions of a person's "coolness." Findings from the experiments revealed that "coolness" ratings are derived entirely from the profile picture. Moreover, the profile text was not found to have any significant impact on user ratings.

In a third experiment, OkCupid manipulated the compatibility percentage that was automatically proffered by their matching algorithm to artificially (and without concern for accuracy) recommend people as much better or worse matches than their actual match score (Wood, 2014). In this mismatching experiment, OkCupid manipulated reporting of algorithm results in a concealed way. As such, the researchers deceived the users. Hence, this was not a website design change. Instead, it was misinformation via falsification. This OkCupid mismatching manipulation was termed "the power of suggestion" and it manipulated the reporting of bad matches (30 percent compatibility) as a 90 percent probability of a good match. Misled users initiating more messages and conversations to potential matches that the users believed were more compatible. This led to concern by OkCupid researchers about whether people were only interacting because of the suggestive power of the manipulated (i.e., fabricated) compatibility level instead of actual outcomes from their matching algorithm. To assess whether this was the case, OkCupid researchers assessed further combinations in which they reported compatibility matches at 30, 60, and 90 percent that were either accurate reports or manipulated reported percentages. They found that the odds of an initial message turning into an actual conversation occurred in the 90% condition. Here, the algorithm produced optimal matches. This allowed the researchers to observe accurate compatibility percentage reports.

Were these OkCupid studies ethical? For much of the study, we can say that they had an adequate design. Some users were randomly segmented into a manipulation condition (e.g., picture-blackout and pictures with/ without text); others were put in a control condition (e.g., typical OkCupid interface). This allowed the OkCupid researchers to investigate whether exposure to the manipulated content changed users' behaviors. It can be argued that the OkCupid design was less than satisfactory in that users were not given an opportunity for informed consent. OkCupid manipulated their experience and did not tell them ahead of time or give them an opportunity to opt out of the experiment. Prior to starting an experiment on a user, researchers typically convey explicitly that they will be participating in a study. Moreover, users as participants in the OkCupid experiments should have been told what procedures would be used. This would have allowed the participants (i.e., users) an opportunity to make an informed decision about whether or not they would take part in a study. Also, the users should have been informed of potential risks and benefits for participating. This would have required an informed consent form that the participants could have signed to indicate that they understand all of this information and were open to being part of the study. The OkCupid researchers may argue that they needed to use deception to get meaningful results. However, this argument requires a level of necessity that they did not adequately display. They could have at least told participants that they were going to be doing a series of studies and participants could have consented.

Another issue is that ethical research typically involves debriefing participants after the study about the ways in which they were deceived. It was not really apparent the extent to which (or if they did so at all) OkCupid debriefed the participants in their studies, though there was an atypical debriefing in that the researchers made their procedures and results publicly known. While cyberpsychologists do disseminate findings publicly via peer-reviewed publications, it is not appropriate to assume that the general public actively and exhaustively reads academic journals. Hence, there is a requirement that researchers debrief each participant directly. Part of the problem for research carried out by companies like OkCupid is that researchers at companies are not required to have their research approved by an ethics review board, a committee that reviews and determines the appropriateness of studies. These committees perform "cost/benefit analyses" to determine that the risk to participants is lower than the benefits of the study. Some would argue that the OkCupid studies would have been less controversial had they passed institutional review board approval. While some companies do have their own internal review processes, it is not apparent that these are similar to conservative university review boards. It is not apparent that OkCupid researchers performed a thorough internal review process for ethical considerations. Again, OkCupid, like so many online dating sites, point to the fact that they did not need to gain consent because users signed the terms of use. However, this is a shallow rejoinder that is almost universally disregarded given that most users do not read terms of use fully. Ultimately, the lack of rigorous ethics review has resulted in a great deal of user dissatisfaction and concerns among academic researchers.

11.3.4   Big Data Concerns for Online Dating Sites

Another area of ethical concern for these large dating sites is their public release of data. A group of Danish researchers publicly released a data set made up of almost 70,000 OkCupid users. In addition to usernames, this data set included a host of identifying information about the users: age, gender, location, relationship preferences, personality traits, and user answers to thousands of profiling questions used by the OkCupid site. Hence, this data dump failed to anonymize the user data to protect user privacy. This was shocking to many researchers and questions were raised to Emil O. W. Kirkegaard (the lead on the project) about anonymization. Kirkegaard's response was couched in terms of the fact OkCupid data is (or was) already publicly available.

As we have found many times in this book, those concerned with privacy and research ethics are disquieted by the ever-increasing release of large data sets to the public. An important, and often overlooked, aspect of this practice is that it fails to recognize that, even if a user reads the terms of service, that user may not have had any idea that private data may be released in a manner that was never intended or agreed on. Unfortunately, data science studies and data releases often fail to meet even the most basic requirements of research ethics: privacy, informed consent, confidentiality, and minimizing harm.

11.4   Digital Citizenship: Ethics for the Connected

Thus far, this chapter has discussed digital access and the need for broadening the ethical concerns of the digital divide from the biosphere's biophysical ecosystem to the infosphere's informational ecosystem made up of informational entities. Moreover, there has been a consideration of those attempting to connect via digital technologies and the ethical considerations of the companies that exploit those efforts. In this section, we turn to those already immersed in a digital world. What are the ethical issues found in digital citizenship? In Floridi's work, we see the infosphere and its presentation of new cognitive processes found in learning, trading, and cultural activities. There is growing research into what it means to be a digital citizen in an ever-evolving and connected digital existence (Stevenson, 2003, 2007; Turner, 2001). What is the Internet's role in digital citizenship? A comprehensive answer to this question is beyond the scope of this chapter (let alone a section of a chapter). Instead, this section considers some rather general observations. That said, there is a growing interest in considering the Internet as a form of digital citizenship (Goode, 2010; Livingstone, 2003).

As early as the 1990s, there were already discussions of concerns arising from "virtual communities" and considerations of the ways in which online interactions present new membership modalities that may or may not have had prior offline existences (Rheingold, 1995; Turkle, 2011). As is apparent in the growth of social media, Internet dating, and Internet-based communities, new technologies present new opportunities for social connections and the development of cultural identity. However, the introduction of novel technologies also raises concerns about the equality of access to, and ethical standards within, these virtual communities. For some, the concern is about the impacts of these digital technologies on reflexive engagement compared to more traditional forms of community (Goode, 2010; Mossberger, Tolbert, & McNeal, 2007; Poster, 2001; Slevin, 2000).

It is important to note that the perspective taken in this book is that the Internet and other digital technologies are not just tools. Instead, they are extensions of our cognitive and affective processes. Given that digital technologies are extensions of our digital selves, they are also part of our digital citizenship. This expands the ethical implications of our interactions and activities in the digital world. An important issue that has developed for digital citizenship is how should persons act toward others while online. For many of us, this is an interesting issue as many people act online in a manner that is far different from how they act when they are physically in another's presence. While this can result in cyber revolutionaries, it can also result in some digital concerns such as cyberbullying.

11.4.1   Hacking

When I was younger, hackers were a bunch of friends crowded around a computer in a basement as we tried to gain unauthorized access to another computer or network. For most of us, this never went further than nonmalicious activities. For a few, things went further as they tried to use code for more nefarious activities. Today, many hackers take part in hacktivism, in which social media is used for good. Some have hacked into social media sites to expose corruption, to amplify important information, and even to instigate revolutions against dictators. The murky ethical waters that surround hacktivism make straightforward ethical considerations problematic. By this, I mean that, like many areas in digital ethics, there are arguments both for and against hacktivism. A well-known example is Julian Assange and his work with WikiLeaks that resulted in national security leaks for multiple world powers. While some view the information provided by WikiLeaks to be important for transparency, others point to the risk of harm to persons who are exposed. For hacktivists like Assange, Anonymous, and Aaron Schwartz, there is not an apparent motivation for vengeance. Instead, they point to personal moral motivations for their actions. A shared view is that all information should be available to the general public.

These hackers are not alone as a number of people share their belief in an ethic of transparency. In fact, some view these hacktivists as heroes and laud their ethical commitments. They argue that, we, as citizens, have a right to know what our governments are doing and whether we can trust governmental disclosures. Nevertheless, most governments do not agree with hacktivism and view hackers as criminals who have hacked into (or attempted to hack into) sensitive government information. Moreover, there are questions of privacy. While hacktivists may be hacking into restricted areas in pursuit of justice, there is still the very real issue that they are acting in a way that can be invasive to another's personal privacy.

One way to approach the issue of hacking can be found in the hypothesis of extended cognition (Clark, 2010a, 2010b; Clark & Chalmers, 1998) and technologies of the extended mind (Fitz & Reiner, 2016; Nagel & Reiner, 2018; Reiner & Nagel, 2017). Accordingly, external artifacts such as smartphones can (under appropriate circumstances) be understood as external feedback loops extending a person's cognitive processes (Palermos, 2014). Carter and Palermos (2016), at the University of Edinburgh, contend that, if the hypothesis of extended cognition is correct, then updates are needed to our ethical theorizing and legal praxes. Such updates would include a broadening of our understanding of personal assault so that it includes intentional harm toward digital technologies that one has appropriately integrated. Consider this personal question: How would you feel, and what actions might you take, if someone intentionally destroyed your smartphone phone, stole your smartwatch, or hacked your laptop in a manner that considerably limited your ability to organize and carry out your activities of daily living? Take this a step further and consider a situation where someone hacked into digital technologies that you rely on daily, because of a congenital or acquired disability, and compromised them to the extent that you were unable to maintain your health behaviors, take your medications, or look up and/or keep your appointments, system preferences, and functionalities. Moreover, what if the hack impacted your contacts list, pictures, notes, and so on. Would you consider this as mere damage to your property? Most likely the answer is no because such a disruption feels more like someone has actually assaulted you. Again, while we can recognize this in healthy populations, consider the impacts hacks may have on a person that relies on these technologies to manage a disability.

Carter and Palermos (2016, p. 549) express an argument for extended assault with two premises and a conclusion:

(P1) Intentional harm to a part of a person responsible for the person's mental and other faculties constitutes personal assault. (Definition)

(P2) Our mental faculties can be partly constituted by external artifacts so long as these artifacts have been appropriately integrated into our overall cognitive system. (From HEC [hypothesis of extended cognition])

(C) Therefore, having our integrated epistemic artifacts intentionally compromised plausibly qualifies as a case of personal assault. (From P1 and P2)

For Carter and Palermos, the argument for extended assault is a logical development of the ethical implications found in technologies of the extended mind. In instances of extended personal assault, whenever one's cognitive faculties and processes "rely for their operation on continuous mutual interactions between some of the individual's organismic faculties and some artifact of the individual's" (2016, p. 555), there is sufficient indication that the person's legal and ethical rights have been violated.

11.4.2   Cyberbullying

Another issue that is important for digital citizenship is the way that we treat others. With the rise of the Internet, social media, and online communities, there has been a concomitant rise in cyberbullying. Opportunity for both good and bad acts are apparent in social networking sites (e.g., Facebook, Twitter), online games, email, blogs, and text messaging. Electronic aggression, and/or online harassment, is an intentional act or behavior that is carried out repeatedly and over time against a victim by an individual or group using digital technologies (Hinduja & Patchin, 2008; Smith et al., 2008). Cyberbullying is a real problem with prevalence estimates in the range of 10–40 percent relative to sampling and measurement (Kowalski et al., 2014). Moreover, there is a growing literature on the significant psychological impact that cyberbullying can have on its victims (Kowalski et al., 2012; Slonje & Smith, 2008; Tokunaga, 2010): depression and lowered self-esteem (Schäfer et al., 2004; Ybarra & Mitchell, 2004; Ybarra et al., 2006); delinquency (McCuddy & Esbensen, 2017; Patchin & Hinduja, 2006); and reduced academic performance (Beran & Li, 2008; Kowalski & Limber, 2013).

Moral philosophers have considered the Internet in general (Lievens, 2011; Plaisance, 2013; Vallor, 2010) and cyberbullying specifically (Harrison, 2015, 2016) from deontological, utilitarian, and virtue ethics approaches to normative ethical inquiry. From a deontological perspective, the emphasis is on "duties" or rules that compel Internet users to perform their duties (Granitz & Loewy, 2007; Lievens, 2011; Lyu, 2012). For the deontologist, moral duties are grounded in self-validating reason. Harrison (2016) has pointed out that school policies and personnel frequently implement deontological-based educational strategies for dealing with online moral issues such as cyberbullying. For example, school personnel may use deontologically based strategies through the promotion of e-safety and enforcing rules related to good and bad online conduct. The efficacy of deontological-based approaches is limited by the fact that digital technologies are advancing rapidly and there is an apparent lack of social consensus about what the duties of digital citizens entail.

From a utilitarian perspective, the emphasis is on consequentialism and cost/benefit analyses of potential outcomes from various actions. Utilitarian-based approaches to dealing with cyberbullying are common in school settings (Stauffer et al., 2012) and include cautioning students about the consequences of cyberbullying (Cross et al., 2012). According to Harrison (2014), a frequently employed method is to appeal to students' sensibilities by emphasizing tangibly the consequences of negative online behaviors. A difficulty for utilitarian approaches is that studies have shown that students (especially younger students) tend to "innocently" cyberbully because they do not realize the potential consequences of their online actions (Mark & Ratliffe, 2011).

Other moral philosophers have turned to virtue ethics for considering digital citizenship (Harrison, 2016; Vallor, 2010) and the potential for virtues to counter cyberbullying. Harrison (2014, 2015, 2016) has argued for approaches to cyberbullying that draw on virtue ethics and the delivery of Aristotelian character education. He has proposed the idea of cyber-phronesis to describe the ability to make good and wise online judgments. This involves the development and administration of educational interventions that aim at enhancing online moral imagination through stories and narratives.

11.5 Conclusions

As mentioned at the beginning of the chapter, persons in Western industrialized countries are progressively exhibiting themselves online and communicating with others in disembodied contexts that span time and space. Posting, tweeting, and blogging are popular platforms for communicating thoughts and feelings with varying levels of anonymity. While a younger-aged person in a developed country may find that these technologies result in digital selves with extended cognition, an older-aged person on the other side of the digital divide may experience fewer changes to self and community. The extent to which one is a techno-optimist (emphasizes positive impacts of technological innovation) versus a techno-pessimist (emphasizes negative effects of innovation) determines one's reaction to the availability of advances in technologies (versus the lack thereof) for a given person and community. To some extent, the ethical implications also reflect ontological perspectives about the nature of being.

PART IV

Applied Ethical Considerations

CHAPTER 12

Virtual Reality Ethics

12.1   Introduction

In this chapter, there is an emphasis on describing some of the ethical concerns that may arise from research, clinical applications, and even personal use of virtual reality and related technologies. Throughout, there will be attempts to offer straightforward recommendations for optimal outcomes and minimal risks. It is important to note that much of virtual reality (research, clinical, and personal applications) is in its infancy. As a result, much of the research to date has been comprised of case studies, open clinical trials, and uncontrolled designs. These issues will be discussed in this chapter and recommendations will be made for focused protocols and consistent reporting standards. The chapter aims to consider the ethical considerations found in the literature, as well as the ethical implications for a brain-based cyberpsychology in the digital era.

The chapter begins with a brief overview of virtual reality for use in cyberpsychology. This introduction includes a discussion of models of presence that reflect findings from the human neurosciences. Next is an examination of the risks in virtual reality research, as well as recommendations for conducting virtual reality. This is followed by an exploration of the uses of virtual environment for investigating ethical dilemmas.

12.2   Brief Overview of Virtual Reality

Virtual reality environments are progressively being used by brain-based cyberpsychologists to simulate everyday activities and interactions. Using virtual reality, researchers can develop ecologically valid, interactive, and multimodal sensory stimulus presentations that maintain experimental control. In a review in the journal *Nature Reviews Neuroscience*, Corey Bohil and colleagues (2011) discuss the potential of virtual reality for the neurosciences:

> The use of VR [virtual reality] in neuroscience research offers several unique advantages. First, and perhaps most importantly, VR allows naturalistic interactive behaviours to take place while brain activity is monitored via imaging or direct recording. This allows researchers to directly address many questions in a controlled environment that would simply not be possible by studying performance "in the wild". Second, VR environments allow researchers to manipulate multimodal stimulus inputs, so the user's sensor-imotor illusion of being "present" in the represented environment is max-imized. (p. 753)

For Bohil and colleagues, virtual reality environments have the potential for enhancing our ability to investigate neurocognitive functioning when persons are faced with everyday activities and situations.

12.2.1   Reduced Cost, Smaller, and Easier-To-Use Equipment

Advances in virtual reality technologies have increased the feasibility and affordability of using simulations in both laboratory research and personal use. Reduced cost, smaller, and easier-to-use equipment is making virtual reality systems increasingly affordable as more and more vendors compete for economic control (Bohil et al., 2011; Parsons & Phillips, 2016; Slater, 2018). Examples of current off-the-shelf virtual reality platforms that use head-mounted (HMDs) displays include the Oculus Rift, HTC VIVE, Google's Daydream View, and Samsung's Gear VR (Parsons, McMahan, & Kane, 2018). While higher-end off-the-shelf units such as Oculus Rift (approximately $400) and HTC VIVE (approximately $500) require computers (approximately $1,500) with at least Nvidia GeForce GTX 970 graphics cards performance (see Table 12.1), there are other HMDs that allow for the three-dimensional presentations using commer-cially available smartphones (approximately $750) such as Google's Daydream with controller (approximately $100) and Samsung's Gear VR (approximately $130).

12.2.2   Models of Immersion and Presence

Given the increased availability of virtual reality platforms, researchers are increasingly able to develop models of virtual reality–based experiences. In the past few decades, a number of cyberpsychologists have investigated the optimal immersion of human sensorimotor channels into simulation environments (Riva et al., 2015). Virtual reality–based experiences allow researchers to immerse participants in simulations that produce a sense or

Table 12.1 *Current popular virtual reality system specifications and hardware requirements (from Parsons, McMahan, & Kane, 2018; reprinted with permission from the publisher)*

System	Hardware	Graphics Card	Operating System	Sensors	Tracking	User Interaction	Resolution	Refresh Rate	Field of View	Connection	Lag
Google Daydream	Google Pixel, Huawei Mate 9 Pro, ZTE Axon 7, Motorola Moto Z	Phone Dependent	Android	Gyroscope, accelerometer, proximity sensor	Head tracking	Controller, Gamepad	Phone Dependent	90 Hz	96 degrees	Wireless	~10 ms
HTC VIVE	Intel i5-4590/ AMD FX 8350, 4GB of RAM	NVIDIA GeForce GTX 970/ AMD Radeon R9 290	Windows 7 or newer	Accelerometer, gyroscope, laser position sensor	Head tracking, room tracking	Controllers	2160 × 1200	90 Hz	110 degrees	Wired	~11 ms
Oculus Rift	Intel i3-6100/ AMD FX 4350, 8GB RAM	NVIDIA GeForce GTX 970/ AMD Radeon R9 290	Windows 7 or newer	Gyroscope, accelerometer, optical sensor	Head tracking, room tracking	Controller, Gamepad	2160 × 1200	90 Hz	110 degrees	Wired	~13 ms
Samsung Gear VR	Samsung phones: Galaxy S8, S8+, Galaxy S7, S7 Edge, S6 Edge +, S6, Galaxy S6 Edge, Note 5	Phone Dependent	Android	Gyroscope, accelerometer, proximity sensor	Head tracking	Gear Controller, Gamepad, Navigation pad	2560 × 1440	60 Hz	101 degrees	Wireless	~20 ms

presence (e.g., "being there"; Waterworth & Riva, 2014). The definition of presence was introduced by Sheridan (1992), who described it as "the effect felt when controlling real world objects remotely" (pp. 123–124). Moreover, cyberpsychologists have described presence in terms of a phenomenological sense of the world and the user's immersion within the environment (Botella et al., 2009; Schubert, Friedmann, & Regenbrecht, 2001).

While some early models promoted a subjective approach that used self-report questionnaires to assess a user's subjective experience of presence and immersion (Witmer & Singer, 1998), others argued that immersion is best understood as an objective psychophysiological property of a system (Slater & Wilbur, 1997). For Mel Slater (2009, 2018), at University College London, higher or lower levels of immersion can be understood as the extent to which a virtual reality system can engender and sustain natural sensorimotor contingencies for perception. Moreover, Slater and colleagues have promoted psychophysiological metrics (over self-reports) as objective measures of presence that do not rely on questionnaires (Slater & Sanchez-Vives, 2016; Slater, Spanlang, & Corominas, 2010).

In addition to debates between subjective self-reports and quantitative psychophysiological approaches, others have focused on developing stimulus–organism–response frameworks that can be used to investigate the impacts of virtual reality stimuli on user states and behaviors. Suh and Prophet (2018) developed a stimulus–organism–response framework (see Figure 12.1) to enhance understanding of the relations among dynamic stimulus presentations from virtual environments (stimuli); neurocognitive and affective profiles of the user (organism); and the impact of using immersive technologies (responses; see Figure 12.1).

12.2.3 Neural Correlates of Immersion and Presence Using Virtual Environments

While these approaches to "presence" have been used to describe a broadly described sensation experienced when immersed in virtual environments, they have been criticized for failing to question why we experience presence and whether it is a specific cognitive process. Critics contend that presence is better understood to be a neuropsychological construct that is not necessarily connected to the experience of a modality (e.g., virtual reality). Instead, the neuropsychological construct of presence may be better viewed as a cognitive control process.

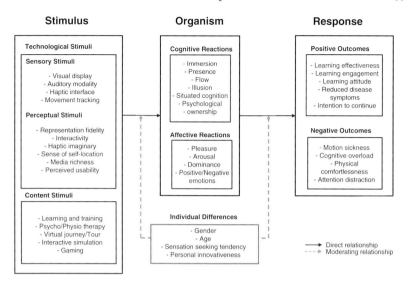

Figure 12.1 Conceptual framework for virtual reality (from Suh & Prophet, 2018; reprinted with permission from the publisher)

12.2.3.1 *Interoceptive Predictive Coding Model*

Anil Seth and colleagues (Seth, Suzuki, & Critchley, 2012), at the University of Sussex's Sackler Centre for Consciousness Science, have developed an interoceptive predictive coding model of presence. In this dual-process model, presence results from the executive inhibition (i.e., controlled cognitive processes) of predictions about interoceptive (affective) signals that were aroused by automatic (e.g., autonomic and bodily) responses to afferent sensory signals. In the interoceptive predictive coding model of conscious presence developed by Seth and colleagues (2012), a large-scale brain network has been suggested for presence. Suggested brain areas contributing to interoceptive predictive coding include cortical (orbitofrontal cortex, insular cortex, and anterior cingulate cortex); subcortical (substantia innominata, nucleus accumbens, amygdala); and brainstem (nucleus of the solitary tract, periaqueductal gray, locus coeruleus) regions. Among these areas, the insular cortex and anterior cingulate cortex are believed to have great import for the experience of presence. The insular cortex is posited as essential to the integration of interoceptive and exteroceptive signals, as well as the formation of subjective feeling states. Furthermore, the anterior cingulate acts as a visceromotor cortex from which autonomic control signals originate. The anterior insula and the

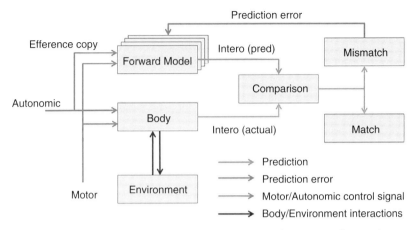

Figure 12.2 Predictive coding applied to interoception for presence (from Seth, Suzuki, & Critchley, 2012; reprinted with permission from the publisher)

anterior cingulate are often coactivated (despite spatial separation) and form a large-scale brain network called the "salience network."

Within this theoretical neural network model, presence is understood as an everyday phenomenon. According to Seth and colleagues' (2012) interoceptive predictive coding model, presence results from the effective inhibition by executive control predictions of informative interoceptive signals evoked by automatic (e.g., autonomic and bodily) responses to afferent sensory signals. In everyday life, presence rests on the continuous executive control prediction of interoceptive (affective) states. When an individual expects a negative encounter (e.g., with a person, place, or object), they make predictions about both their negative affective responses (e.g., fear, anxiety, frustration) and the biological change they will experience (e.g., autonomic responses such as cardiovascular reactivity). When encountering the negative stimulus, the individual compares the predicted state with the actual interoceptive state that they experienced. Seth and colleagues point out that, most of the time, there will be a certain degree of mismatch between the predicted and the actual interoceptive state. For them, presence results from the successful suppression of this mismatch (see Figure 12.2).

12.2.3.2   *Forward-Inverse Model of Presence*
Guiseppe Riva (see Parsons, Gaggioli, & Riva, 2017) has argued for a model of presence that comports well with Seth's dual-process approach. For Riva, the feeling (automatic processes) of presence provides (to the controlled

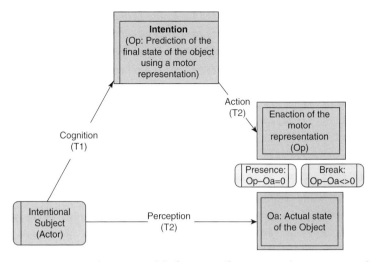

Figure 12.3 Forward-inverse model of presence (from Riva et al., 2015; reprinted with permission from the publisher)

processes) feedback about the status of activities. He first describes various intentions in a virtual environment: (1) distal intentions (D-intentions are controlled brain processes that are future-directed); (2) proximal intentions (P-intentions are controlled brain processes for present-directed intentions); and (3) motor intentions (M-intentions are automatic [unconscious] brain processes that guide and monitor). Next, he contends that the user perceives changes in feelings of presence and the user's activities are modified accordingly. According to this forward-inverse model (see Figure 12.3), presence is achieved as follows:

1) Given the current states of the system and environment, the agent produces a motor command to achieve a desired state
2) An efference copy of the motor command is fed forward and generates a prediction of the consequences of performing this motor command
3) The predicted state is compared with the actual sensory feedback. Variance (error) between the desired and actual states update the model and improve performance.

To develop and validate presence as a neuropsychological construct, there is need for neuroimaging studies to establish the neural correlates of presence and immersion. As early as 2005, Sanchez-Vives and Slater (2005) called for the collective use of neuroimaging and virtual environments for direct manipulation of presence. An increasing number of studies over the years have answered that call: Baumgartner and colleagues (2008) found a distributed network of brain regions related to reported presence while participants experienced a virtual reality rollercoaster; Aardema and colleagues (2010) found that immersion in virtual environments modulates the neural mechanisms underpinning presence; and neuroimaging studies using virtual environment have found relations between presence and agency (Gutierrez-Martinez, Gutierrez-Maldonado, & Loreto-Quijada, 2011; Lallart, Lallart, & Jouvent, 2009).

12.2.4   Social Presence

In addition to neuroimaging studies, findings from clinical, affective, and social neurosciences are increasingly informing a brain-based approach to cyberpsychology research (Parsons, 2015a, 2017; Parsons, Gaggioli, & Riva, 2017). This is important because some virtual reality experiences also involve social presence. Short, Williams, and Christie (1976) originally formulated the concept of social presence to describe the degree of salience between two communicators using a communication medium. Social presence has been applied to virtual environments to represent the construct used to understand how users perceive the presence of another as social entities (living or synthetic) in a virtual environment (Parsons, Gaggioli, & Riva, 2017).

Giuseppe Riva and colleagues (see Riva & Mantovani, 2012, 2014; Riva et al., 2015) have developed a model of social presence that includes three different layers/subprocesses that are phylogenetically different but mutually inclusive:

- Other's Presence (Other vs. the Self – M-intentions);
- Interactive Presence (Other toward the Self – P-intentions);
- Shared Presence (Other is like the Self – D-intentions).

These three levels of social presence are associated with concurrent impacts on the user's capacity for social interaction. According to Waterworth and Riva (2014),

> if this shift offers a valuable opportunity, the subject can act to increase his level of social presence. For example, if a girl starts staring at me at a party, I immediately become aware of the shift from other's presence (the girl is at the same party as me) to interactive presence (the girl is looking at me). If the girl is interesting, I can approach her and talk to her in order to understand her intentions. Is she looking at me because she likes me or because I have a stain on my jacket? (p. 112)

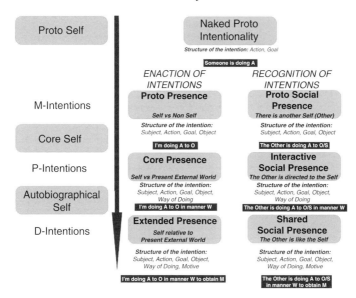

Figure 12.4 Riva's model of social presence: the evolution of self, presence, and social presence (from Riva et al., 2015; reprinted with permission from the publisher)

The experience of this varies relative to the level of social presence experienced by the user. While the role of social presence in determining the characteristics of the user's actions is automatic and preconscious, the user consciously perceives the shift from one level of social presence to another in social interactions (see Figure 12.4).

12.3   Virtual Reality as a Technology of the Extended Mind

Virtual reality can be a technology of the extended mind. As discussed in Chapter 3, this would involve the addition of algorithmic computational processing in adaptive virtual environments. While only a few virtual environments available today are truly adaptive, there is a growing interest in approaches to adaptive virtual environments for neuropsychological assessment and training (Parsons & Courtney, 2011; Parsons & Reinebold, 2012; Wu et al., 2010), learning technologies (Lin & Parsons, 2018; Moghim et al., 2015), and even neurogaming (McMahan, Parberry, & Parsons, 2015; Parsons, McMahan, & Parberry, in press). Adaptive virtual environments with learning algorithms comport well with the extended mind hypothesis (see Chapter 3 of this book) because these algorithms consist of the rules, strategies, and procedures that a person

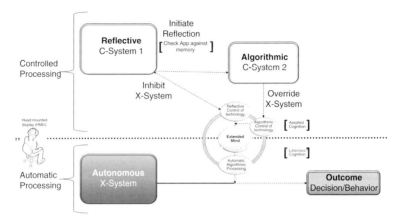

Figure 12.5 Framework for understanding technologies of the extended mind

can retrieve from memory to aid problem-solving, which allows for additional contributions (in addition to the brain) to conceptions of mental processing.

In Figure 12.5, there is a framework for understanding virtual reality technologies of the extended mind. What type of virtual environments can be considered technologies of the extended mind? Not every virtual environment has sophisticated algorithmic function for (external to the brain) extended minds. Instead, it is preferable to conceptualize technologies of the extended mind as a fairly continuous interface between brain and algorithm, in which the person immersed in the virtual environment perceives the algorithm adapting the experience as being an actual extension of her or his mind.

As can be seen in Figure 12.5, the virtual environment adapts algorithmically using the immersed user's automatic algorithmic processes from the virtual environment to the autonomous (automatic), reflective, and algorithmic processing of the tripartite model (see Chapter 3 in this book). For the virtual environment to be a technology of the extended mind, the adaptive algorithms must be learning algorithms that become automated and algorithmic couplings of the brain and virtual reality platforms. When the user is first immersed into the virtual environment, there is a period during which the user relies on controlled cognitive processes to inhibit and override automatic processes initiated by the virtual environment (see reflective and algorithmic control of technology in Figure 12.5). After using the virtual environment for a period of time, the adaptive operations become overlearned and more or less automatic.

We can extend the idea of a driver using GPS as a technology of the extended mind found in Chapter 3 of this book to an updated scenario in which Valerie takes a virtual trip to a virtual reality simulation of a museum. In this updated scenario, Valerie is immersed in the virtual museum and is informed that she can navigate the virtual museum to various virtual exhibits where virtual human docents can tell her more about the art. If she is having difficulty finding an exhibit, the adaptive system can superimpose arrows on the floor, directing her to her desired destination. Valerie remains alert (see controlled/reflective processing in Figure 12.5) to her environment and that she needs to use her controllers to move herself around in the virtual museum environment. Given the newness of the controls, she is very much aware of the head-mounted display, which causes regular breaks in presence.

After some time, Valerie begins to acclimate herself to the hardware and can easily navigate without consciously thinking of every move (automatic processing and presence). Moreover, the learning algorithms in the adaptive environment are learning from her and adjusting refresh rates, as well as adapting the presentation of stimuli to personalize Valerie's experience. At times, she catches herself and reminds herself that she is in a simulation (see inhibition and override of technology with breaks in presence using reflective and algorithmic control of technology in Figure 12.5). Is Valerie's experience of the virtual environment the same as experiencing a technology of the extended mind? While the adaptive virtual environment and its learning algorithms are undoubtedly performing computations that are external to Valerie's brain, the breaks in presence suggest more cognitive assistance than being fully immersion and present in another reality. Why is this the case? The answer is that neither the algorithmic calculations from the virtual environment platform nor Valerie's use of them are automated with Valerie's cognitive processes (see algorithmic control of technology in Figure 12.5). Now consider a different scenario in which Valerie has experienced a number of virtual exhibits over the course of the past month. Even though she now has slightly more knowledge of the virtual museum, it is immense (an open virtual world) and she tends to rely more and more on guidance from the virtual environment as it predicts, classifies, and adapts her experience. In fact, the learning algorithms at this point actually automate procedural content generation relative to Valerie's interests. At this point, when the system suggests a new virtual exhibit to her, she automatically follows the arrows to the virtual destination suggested by her virtual environment and readily receives information about the art. The adaptive virtual environment is beginning to function as a technology of the extended mind because Valerie has integrated its algorithmic processes into the working of her mind.

12.4   Risks and Recommendations for Virtual Reality in Controlled Settings

What are the potential ethical implications of Valerie using an adaptive virtual environment that personalizes her experiences based on its learning algorithms? How does this relate to the increasing evidence for neural correlates of a user's experience of presence while immersed in virtual environments? What are the ethical implications? It is important to note that the virtual reality ethics literature includes several general approaches to ethical guidelines (Behr et al., 2005; Spiegel, 2017), legal codes (Mitrović, 2017), and ethical codes of conduct (Kuntze et al., 2002; Madary & Metzinger, 2016). Moreover, there are focused discussions of ethical issues related to privacy (Adams et al., 2018; Heimo et al., 2014; O'Brolcháin, 2016), clinical virtual reality (Rizzo, Schultheis, & Rothbaum, 2002; Vines et al., 2016; Whalley, 1995; Yellowlees, Holloway, & Parish, 2012), virtual reality games (Kade, 2015), virtual human avatars (Ewell et al., 2016), representation (Brey, 1999), and cyber-learning (Cheshire, 2010; Ruggeroni, 2001; Parsons, Lin, & Cockerham, 2019; Southgate, Smith, & Scevak, 2017). In the following, attempts are made to extend these ethics considerations in light of advances in adaptive virtual environments using learning algorithms for the personalization of content for enhanced presence.

12.4.1   Adverse Side Effects

The ethical use of virtual reality involves the limitation of potential adverse side effects. This is important because side effects can limit the applicability of virtual environments for certain cohorts (e.g., clinical populations, older-age participants). There are two common types of side effects associated with virtual reality: cybersickness and the aftereffects depersonalization and derealization.

12.4.1.1   Cybersickness

Cybersickness (also known as simulator sickness) is a subtype of motion sickness that can result when persons are immersed in virtual reality. Cybersickness is an unpleasant side effect of virtual reality that can be described as a group of symptoms such as motion sickness, fatigue, headache, eye strain, and/or nausea (Davis, Nesbitt, & Nalivaiko, 2014, 2015). These symptoms can occur alone or together during and/or after exposure to a virtual environment (Cobb et al., 1999; Kennedy, Berbaum, & Drexler, 1994). The neural correlates of motion sickness in general, as well as visually induced cybersickness specifically, are unknown currently. Various theories have hypothesized diverse factors that may account for cybersickness. Table 12.2 presents some notable proposals aimed at explaining cybersickness: sensory mismatch, postural instability, rest frame, and poison.

It is important to note that sensory mismatch and postural instability are often pointed to as potential causes. Perhaps the most common theoretical explanation can be found in Reason and Brand's (1975), as well as Reason's (1978), "sensory conflict" theory, in which motion sickness is argued to arise in situations where "the motion signals transmitted by the eyes, the vestibular system and the nonvestibular proprioceptors are at variance one with another, and hence with what is expected on the basis of previous transactions with the spatial environment" (p. 820). Building on Reason and Brand's work, Bos, Bles, and Groen (2008) put forth a "vertical mismatch" theory to provide an advanced framework for describing and predicting visually induced motion sickness. One hope is that future possible virtual environments with adaptive algorithms will be able to reduce cybersickness via learning algorithms that adapt the simulations in real time relative to the user's experience.

Table 12.2 *Cybersickness theories (from Rebenitsch & Owen, 2016; reprinted with permission from the publisher)*

	Posits	Most Related Virtual Aspects
Sensory mismatch	If the stimuli from the outside environment are being perceived differently by different senses, symptoms will occur	Tracking, vection, and navigation
Postural instability	If a person is unable to maintain the posture necessary given the stimuli from the outside environment, symptoms will occur	Orientation cues and position during immersion
Rest frame	If the direction a person perceives as up is different from the up due to gravity, symptoms will occur	Habituation and orientation cues
Poison	If an incorrectly perceived environment could have been due to the effect of poison in the past, symptoms will occur	Realism, tracking, and navigation

12.4.1.2   Depersonalization and Derealization

Frederick Aardema and colleagues (2010) have argued that the effects of virtual reality are similar to symptoms found in dissociative disorders (depersonalization and derealization). For example, virtual reality may result in feelings of detachment from one's sense of self (depersonalization) and one's environment. Aardema and colleagues (2010) argue that the effects of virtual reality may impact the agency and responsibility needed for a moral life. While there is not much evidence that virtual reality can cause such effects in most users, some have pointed to the negative effects of problematic video gaming (Gentile et al., 2011) as suggesting the potential pitfalls of virtual reality use (Spiegel, 2017). Moreover, when one considers the potential of adaptive virtual environments for personalizing experiences that enhance presence, it may become increasingly difficult to stay present in the real world.

12.4.2   Social Exclusion

Social exclusion and ostracism may result from interactions with virtual characters. Take, for example, the virtual game *Cyberball*, which consistently elicits feelings of social exclusion at various levels: affective (Wesselmann et al., 2012; Williams, 2007), neurobiological (Eisenberger, 2012), psychophysiological (Moor, Crone, & Van der Molen, 2010; Sijtsema, Shoulberg, & Murray-Close, 2011), and hormonal (Geniole, Carré, & McCormick, 2011; Zwolinski, 2012). Throughout the *Cyberball* task, the participant is represented by an avatar that is playing catch with two other avatars. The two other avatars ostensibly represent two other human participants. Participants are either included or ostracized during the *Cyberball* tossing game by two or three other players who are, in fact, controlled by an experimenter. The virtual *Cyberball* game starts with each avatar catching and throwing a ball (each about a third of the time). During the "inclusion" condition, the participant continues to catch and throw the ball about a third of the time. However, during the "exclusion" condition, the other two avatars throw the ball back and forth and ignore (neither avatar looks at or throws the ball to) the participant.

It is interesting to note that telling participants that the avatars in the *Cyberball* game are controlled by a computer does not change the effects of ostracism. In fact, the ostracism delivered by computers was judged by participants to be just as unpleasant as ostracism by humans. Further, it did not matter to participants whether the human-controlled or computer-controlled players had a choice as to whom they threw the ball (Zadro, Williams, & Richardson, 2004).

Findings from neuroimaging studies have revealed that social exclusion activates a ventral affective salience network that involves a number of interconnected brain hub areas, including the medial prefrontal cortex, anterior cingulate cortex, amygdala, and anterior insula. Furthermore, being excluded during a *Cyberball* game has been found to be associated with ventrolateral areas of the prefrontal cortex involved in the regulation of social distress (Eisenberger, 2013). Neuroimaging studies have also found that the experience of being excluded from ball-tossing reliably evokes increased activation of the dorsal anterior cingulate and anterior insula, which correlates with self-reports of physical pain (Eisenberger, 2012). Moreover, during *Cyberball*-based social exclusion, nociceptive stimuli and social rejection both reveal commonalities (Cacioppo et al., 2013; Eisenberger, 2015; Rotge et al., 2014).

As virtual environments increase in graphics quality, fidelity, and adaptive abilities there may also be an increase in feelings of social rejection. This may be especially apparent in sensitive populations (Parsons, Gaggioli, & Riva, 2017; Venturini et al., 2016; Venturini & Parsons, in press). An immersive virtual environment version of *Cyberball* places the participant into a virtual environment with interactive virtual humans (Kassner et al., 2012). Results revealed that the more immersive virtual environments induced feelings of ostracism in participants. In addition to prompting feelings of ostracism that are consistent with negative effects found in minimalist environments, the immersive virtual environment effect sizes were medium to large in magnitude.

In addition to these robust effects, the immersive virtual environment of the *Cyberball* paradigm offers researchers the ability to control aspects (proxemics and nonverbal communication) of the social context that cannot be accomplished in minimalist ostracism paradigms. The inclusion of immersive virtual environments in *Cyberball* paradigms may allow for enhanced flexibility in the manipulation of social information about the confederate's avatars, virtual humans, and/or their behaviors (Wirth et al., 2010). Further, the inclusion of virtual humans enhances the *Cyberball* paradigm because it allows for additional social information such as nonverbal (e.g., eye-gaze) information that has been found to convey ostracism (Wirth et al., 2010).

12.4.3 Beneficence, Nonmaleficence, and Autonomy in Virtual Environments

Given the potential of virtual environments to induce cybersickness, there is an important ethical consideration related to the principles of beneficence and nonmaleficence (Behr et al., 2005; Singer & Vinson, 2002). As discussed in Chapter 2, beneficence (*salus aegroti suprema lex* [patient safety is the supreme

law]) calls for optimizing benefits of virtual environments while nonmaleficence (*primum nil nocere* [first, do no harm]) dictates that harms and risks be
curtailed for the users of these platforms. Cybersickness is a potential harm.
Efforts to increase beneficence require the minimization of cybersickness.

Another concern about virtual reality involves the tension between beneficence and autonomy in applied ethics (Beauchamp & Childress, 2013). As
discussed, virtual reality can impact the brain and manipulate psychological
experiences. As a result, virtual reality can be applied to benefit patients
through positive behavioral and psychological manipulations. In fact, there is
now a good deal of research suggesting that virtual reality exposure has promise
for treating social phobias (Opris et al., 2012; Parsons, 2015b; Parsons et al.,
2008; Powers & Emmelkamp, 2008); pain (Parsons & Trost, 2014; Pourmand
et al., 2018; Trost & Parsons, 2014); and cognitive disorders (Aida, Chau, &
Dunn, 2018; Dahdah et al., 2017a, 2017b; Parsons et al., 2009; Salisbury et al.,
2016; Tieri et al., 2018). When patients are immersed in a virtual environment,
they can be systematically exposed to specific affect-inducing stimuli within
a contextually relevant setting (Courtney et al., 2009; Parsons et al., 2009).
Virtual reality exposure therapy comports well with the emotion-processing
model, which holds that the fear network must be activated through con-
frontation with threatening stimuli and that new, incompatible information
must be added into the emotional network. It is important to note, though,
that there may be situations in which patients do wish to experience the
benefits of psychological manipulations. In such situations, it is permissible
that virtual reality exposure may violate the person's autonomy.

12.5   Therapeutic Misconceptions

A concern for cyberpsychologists using virtual reality for research and
applied applications is that participants may develop therapeutic misconceptions about what virtual reality interventions can actually offer
(Appelbaum & Lidz, 2008; Dunn et al., 2006; Henderson et al., 2007).
For example, a veteran struggling with combat stress symptoms may
believe that treatment using virtual reality is better than traditional interventions merely because of the novelty of virtual reality exposure therapy.
However, these expectations may be misguided. A randomized clinical trial
was completed to evaluate the efficacy of virtual reality exposure therapy
through comparison to prolonged exposure therapy (i.e., traditional talk
therapy) for the treatment of posttraumatic stress disorder in active duty
soldiers with combat-related trauma (Reger et al., 2016). Results revealed
that virtual reality exposure was actually inferior to talk therapy using

prolonged exposure. In fact, prolonged exposure-based talk therapy was found to be significantly better at reducing symptoms than virtual reality exposure at three- and six-month follow-up. Given the potential for therapeutic misconceptions, researchers and clinicians using virtual reality should be cognizant of established techniques for countering therapeutic misconception in their participants.

12.6   Virtual Reality–Based Neuropsychological Assessment

An interesting flipside to ethical considerations of virtual environments in clinical settings is virtual reality–based neuropsychological assessment devices (Parsons, 2016; Parsons & Kane, 2017; Parsons, McMahan, & Kane, 2018). These virtual environments have heightened computational abilities for the efficient administration of assessments and treatments: stimulus presentation, automated response logging, and data analytic processing. This enhanced computation capability results in improved ability for producing perceptual environments that systematically present and record neurobehavioral responses to dynamic stimuli. This is important because past stimulus presentations have been limited to static stimuli with little (more often no) adaptive interaction. Developments in virtual reality technologies proffer advanced platforms in which three-dimensional stimuli are presented in a dynamic, consistent, and precise manner. Moreover, the virtual environment provides the cyberpsychologist with an ecologically valid platform for presenting dynamic stimuli that simulate real-life situations (Jovanovski et al., 2012a, 2012b; Parsons, 2015a). In sum, virtual environments can balance naturalistic observation with the need for exacting control over key variables (Parsons, 2015a, 2016, 2017). The primary ethical concern for these virtual environments surrounds the use of head-mounted displays. Given that some participants (especially older-aged participants) may have sensitivities to adverse effects (e.g., cybersickness) from using head-mounted displays, it may be better to present simulations via desktop platforms.

12.7   Informed Consent

Over the past couple of decades, various codes of ethics and ethical guidelines have been written and disseminated. Moreover, professional societies have developed specialty-oriented guidelines and policies to safeguard research participants and ensure the appropriate conduct of studies. For the cyberpsychologist, the predominant communication has been that ethical research affords protections against research-related harm, violations to autonomy, and risks of the participant. Furthermore, cyberpsychologists must obtain informed consent from participants (research settings) and clients (in clinical settings) using language the participants/clients can understand, and consenting is to be performed as soon as possible (American Psychological Association, 2010). The American Psychological Association's ethics code designates informed consent, in part, as follows:

> Informed Consent, psychologists inform participants about (1) the purpose of the research, expected duration and procedures; (2) their right to decline to participate and to withdraw from the research once participation has begun; (3) the foreseeable consequences of declining or withdrawing; (4) reasonably foreseeable factors that may be expected to influence their willingness to participate such as potential risks, discomfort or adverse effects; (5) any prospective research benefits; (6) limits of confidentiality; (7) incentives for participation; and (8) whom to contact for questions about the research and research participants' rights. They provide opportunity for the prospective participants to ask questions and receive answers. (n.p.)

For example, informed consent is a vital component in virtual reality exposure therapy. The consenting process ensures that, prior to exposure, the participant understands the purpose of the virtual reality protocol, procedures used, and the duration of the virtual reality exposure therapy. Moreover, clients must be informed of their right to decline to participate and/or withdraw from the virtual reality exposure and what the foreseeable consequences might be for declining or withdrawing. Furthermore, informed consent comports well with what Dattillio and Hanna (2012) refer to as collaborative empiricism, or the process of the therapist and client working together to establish common goals and any prospective research benefits. The thorough discussions found in the consenting process allow for increased treatment effectiveness, improved cooperation, enhanced trust, and opportunities for participants to guide the next steps in treatment.

12.8   Virtual Reality with Vulnerable Populations

This is a good place to point out that vulnerable populations (children and older adults) call for unique ethical considerations regarding informed consent. According to the American Psychological Association's Code of Ethics, persons who are legally incapable of giving informed consent (e.g., children, older adults) should still be asked to give their assent (American Psychological Association, 2010). It may be particularly difficult for persons from such vulnerable populations (e.g., children, older adults) to completely grasp what exposure therapy entails and the rationale for treatment. Jennifer Gola and colleagues (2016), at the Center for Emotional Health in Philadelphia, discuss the ethical considerations for exposure therapy in children. As they point out, even though there is a good deal of research supporting the efficacy, safety, tolerability, and minimal risk of exposure therapy for childhood anxiety disorders (including obsessive compulsive disorders), there are unique ethical considerations in exposure therapy with children. They provide ethical parameters around exposure therapy for youth (see Table 12.3).

Table 12.3 *Ethical issues for virtual reality exposure therapy with children (from Gola et al., 2016; reprinted with permission from the publisher)*

Ethical Standards	Potential Challenges	Recommendations
Informed consent and assent	• Exposure therapy may be viewed as harmful, unsafe, or ineffective. • Children may not fully understand treatment and rationale. • Children may be unwilling to engage in exposure therapy.	• Provide comprehensive information about treatment research, benefits and "side effects," and rationale, describe parents' role. • Describe specific steps in treatment and rationale in age-appropriate terms. Use child-friendly and personable analogies. • Empathize with difficulty of exposures. Frame the exposures as hypotheses or suggest a "trial run." Emphasize treatment is at the client's pace. Use motivational interviewing strategies, values work, or work with parents in reducing accommodations.
Competence	• Not challenging the client enough. • Not thinking through the logistics or potential pitfalls. • Conducting too challenging of an exposure too early on. • A therapist may not be able to be emotionally tolerant to the client's anxiety or may share the same fear as the client.	• Examine one's own beliefs about exposure and what it means for a client to be anxious. • Discuss in supervision. • Think through the potential obstacles and pitfalls before conducting an exposure and discuss with the client or family. • Create anchors for subjective units of distress (SUDS). Take a calm and accepting approach when an exposure was not successful. Take ownership when not successful. • Determine whether you possess the emotional tolerance to do this work. Keep in mind the value of exposure and rationale. Use supervision to discuss discomfort. Conduct exposures to fear.

Table 12.3 (cont.)

Ethical Standards	Potential Challenges	Recommendations
Beneficence and nonmaleficence	Minimize risk of exposure therapy and maximize the benefit.	• Collaboratively create exposures, choose the next exposure, and agree on the specifics of exposure. • Think through potential obstacles. • Help the client understand that there are no guarantees. • Anticipate that exposures may not go as planned; emphasize the goal of being able to tolerate anxiety. • First exposure should be challenging but feasible. • Modify exposures that were unsuccessful. • Create "above and beyond" top of the hierarchy exposures that fully target core fear but are not truly harmful or unsafe. • Consult with colleagues, poll others, consult with other professionals, discuss with family to determine appropriateness of exposure.
Confidentiality	Out-of-office exposures increase the risk of confidentiality breaches.	• Discuss concerns with client and family before engaging in exposure. • Remind clients that they have a right to refuse out-of-office exposures. • Take steps to deidentify self, such as removing badges, coats, and ties; avoid visibly recording SUDS. • Develop a cover story. • Conduct the exposure in another neighborhood or at a time when there is less chance of people being around.
Boundaries	Boundaries may be more easily blurred when conducting exposure therapy.	• Remember that casual conversations and settings outside of the office may be necessary or appropriate in an exposure. • Address this issue during consent. • Gain approval from parents for all steps in the exposure. • Consider a cost/benefit analysis when a boundary is informed crossed. • Take a neutral stance when asked personal questions by children.

While Gola and colleagues developed the considerations set out in Table 12.3 for general exposure therapy, the material is also relevant for virtual reality exposure therapy with special populations.

In review, during the consenting process, it is important that the cyberpsychologist proffer straightforward and accurate information on what the study (and/or treatment) entails, the potential benefits and side effects of virtual reality exposure therapy, and alternative treatment options. Participants should be informed that, as in any in vivo exposure therapy, although they will likely experience increased anxiety during the treatment, addressing anxiety-invoking scenarios can enhance their capacity for tolerating anxiety. Moreover, as the therapy progresses, the participant will eventually have greater control over anxiety and phobias.

12.9   Virtual Environments for Investigating Ethical Dilemmas

Another area for ethics and virtual reality can be found in moral judgments and decision-making using simulations of moral dilemmas. Studies using virtual reality scenarios have shown that participants immersed in virtual reality–based moral scenarios experience significant changes in subjective experience, behavior, and physiological responses. For example, Mel Slater and colleagues (2006) developed a virtual reality–based replication of Milgram's 1963 obedience experiment. Slater and colleagues followed the methodology of the original experiments and had participants administer a series of word-association memory tests to the virtual human that represented an unknown female. The participants were instructed to administer her with an "electric shock" when she answered incorrectly. Further, participants were instructed to continually increase the voltage each time. Each time, the virtual human reacted with cumulative discomfort and protests. She eventually demanded that the experiment be terminated. Their results revealed that the participants who saw and heard the virtual human female tended to respond to the situation at the subjective, behavioral, and physiological levels as if the virtual human and experiment were real (see Figure 12.6).

Another example is virtual reality simulations of the classic Trolley and Footbridge Dilemmas (see Chapter 2 of this book) that have been developed and evaluated (Navarrete et al., 2012; Patil et al., 2014; Skulmowski et al., 2014). In these dilemmas, participants are immersed in a virtual environment, in which a runaway trolley is heading for five immobile

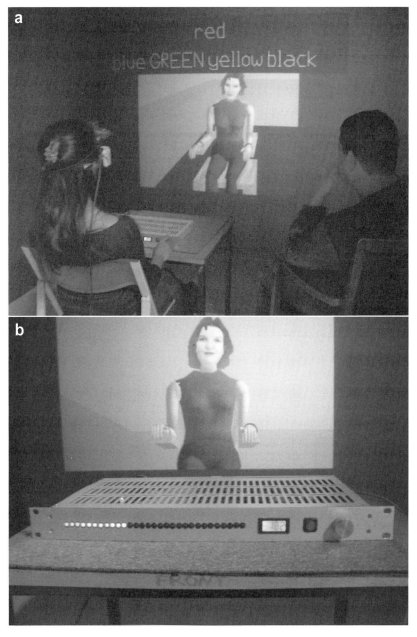

Figure 12.6 Virtual Milgram obedience study (from Slater et al., 2006; reprinted
with permission from the publisher)

people on its tracks. If the trolley is allowed to continue unmoved from its course, it will kill the five virtual humans. In the virtual Footbridge Dilemma, the participant is standing next to a very large stranger on a footbridge spanning the tracks through which the trolley will travel, and the participant's only option for saving the five defenseless virtual humans is to heave the large stranger off the footbridge. While this will kill the large person, it also has the value of blocking the trolley from killing the five helpless persons. Participants immersed in these virtual scenarios often find it difficult to decide that one answer (kill the large person to save the other five persons) is preferable to the other (save the large person but let the other five die).

A dual-process theory has been proposed to describe the processes involved in resolving these moral dilemmas. According to the dual-process perspective, both controlled cognitive responses and automatic affective responses perform essential roles in moral decision-making (see also Greene et al., 2004, 2008):

1) Automatic processes (hot affective) drive nonutilitarian processes and reflect prohibition of harm, in which negative affective responses are generated in the medial prefrontal cortex and the amygdala
2) Controlled processes (cold cognitive) evaluations drive utilitarian judgments and weigh the costs and benefits associated with an action.

While judgments of correct actions when immersed in these virtual Trolley Dilemmas tend to involve controlled (e.g., Cold) cognitive processes, the decision to apply direct physical force triggers automatic (e.g., Hot) affective responses.

Virtual environments allow for observations of morally relevant decision-making behaviors in realistic three-dimensional simulations. With virtual environments, researchers can perform real-time assessment of the cognitive and affective factors inherent in explicit moral behaviors. Patil and colleagues (2014) compared traditional text-based approaches to a virtual environment version of the Trolley Dilemma. They found a modality-specific difference in that participant behavior in the virtual environment reflected a utilitarian approach but, in the text-based descriptions, the same moral dilemmas resulted in nonutilitarian decisions. Further, autonomic arousal was greater in virtual environments. These differences suggest that text-based scenario presentation does not include dynamic visual information that is available to persons in real-world environments. With virtual environments, there appears to be an enhanced capacity for the context-dependent knowledge that is critical for moral decision-making.

Navarrete and colleagues (2012) used virtual environments to observe behaviors and record the autonomic arousal of participants as they confronted moral dilemmas. Specifically, they immersed participants into a virtual reality version of the Trolley Dilemma. Participants were given the choice of whether or not to pull a lever that would determine the fate (e.g., death or safety) of some number of people. The virtual environment included virtual human agents that were capable of movement and sound in real time. The validity of the virtual trolley paradigm was apparent in that results were consistent with the behavioral pattern observed in studies using text versions of the Trolley Dilemma. Results also revealed that affective arousal was (1) associated with a reduced likelihood that participants were acting to achieve a utilitarian outcome and (2) greater when participants were attempting to behaviorally resolve a dilemma that required committing an act than when participants were omitting an action. An important aspect of these findings is that they provide support for a relation between Hot affective processing and moral action. These findings also suggest that similar neurophysiological processes may mediate Cold processing of moral judgments and actions. Virtual environment–based moral dilemmas appear to offer an empirical platform for investigating the contents and contexts in which Hot affective and Cold cognitive processing occur.

In a study that builds on Navarrete and colleagues' (2012) paradigm, Skulmowski and colleagues (2014) developed a virtual reality–based Trolley Dilemma that utilized a first-person perspective of the forced-choice

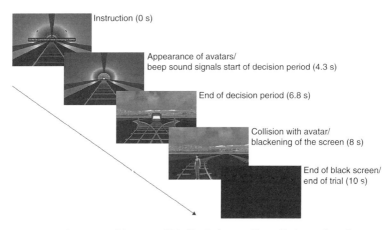

Figure 12.7 Overview of the Virtual Trolley Dilemma (from Skulmowski et al., 2014; reprinted with permission from the publisher)

decision-making paradigm. A novel aspect of the Skulmowski design is that the participants were the drivers of the train (see Figure 12.7). This approach was chosen because research on presence and immersion in virtual environments has found that first-person perspectives elicit a greater sense of presence and involvement (Slater, Spanlang, & Corominas, 2010). The study also included psychophysiological assessment metrics drawn from pupillometry that were integrated into the virtual environment paradigm. Like Navarrete and colleagues' virtual trolley study, Skulmowski's experiment replicated the behavioral pattern found in studies using text-based versions of the Trolley Dilemma (see Figure 12.6). This further validated the use of the virtual trolley platform for research on moral decision-making. Additional findings included a peak in the level of arousal related to the moment that the moral decision was made. Furthermore, eye-tracking revealed context-dependent gaze durations during decisions to sacrifice. These findings comport well with dual-process theories. Since decision time frames were able to be held constant in the virtual environment paradigm, events could be logged and marked for comparison to pupillometric measurements. This approach offers promise for moving beyond paper-and-pencil (e.g., text-based) approaches in which participants read scenario descriptions at varying speeds.

12.10 Conclusions

In summary, mere judgments about moral dilemmas result in a limited understanding. The hypothetical and text-based vignettes attempt to stimulate the imagination of participants and then use questionnaires or experiments involving low-level manipulations of harm to enhance understanding. The addition of virtual environments allows researchers to assess the expression of decision-making processes via the real-time logging of behaviors. Given that virtual environments are more dynamic than text-based scenarios and that they do not involve the potential for harmful outcomes, they may bridge the gap between judgment and behavior via explorations of the underlying mechanisms. While the virtual environment approach does not offer a definitive solution to the long-standing trade-off between laboratory control and real-world behaviors, it does allow researchers a methodology for presenting participants with auditory and visual representations of real-world activities.

CHAPTER 13

Video Games, Video Gamers, and the Ethics of Video Game Design

13.1   Introduction

Are video games ethical? Is it ethical to play violent video games? These questions are at the heart of many discussions and research studies related to video games. Warnings abound as popular media outlets promote salacious headlines about the harmful and negative impacts of video game play. Although the cautions circulating in the popular media offer interesting headlines, not all stand up to research scrutiny. In this chapter, there will be a focus on both the ethical issues of video games and the ways in which ethical dilemmas are represented in video games. However, before diving too deep into these ethical questions and concerns, it is important to note that there are several different game genres and platforms. There are millions of video games that have been designed to allow players to actively engage with them in an interactive manner. Some games are competitive, while others require cooperative play.

Given the diversity of genres and dimensions on which video games can vary, Granic, Lobel, and Engels (2014) provide a conceptual map that depicts most of the genres (with examples) along two dimensions: the level of complexity and the extent of social interaction (see Figure 13.1).

It is important to note that Figure 13.1 represents more of a simplified conceptual overview than an exhaustive taxonomy of games. Several video games also vary on other significant dimensions and, progressively, commercial video games can be played on both a social basis and nonsocially, cooperatively, and competitively. Moreover, video game complexity is frequently contingent on the ways in which the gamer takes part in these assorted gaming contexts.

13.2   Contamination Thesis

From an ethical perspective, a common approach to assessing the moral worth and impacts of video games is to consider the content of the video

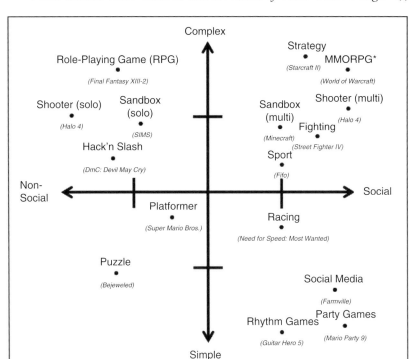

Figure 13.1 Conceptual map of the main genres of video games (with examples)
(from Granic, Lobel, & Engels, 2014; reprinted with permission from the publisher)
Note: This figure was organized according to two dimensions: complexity level and
social interaction. This is not an exhaustive compilation of genres. *Halo 4* is
deliberately recurring to emphasize that many games can be either a single- or
a multiplayer. MMORPG = massive multiplayer online role-playing game.

games and the relations between playing a video game and that content and
behavior in the real world (Gotterbarn, 2010). These video game contents
are judged by largely accepted moral norms that disallow certain actions.
Some have referred to this contamination thesis (Coeckelbergh, 2007;
Goerger, 2017) in terms of the following: If video game contents are
harmful, surely we are obliged to prevent them from spilling over from
the virtual world into the real world? Following this thesis, the assessment
of the morality of decisions and actions in video games is done relative to
imagined decisions and actions taking place in the real world.

In the cyberpsychology arena, a number of researchers offer support for
the contagion thesis in their arguments that there are many negative effects
resulting from video games. Findings have revealed negative impacts for

addiction (Kuss, 2013); the impact of sexist content (Fox & Tang, 2014, 2017); and the influence of violent content (Brockmyer, 2015; Gentile & Stone, 2005). It is this latter issue of violence in video games that has garnered a good deal of concern. Violent video games have been associated with sleep disruption (Lam, 2014) and decreased neurocognitive and affective responses to negative stimuli (Montag et al., 2012). Moreover, the violent content found in some video game narratives has prompted concern that video gamers may imitate video game scenarios in real life (Ybarra et al., 2014). Research has also shown that video gamers are more likely to engage in risky driving behaviors after playing street-racing games (Vingilis et al., 2013).

Nevertheless, several studies have found enhanced neurocognitive processing in video gamers (see Parsons, 2017). Moreover, there is increasing interest in the therapeutic and rehabilitative potential of video games for a variety of nervous system disorders (Horne-Moyer et al., 2014; Primack et al., 2012) in both younger (Charlier et al., 2016; Franceschini et al., 2013) and older-aged (Anguera et al., 2013; Anguera & Gazzaley, 2015; Mishra, Anguera, & Gazzaley, 2016) cohorts. A recent meta-analysis by Bediou and colleagues (2018) showed that action video game play robustly enhances executive functioning, attentional processing, and spatial cognition, as well as encouraging results for perceptual processes. Video games for interventional and rehabilitation purposes have been evaluated in various cohorts, including traumatic and acquired brain injury (Llorens et al., 2015), degenerative ataxia (Synofzik et al., 2013), dyslexia (Franceschini et al., 2013), stroke (Cho, Lee, & Song, 2012), autism (Crowder & Merritte, 2013), and aging (Anguera et al., 2013; Basak et al., 2008; Marston & Smith, 2012). Serious games have also successfully been applied to counter depression (Fleming et al., 2012; Kühn et al., 2018a) and social isolation in an older age cohort (Harley et al., 2010). Moreover, there is increasing interest in the use of off-the-shelf video games as potential applications in preventive and therapeutic medicine (Colder Carras et al., 2018).

While a meta-analysis by Ferguson and Kilburn (2010) argued against what they called the misestimation and overinterpretation of violent video game effects in Eastern and Western nations, a task force of the American Psychological Association more recently summarized findings related to violent video games that suggested risk factors for adverse outcomes such as desensitization and decreased empathy (Calvert et al., 2017). However, a longitudinal neuroimaging study that allowed for actual assessment of causal conclusions showed no evidence for a desensitization effect in neural signals during empathy for pain. The issue of whether violent video games will result in violent behaviors in the real world has recently been described as part of the replication crisis in psychology research (Hengartner, 2018). This may be due to the fact that previous experimental studies were on short-term effects of violent video game play. The emergence of long-itudinal studies investigating the impacts of long-term violent video game play does not appear to have evidence of significant negative impacts. In another longitudinal study, Smith, Ferguson, and Beaver (2018) performed a longitudinal analysis of shooter games and their relationship with con-duct disorder and self-reported delinquency. Their results revealed that exposure to shooter games did not predict adolescent conduct disorder or criminal behavior. Kühn and colleagues (2018b) at the Max Planck Institute for Human Development, in Berlin, Germany, completed a longitudinal intervention study using large batteries of tests (question-naires; behavioral measures of aggression, sexist attitudes, empathy and interpersonal competencies, impulsivity, depression, anxiety, executive control functions) to assess for aggression before and after two months of game play. Their results showed that playing violent video games did not cause aggression. Hence, there appears to be less and less evidence for the contagion thesis.

In addition to the cyberpsychology literature, Coeckelbergh (2007) has suggested several problems with the contamination approach. First, it depends on the empirical claim that there is a causal relation between playing the game and violent behavior. As noted, this does not appear to be the case. At best, the empirical evidence is controversial. At worst, the lack of support from recent longitudinal studies makes the thesis mute. According to Coeckelbergh, both the utilitarian consequentialist, who weighs the benefits against the potential harms, and the Kantian deon-tologist, who understands such harms in terms of a disrespect for (real) persons as ends, are contingent on the currently lacking empirical proof that there are, or that there are not, harmful consequences for the player and/or for others. Coeckelbergh's second concern is that the problems with the contamination thesis are not limited to consequentialism and/or deontology. Pace McCormick (2001), virtue theory tenders a reasonable way of considering the issue: violent video games may not erode one's character and make it problematic to live the good life. Coeckelbergh's third objection is that the contamination thesis is too general if it is made on account of the violent content in video games alone. He argues that if content is all that matters, then the contamina-tion thesis can be applied to other media as well (e.g., novels, television, board games, etc.).

Likewise, Schulzke (2010) sees limitations in the contamination thesis on both theoretical and empirical grounds. He contends that arguments against violent video games suffer from a number of significant short-comings that make them ineffective. Instead, he promotes the view that video games are defensible from moral perspectives found in Kantian deontological claims, utilitarian analyses, and virtue theory.

13 3   Kant and Video Games

Starting with Kantian deontological moral reasoning, the emphasis is on the ways in which players treat others in the digital video game world and what intentions inform the players' actions. You may recall from Chapter 2 that Immanuel Kant developed the Categorical Imperative (unconditional command), an authoritative moral code that is universal and without exception. In his book *Foundations of the Metaphysics of Morals*, Kant offers multiple formulations of the categorical imperative. The two most well-known versions are as follows:

1) "Act only in accordance with that maxim through which you can at the same time will that it become a universal law" (Kant, 1785/1998, p. 421).
2) "Act so that you use humanity, in your own person as well as in that of another, always also as an end and never only as a means" (Kant, 1785/1998, p. 429).

The core idea of the categorical imperative is that our capacity for reason makes all human beings alike and reason also makes us distinct from anything else in the natural world. Given the fundamental similarity found among persons, there is a requirement that persons abide by a distinct set of rules that apply only to humans.

According to Kant, persons have duties to themselves as animals and as moral beings. He writes of the vices contrary to the duties to oneself:

> These [vices] adopt principles that are directly contrary to his character as a moral being, that is, to inner freedom, the innate dignity of a human being, which is tantamount to saying that they make it one's basic principle to have no basic principle and hence no character, that is, to throw oneself away and make oneself an object of contempt. (Kant, 1797/1996, p. 545)

For Kant, insincerity, avarice, and false humility are examples of vices that are contrary to one's duties to oneself. That said, any vice that is harmful to one's character as a moral being would most likely be sufficient. Hence, if a player acts cruelly while playing an ultraviolent video game, this could constitute a violation of the player's duty to oneself. Waddington (2007) considers two Kantian grounds for concern with video games. First, there are times when video games involve acts of cruelty that violate our duties to ourselves. The second is that video game characters, like animals, may be analogues of humanity. If we choose not to treat human analogues with respect, we may decrease the likelihood that we will perform our duties toward other human beings.

McCormick (2001) draws on Kant's second formulation of the categorical imperative, in which humanity is viewed as end in itself: "Act so that you use humanity, in your own person as well as in that of another, always also as an end and never only as a means" (Kant, 1785/1998, p. 429). In other words, the second formulation of the categorical imperative is stating that it is unethical for one individual to use another person. Instead, the ethical inter-action with another must respect them as rational persons. For McCormick, this means that what makes for moral or immoral players is whether opponents are respected. For example, when Tommy gloats over a victory or uses it against his fellow player, he is behaving poorly because his focus is on personal interest and he is treating his fellow player as a means to gratification.

Cogburn and Silcox (2009) give the example of the video game *The Sims*. Although the player is not given an explicit set or goals for "winning" this game, there are a number of implied recommendations. In the first release of *The Sims* video game, the player starts with just enough resources to construct a small house with a limited number of inexpensive appliances. This occurs in a neighborhood that already includes a huge and extravagantly furnished home that is awaiting occupants. Several game players quickly uncovered a helpful strategy for occasioning the success of their own preferred Sims as quickly as possible. The strategy was to put up two distinct tiny households, each one inhabited by new citizens of the *Sim* game world. The player would systematically use the resources and personalities of one household to increase the fortunes of the other. The player's preferred Sim family can contact the less favored neighbors to banter or flirt whenever they need to maintain high social interaction scores or just show up to borrow resources. This exploitation of one's *Sim* friends reflects a violation of the second version of Kant's categorical imperative because it is using others as a means without considering their (game-relative) ends.

13.4 Utilitarian Video Game Play

From a utilitarian perspective, there is a cost/benefit analysis; even if games increase the risk of violent incidents, the potential harm must be weighed against the positive benefits. As discussed in Chapter 2 of this book, the classic utilitarians Jeremy Bentham (1789) and John Stuart Mill (1861) argued for the utilitarian principle of utility (i.e., the Greatest Happiness Principle) in terms of pleasure and pain resulting from an agent's actions. Mill (1859/1991) formulated the utilitarian principle as follows:

> Actions are right in proportion as they tend to promote happiness; wrong as they tend to produce the reverse of happiness. By happiness is intended pleasure and the absence of pain; by unhappiness pain and the privation of pleasure. (p. 66)

In our everyday moral decision-making, this principle of maximizing happiness appears to cover most ethical questions.

In video games, utilitarianism can be used to rank the cost/benefit of game play alternatives according to their goodness. Moreover, the video game player's happiness can be argued to be a consequence (Richter, 2010). From a consequentialist perspective, the optimal outcome of video game play is happiness, and the appropriateness of the consequences of a player's actions can be found in the degree to which happiness was produced for those players impacted by an action. For some consequentialists, calling a video game "violent" is mere ethical emotivism. For example, Tavinor (2007) has argued that video game events are not relevant to the ethical evaluation of the game:

> The apparent violent, sadistic, and otherwise criminal events that occur within games cannot be factored into the consequentialist account for the very simple reason that the worlds and events of video gaming are fictional. Grand Theft Auto, for example, has repeatedly been condemned for allowing its players to perform acts of theft, assault, murder, and worse. But these apparent actions are fictional ones, and really there are no such things involved in the game. Grand Theft Auto, and similar games, might be thought of as crime simulators, in that similar to flight simulators, they allow their players to indulge in immediately non-consequential behavior that pursued in reality can be quite dangerous. (p. 30)

Furthermore, Tavinor suggests that untying video game playing behavior from the sorts of consequences experienced in the real world is a prerequisite for a player's ability to derive pleasure from it. Hence, from a consequentialist perspective, the consequences following a video game player's action in a game are to be considered as right or wrong relative to the enjoyment the player experiences.

Video games are pleasurable and have a positive value in entertaining video game players that can outweigh some costs that they might incur. According to Reynolds (2002), a utilitarian analysis of *Grand Theft Auto III* may offend and degrade different groups but this cannot be considered from a utilitarian perspective without also considering the pleasure players get from taking part in the video game. Reynolds contends that the entertainment value is greater than any harm as these video games give what he estimates to be more than a billion hours of entertainment to millions of persons. Given the numbers, video game sales keep a multibillion-dollar industry strong and fuels the economy. Moreover, the success of video games results in the development of ever newer technologies that may benefit persons outside the entertainment industry. Added to these societal benefits, there are a number of studies suggesting that video game play robustly enhances cognitive functioning (Bediou et al., 2018), countering depression (Fleming et al., 2012; Kühn et al., 2018a) and social isolation (Harley et al., 2010), and there is increasing interest in the use of off-the-shelf video games as potential applications in preventive and therapeutic medicine (Colder Carras et al., 2018).

13.5   Virtuous Gamers

As we saw in Chapter 2 of this book, Aristotle developed a virtue theory, in which morality is understood in terms of the agent's character traits displayed in action. A video gamer's possession and exercise of virtues determine the player's ethical decision-making. The virtue ethics approach conceptualizes a virtuous gamer as one possessing ideal character traits that are the consequence of natural tendencies. Virtual ethics may be understood in contrast to deontological and consequentialist approaches. From a virtue ethics perspective, there is little emphasis on universal duties that constrain actions. Instead, the virtue ethicist considers the wider implications related to one's actions. McCormick (2001) sees little hope for defending violent video games from an Aristotelian perspective. He contends that a virtue theorist would argue that taking part in a video game that simulates extreme, decadent, and wrongful acts does not promote the cultivation of optimal character.

Others think that McCormick overstates the virtue theorist's disdain for simulated violence (Cogburn & Silcox, 2009; Sicart, 2009). For example, Cogburn and Silcox (2009) argue that Aristotle only opposed particular demonstrations of violence. In fact, some virtues (e.g., combat) can be found in a soldier going into battle. Cogburn and Silcox (2009) use *Oedipus the King* as an example. In the play, Oedipus unintentionally weds his own mother. On learning the identity of his bride, he moves offstage and gouges out his own eyes; he then reappears in front of the audience so that they can see his gory face. While a fifth century BCE audience probably experienced this the same way that players of *Mortal Kombat* or *Soldier of Fortune* first experienced gruesome "fatalities," Aristotle appears to have considered this sort of explicit alarm as something that could play an ethically helpful function for the citizens of ancient Greece. Perhaps this is analogous to reports from first-person–shooter fans about the perceived value of these violent games for purging hostile sentiments.

Furthermore, Aristotle and other virtue ethicists focus on learning virtue through practice. For Coeckelbergh (2007), video games could be designed in a manner that aims to engross the player in character-developing scenarios that will enhance the player's capacity for empathy and cosmopolitan thinking. From a virtue ethics perspective, Schulzke (2010) argues that there is much to praise in games that provide simulations of moral dilemmas. He gives *Fallout 3* as an example because each quest has multiple potential outcomes that proceed to separate pathways contingent on whether the video game player chooses to be moral or immoral. *BioShock* is another example of character development in a video game. Throughout the game, the player is confronted with one radical choice that recurs throughout the game: Should the player harm a virtual human child for the sake of character improvement or be a virtuous player that develops gradually (see Tavinor, 2009)?

Christopher Bartel (2015) points to several examples from *The Elder Scrolls V: Skyrim* (2011) to *BioShock Infinite* (2013) to reflect the opportunities for developing virtuous characters in violent video games. In the massive *The Elder Scrolls V: Skyrim* (2011) video game, there are several cities, landscapes, and deep, dark places to experience. There are numerous ways that a player can develop their player-character throughout the game play. At the start of the video game, the player is only invited to choose the race, gender, and physical appearance of their character. They are not asked to decide on the player-character's class at this point. Instead, the player is free to develop her own style as she takes part in the game. This allows the player a greater freedom for developing into a player-character relative to the circumstances found in the game.

Bartel also offers *BioShock Infinite* (2013) as an example of a protagonist who is pulled into a clash between the fascist Founders and the rebel Vox Populi. In this game, however, the player travels through alternative realities that require them to fight on both sides of this conflict at different times in the game. As a result of never being in a place to choose to align himself with one side or the other permanently, the player is given opportunities to develop the character relative to available information and connections. In summary, some violent video games have value as a source of moral development. This potential is contingent on the extent to which game scenarios are designed in a manner that permits players to practice working through moral dilemmas that are similar to those that may occur in real-life situations.

Yupanqui Muñoz and Charbel El-Hani (2012) see a great deal of promise in bringing video games into science classrooms to encourage culturally sensitive ethics and citizenship education. It is important to note that the types of video games they endorse are not "educational" games. Instead, Muñoz and El-Hani include games such as *Fallout 3* because they are popular games that include violent representations of gender, race, class, nationality, science, and technology. They argue that these video games offer the player a powerful experience in which the player has opportunities to foster a practical wisdom (*phronesis*) that may lead them to becoming a virtuous being. They also point out that the narratives found in these video games can also be harmful to the moral development of the players when unethical narratives fail to visibly and expressly denounce violent content, sexism, racism, and/or xenophobia. The main idea is that instead of banning violent video games, one may highlight their role in the education of critical, socially responsible, moral, and politically active citizenship, specifically since they include opportunities for moral development as well as science, technology, and societal considerations.

13.6 The Importance of Narrative for Video Game Ethics

Following Coeckelbergh (2007) and Schulzke (2010), Goerger (2017) contends that the limitations of the contamination thesis should not preclude one from viewing some violent video games as morally inappropriate. Goerger argues that, instead of emphasizing violent imagery and the effects of video game play on the user, it is better to consider the ways in which specific video games integrate violence into their narratives. While some video games have violent imagery (e.g., *The Last of Us*), their gaming narratives are less morally questionable than other video games with low violent imagery but narratives that involve crimes, hijacking cars, drugs, alcohol, and acts against vulnerable populations (e.g., *Grand Theft Auto V*).

The importance of video game narrative is apparent in the work of Miguel Sicart, a professor and information ethicist at the IT University of Copenhagen. Sicart (2009) developed a model of video game ethics from

Espen Aarseth's (2003) three-level model of game analysis (that can be analyzed individually or together):

1) Game play: a player's motives, strategies, and actions
2) Game structure: a game's rules and structure
3) Game world: a video game's fictional context, topology, and level design.

The player's motives represent a first-tier element within this system. The three corresponding levels work together to produce the video game experience. Sicart adopted this model to develop a system of video game ethics that includes representations of ethics within each of Aarseth's layers:

1) Game system: rule-based structure, in which the narration of a game includes ethical issues. The players are faced with decisions about whether or not to act in a certain way. These decisions impact the subsequent narrative.
2) Game platform: the influence of the game developer's real-world ethical convictions is evident.
3) Player experience: the ethical game play elements of the player–game interaction, as well as the player's establishment of a particular ethical culture (e.g., creation of implicit rules between players of multiplayer online games).

   While Sicart's model presents a range of potential approaches to the examination of video game ethics, video game ethicists often emphasize human players' activities and the situational aspects of moral decision-making in the games (Evans, 2010; Gotterbarn & Moor, 2009; McCormick, 2001; Sicart, 2005). Given that the players can act in these gaming environments, a video game may be thought of as a designed experience (Squire, 2006) or a simulation (Frasca, 2003) in with ethical choices occur.

   Jerry Banks (1998) defines a simulation as a platform that can be used for resolving real-world concerns:

> The imitation of the operation of a real-world process or system over time. Simulation involves the generation of an artificial history of the system and the observation of that artificial history to draw inferences concerning the operational characteristics of the real system that is represented. Simulation is an indispensable problem-solving methodology for the solution of many real-world problems. Simulation is used to describe and analyze the behavior of a system, ask what-if questions about the real system, and aid in the design of real systems. Both existing and conceptual systems can be modeled with simulation. (pp. 3–4)

As is apparent, Banks sees simulations (e.g., video games for our modality) as enablers of virtual decision processes by providing the user with information about the simulated world. The result is an artificial history of the system from which the user can draw inferences about the operational characteristics of the real systems that are represented. Hence, game narratives are important for the development of coherent game worlds. In computer game studies, this connection between the game's narrative and players' actions is referred to as ergodic (Aarseth, 1997). Two fundamental issues can be gleaned for an ethical analysis of video games: (1) the ethical dimension of game play and (2) reflections on the narrative depictions of ethical dilemmas and their use. Moreover, as the video game narrative immerses the player into a meaningful virtual environment, the player's ethical reasonings have greater import (Squire, 2006).

Goerger (2017) argues that, while the contamination thesis fails, some video games have more ethical import than others. This ties in with the narrative argument in which games that present violent narratives and disrespect values are more objectionable than violent games that include narratives that reinforce or cultivate those values. In his comparison of the narratives found in *The Last of Us* and *Grand Theft Auto*, we see the juxtaposition of *Grand Theft Auto*'s narrative, which disrespects values, with the narrative found in *The Last of Us*, which reinforces and/or cultivates those values. The narrative found in *Grand Theft Auto* takes place in major cities (Los Angeles, Miami, New York, and London, depending on the iteration). Within the narrative, the player takes part in various criminal behaviors, drug use, sex acts, gang activity, and urban violence. The game's narrative includes depictions of illicit drug and gang-related violence in a largely consequence-free environment. Moreover, these criminal activities are representations of real-world crimes and criminal enterprises that presently dominate far-reaching areas of large metropolitan areas.

In contrast, the narrative in *The Last of Us* involves a fictional post-apocalyptic world and includes a complex survival storyline. It includes violence to underscore the fragility of the virtual character as they experience a digital world in chaos. Moreover, the violence included in the narrative accentuates the significance of the moral choices faced by game characters. Goerger argues that each instance of violence within the game's narrative is detrimental and painful for the player as the moral realities of a postapocalyptic world are contrasted with those of the world in which we live. In sum, the narrative found in *The Last of Us* compels players to participate in moral deliberation and to encounter the realities of the human condition in an unparalleled and persuasive manner.

Grand Theft Auto and *The Last of Us* connect with players in meaningfully dissimilar ways. Narrative differences impact the ways in which players experience the violence. As Goerger (2017) and Sicart (2009) argue, some may want to lump both games together due to their violent imagery. This lack of consideration of narratives may limit understandings of many representational features of a game such as the background narrative, the foreground narrative in the presentation of persons, and whether violent acts and decisions have consequences. Hence, each video game should be evaluated individually and the violence found in the narratives evaluated to assess its representational context.

13.7   Extended Mind Perspective

In Chapter 3 of this book, "Digital and Extended Selves in Cyberspace," the focus was on extending our understandings of human conscious processing of information using an extended cognition (also known as an "extended mind") approach. According to the extended mind approach, ethical decision-making in video games consists of complex feedback (including feedforward and feed-around) loops among brain, body, and the external world where the player is experiencing the video game (see Clark, 2008; Clark & Chalmers, 1998). Following the extended mind approach, ethical decision-making and related cognitive processes go beyond wetware (i.e., one's brain) to video game software and hardware used by the player's brain. Moreover, cognition can be viewed as something being processed by a system that is coupled with the video game (Clark, 2008; Clark & Chalmers, 1998). The cyberpsychologist can answer ethical questions about video game play by using an extended mind approach in which the video game player's interactions during video game play form an extended cognitive system that performs functions that would otherwise be accomplished via the action of internal brain-based cognitive processes. The extension of mental processes outside of the brain (e.g., technologies of the extended mind) means that mental processes cannot be fully reduced to brain processes. According to Andy Clark (2003), we are naturally born cyborgs. So, the addition of neuroethical formulations (see Chapter 4) to a brain-based cyberpsychology perhaps takes us closer to a need for cyborg ethics.

Andy Clark and David Chalmers (1998) illustrate three varied approaches that a player could possibly take to play the video game *Tetris*:

1. Visualize the *Tetris* game pieces rotating in mid-air
2. Use a computer mouse to manipulate representations of *Tetris* game pieces on a monitor
3. Access a brain–computer interface to perform the rotation operation as rapidly as the computer does.

According to Clark and Chalmers, all three approaches consist of the same types of cognitive processes. Additionally, it would appear completely natural to most persons to say about the first case that all aspects of game play were going on "inside" of the player's mind, even though it is a good deal easier to play *Tetris* using a computer mouse as in case 2. Given the *Tetris* video game scenario, the extended mind thesis is very rapid and, as *Tetris* players gain in skill, it becomes more automatic. The mind starts with controlled processing in case 1 until it, paradigmatically, after a good deal of game play, automatically performs computational tasks to move the mouse to manipulate representations. Here again, a quote from Daniel Dennett (1996) points out that the brain frequently extends our cognitive processes into the environment by

> off-loading as much as possible of our cognitive tasks into the environment itself – extruding our minds (that is, our mental projects and activities) into the surrounding world, where a host of peripheral devices we construct can store, process and re-represent our meanings, streamlining, enhancing, and protecting the processes of transformation that are our thinking. This widespread practice of off-loading releases us from the limitations of our animal brains. (pp. 134–135)

In line with Dennett and the extended mind thesis, one may view the cognitive processes as being performed by both the brain and the video game working in tandem. Moreover, the human mind can be viewed as an extremely influential but relatively disparate assemblage of psychological affects coupled with external props to our cognitive processes such as the *Tetris* player's desktop mouse.

Cogburn and Silcox (2009) argue for the application of the extended mind thesis to external entities like video game characters that we play in *World of Warcraft* as parts of our very selves. For many gamers, it is probably easy to think of their avatars as extensions of their own identity. Video game players often feel close connections to their avatars and some certainly act as if they are extensions of themselves. Marcus Johansson (2009), at Linköping University, uses the extended mind argument to support the idea that punishing avatars for their actions can be morally justified and perhaps even represents an obligation. Likewise, an argument can be made for harm done to an avatar to be experienced as harm done against the game player.

An example of the ethical impact of video games of the extended mind can be found in Bartel's (2015) consideration of the "airport massacre" mission in *Call of Duty: Modern Warfare 2* (2009) – the "No Russian" mission. During this notorious gaming scenario, the player plays the role of an undercover American CIA agent who is endeavoring to subvert a group of Russian terrorists. During the game play, the group arrives at a packed airport and butchers scores of unarmed civilians. The player has the choice of participating in the massacre or to abstain with no penalty to their progress or achievements in the game. The reaction in the gaming community was highly controversial and many players felt very uncomfortable opening fire on virtual civilians. Why would anyone feel uncomfortable playing a game in which virtual characters are killed and there is no real-world harm? The answer may be that the games we play become extensions of ourselves.

13.8   Conclusions

In this chapter, there has been a discussion of the contamination thesis and the unlikeliness that the argument holds given the empirical and theoretical arguments against it. Also in this chapter, attempts have been made to consider video games in light of some of the main approaches to moral philosophy, as found in Kantian deontological ethics, utilitarianism, and virtue ethics. For the Kantian deontologist, emphasis is placed on the ways in which players should treat each other in the game world. As long as players treat each other with respect, playing video games does not result in unambiguous harm. For the utilitarian, several claims about the potential harms and negative consequences of video game play are negated due to the robust empirical evidence of benefits that outweigh the less substantiated shortcomings. For the virtue ethicist, we discussed an emphasis on what kinds of virtues or vices players are trained to emulate.

Ultimately, the background narratives of game violence must be considered. While some may want to lump various games together due to their violent imagery, this lack of consideration of narratives may limit understandings of many representational aspects of a game. It is important to consider that reflections on game violence should include the background narrative, the foreground narrative in the presentation of persons, and whether violent acts and decisions have consequences. Taken together, these features determine the moral acceptance of various violent video games. Each video game should be evaluated individually and the violence found in the narratives evaluated to assess its representational context.

Finally, there was a discussion of the ways in which video game avatars can be understood as technologies of the extended mind. As such, the relations that develop between the game player and the extended avatar can develop to a point that there are very much complex feedback (including feedforward and feed-around) loops among brain, controllers, and the digital world of the video game.

References

Aardema, F., O'Connor, K., Côté, S., & Taillon, A. (2010). Virtual reality induces dissociation and lowers sense of presence in objective reality. *Cyberpsychology, Behavior, and Social Networking*, 13(4), 429–435.

Aarseth, E. (1997). *Cybertext: Perspectives on Ergodic Literature.* Baltimore, MD: Johns Hopkins University Press.

Aarseth, E. (2003). Playing research: Methodological approaches to game analysis. Paper presented at the 5th International Digital Arts and Culture Conference, Melbourne, Australia, May 19–23.

Abbott, J. A. M., Klein, B., & Ciechomski, L. (2008). Best practices in online therapy. *Journal of Technology in Human Services*, 26(2–4), 360–375.

Aboujaoude, E., Salame, W., & Naim, L. (2015). Telemental health: A status update. *World psychiatry*, 14(2), 223–230.

Achterhuis, H. (ed.). (2001). *American Philosophy of Technology: The Empirical Turn.* Bloomington: Indiana University Press.

Adams, D., Bah, A., Barwulor, C., Musabay, N., Pitkin, K., & Redmiles, E. M. (2018). Ethics emerging: The story of privacy and security perceptions in virtual reality. In *Fourteenth Symposium* on Usable Privacy and Security ({SOUPS} 2018) (pp. 427–442).

Adolphs, R. (2003). Cognitive neuroscience of human social behaviour. *Nature Review Neuroscience*, 4(3), 165–178.

Ahuja, M. K. (2002). Women in the information technology profession: A literature review, synthesis and research agenda. *European Journal of Information Systems*, 11(1), 20–34.

Aida, J., Chau, B., & Dunn, J. (2018). Immersive virtual reality in traumatic brain injury rehabilitation: A literature review. *NeuroRehabilitation*, 42(4), 441–448.

Aivazpour, Z., Valecha, R., & Rao, R. H. (2017). Unpacking privacy paradox: A dual process theory approach. In *Proceedings of the AMCIS, Boston (2017)* .

Akil, H., Gordon, J., Hen, R., Javitch, J., Mayberg, H., McEwen, B., . . . & Nestler, E. J. (2017). Treatment resistant depression: A multi-scale, systems biology approach. *Neuroscience & Biobehavioral Reviews*, 84, 272–288.

Alderson, P. & Morrow, V. (2004). *Ethics, Social Research and Consulting with Children and Young People.* London: Barnardo's.

Allen, M. W., Armstrong, D. J., Riemenschneider, C. K., & Reid, M. F. (2006). Making sense of the barriers women face in the information technology work force: Standpoint theory, self-disclosure, and causal maps. *Sex Roles*, 54(11–12), 831–844.

Allied Control Council. (1949). *Trials of War Criminals Before the Nuernberg Military Tribunals Under Control Council Law No. 10.* Washington, DC: US Government Printing Office.

American Counseling Association. (1999). *Ethical Standards for Internet Online Counseling.* Alexandria, VA: American Counselling Association.

American Psychiatric Association. (2013). *Diagnostic and Statistical Manual of Mental Disorders* (5th edn). Washington, DC: American Psychiatric Association.

American Psychological Association. (2002). Ethical principles of psychologists and code of conduct. *American Psychologist*, 57(12), 1060–1073.

American Psychological Association. (2010). *American Psychological Association Ethical Principles of Psychologists and Code of Conduct.* www.apa.org/ethics/code/

American Psychological Association. (2013a). *Guidelines and Principles for Accreditation of Programs in Professional Psychology.* Washington, DC: American Psychological Association.

American Psychological Association. (2013b). *Guidelines for the Practice of Telepsychology.* www.apa.org/practice/guidelines/telepsychology.aspx.

American Psychological Association. (2013c). *Telepsychology 50-State Review.* www.apapracticecentral.org/advocacy/state/telehealth-slides.pdf

American Psychological Association. (2017). *Ethical Principles of Psychologists and Code of Conduct.* www.apa.org/ethics/code/ethics-code-2017.pdf

American Psychological Association Presidential Task Force on Evidence-Based Practice. (2006). Evidence-based practice in psychology. *American Psychologist*, 61(4), 271–285.

American Telemedicine Association. (2009). *Practice Guidelines for Videoconferencing-Based Telemental Health.* https://telehealth.org/wp-content/uploads/2013/11/ATA-guidelines.pdf

Andrews, C. (2012). Social media recruitment. *Applied Clinical Trials*, 21(11), 32–42.

Angle, S. & Slote, M. (eds.). (2013). *Virtue Ethics and Confucianism.* New York: Routledge.

Anguera, J. A., Boccanfuso, J., Rintoul, J. L., Al-Hashimi, O., Faraji, F., Janowich, J., . . . & Gazzaley, A. (2013). Video game training enhances cognitive control in older adults. *Nature*, 501(7465), 97.

Anguera, J. A. & Gazzaley, A. (2015). Video games, cognitive exercises, and the enhancement of cognitive abilities. *Current Opinion in Behavioral Sciences*, 4, 160–165.

Anscombe, G. E. M. (1958). Modern moral philosophy. *Philosophy*, 33(124), 1–19.

Appelbaum, P.S., & Lidz, C. (2008). The therapeutic misconception. In E. J. Emanuel, C. Grady, R. A. Crouch, R. K. Lie, F. G. Miller, & D. Wendler (eds.), *The Oxford Textbook of Clinical Research Ethics* (pp. 633–644). New York: Oxford University Press.

Aristotle (1998). *Nicomachean Ethics*. Ed. and trans. by J. L. Ackrill, J. O. Urmson, & D. Ross. New York: Oxford University Press.

Artz, J. M. (1994). Virtue vs. utility: Alternative foundations for computer ethics. Paper presented at the Conference on Ethics in the Computer Age, Gatlinburg, TN, USA, November 11–13. https://doi.org/10.1145/199544.199553

Association of State and Provincial Psychology Boards. (2005). *ASPPB Code of Conduct*. Montgomery, AL: Association of State and Provincial Psychology Boards.

Attrill, A. (ed.). (2015). *Cyberpsychology*. Oxford: Oxford University Press.

Attrill, A. & Fullwood, C. (eds.). (2016). *Applied Cyberpsychology: Practical Applications of Cyberpsychological Theory and Research*, New York: Palgrave Macmillan.

Baddeley, A. (1981). The cognitive psychology of everyday life. *British Journal of Psychology*, 72(2), 257–269.

Bagozzi, R. P., Verbeke, W. J. M. I., Dietvorst, R. C., Belschak, F. D., van den Berg, W. E., & Rietdijk, W. J. R. (2013). Theory of mind and empathic explanations of Machiavellianism: A neuroscience perspective. *Journal of Management*, 39, 1760–1798.

Banks, J. (ed.). (1998). Handbook of Simulation: Principles, Methodology, Advances, Applications, and Practice. New York: John Wiley & Sons.

Barchard, K. A. & Williams, J. (2008). Practical advice for conducting ethical online experiments and questionnaires for United States psychologists. *Behavior Research Methods*, 40(4), 1111–1128.

Barnett, J. E. & Kolmes, K. (2016). The practice of tele-mental health: Ethical, legal, and clinical issues for practitioners. *Practice Innovations*, 1(1), 53–66.

Barsky, A., Kaplan, S. A., & Beal, D. J. (2011). Just feelings? The role of affect in the formation of organizational fairness judgments. *Journal of Management*, 37, 248–279.

Bartel, C. (2015). Free will and moral responsibility in video games. *Ethics and Information Technology*, 17(4), 285–293.

Basak, C., Boot, W. R., Voss, M. W., & Kramer, A. F. (2008). Can training in a real-time strategy video game attenuate cognitive decline in older adults? *Psychology and Aging*, 23(4), 765–777.

Bashshur, R., Shannon, G., Krupinski, E., & Grigsby, J. (2011). The taxonomy of telemedicine. *Telemedicine and e-Health*, 17(6), 484–494.

Battro, A. M. & Fischer, K. W. (2012). Mind, brain, and education in the digital era. *Mind, Brain, and Education*, 6(1), 49–50.

Baumgartner, T., Speck, D., Wettstein, D., Masnari, O., Beeli, G., & Jäncke, L. (2008). Feeling present in arousing virtual reality worlds: Prefrontal brain regions differentially orchestrate presence experience in adults and children. *Frontiers in Human Neuroscience*, 2(8), 1–12.

Bayer, J. B., Ellison, N. B., Falk, E. B., & Schoenebeck, S. Y. (2015). Sharing the small moments: Ephemeral social interaction on Snapchat. *Information, Communication & Society*, 19(7), 956–977.

Beauchamp, T. L. & Childress, J. F. (1978). *Principles of Biomedical Ethics*, 1st ed. New York: Oxford University Press.

Beauchamp, T. L. & Childress, J. F. (2001). *Principles of Biomedical Ethics*, 6th ed. New York: Oxford University Press.

Beauchamp, T. L. & Childress, J. F. (2013). *Principles of Biomedical Ethics*, 7th ed. New York: Oxford University Press.

Bechara, A. & Damasio, A. R. (2005). The somatic marker hypothesis: A neural theory of economic decision. *Games and Economic Behavior*, 52, 336–372.

Bechara, A., Tranel, D., Damasio, H., & Damasio, A. R. (1996). Failure to respond autonomically to anticipated future outcomes following damage to prefrontal cortex. *Cerebral Cortex*, 6, 215–225.

Bediou, B., Adams, D. M., Mayer, R. E., Tipton, E., Green, C. S., & Bavelier, D. (2018). Meta-analysis of action video game impact on perceptual, attentional, and cognitive skills. *Psychological Bulletin*, 144(1), 77–110.

Behr, K.-M., Nosper, A., Klimmt, C., & Hartmann, T. (2005). Some practical considerations of ethical issues in VR research. *Presence*, 14, 668–676.

Bell, F. & Adam, A. (2004). Whatever happened to information systems ethics?: Caught between the devil and the deep blue sea. In B. Kaplan, D. Truex, D. Wastell, A.T. Wood-Harper, & J. DeGross (eds.), *Information Systems Research: Relevant Theory and Informed Practice* (pp. 159–174). Boston: Kluwer Academic.

Bellman, S., Johnson, E. J., Kobrin, S. J., & Lohse, G. L. (2004). International differences in information privacy concerns: A global survey of consumers. *The Information Society*, 20(5), 313–324.

Benbunan-Fich, R. (2017). The ethics of online research with unsuspecting users: From A/B testing to C/D experimentation. *Research Ethics*, 13(3–4), 200–218.

Beninger, K. (2017). Social media users' views on the ethics of social media research. In L. Sloan & A. Quan-Hasse (eds.), *The SAGE Handbook of Social Media Research Methods* (pp. 57–73). London: Sage.

Bentham, J. (1789). *Principles of Morals and Legislation*. Oxford: Clarendon Press.

Beran, T. & Li, Q. (2008). The relationship between cyberbullying and school bullying. *The Journal of Student Wellbeing*, 1(2), 16–33.

Berdichevsky, D. & Neuenschwander, E. (1999). Toward an ethics of persuasive technology. *Communications of the ACM*, 42(5), 51–58.

Berg, J. W., Mehlman, M. J., Rubin, D. B., & Kodish, E. (2009). Making all the children above average: Ethical and regulatory concerns for pediatricians in pediatric enhancement research. *Clinical Pediatrics*, 48(5), 472–480.

Bermudes, R. A., Lanocha, K. I., & Janicak, P. G. (eds.). (2017). *Transcranial Magnetic Stimulation: Clinical Applications for Psychiatric Practice*. Washington, DC: American Psychiatric Association Publishing.

Bernecker, S. (2014). How to understand the extended mind. *Philosophical Issues*, 24(1), 1–23.

Berners-Lee, T., Hendler, J., & Lassila, O. (2001). The semantic web. *Scientific American*, 284(5), 28–37.

Bernhardt, B. C. & Singer, T. (2012). The neural basis of empathy. *Annual Review of Neuroscience*, 35, 1–23.

Bharucha, A. J., Anand, V., Forlizzi, J., Dew, M. A., Reynolds, C. F., III, Stevens, S., & Wactlar, H. (2009). Intelligent assistive technology applications to dementia care: Current capabilities, limitations, and future challenges. *American Journal of Geriatric Psychiatry*, 17(2), 88–104.

Bhugra, D. & Ventriglio, A. (2017). Mind and body: Physical health needs of individuals with mental illness in the 21st century. *World Psychiatry*, 16(1), 47–48.

Bidmon, S., Terlutter, R., & Röttl, J. (2014). What explains usage of mobile physician-rating apps? Results from a web-based questionnaire. *Journal of Medical Internet Research*, 16(6), e148. https://doi.org/10.2196/jmir.3122

Billieux, J., Philippot, P., Schmid, C., Maurage, P., De Mol, J., & Van der Linden, M. (2015). Is dysfunctional use of the mobile phone a behavioural addiction? Confronting symptom-based versus process-based approaches. *Clinical Psychology & Psychotherapy*, 22(5), 460–468.

Billieux, J., Schimmenti, A., Khazaal, Y., Maurage, P., & Heeren, A. (2015). Are we overpathologizing everyday life? A tenable blueprint for behavioral addiction research. *Journal of Behavioral Addictions*, 4, 142–144.

Billieux, J., Thorens, G., Khazaal, Y., Zullino, D., Achab, S., & Van der Linden, M. (2015). Problematic involvement in online games: A cluster analytic approach. *Computers in Human Behavior*, 43, 242–250.

Billieux, J., Van der Linden, M., Achab, S., Khazaal, Y., Paraskevopoulos, L., Zullino, D., & Thorens, G. (2013). Why do you play World of Warcraft? An in-depth exploration of self-reported motivations to play online and in-game behaviours in the virtual world of Azeroth. *Computers in Human Behavior*, 29 (1), 103–109.

Biswas-Diener, R., Kashdan, T. B., & King, L. A. (2009). Two traditions of happiness research, not two distinct types of happiness. The Journal of Positive Psychology, 4(3), 208–211.

Blair, J., Marsh, A. A., Finger, E., Blair, K. S., & Luo, J. (2006). Neuro-cognitive systems involved in morality. *Philosophical Explorations*, 9(1), 13–27.

Blair, R. J. (2007). The amygdala and ventromedial prefrontal cortex in morality and psychopathy. *Trends in Cognitive Science*, 11, 387–392.

Blazer, D., Le, M., Maslow, K., & Eden, J. (eds.). (2012). *The Mental Health and Substance Use Workforce for Older Adults: In Whose Hands?*. Washington, DC: National Academies Press.

Bleakley, C. M., Charles, D., Porter-Armstrong, A., McNeill, M. D., McDonough, S. M., & McCormack, B. (2015). Gaming for health: A systematic review of the physical and cognitive effects of interactive computer games in older adults. *Journal of Applied Gerontology*, 34(3), NP166–NP189.

Bohil, C. J., Alicea, B., & Biocca, F. A. (2011). Virtual reality in neuroscience research and therapy. *Nature reviews neuroscience*, 12(12), 752–762.

Böhme, R. & Köpsell, S. (2010). Trained to accept?. In *Proceedings of the 28th International Conference on Human Factors in Computing Systems – CHI 2010* (pp. 2403–2406). New York: ACM Press.

Bojnec, Š. & Fertő, I. (2012). Broadband availability and economic growth. *Industrial Management & Data Systems*, 112(9), 1292–1306.

Bonnefon, J. F., Shariff, A., & Rahwan, I. (2016). The social dilemma of autonomous vehicles. *Science*, 352(6293), 1573–1576.

Bos, J. E., Bles, W., & Groen, E. L. (2008). A theory on visually induced motion sickness. *Displays*, 29(2), 47–57.

Bostrom, N. (2008). Drugs can be used to treat more than disease. *Nature*, 451 (7178), 520.

Bostrom, N. & Sandberg, A. (2006). Converging cognitive enhancements. *Annals of the New York Academy of Sciences*, 1093, 201–227.

Bostrom, N., & Sandberg, A. (2009). Cognitive enhancement: Methods, ethics, regulatory challenges. *Science and Engineering Ethics*, 15(3), 311–341.

Bostrom, N. & Savulescu, J. (2009). *Human enhancement ethics: The state of the debate*. In J. Savulescu & N. Bostrom (eds.), *Human Enhancement* (pp. 1–22). Oxford: Oxford University Press.

Botella C., Garcia-Palacios A., Baños R. M., Quero S. (2009). Cybertherapy: Advantages, limitations, and ethical issues. *PsychNology Journal*, 7, 77–100.

Botella, C., Riva, G., Gaggioli, A., Wiederhold, B. K., Alcaniz, M., & Banos, R. M. (2012). The present and future of positive technologies. *Cyberpsychology, Behavior, and Social Networking*, 15(2), 78–84.

Bouma, H. (1992). Gerontechnology: Making technology relevant for the elderly. *Gerontechnology*, 3, 1–5.

Bouma, H. (2010). Professional ethics in gerontechnology: A pragmatic approach. *Gerontechnology*, 9(4), 429–432.

Bouma, H., Fozard, J. L., Bouwhuis, D. G., & Taipale, V. (2007). Gerontechnology in perspective. *Gerontechnology*, 6(4), 190–216.

Boyd, D. & Crawford, K. (2012). Critical questions for big data: Provocations for a cultural, technological, and scholarly phenomenon. *Information, Communication & Society*, 15(5), 662–679.

Boyd, D. M. & Ellison, N. B. (2007). Social network sites: Definition, history, and scholarship. *Journal of Computer-Mediated Communication*, 13 (1), 210–230.

Boyle, E., Terras, M. M., Ramsay, J., & Boyle, J. M. (2013). Executive functions in digital games. In *Psychology, Pedagogy, and Assessment in Serious Games* (pp. 19–46). Hershey, PA: IGI Global.

Bradley, M. M. & Lang, P. J. (2000). Measuring emotion: Behavior, feeling, and physiology. *Cognitive Neuroscience of Emotion*, 25, 49–59.

Brand, M., Young, K. S., Laier, C., Wölfling, K., & Potenza, M. N. (2016). Integrating psychological and neurobiological considerations regarding the development and maintenance of specific Internet-use disorders: An Interaction of Person-Affect-Cognition-Execution (I-PACE) model. *Neuroscience & Biobehavioral Reviews*, 71, 252–266.

Branley, D. B. & Covey, J. (2018). Risky behavior via social media: The role of reasoned and social reactive pathways. *Computers in Human Behavior*, 78, 183–191.

Brasher B. E. (2004). *Give Me That Online Religion*. New Brunswick, NJ: Rutgers University Press.

Braun, M. T. (2013). Obstacles to social networking website use among older adults. *Computers in Human Behavior*, 29(3), 673–680.

Bray, A. (2008). The extended mind and borderline personality disorder. *Australasian Psychiatry*, 16, 8–12.

Brey, P. (1999). The ethics of representation and action in virtual reality. *Ethics and Information technology*, 1(1), 5–14.

Brey, P. (2010). Philosophy of technology after the empirical turn. *Techné: Research in Philosophy and Technology*, 14(1), 36–48.

Brockmyer, J. F. (2015). Playing violent video games and desensitization to violence. *Child and Adolescent Psychiatric Clinics of North America*, 24(1), 65–77.

Bronswijk, J. E., Bouma, H., Fozard, J. L., Kearns, W. D., Davison, G. C., & Tuan, P. C. (2009). Defining gerontechnology for R&D purposes. *Gerontechnology*, 8(1), 3–10.

Brown, A., López, G., & Lopez, M. H. (2016). Digital divide narrows for Latinos as more Spanish speakers and immigrants go online. Pew Research Center. www.pewhispanic.org/2016/07/20/digital-divide-narrows-for-latinos-as-more-spanish-speakers-and-immigrants-go-online/.

Bruckman, A. (2002). Studying the amateur artist: A perspective on disguising data collected in human subjects research on the internet. *Ethics and Information Technology*, 4(3), 217–231.

Buchanan, A., Brock, D. Daniels, N. & Wikler, D. (2001). *From Chance to Choice*. Cambridge: Cambridge University Press.

Buchanan, E. A. & Ess, C. (2008). Internet research ethics: The field and its critical issues. In K. E. Himma & H. T. Tavani (eds.), *The Handbook of Information and Computer Ethics* (pp. 273–292). New Jersey: John Wiley & Sons.

Buckwalter, J. G., Forgatch, G., Carter, S., Parsons, T. D., & Warren, N. C. (2004). U.S. Patent No. 6735568. Washington, DC: US Patent and Trademark Office.

Buckwalter, J. G., Forgatch, G., Carter, S., Parsons, T. D., & Warren, N. C. (2014). U.S. Patent No. 0180942 A1. Washington, DC: US Patent and Trademark Office.

Bunt, G. R. (2009). *iMuslims: Rewiring the House of Islam*. Chapel Hill: University of North Carolina.

Buon, M., Seara-Cardoso, A., & Viding, E. (2016). Why (and how) should we study the interplay between emotional arousal, Theory of Mind, and inhibitory control to understand moral cognition?. *Psychonomic Bulletin & Review*, 23(6), 1660–1680.

Bzdok, D., Schilbach, L., Vogeley, K., et al. (2012). Parsing the neural correlates of moral cognition: ALE meta-analysis on morality, theory of mind, and empathy. *Brain Structure & Function*, 217, 783–796.

Cacioppo, S., Frum, C., Asp, E., Weiss, R. M., Lewis, J. W., & Cacioppo, J. T. (2013). A quantitative meta-analysis of functional imaging studies of social rejection. *Scientific Reports*, 3, 1–3.

Cahn, S. M. & Forcehimes, A. (eds.). (2017). *Principles of Moral Philosophy: Classic and Contemporary Readings in Normative Ethics*. New York: Oxford University Press.

Calvert, S. L., Appelbaum, M., Dodge, K. A., Graham, S., Nagayama Hall, G. C., Hamby, S., ... & Hedges, L. V. (2017). The American Psychological Association Task Force assessment of violent video games: Science in the service of public interest. *American Psychologist*, 72(2), 126–143.

Calvo, R. A. & D'Mello, S. (2010). Affect detection: An interdisciplinary review of models, methods, and their applications. *IEEE Transactions on Affective Computing*, 1(1), 18–37.

Calvo, R. A., D'Mello, S. K., Gratch, J., & Kappas, A. (2015). Introduction to affective computing. In R. A. Calvo, S. K. D'Mello, J. Gratch, & A. Kappas (eds.), *The Oxford Handbook of Affective Computing* (pp. 1–10). Oxford: Oxford University Press.

Campos-Castillo, C. (2015). Revisiting the first-level digital divide in the United States: Gender and race/ethnicity patterns, 2007–2012. *Social Science Computer Review*, 33, 423–439.

Canellopoulou-Bottis, M. & Himma, K. E. (2008). The digital divide: A perspective for the future. In K. E. Himma & H. T. Tavani (eds.), *The Handbook of Information and Computer Ethics* (pp. 621–637). New Jersey: Wiley Press.

Caplan A. & Seife C. (2014). Facebook experiment used Silicon Valley trickery. *NBC News*, June 30. www.nbcnews.com/health/mental-health/opinion-facebook-experiment-used-silicon-valley-trickery-n144386

Carpenter, B. D. & Buday, S. (2007). Computer use among older adults in a naturally occurring retirement community. *Computers in Human Behavior*, 23(6), 3012–3024.

Carter, J. A., Clark, A., Kallestrup, J., Palermos, S. O., & Pritchard, D. (eds.). (2018). *Extended Epistemology*. Oxford: Oxford University Press.

Carter, J. A., Clark, A., & Palermos, S. O. (2018). New humans? Ethics, trust, and the extended mind. In J. A. Carter, A. Clark, J. Kallestrup, S. O. Palermos, & D. Pritchard (eds.), *Extended Epistemology* (pp. 331–351). Oxford: Oxford University Press.

Carter, J. A. & Palermos, S. O. (2016). Is having your computer compromised a personal assault? The ethics of extended cognition. *Journal of the American Philosophical Association*, 2(4), 542–560.

Carvalho, D., Bessa, M., Oliveira, L., Guedes, C., Peres, E., & Magalhães, L. (2012). New interaction paradigms to fight the digital divide: a pilot case study regarding multi-touch technology. *Procedia Computer Science*, 14, 128–137.

Casas, R., Marco, A., Falco, J. L., Artigas, J. I., & Abascal, J. (2006). Ethically aware design of a location system for people with dementia. In K. Miesenberger et al. (eds.), *International Conference on Computers for Handicapped Persons* (pp. 777–784). Berlin: Springer.

Casey, B., Craddock, N., Cuthbert, B., Hyman, S, Lee, F., & Ressler, K. (2013). DSM-5 and RDoC: progress in psychiatry research?. *Nature Reviews Neuroscience*, 14, 810–814.

Cavanna, A. E. (2018). The mind-body problem. In A. E. Cavanna (ed.), *Motion and Emotion* (pp. 29–44). Cham: Springer.

Ceyhan, A. A. & Ceyhan, E. (2008). Loneliness, depression, and computer self-efficacy as predictors of problematic internet use. *Cyber Psychology & Behavior*, *11*, 699–701.

Chalmers, D. (2011). Foreword. In A. Clark (ed.), *Supersizing the Mind: Embodiment, Action, and Cognitive Extension* (pp. ix–xvi). Oxford: Oxford University Press.

Charlier, N., Zupancic, N., Fieuws, S., Denhaerynck, K., Zaman, B., & Moons, P. (2016). Serious Games for improving knowledge and self-management in young people with chronic conditions: A systematic review and meta-analysis. *Journal of the American Medical Informatics Association*, *23*(1), 230–239.

Cheshire, W. P., Jr. (2010). Doing no harm to Hippocrates: Reality and virtual reality in ethics education. *Ethics and Medicine*, *26*(3), 137–142.

Cho, K. H., Lee, K. J., & Song, C. H. (2012). Virtual-reality balance training with a video-game system improves dynamic balance in chronic stroke patients. *The Tohoku Journal of Experimental Medicine*, *228*(1), 69–74.

Chopik, W. J. (2016). The benefits of social technology use among older adults are mediated by reduced loneliness. *Cyberpsychology, Behavior, and Social Networking*, *19*(9), 551–556.

Christman, J. (2004). Relational autonomy, liberal individualism, and the social constitution of selves. *Philosophical Studies*, *117*(1), 143–164.

Churchland, P. (1986). *Neurophilosophy: Toward a Unified Science of the Mind–Brain*. Cambridge, MA: MIT Press.

Churchland, P. (1988). *Matter and Consciousness*. Cambridge, MA: MIT Press.

Churchland, P. (1994). Can neurobiology teach us anything about consciousness? *Proceedings and Addresses of the American Philosophical Association*, *67*, 23–40.

Churchland, P. (2002). *Brainwise: Studies in Neurophilosophy*. Cambridge, MA: MIT Press.

Churchland, P. S. & Churchland, P. M. (2002). Neural worlds and real worlds. *Nature Reviews Neuroscience*, *3*, 903–907.

Ciaramelli, E., Muccioli, M., Ladavas, E., & di Pellegrino, G. (2007). Selective deficit in personal moral judgment following damage to ventromedial prefrontal cortex. *Social Cognitive and Affective Neuroscience*, *2*(2), 84–92.

Clark, A. (2003). *Natural-Born Cyborgs: Minds, Technologies, and the Future of Human*. Oxford: Oxford University Press.

Clark, A. (2008). *Supersizing the Mind: Embodiment, Action, and Cognitive Extension*. Oxford: Oxford University Press.

Clark, A. (2010a). Out of our brains, *New York Times*, December 12. http://opinionator.blogs.nytimes.com/2010/12/12/out-of-our-brains/

Clark, A. (2010b). Memento's revenge: The extended mind extended. In R. Menary (ed.), *The Extended Mind* (pp. 43–66). Cambridge, MA: MIT Press.

Clark, A. & Chalmers, D. (1998). The extended mind. *Analysis*, *58*(1), 7–19.

Clark, D. (2004). What if you meet face to face? A case study in virtual/material research ethics. In E. Buchanan (ed.), *Readings in Virtual Research Ethics*: Issues and Controversies (pp. 246–261). Hershey, PA: Idea Group.

Clausen, J. (2010). Ethical brain stimulation: Neuroethics of deep brain stimulation in research and clinical practice. *European Journal of Neuroscience*, 32(7), 1152–1162.

Clausen, J. & Levy, N. (eds.). (2015). *Handbook of Neuroethics*. Dordrecht: Springer.

Clewis, R. R. (2017). Does Kantian ethics condone mood and cognitive enhancement?. *Neuroethics*, 10(3), 349–361.

Clouser, K. D. & Gert, B. (1990). A critique of principlism. *The Journal of Medicine and Philosophy*, 15(2), 219–236.

Clowes, R. (2013). The cognitive integration of e-memory. *Review of Philosophy and Psychology*, 4(1), 107–133.

Clowes, R. (2015). Thinking in the cloud: The cognitive incorporation of cloud-based technology. *Philosophy & Technology*, 28(2), 261–296.

Cobb, S. V., Nichols, S., Ramsey, A., & Wilson, J. R. (1999). Virtual reality-induced symptoms and effects (VRISE). *Presence: Teleoperators & Virtual Environments*, 8(2), 169–186.

Coeckelbergh, M. (2007). Violent computer games, empathy, and cosmopolitanism. *Ethics and Information Technology*, 9(3), 219–231.

Coeckelbergh, M. (2015). Language and technology: Maps, bridges, and pathways. *AI & Society*, 32(2), 175–189.

Coeckelbergh, M. (2017). *Using Words and Things: Language and Philosophy of Technology*. New York: Routledge.

Coeckelbergh, M. (2018). Technology games: Using Wittgenstein for understanding and evaluating technology. Science and Engineering Ethics, 24(5), 1503–1519.

Cogburn, J. & Silcox, M. (2009). *Philosophy Through Video Games*. New York: Routledge.

Colder Carras, M., Van Rooij, A. J., Spruijt-Metz, D., Kvedar, J., Griffiths, M. D., Carabas, Y., & Labrique, A. (2018). Commercial video games as therapy: A new research agenda to unlock the potential of a global pastime. *Frontiers in Psychiatry*, 8(300), 1–7.

Colombetti, G. & Roberts, T. (2015). Extending the extended mind: The case for extended affectivity. *Philosophical Studies*, 172, 1243–1263.

Compaine, B. M. (ed.). (2001a). *The Digital Divide: Facing a Crisis or Creating a Myth?*. Cambridge, MA: MIT Press.

Compaine, B. M. (2001b). Information gaps: Myth or reality?. In B. M. Compaine (ed.), *The Digital Divide: Facing a Crisis or Creating a Myth?* (pp. 105–118). Cambridge, MA: MIT Press.

Connolly, I., Palmer, M., Barton, H., & Kirwan, G. (eds.). (2016). *An Introduction to Cyberpsychology*. New York: Routledge.

Cooper, W. (2004). Internet culture. In L. Floridi (ed.), *The Blackwell Guide to the Philosophy of Computing and Information* (pp. 92–105). Oxford: Blackwell Publishing.

Corgnet, B., Hernán Gonzalez, R., & Mateo, R. (2015). Cognitive reflection and the diligent worker: An experimental study of Millennials. *PLoS One*, 10: e0141243.

Cotten, S. R., Anderson, W. A., & McCullough, B. M. (2013). Impact of Internet use on loneliness and contact with others among older adults: Cross-sectional analysis. *Journal of Medical Internet Research*, 15, e39.

Courtney, C., Dawson, M., Schell, A., & Parsons, T. D. (2009). Affective virtual reality exposure: Psychophysiological support for increased elicitation of negative emotions in high and low fear subjects. *Lecture Notes in Artificial Intelligence*, 5638, 459–468.

Crick, F. (1994). *The Astonishing Hypothesis: The Scientific Search for the Soul*. New York: Touchstone.

Crick, F. & Koch, C. (2003). A framework for consciousness. *Nature Neuroscience*, 6, 119–126.

Critchley, H. D. (2002). Electrodermal responses: What happens in the brain. *The Neuroscientist*, 8(2), 132–142.

Cromwell, H. C. & Panksepp, J. (2011). Rethinking the cognitive revolution from a neural perspective: How overuse/misuse of the term 'cognition' and the neglect of affective controls in behavioral neuroscience could be delaying progress in understanding the BrainMind. *Neuroscience & Biobehavioral Reviews*, 35(9), 2026–2035.

Cross, E., Piggin, R., Douglas, T., & Vonkaenel-Flatt, J. (2012). *Virtual Violence II: Progress and Challenges in the Fight against Cyberbullying*. London: Beatbullying.

Crowder, S. A. & Merritte, K. (2013). The possible therapeutic benefits of utilizing motion gaming systems on pediatric patients presenting autism. *Journal of the Tennessee Medical Association*, 106(8), 41–43.

Cushman, F., Young, L., & Hauser, M. (2006). The role of conscious reasoning and intuition in moral judgment: Testing three principles of harm. *Psychological Science*, 17(12), 1082–1089.

Czaja, S. J. & Lee, C. C. (2007). Information technology and older adults. In A. Sears & J. A. Jacko (eds.), *Human-Computer Interaction Handbook: Fundamentals, Evolving Technologies and Emerging Applications*, 2nd ed. (pp. 777–792). Mahwah, NJ: Lawrence Erlbaum Associates.

Dahdah, M., Bennett, M., Prajapati, B., Parsons, T. D., Sullivan, E., & Driver, S. (2017a). Application of virtual environments in a multi-disciplinary day neurorehabilitation program to improve executive functioning using the Stroop task. *Neurorehabilitation*, 41, 721–734.

Dahdah, M., Bennett, M., Prajapati, P., Parsons, T. D., Sullivan, E., & Driver, S. (2017b). Application of virtual environments in a multi-disciplinary day neurorehabilitation programme. *Brain Injury*, 31, 918–919.

Damasio, A. R. (1994). *Descartes' Error: Emotion, Reason, and the Human Brain*. New York: Putnam.

Damasio, H., Grabowski, T., Frank, R., Galaburda, A. M., & Damasio, A. R. (1994). The return of Phineas Gage: Clues about the brain from the skull of a famous patient. *Science*, 264, 1102–1105.

Daniels, J. (2013). Race and racism in Internet studies: A review and critique. New Media & Society, 15(5), 695–719.

Daniels, N. (2008). *Just Health*. New York: Cambridge University Press.

D'Arcy, A. & Young, T. M. (2012). Ethics and social media: Implications for sociolinguistics in the networked public. *Journal of Sociolinguistics*, 16(4), 532–546.

Dattilio, F. M. & Hanna, M. A. (2012). Collaboration in cognitive-behavioral therapy. *Journal of Clinical Psychology*, 68(2), 146–158.

D'Aubin, A. (2007). Working for barrier removal in the ICT area: Creating a more accessible and inclusive Canada: A position statement by the Council of Canadians with Disabilities. *The Information Society*, 23(3), 193–201.

Davis, K., Hu, J., Feijs, L., & Owusu, E. (2015). Social hue: A subtle awareness system for connecting the elderly and their caregivers. Paper presented at the IEEE International Conference on Pervasive Computing and Communication Workshops (PerCom Workshops), St. Louis, MO, March 23–27.

Davis, S., Nesbitt, K., & Nalivaiko, E. (2014). A systematic review of cybersickness. In K. Blackmore, K. Nesbitt, & S. P. Smith (eds.), *Proceedings of the 2014 Conference on Interactive Entertainment* (pp. 1–9). New York: ACM.

Davis, S., Nesbitt, K., & Nalivaiko, E. (2015). Comparing the onset of cybersickness using the Oculus Rift and two virtual roller coasters. In Y. Pisan, K. Nesbitt, & K. Blackmore (eds.), *Proceedings of the 11th Australasian Conference on Interactive Entertainment* (pp. 3–14). Sydney: Conferences in Research and Practice in Information Technology (CRPIT).

Dawkins, R. (1982). *The Extended Phenotype*. Oxford: Oxford University Press.

Decety, J., Michalska, K. J., & Kinzler, K. D. (2011). The contribution of emotion and cognition to moral sensitivity: A neurodevelopmental study. Cerebral Cortex, 22(1), 209–220.

Dees, R. H. (2007). Better brains, better selves? The ethics of neuroenhancements. *Kennedy Institute of Ethics Journal*, 17(4), 371–395.

Dehaene, S. & Naccache, L. (2001). Towards a cognitive neuroscience of consciousness: Basic evidence and a workspace framework. *Cognition*, 79 (1–2), 1–37.

Delello, J. A. & McWhorter, R. R. (2017). Reducing the digital divide: Connecting older adults to iPad technology. *Journal of Applied Gerontology*, 36(1), 3–28.

Dennett, D. C. (1987). *The Intentional Stance*. Cambridge, MA: MIT Press.

Dennett, D. C. (1991). *Consciousness Explained*. New York: Penguin Books.

Dennett, D. C. (1996). *Kinds of Minds*. New York: Basic Books.

Department of Health, Education, and Welfare. (2014). The Belmont Report: Ethical principles and guidelines for the protection of human subjects of research. *The Journal of the American College of Dentists*, 81(3), 4–13.

Descartes, R. (1641/1996). *Meditations on First Philosophy* (trans. John Cottingham). Cambridge: Cambridge University Press.

Dewan, S. & Riggins, F. J. (2005). The digital divide: Current and future research directions. *Journal of the Association for Information Systems*, 6(12), 298–337.

D'Hondt, F. & Maurage, P. (2017). Electrophysiological studies in Internet addiction: A review within the dual-process framework. *Addictive Behaviors*, 64, 321–327.

DiMaggio, P. & Hargittai, E. (2001). From the "digital divide" to "digital inequality": Studying Internet use as penetration increases. Working Paper Series 15, Princeton University, Woodrow Wilson School of Public and International Affairs, Center for Arts and Cultural Policy Studies.

DiMaggio, P., Hargittai, E., Celeste, C., & Shafer, S. (2004). Digital inequality: From unequal access to differentiated use. In K. Neckerman (ed.), *Social Inequality* (pp. 355–400). New York. Russell Sage.

Dimoka, A. (2012). How to conduct a functional magnetic resonance (FMRI) study in social science research. *MIS Quarterly*, 36(3), 811–840.

Drayson, Z. (2009). Embodied cognitive science and its implications for psychopathology. *Philosophy, Psychiatry, & Psychology*, 16, 329–340.

Dreyfuss, E. (2015). How to check if you or a loved one were exposed in the Ashley Madison hack. *Wired*, August 19. www.wired.com/2015/08/check-loved-one-exposed-ashley-madison-hack/

Drum, K. B. & Littleton, H. L. (2014). Therapeutic boundaries in telepsychology: Unique issues and best practice recommendations. *Professional Psychology: Research and Practice*, 45(5), 309–315.

Dueck, A. & Parsons, T. D. (2004). Integration discourse: Modern and postmodern. *The Journal of Psychology and Theology*, 32, 232–247.

Dum, R. P., Levinthal, D. J., & Strick, P. L. (2016). Motor, cognitive, and affective areas of the cerebral cortex influence the adrenal medulla. *Proceedings of the National Academy of Sciences*, 113(35), 9922–9927.

Dunn, L. B., Palmer, B. W., Keehan, M., Jeste, D. V., & Appelbaum, P. S. (2006). Assessment of therapeutic misconception in older schizophrenia patients with a brief instrument. *American Journal of Psychiatry*, 163(3), 500–506.

Edelman, G. M. (2004). Wider than the sky: The phenomenal gift of consciousness. New Haven, CT: Yale University Press.

Eisenberger, N. I. (2012). The neural bases of social pain: Evidence for shared representations with physical pain. *Psychosomatic Medicine*, 74, 126–135.

Eisenberger, N. I. (2013). An empirical review of the neural underpinnings of receiving and giving social support: Implications for health. *Psychosomatic Medicine*, 75(6), 545–556.

Eisenberger, N. I. (2015). Social pain and the brain: Controversies, questions, and where to go from here. *Annual Review of Psychology*, 66, 601–629.

El Ayadi, M., Kamel, M. S., & Karray, F. (2011). Survey on speech emotion recognition: Features, classification schemes, and databases. *Pattern Recognition*, 44(3), 572–587.

Elhai, J. D. & Hall, B. J. (2015). How secure is mental health providers' electronic patient communication? An empirical investigation. *Professional Psychology: Research and Practice*, 46(6), 444–450.

Ellul, J. (1964). *The Technological Society* (trans. John Wilkinson). New York: Vintage Books.

Eltis, K. (2005). Predicating dignity on autonomy: The need for further inquiry into the ethics of tagging and tracking dementia patients with GPS technology. Elder Law Journal, 13, 387–411.

Eng, J. (2014). Snapchat hacked, info on 4.6 million users reportedly leaked. *NBC News*, January 1. www.nbcnews.com/business/snapchathacked-info-4-6-million-users-reportedlyleaked-2D11833474.

Epstein, R. (2007). The truth about online dating. *Scientific American Mind*, 18(1), 28–35.

Ermann, D., Williams, M., & Shauf, M. (1997). *Computers, Ethics, and Society*. Oxford: Oxford University Press.

Ernst, M., Bolla, K., Mouratidis, M., et al. (2002). Decision-making in a risk-taking task: A PET study. *Neuropsychopharmacology* 26, 682–691.

Ess, C. (2009). *Digital Media Ethics*. Malden, MA: Polity Press.

Evans, M. (2010). Murder, ransom, theft and grief: Understanding digital ethics in games. In D. Riha (ed.), *Videogame Cultures and the Future of Interactive Entertainment* (pp. 81–89). Oxford: Inter-Disciplinary Press.

Evers, K. (2017). The contribution of neuroethics to international brain research initiatives. *Nature Reviews Neuroscience*, 18(1), 1–2.

Ewell, P. J., Guadagno, R. E., Jones, M., & Dunn, R. A. (2016). Good person or bad character? Personality predictors of morality and ethics in avatar selection for video game play. *Cyberpsychology, Behavior, and Social Networking*, 19(7), 435–440.

Ewing, A. C. (1965). *Ethics*. New York: Free Press.

Eyal, N. (2014). *Hooked: How to Build Habit-Forming Products*. New York: Penguin.

Facebook. (2014). Introducing graph search. www.facebook.com/about/graphsearch

Facebook Inc. (2015). Key facts about Facebook. http://newsroom.fb.com/keyfacts

Faden, R. R., & Beauchamp, T. L. (1986). *A History and Theory of Informed Consent*. New York: Oxford University Press.

Farah, M. J. (2005). Neuroethics: the practical and the philosophical. Trends in Cognitive Sciences, 9(1), 34–40.

Farah, M. J. (2012). Neuroethics: The ethical, legal, and societal impact of neuroscience. *Annual Review of Psychology*, 63, 571–591.

Farah, M. J. (2015a). The unknowns of cognitive enhancement. *Science*, 350(6259), 379–380.

Farah, M. J. (2015b). An ethics toolbox for neurotechnology. *Neuron*, 86(1), 34–37.

Farah, M. J., Illes, J., Cook-Deegan, R., Gardner, H., Kandel, E., King, P., . . . & Wolpe, P. R. (2004). Neurocognitive enhancement: What can we do and what should we do?. *Nature Reviews Neuroscience*, 5(5), 421–425.

Faurholt-Jepsen, M., Vinberg, M., Frost, M., Debel, S., Margrethe Christensen, E., Bardram, J. E., & Kessing, L. V. (2016). Behavioral activities collected through smartphones and the association with illness activity in bipolar disorder. *International journal of Methods in Psychiatric Research*, 25(4), 309–323.

Feenberg, A. (1995). Alternative Modernity: The Technical Turn in Philosophy and Social Theory. Berkeley: University of California Press.

Feenberg, A. (1999). Questioning Technology. New York: Routledge.

Feiler, J. B. & Stabio, M. E. (2018). Three pillars of educational neuroscience from three decades of literature. *Trends in Neuroscience and Education*, 13, 17–25. https://doi.org/10.1016/j.tine.2018.11.001

Feliciano, C., Lee, R., & Robnett, B. (2011). Racial boundaries among Latinos: Evidence from internet daters' racial preferences. *Social Problems*, 58, 189–212.

Feliciano, C., Robnett, B., & Komaie, G. (2009). Gendered racial exclusion among White internet daters. *Social Science Research*, 38, 39–54.

Ferguson, C. J., Coulson, M., & Barnett, J. (2011). A meta-analysis of pathological gaming prevalence and comorbidity with mental health, academic and social problems. *Journal of Psychiatric Research*, 45, 1573–1578.

Ferguson, C. J. & Kilburn, J. (2010). Much ado about nothing: The misestimation and overinterpretation of violent video game effects in eastern and western nations: comment on Anderson et al. (2010). *Psychological Bulletin*, 136, 174–178.

Fernback, J. & Papacharissi, Z. (2007. Online privacy as legal safeguard: The relationship among consumer, online portal, and privacy policies. *New Media & Society*, 9(5), 715–734.

Ferro, E., Helbig, N. C., & Gil-Garcia, J. R. (2011). The role of IT literacy in defining digital divide policy needs. *Government Information Quarterly*, 28 (1), 3–10.

Fiddick, L., Spampinato, M. V., & Grafman, J. (2005). Social contracts and precautions activate different neurological systems: An fMRI investigation of deontic reasoning. *NeuroImage*, 28(4), 778–786.

Finkel, E. J., Eastwick, P. W., Karney, B. R., Reis, H. T., & Sprecher, S. (2012). Online dating: A critical analysis from the perspective of psychological science. *Psychological Science in the Public Interest*, 13(1), 3–66.

Fins, J. J. (2008). Neuroethics and neuroimaging: Moving toward transparency. *The American Journal of Bioethics*, 8(9), 46–52.

Firth, J., Torous, J., Nicholas, J., Carney, R., Pratap, A., Rosenbaum, S., & Sarris, J. (2017). The efficacy of smartphone-based mental health interventions for depressive symptoms: A meta-analysis of randomized controlled trials. *World Psychiatry*, 16(3), 287–298.

Fischer, K. W. & Bidell, T. (2006). Dynamic development of action and thought. In W. Damon & R. Lerner (eds.), *Handbook of Child Psychology, Vol. 1: Theoretical Models of Human Development*, 6th ed. (pp. 313–399). Hoboken, NJ: Wiley.

Fitz, N. S. & Reiner, P. B. (2016). Perspective: Time to expand the mind. *Nature*, 531(7592), S9–S9.

Fleischman, J. (2002). *Phineas Gage: A Gruesome but True Story about Brain Science*. New York: Houghton Mifflin.

Fleming, T., Dixon, R., Frampton, C., & Merry, S. (2012). A pragmatic randomized controlled trial of computerized CBT (SPARX) for symptoms of depression among adolescents excluded from mainstream education. Behavioural and Cognitive Psychotherapy, 40(5), 529–541.

Flick, C. (2013). Informed consent in information technology. In J. Weckert (ed.), *The Importance of Being Professional: Professionalism in the ICT Industry*. Canberra: ANU E-Press.

Flick, C. (2016). Informed consent and the Facebook emotional manipulation study. *Research Ethics*, 12(1), 14–28.

Floridi, L. (1999). Information ethics: On the philosophical foundation of computer ethics. *Ethics and Information Technology*, 1(1), 33–52.

Floridi, L. (2001). Ethics in the Infosphere. *The Philosophers' Magazine*, 6(16), 18–19.

Floridi, L. (2002). Information ethics: An environmental approach to the digital divide. *Philosophy in the Contemporary World*, 9(1), 39–45.

Floridi, L. (2005). The ontological interpretation of informational privacy. *Ethics and Information Technology*, 7(4), 185–200.

Floridi, L. (2006a). Four challenges for a theory of informational privacy. *Ethics and Information Technology*, 8(3), 109–119.

Floridi, L. (2006b). Information ethics, its nature and scope. *ACM SIGCAS Computers and Society*, 36(3), 21–36.

Floridi, L. (2008a). Foundations of information ethics. In K. Himma & H. Tavani (eds.), *The Handbook of Information and Computer Ethics* (pp. 3–24). Hoboken, NJ: Wiley.

Floridi, L. (2008b). Information ethics: Its nature and scope. In J. van den Hoven & J. Weckert (eds.), *Information Technology and Moral Philosophy* (pp. 40–65). Cambridge: Cambridge University Press.

Floridi, L. (2013). *The Ethics of Information*. Oxford: Oxford University Press.

Floridi, L. (2014). *The Fourth Revolution: How the Infosphere Is Reshaping Human Reality*. Oxford: Oxford University Press.

Floridi, L. (2015). *The Online Manifesto: Being Human in a Hyperconnected Era*. Cham: Springer.

Floridi, L. & Sanders, J. W. (2001). Artificial evil and the foundation of computer ethics. *Ethics and Information Technology*, 3(1), 55–66.

Floridi, L. & Sanders, J. W. (2004). On the morality of artificial agents. *Minds and Machines*, 14(3), 349–379.

Floridi, L. & Sanders, J. W. (2005). Internet ethics: The constructionist values of homo poieticus. In R. Cavalier (ed.), *The Impact of the Internet on Our Moral Lives* (pp. 195–215). New York: SUNY Press.

Fogel, J. & Nehmad, E. (2009). Internet social network communities: Risk taking, trust, and privacy concerns. *Computers in Human Behavior*, 25(1), 153–160.

Fogg, B. J. (2002). Persuasive technology: Using computers to change what we think and do. Ubiquity, 2002(December), 5.

Foot, P. (1978). The problem of abortion and the doctrine of the double effect. In P. Foot, *Virtues and Vices and Other Essays in Moral Philosophy* (pp. 19–32). Berkeley: University of California Press.

Ford, S. G & Ford, G. S. (2009). *Internet Use and Depression Among the Elderly*. Phoenix Center Policy Paper.

Forlini, C., Gauthier, S., & Racine, E. (2013). Should physicians prescribe cognitive enhancers to healthy individuals?. *Canadian Medical Association Journal*, 185(12), 1047–1050.

Forson, C. & Özbilgin, M. (2003). Dot-com women entrepreneurs in the UK. *The International Journal of Entrepreneurship and Innovation*, 4(1), 13–24.

Fox, S. (2011). *Americans Living with Disability and Their Technology Profile*. Report. Pew Research Center. www.pewinternet.org/~/media//Files/Reports/2011/PIP_Disability.pdf.

Fox, J. & Tang, W. Y. (2014). Sexism in online video games: The role of conformity to masculine norms and social dominance orientation. *Computers in Human Behavior*, 33, 314–320.

Fox, J. & Tang, W. Y. (2017). Women's experiences with general and sexual harassment in online video games: Rumination, organizational responsiveness, withdrawal, and coping strategies. *New Media & Society*, 19(8), 1290–1307.

Fozard, J. L. (2005). Impacts of technology interventions on health and self-esteem. *Gerontechnology*, 4(2), 63–76.

Franceschini, S., Gori, S., Ruffino, M., Viola, S., Molteni, M., & Facoetti, A. (2013). Action video games make dyslexic children read better. *Current Biology*, 23, 462–466.

Frankel, M. S., & Siang, S. (1999). *Ethical and Legal Aspects of Human Subjects Research on the Internet*. Washington, DC: American Association for the Advancement of Science.

Frankish, K., & Evans, J. S. B. T. (2009). The duality of mind: An historical perspective. In J. S. B. T. Evans & K. Frankish (eds.), *In Two Minds: Dual Processes and Beyond* (pp. 1–29). Oxford: Oxford University Press.

Frasca, G. (2003). Simulation versus narrative: Introduction to Ludology. In M. J. P. Wolf & B. Perron (eds.), *The Video Game Theory Reader* (pp. 221–236). London: Routledge.

Friedman, B. & Kahn, P. H. (2012). Human values, ethics and design. In J. A. Jacko & A. Sears (eds.), *The Human-Computer Interaction Handbook*, 3rd ed. (pp. 1241–1266). Mahwah, NJ: Lawrence Erlbaum Associates.

Frith, C. D. & Frith, U. (2007). Social cognition in humans. *Current Biology*, 17 (16), R724–R732.

Frith, C. D. & Singer, T. (2008). The role of social cognition in decision making. Philosophical Transactions of the Royal Society of London. *Series B, Biological Sciences*, 363(1511), 3875–3886.

Fumagalli, M. & Priori, A. (2012). Functional and clinical neuroanatomy of morality. *Brain*, 135(7), 2006–2021.

Gamble, N. & Morris, Z. A. (2014). Ethical and competent practice in the online age. *InPsych*, 36, 18–19. www.psychology.org.au/Content.aspx?ID=5851

Gaucher, N., Payot, A., & Racine, E. (2013). Cognitive enhancement in children and adolescents: Is it in their best interests?. *Acta Paediatrica*, 102(12), 1118–1124.

Gavison, R. (1980). Privacy and the limits of law. *The Yale Law Journal*, 89(3), 421–471.

Gelinas, L., Pierce, R., Winkler, S., Cohen, I. G., Lynch, H. F., & Bierer, B. E. (2017). Using social media as a research recruitment tool: Ethical issues and recommendations. *The American Journal of Bioethics*, 17(3), 3–14.

Geniole, S. N., Carré, J. M., & McCormick, C. M. (2011). State, not trait, neuroendocrine function predicts costly reactive aggression in men after social exclusion and inclusion. *Biological Psychology*, 87(1), 137–145.

Gentile, D. A., & Stone, W. (2005). Violent video game effects on children and adolescents. A review of the literature. *Minerva Pediatrica*, 57(6), 337–358.

Gentile, D., Choo, H., Liau, A., Sim, T., Li, D., Fung, D., & Khoo, A. (2011). Pathological videogame use among youths: A two-year longitudinal study. *Pediatrics*, 127, 319–329.

Gert, B. (1998). *Morality: Its Nature and Justification*. Oxford: Oxford University Press.

Ghadially, R. (ed.). (2007). *Urban Women in Contemporary India: A Reader*. New Delhi: Sage.

Ghobadi, S. & Ghobadi, Z. (2015). How access gaps interact and shape digital divide: A cognitive investigation. *Behaviour & Information Technology*, 34(4), 330–340.

Giordano, J. (2008). Technology in pain medicine: Research, practice, and the influence of the market. *Practical Pain Management*, 8, 56–59.

Gjoreski, M., Luštrek, M., Gams, M., & Gjoreski, H. (2017). Monitoring stress with a wrist device using context. *Journal of Biomedical Informatics*, 73, 159–170.

Glannon, W. (2006). Neuroethics. *Bioethics*, 20(1), 37–52.

Goel, V. (2014). As data overflows online, researchers grapple with ethics. *New York Times*, August 12. www.nytimes.com/2014/08/13/technology/the-boon-of-online-data-puts-social-science-in-a-quandary.html

Goel, V., Buchel, C., Frith, C., & Dolan, R. J. (2000). Dissociation of mechanisms underlying syllogistic reasoning. *Neuroimage*, 12(5), 504–514.

Goel, V., & Dolan, R. J. (2003). Explaining modulation of reasoning by belief. *Cognition*, 87(1), B11–B22.

Goerger, M. (2017). Value, violence, and the ethics of gaming. *Ethics and Information Technology*, 19(2), 95–105.

Gola, J. A., Beidas, R. S., Antinoro-Burke, D., Kratz, H. E., & Fingerhut, R. (2016). Ethical considerations in exposure therapy with children. *Cognitive and Behavioral Practice*, 23(2), 184–193.

González-Bueso, V., Santamaría, J. J., Fernández, D., Merino, L., Montero, E., & Ribas, J. (2018). Association between internet gaming disorder or pathological video-game use and comorbid psychopathology: A comprehensive review. *International Journal of Environmental Research and Public Health*, 15(4), 668.

Goode, L. (2010). Cultural citizenship online: The Internet and digital culture. *Citizenship Studies*, 14(5), 527–542.

Gotterbarn, D. (2010). The ethics of video games: Mayhem, death, and the training of the next generation. *Information Systems Frontiers*, 12(4), 369–377.

Gotterbarn, D. & Moor, J. (2009). Virtual decisions: Video game ethics, just consequentialism, and ethics on the fly. *Computers and Society*, 39(3), 27–42.

Graf, W. D., Nagel, S. K., Epstein, L. G., Miller, G., Nass, R., & Larriviere, D. (2013). Pediatric neuroenhancement: Ethical, legal, social, and neurodevelopmental implications. *Neurology*, 80(13), 1251–1260.

Graham, M., Hale, S., & Stephens, M. (2012). Featured graphic: Digital divide: the geography of Internet access. Environment and Planning A, 44(5), 1009–1010.

Granic, I., Lobel, A., & Engels, R. C. (2014). The benefits of playing video games. *American psychologist*, 69(1), 66.

Granitz, N., & Loewy, D. (2007). Applying ethical theories: Interpreting and responding to student plagiarism. *Journal of Business Ethics*, 72(3), 293–306.

Greely, H. T., Ramos, K. M., & Grady, C. (2016). Neuroethics in the age of brain projects. *Neuron*, 92(3), 637–641.

Greene, J. D. (2007). The secret joke of Kant's soul. In W. Sinnott-Armstrong (ed.), *Moral Psychology, Vol. 3: The Neuroscience of Morality: Emotion, Brain Disorders, and Development* (pp. 35–80). Cambridge, MA: MIT Press.

Greene, J. D. (2015). The cognitive neuroscience of moral judgment and decision making. In J. Decety & T. Wheatley (eds.), *The Moral Brain: A Multidisciplinary Perspective* (pp. 197–220). Cambridge, MA: MIT Press.

Greene, J. D., Morelli, S. A., Lowenberg, K., Nystrom, L. E., & Cohen, J. D. (2008). Cognitive load selectively interferes with utilitarian moral judgment. *Cognition*, 107, 1144–1154.

Greene, J. D., Nystrom, L. E., Engell, A. D., Darley, J. M., & Cohen, J. D. (2004). The neural bases of cognitive conflict and control in moral judgment. *Neuron*, 44(2), 389–400.

Greene, J. D., Sommerville, R. B., Nystrom, L. E., Darley, J. M., & Cohen, J. D. (2001). An fMRI investigation of emotional engagement in moral judgment. *Science*, 293(5537), 2105–2108.

Griffiths, M. D., van Rooij, A., Kardefelt-Winther, D., et al. (2016). Working towards an international consensus on criteria for assessing Internet gaming disorder: A critical commentary on Petry et al. (2014). *Addiction*, 111, 167–178.

Grimmelmann, J. (2014). The Facebook emotional manipulation study: sources. The Laboratorium, June 30. http://laboratorium.net/archive/2014/06/30/the_facebook_emotional_manipulation_study_source

Grimmelmann, J. (2015). The law and ethics of experiments on social media users. *Journal on Telecommunications & High Technology Law*, 13, 219–271.

Grodzinsky, F. (2001). The practitioner from within: Revisiting the virtues. In A. R. Spinello & T. H. Tavani (eds.), *Readings in Cyberethics* (pp. 580–591). Sudbury, MA: Jones & Bartlett.

Gros, D. F., Morland, L. A., Greene, C. J., et al. (2013). Delivery of evidence-based psychotherapy via video telehealth. *Journal of Psychopathology and Behavioral Assessment*, 35(4), 506–521.

Grossman, L. (2009). Iran protests: Twitter, the medium of the movement. *Time*, June 17. www.time.com/time/world/article/0,8599,1905125,00.html.

Grunwald, A. (2014). Technology assessment for responsible innovation. In L. van den Hoven, N. Doorn, T. Swierstra, B. J. Koops, & H. Romijn (eds.), *Responsible Innovation 1: Innovative Solutions for Global Issues* (pp. 15–31). Dordrecht: Springer.

Gupta, K., Sinha, A., & Bhola, P. (2016). Intersections between ethics and technology: Online client–therapist interactions. In P. Bhola & A. Raguram (eds.), *Ethical Issues in Counselling and Psychotherapy Practice* (pp. 169–186). Singapore: Springer.

Gutierrez-Martinez, O., Gutierrez-Maldonado, J., & Loreto-Quijada, D. (2011). Control over the virtual environment influences the presence and efficacy of a virtual reality intervention on pain. *Studies in Health Technology and Informatics*, 167, 111–115.

Hadlington, L. (2017). *Cybercognition: Brain, Behaviour and the Digital World*. London: Sage.

Haidt, J. (2001). The emotional dog and its rational tail: A social intuitionist approach to moral judgment. *Psychological Review*, 108(4), 814–834.

Hammer J. (2015). Marriage in American Muslim communities. *Religion Compass*, 9, 35–44.

Hardiman, M., Rinne, L., Gregory, E., & Yarmolinskaya, J. (2012). Neuroethics, neuroeducation, and classroom teaching: Where the brain sciences meet pedagogy. *Neuroethics*, 5(2), 135–143.

Hargittai, E. (2015), Is bigger always better? Potential biases of big data derived from social network sites. *The Annals of the American Academy of Political and Social Science*, 659(1), 63–76.

Hargittai, E. & Hinnant, A. (2008). Digital inequality: Differences in young adults' use of the Internet. *Communication Research*, 35, 602–621.

Harley, D., Fitzpatrick, G., Axelrod, L., White, G., & McAllister, G. (2010). Making the Wii at home: Game play by older people in sheltered housing. In Symposium of the Austrian HCI and Usability Engineering Group (pp. 156–176). Berlin: Springer.

Harlow, J. M. (1848). Passage of an iron rod through the head. *Boston Medical Surgery Journal*, 39, 389–393.

Harrington, T. L. & Harrington, M. K. (2000). *Gerontechnology: Why and How*. Maastricht: Shaker.

Harris, J. (2010). *Enhancing Evolution: The Ethical Case for Making Better People*. Princeton: Princeton University Press.

Harrison, T. (2014). *The Influence of the Internet on the Character Virtues of 11–14 Year Olds*. Birmingham, AL: University of Birmingham.

Harrison, T. (2015). Virtuous reality: Moral theory and research into cyber-bullying. *Ethics and Information Technology*, 17(4), 275–283.

Harrison, T. (2016). Cultivating cyber-phronesis: A new educational approach to tackle cyberbullying. *Pastoral Care in Education*, 34(4), 232–244.

Hauser, M. D. (2006a). The liver and the moral organ. *Social Cognitive and Affective Neuroscience*, 1(3), 214–220.

Hauser, M. D. (2006b). *Moral Minds: The Nature of Right and Wrong*. New York: Harper Perennial.

Hauser, M., Cushman, F., Young, L., Kang-Xing Jin, R., & Mikhail, J. (2007). A dissociation between moral judgments and justifications. *Mind & Language*, 22(1), 1–21.

Heersmink, R. (2015). Dimensions of integration in embedded and extended cognitive systems. *Phenomenology and the Cognitive Sciences*, 14(3), 577–598.

Heersmink, R. (2017). Extended mind and cognitive enhancement: Moral aspects of cognitive artifacts. *Phenomenology and the Cognitive Sciences*, 16(1), 17–32.

Heersmink, R. & Carter, J. A. (2017). The philosophy of memory technologies: Metaphysics, knowledge, and values. *Memory Studies*. https://doi.org/10.1177/1750698017703810

Heersmink, R. & Knight, S. (2018). Distributed learning: Educating and assessing extended cognitive systems. *Philosophical Psychology*, 31(6), 969–990.

Heidegger, M. (1954). The question concerning technology. In C. Hanks (ed.), *Technology and Values: Essential Readings* (pp. 99–113). London: John Wiley & Sons.

Heimo, O. I., Kimppa, K. K., Helle, S., Korkalainen, T., & Lehtonen, T. (2014). Augmented reality: Towards an ethical fantasy?. Paper presented at the 2014 IEEE International Symposium on Ethics in Science, Technology and Engineering, Chicago, IL, May 23–24.

Henderson, G. E., Churchill, L. R., Davis, A. M., et al. (2007). Clinical trials and medical care: Defining the therapeutic misconception. *PLoS Medicine*, 4(11), e324.

Hengartner, M. P. (2018). Raising awareness for the replication crisis in clinical psychology by focusing on inconsistencies in psychotherapy research: How much can we rely on published findings from efficacy trials?. *Frontiers in Psychology*, 9(256), 1–5.

Henrich, J., Heine, S. J., & Norenzayan, A. (2010). The weirdest people in the world? *Behavioral and Brain Sciences*, 33, 61–83.

Herring, S. C. (1996). Linguistic and critical analysis of computer-mediated communication: Some ethical and scholarly considerations. *The Information Society*, 12(2), 153–168.

Hilbert, M. (2011). Digital gender divide or technologically empowered women in developing countries? A typical case of lies, damned lies, and statistics. *Women's Studies International Forum*, 34(6), 479–489.

Hill, R., Betts, L. R., & Gardner, S. E. (2015). Older adults' experiences and perceptions of digital technology: (Dis)empowerment, wellbeing, and inclusion. *Computers in Human Behavior*, 48, 415–423.

Himma, K. E. (2007). The information gap, the digital divide, and the obligations of affluent nations. *African Information Ethics in the Context of the Global Information Society*, 7, 63–76.

Hinduja, S. & Patchin, J. W. (2008). Cyberbullying: An exploratory analysis of factors related to offending and victimization. *Deviant Behavior*, 29, 129–156.

Hoeft, F., Watson, C. L., Kesler, S. R., Bettinger, K. E., & Reiss, A. L. (2008). Gender differences in the mesocorticolimbic system during computer game-play. *Journal of Psychiatric Research*, 42, 253–258.

Hoffman, G. A. (2016). Out of our skulls: How the extended mind thesis can extend psychiatry. *Philosophical Psychology*, 29(8), 1160–1174.

Holt, L. (2004). The "voices" of children: De-centring empowering research relations. *Children's Geographies*, 2(1), 13–27.

Hong, S. B., Kim, J. W., Choi, E. J., et al. (2013). Reduced orbitofrontal cortical thickness in male adolescents with internet addiction. *Behavioral and Brain Functions*, 9(1), 1–5.

Hordyk, S. R. (2017). "This feels like school!" Revisiting assent and motivation in research with child participants. *Child and Adolescent Social Work Journal*, 34(6), 583–595.

Horn, G. (2008). *Brain Science, Addiction and Drugs*. London: Academy of Medical Sciences.

Horne-Moyer, H. L., Moyer, B. H., Messer, D. C., & Messer, E. S. (2014). The use of electronic games in therapy: A review with clinical implications. *Current Psychiatry Reports*, 16(12), 1–9.

Hossain, M. A. & Ahmed, D. T. (2012). Virtual caregiver: An ambient-aware elderly monitoring system. *IEEE Transactions on Information Technology in Biomedicine*, 16(6), 1024–1031.

Howard, P. N. (2015). *Pax Technica: How the Internet of Things May Set Us Free or Lock Us Up*. New Haven, CT: Yale University Press.

Howard-Jones, P. (2010). *Introducing Neuroeducational Research: Neuroscience, Education and the Brain from Contexts to Practice*. New York: Routledge.

Howard-Jones, P. A. & Fenton, K. D. (2012). The need for interdisciplinary dialogue in developing ethical approaches to neuroeducational research. *Neuroethics*, 5(2), 119–134.

Howard-Jones, P. A., Varma, S., Ansari, D., Butterworth, B., De Smedt, B., Goswami, U., Thomas, M. S. et al. (2016). The principles and practices of educational neuroscience: Comment on Bowers (2016). *Psychological Review*, 123(5), 620–627.

Hughes, R. (2008a). Electronic surveillance and tagging people with dementia. *International Journal of Palliative Nursing*, 4, 74–76.

Hughes, R. (2008b). Using surveillance and tracking technology in care homes. *Nursing and Residential Care*, 10, 341–345.

Hughes, J. C., Newby, J., Louw, S. J., Campbell, G. & Hutton, J. (2008). Ethical issues and tagging in dementia: A survey. *Journal of Ethics in Mental Health*, 3, 1–6.

Hume, D. (1739/1978). *A Treatise of Human Nature*. Oxford: Oxford University Press.

Hume, D. (1748). *Philosophical Essays Concerning Human Understanding*, 1st ed. London: A. Millar.

Huyer, S., Hafkin, N., Ertl, H., & Dryburgh, H. (2005). Women in the information society. In G. Sciadas (ed.), *From the Digital Divide to Digital Opportunities: Measuring Infostates for Development* (pp. 135–196). Ottawa: NRC Research Press.

Ihde, D. (1990). *Technology and the Lifeworld: From Garden to Earth*. Bloomington: University of Indiana Press.

Ihde, D. (1993). *Postphenomology*. Evanston, IL: Northwestern University Press.

Illes, J. (ed.). (2017). *Neuroethics: Anticipating the Future*. New York: Oxford University Press.

Illes, J. & Bird, S. J. (2006). Neuroethics: A modern context for ethics in neuroscience. *Trends in Neurosciences*, 29(9), 511–517.

Illes, J., Kirschen, M. P., & Gabrieli, J. D. (2003). From neuroimaging to neuroethics. *Nature Neuroscience*, 6(3), 205.

Immordino-Yang, M. H. (2008). The smoke around mirror neurons: Goals as sociocultural and emotional organizers of perception and action in learning. *Mind, Brain, and Education*, 2(2), 67–73.

Immordino-Yang, M. H. & Singh, V. (2011). Perspectives from social and affective neuroscience on the design of digital learning technologies. In R. A. Calvo & S. K. D'Mello (eds.), *New Perspectives on Affect and Learning Technologies* (pp. 233–241). New York: Springer.

Insel, T., Cuthbert, B., Garvey, M., Heinssen, R., Pine, D, Quinn, K., et al. (2010). Research Domain Criteria (RDoC): Toward a new classification framework for research on mental disorders. *American Journal of Psychiatry*, 167, 748–751.

International Society for Mental Health Online. (2009). *Suggested Principles for the Online Provision of Mental Health Services*. www.ismho.org/suggestions.asp.

Internet Society. (2012). *Internet Accessibility Internet Use by Persons with Disabilities: Moving Forwards*. Report. November 1. www.internetsociety.org/resources/doc/2012/internet-accessibility-internet-use-by-persons-with-disabilities-moving-forward/

Istepanian, R. S., Jovanov, E., & Zhang, Y. T. (2004). Guest editorial introduction to the special section on m-health: Beyond seamless mobility and global wireless health-care connectivity. *IEEE Transactions on Information Technology in Biomedicine*, 8(4), 405–414.

Istepanian, R. S. & Lacal, J. C. (2003). Emerging mobile communication technologies for health: Some imperative notes on m-health. In *Engineering in Medicine and Biology Society, Proceedings of the 25th Annual International Conference of the IEEE*, Vol. 2 (pp. 1414–1416), Cancun: IEEE.

Ivanhoe, P. J. (2013). Virtue ethics and the Chinese Confucian tradition. In D. Russell (ed.), *The Cambridge Companion to Virtue Ethics* (pp. 49–69). Cambridge: Cambridge University Press.

Jacobsen, L. A., Kent, M., Lee, M., & Mather, M. (2011). *America's Aging Population*: Washington, DC: Population Reference Bureau.

Januszewski, A. & Molenda, M. (eds.). (2007). *Educational Technology: A Definition with Commentary*, 2nd ed. New York: Routledge.

Java, A., Song, X., Finin, T., & Tseng, B. (2007). Why we Twitter: Understanding microblogging usage and communities. In *Proceedings of the 9th WebKDD and 1st SNA-KDD 2007 Workshop on Web Mining and Social Network Analysis* (pp. 56–65). San Jose, CA: ACM.

Jenks, C. (2000). Zeitgeist. In P. Christensen & A. James (eds.), *Research with Children: Perspectives and Practices* (pp. 62–76). London: Falmer Press.

Jerritta, S., Murugappan, M., Nagarajan, R., & Wan, K. (2011). Physiological signals based human emotion recognition: A review. In *Proceedings: 2011 IEEE 7th International Colloquium on Signal Processing and Its Applications, CSPA 2011* (pp. 410–415). Penang: IEEE.

Jiménez-Murcia, S., Fernández-Aranda, F., Granero, R., Chóliz, M., La Verde, M., Aguglia, E., . . . & del Pino-Gutiérrez, A. (2014). Video game addiction in gambling disorder: Clinical, psychopathological, and personality correlates. *BioMed Research International*, 2014, 1–11.

Jimoh, L., Pate, M. A., Lin, L., & Schulman, K. A. (2012). A model for the adoption of ICT by health workers in Africa. *International Journal of Medical Informatics*, 81(11), 773–781.

Johansson, M. (2009). Why unreal punishment in response to unreal crimes might actually be a really good thing. *Ethics and Information Technology*, 11(1), 71–79.

Johnson, D. (2001). *Computer Ethics*. Upper Saddle River, NJ: Prentice Hall.

Johnson, D. & Nissenbaum, H. (1995). *Computers, Ethics and Social Values*. Englewood Cliffs, NJ: Prentice Hall.

Johnson, S. C., Baxter, L. C., Wilder, L. S., Pipe, J. G., Heiserman, J. E., & Prigatano, G. P. (2002). Neural correlates of self-reflection. *Brain: A Journal of Neurology*, 125, 1808–1814.

Joint Task Force. (2013).Guidelines for the practice of telepsychology. *American Psychologist*, 68(9), 791–800.

Jovanovski, D., Zakzanis, K., Campbell, Z., Erb, S., & Nussbaum, D. (2012a). Development of a novel, ecologically oriented virtual reality measure of executive function: The multitasking in the city test. *Applied Neuropsychology: Adult*, 19, 171–182.

Jovanovski, D., Zakzanis, K., Ruttan, L., Campbell, Z., Erb, S., & Nussbaum, D. (2012b). Ecologically valid assessment of executive dysfunction using a novel virtual reality task in patients with acquired brain injury. *Applied Neuropsychology: Adult*, 19, 207–220.

Juel Vang, K. (2013). Ethics of Google's Knowledge Graph: Some considerations. *Journal of Information, Communication and Ethics in Society*, 11(4), 245–260.

Juengst E. (1998). What does enhancement mean? In E. Parens (ed.), *Enhancing Human Traits: Ethical and Social Implications* (pp. 29–47). Washington, DC: Georgetown University Press.

Jung, J. Y., Qiu, J. L., & Kim, Y. C. (2001). Internet connectedness and inequality beyond the "divide." *Communication Research*, 28, 507–535.

Kade, D. (2015). Ethics of virtual reality applications in computer game production. *Philosophies*, 1(1), 73–86.

Kadosh, R. C., Levy, N., O'Shea, J., Shea, N., & Savulescu, J. (2012). The neuroethics of non-invasive brain stimulation. *Current Biology*, 22(4), R108–R111.

Kalberg, S. (1946). *The Protestant Ethic and the Spirit of Capitalism*, 3rd ed. Los Angeles: Roxbury Publishing Company.

Kane, R. L. & Parsons, T. D. (eds.). (2017). *The Role of Technology in Clinical Neuropsychology*. Oxford: Oxford University Press.

Kant, I. (1996). *The Metaphysics of Morals* (trans. and ed. M. Gregor). Cambridge: Cambridge University Press.

Kant, I. (1781/1998). *The Critique of Pure Reason* (trans. and ed. Paul Guyer & Allen W. Wood). New York: Cambridge University Press.

Kant, I. (1785/1998). *Groundwork of the Metaphysics of Morals* (trans. and ed. Paul Guyer & Allen W. Wood). New York: Cambridge University Press.

Kashdan, T. B., Biswas-Diener, R., & King, L. A. (2008). Reconsidering happiness: The costs of distinguishing between hedonics and eudaimonia. The Journal of Positive Psychology, 3(4), 219–233.

Kassner, M. P., Wesselmann, E. D., Law, A. T., & Williams, K. D. (2012). Virtually ostracized: Studying ostracism in immersive virtual environments. *Cyberpsychology, Behavior, and Social Networking*, 15(8), 399–403.

Kätsyri, J., Hari, R., Ravaja, N., & Nummenmaa, L. (2013). The opponent matters: Elevated fMRI reward responses to winning against a human versus a computer opponent during interactive video game playing. *Cerebral Cortex*, 23(12), 2829–2839.

Kaufman, J. (2008). *Tastes, Ties, and Time: Facebook Data Release*. Berkman Center for Internet & Society. https://cyber.harvard.edu/node/94446

Kelley, K. J. & Gruber, E. M. (2012). Problematic Internet use and physical health. *Journal of Behavioral Addictions*, 2, 108–112.

Kennedy, R. S., Berbaum, K. S., & Drexler, J. (1994). Methodological and measurement issues for identification of engineering features contributing to virtual reality sickness. Paper presented at In Image 7 Conference, Tucson, AZ, June.

Kern, J. (2006). Evaluation of teleconsultation systems. *International Journal of Medical Informatics*, 75(3–4), 330–334.

Kiel, J. M. (2005). The digital divide: Internet and e-mail use by the elderly. *Medical Informatics and the Internet in Medicine*, 30(1), 19–23.

Kim, E., Lee, B., & Menon, N. M. (2009). Social welfare implications of the digital divide. *Government Information Quarterly*, 26(2), 377–386.

King, J. A., Blair, R. J., Mitchell, D. G., Dolan, R. J., & Burgess, N. (2006). Doing the right thing: A common neural circuit for appropriate violent or compassionate behavior. *NeuroImage*, 30, 1069–1076.

King, L. A. (2011). Are we there yet? What happened on the way to the demise of positive psychology. In K. M. Sheldon, T. B. Kashdan, & M. F. Steger (eds.), *Designing Positive Psychology: Taking Stock and Moving Forward* (pp. 439–446). New York: Oxford University Press.

King, S. A. (1996). Researching Internet communities: Proposed ethical guidelines for the reporting of results. *The Information Society*, 12(2), 119–128.

Kliemann, D. & Adolphs, R. (2018). The social neuroscience of mentalizing: challenges and recommendations. Current Opinion in Psychology, 24, 1–6.

Klopfer, E., Perry, J., Squire, K., Jan, M. F., & Steinkuehler, C. (2005). Mystery at the museum: a collaborative game for museum education. In *Proceedings of the 2005*

Conference on Computer Support for Collaborative Learning: Learning 2005: The Next 10 Years! (pp. 316–320). Taipei: International Society of the Learning Sciences.

Ko, C. H., Yen, J. Y., Yen, C. F., Chen, C. S., & Chen, C. C. (2012). The association between Internet addiction and psychiatric disorder: A review of the literature. *European Psychiatry*, 27(1), 1–8.

Koch, C. (2004). *The Quest for Consciousness: A Neurobiological Approach.* Englewood, CO: Roberts & Company.

Koenigs, M. & Tranel, D. (2007). Irrational economic decision-making after ventromedial prefrontal damage: Evidence from the Ultimatum Game. *The Journal of Neuroscience*, 27(4), 951–956.

Koenigs, M., Young, L., Adolphs, R., Tranel, D., Cushman, F., Hauser, M., & Damasio, A. (2007). Damage to the prefrontal cortex increases utilitarian moral judgements. *Nature*, 446(7138), 908–911.

Koepp, M. J., Gunn, R. N., Lawrence, A. D., Cunningham, V. J., Dagher, A., Jones, T., . . . & Grasby, P. M. (1998). Evidence for striatal dopamine release during a video game. *Nature*, 393(6682), 266–268.

Kolmes, K. (2012). Social media in the future of professional psychology. *Professional Psychology: Research and Practice*, 43(6), 606.

Kononova, A. G. (2013). Effects of distracting ads and cognitive control on the processing of online news stories with stereotype-related information. *Cyberpsychology, Behavior, and Social Networking*, 16(5), 321–328.

Kosinski, M., Matz, S. C., Gosling, S. D., Popov, V., & Stillwell, D. (2015). Facebook as a research tool for the social sciences: Opportunities, challenges, ethical considerations, and practical guidelines. *American Psychologist*, 70(6), 543–556.

Kotzee, B. (2018). Cyborgs, knowledge and credit for learning. In J. A. Carter, A. Clark, J. Kallestrup, S. o. Palermos, & D. Pritchard (eds.), *Extended Epistemology*. Oxford: Oxford University Press.

Kowalski, R. M., Giumetti, G. W., Schroeder, A. N., & Lattanner, M. R. (2014). Bullying in the digital age: A critical review and meta-analysis of cyberbullying research among youth. *Psychological Bulletin*, 140(4), 1073.

Kowalski, R. M. & Limber, S. P. (2013). Psychological, physical, and academic correlates of cyberbullying and traditional bullying. *Journal of Adolescent Health*, 53(1), S13–S20.

Kowalski, R. M., Limber, S. P., Limber, S., & Agatston, P. W. (2012). *Cyberbullying: Bullying in the Digital Age*. London: John Wiley & Sons.

Koziol, L. F., & Budding, D. E. (2009). *Subcortical Structures and Cognition: Implications for Neuropsychological Assessment*. New York: Springer Science & Business Media.

Kramer, A. D. (2014). OK so. A lot of people have asked me about my and Jamie and Jeff's recent study published in PNAS, and I wanted to give a brief public explanation (Facebook post), June 29. www.facebook.com/akramer/posts/10152987150867796

Kramer, A. D., Guillory, J. E., & Hancock, J. T. (2014). Experimental evidence of massive-scale emotional contagion through social networks. *Proceedings of the National Academy of Sciences*, 111(24), 8788–8790.

Krueger, F. & Hoffman, M. (2016). The emerging neuroscience of third-party punishment. *Trends in Neurosciences*, 39(8), 499–501.

Kühn, S., Berna, F., Lüdtke, T., Gallinat, J., & Moritz, S. (2018a). Fighting depression: Action video game play may reduce rumination and increase subjective and objective cognition in depressed patients. *Frontiers in Psychology*, 9, 129, 1–10.

Kühn, S., Kugler, D. T., Schmalen, K., Weichenberger, M., Witt, C., & Gallinat, J. (2018b). Does playing violent video games cause aggression? A longitudinal intervention study. *Molecular Psychiatry*, 1, 1–15.

Kuntze, M. F., Stoermer, R., Mueller-Spahn, F., & Bullinger, A. H. (2002). Ethical codes and values in a virtual world. *Cyberpsychology & Behavior*, 5(3), 203–206.

Kurniawan, S. (2008). Older people and mobile phones: A multi-method investigation. *International Journal of Human-Computer Studies*, 66, 889–901.

Kurzweil, R. (2010). *The Singularity Is Near: When Humans Transcend Biology*. New York: Penguin Group.

Kuss, D. J. & Lopez-Fernandez, O. (2016). Internet addiction and problematic Internet use: A systematic review of clinical research. *World Journal of Psychiatry*, 6, 143–176.

Kuss, D. J. (2013). Internet gaming addiction: Current perspectives. *Psychology Research and Behavior Management*, 6, 125–137.

Kvasny, L. (2006). Cultural (re) production of digital inequality in a U.S. community technology initiative. *Information, Communication & Society*, 9, 160–181.

Kwon, M., Lee, J. Y., Won, W. Y., Park, J. W., Min, J. A., Hahn, C., . . . & Kim, D. J. (2013). Development and validation of a smartphone addiction scale (SAS). *PLoS One*, 8(2), e56936.

Laguna, K. & Babcock, R. L. (1997). Computer anxiety in young and older adults: Implications for human-computer interactions in older populations. *Computers in Human Behavior*, 13(3), 317–326.

Lalancette, H. & Campbell, S. R. (2012). Educational neuroscience: Neuroethical considerations. *International Journal of Environmental and Science Education*, 7 (1), 37–52.

Lallart, E., Lallart, X., & Jouvent, R. (2009). Agency, the sense of presence, and schizophrenia. *Cyberpsychology & Behavior*, 12(2), 139–145.

Lam, L. T. (2014). Internet gaming addiction, problematic use of the internet, and sleep problems: A systematic review. *Current Psychiatry Reports*, 16(4), 1–9.

Lamme, V. A. F. (2006). Towards a true neural stance on consciousness. *Trends in Cognitive Sciences*, 10, 494–501.

Lanaj, K., Johnson, R. E., & Barnes, C. M. (2014). Beginning the workday yet already depleted? Consequences of late-night smartphone use and sleep. *Organizational Behavior and Human Decision Processes*, 124(1), 11–23.

Lannin, D. G. & Scott, N. A. (2013). Social networking ethics: Developing best practices for the new small world. *Professional Psychology: Research and Practice*, 44(3), 135–141.

Latour, B. (1993). *We Have Never Been Modern*. Cambridge, MA: Harvard University Press.

Latour, B. (1994). On technical mediation: Philosophy, sociology, genealogy. *Common Knowledge*, 3(2), 29–64.

Lee, S. Y. T., Gholami, R., & Tong, T. Y. (2005). Time series analysis in the assessment of ICT impact at the aggregate level–lessons and implications for the new economy. *Information & Management*, 42(7), 1009–1022.

Leetaru, K. (2016). Are research ethics obsolete in the era of big data? *Forbes*, June 17. www.forbes.com/sites/kalevleetaru/2016/06/17/are-research-ethics-obsolete-in-the-era-of-big-data/#75acb4cb7aa3

Lengsfeld, J. H. B. (2011). An econometric analysis of the sociodemographic topology of the digital divide in Europe. *The Information Society*, 27(3), 141–157.

Levy, N. (2007a). Rethinking neuroethics in the light of the extended mind thesis. *American Journal of Bioethics*, 7(9), 3–11.

Levy N (2007b). *Neuroethics: Challenges for the 21th Century*. Cambridge: Cambridge University Press.

Levy, N. (2011). Neuroethics and the extended mind. In J. Illes & S. Hossain (eds.), *Neuroethics: Anticipating the Future* (pp. 285–294). Oxford: Oxford University Press.

Levy, S. (1984). *Hackers: Heroes of the Computer Revolution*, Vol. 14. Garden City, NY: Anchor Press/Doubleday.

Lewis, K., Kaufman, J., Gonzalez, M., Wimmer, A., & Christakis, N. (2008). Tastes, Ties, and time: A new social network dataset using Facebook. com. *Social Networks*, 30(4), 330–342.

Lieberman, M. D. (2007). Social cognitive neuroscience: A review of core processes. *Annual Review of Psychology*, 58(1), 259–289.

Lievens, E. (2011). Risk-reducing regulatory strategies for protecting minors in social networks. *Strategy for Telecommunications, Information and Media*, 13(6), 43–54.

LiKamWa, R., Liu, Y., Lane, N. D., & Zhong, L. (2013). Moodscope: Building a mood sensor from smartphone usage patterns. In *Proceeding of the 11th Annual International Conference on Mobile Systems, Applications, and Services* (pp. 389–402). Taipei: ACM.

Lin, L. & Parsons, T. D. (2018). Ecologically valid assessments of attention and learning engagement in media multitaskers. *TechTrends*, 62(5), 518–524.

Lin, P. & Allhoff, F. (2008). Untangling the debate: The ethics of human enhancement. *NanoEthics*, 2(3), 251.

Lin, Y. H., Lin, Y. C., Lee, Y. H., Lin, P. H., Lin, S. H., Chang, L. R., ... & Kuo, T. B. (2015). Time distortion associated with smartphone addiction: Identifying smartphone addiction via a mobile application (App). *Journal of Psychiatric Research*, 65, 139–145.

Liu, A., & Li, T. M. (2016). Develop habit-forming products based on the Axiomatic Design Theory. Procedia CIRP, 53, 119–124.

Livingstone, S. (2003). Children's use of the internet: Reflections on the emerging research agenda. *New Media & Society*, 5(2), 147–166.

Livingstone, S., Byrne, J., & Carr, J. (2016). *One in Three: Internet Governance and Children's Rights*, Innocenti Discussion Papers No. 2016–01, UNICEF Office of Research – Innocenti, Florence.

Llorens, R., Noé, E., Ferri, J., & Alcañiz, M. (2015). Videogame-based group therapy to improve self-awareness and social skills after traumatic brain injury. *Journal of Neuroengineering and Rehabilitation*, 12(1), 1–9.

Louis, J. J., & Adams, P. (2017). U.S. Patent No. 9,609,072. Washington, DC: U.S. Patent and Trademark Office.

Luber, B. & Lisanby, S. H. (2014). Enhancement of human cognitive performance using transcranial magnetic stimulation (TMS). *Neuroimage*, 85, 961–970.

Lupton, D. (2014). *Digital Sociology*. New York: Routledge.

Lustgarten, S. D. (2015). Emerging ethical threats to client privacy in cloud communication and data storage. *Professional Psychology: Research and Practice*, 46(3), 154.

Lustgarten, S. D. & Colbow, A. J. (2017). Ethical concerns for telemental health therapy amidst governmental surveillance. *American Psychologist*, 72(2), 159–170.

Lustgarten, S. D. & Elhai, J. D. (2018). Technology use in mental health practice and research: Legal and ethical risks. *Clinical Psychology: Science and Practice*, e12234.

Lynch, G., Palmer, L. C., & Gall, C. M. (2011). The likelihood of cognitive enhancement. *Pharmacology Biochemistry and Behavior*, 99(2), 116–129.

Lyu, H. (2012). Internet policy in Korea: A preliminary framework for assigning moral and legal responsibility to agents in Internet activities. *Government Information Quarterly*, 29(3), 394–402.

MacIntyre, A. (1985). *After Virtue*, 2nd ed. London: Duckworth.

Mackenzie, C. (2010). Imagining oneself otherwise. In C. Mackenzie & N. Stoljar (eds.), *Relational Autonomy: Feminist Perspectives on Autonomy, Agency, and the Social Self* (pp.124–150). New York: Oxford University Press.

MacMillan, M. (2000). *An Odd Kind of Fame: Stories of Phineas Gage*. Cambridge: Cambridge University Press.

Madary, M. & Metzinger, T. K. (2016). Real virtuality: A code of ethical conduct. recommendations for good scientific practice and the consumers of vr-technology. *Frontiers in Robotics and AI*, 3, 1–23.

Madelin, R. (2011). The evolving social responsibilities of internet corporate actors: Pointers past and present. *Philosophy & Technology*, 24(4), 455–461.

Maher, B. (2008). Poll results: Look who's doping. *Nature*, 452(7188), 674–676.

Maheu, M. M., Pulier, M. L., Wilhelm, F. H., McMenamin, J. P., & Brown-Connolly, N. E. (2004). *The Mental Health Professional and the New Technologies: A Handbook for Practice Today*. New York: Routledge.

Majumder, S., Aghayi, E., Noferesti, M., Memarzadeh-Tehran, H., Mondal, T., Pang, Z., & Deen, M. J. (2017). Smart homes for elderly healthcare: Recent advances and research challenges. *Sensors*, 17(11), 1–32.

Maley, T. (2004). Max Weber and the iron cage of technology. *Bulletin of Science, Technology & Society*, 24(1), 69–86.

Manson, N. C. & O'Neill, O. (2007). *Rethinking Informed Consent in Bioethics.* New York: Cambridge University Press.

Marcus, H. (1968). *One-Dimensional Man: Studies in the Ideology of Advanced Industrial Society.* Boston: Beacon Press.

Mariën, I. & Prodnik, J. A. (2014). Digital inclusion and user (dis)empowerment: A critical perspective. *Info*, 16(6), 35–47.

Mark, L. & Ratliffe, K. (2011). Cyberworlds: New playgrounds for bullying, computers in the schools. *Computers in the Schools: Interdisciplinary Journal of Practice, Theory, and Applied Research*, 28, 92–116.

Marston, H. R. & Smith, S. T. (2012). Interactive videogame technologies to support independence in the elderly: A narrative review. *Games For Health: Research, Development, and Clinical Applications*, 1(2), 139–152.

Mathiak, K. & Weber, R. (2006). Toward brain correlates of natural behavior: fMRI during violent video games. *Human Brain Mapping*, 27, 948–956.

Mayberg, H. S. (2009). Targeted modulation of neural circuits: A new treatment strategy for depression. *Journal of Clinical Investigation*, 119(4), 717–725.

Mayberg, H. S., Lozano, A. M., Voon, V., McNeely, H. E., Seminowicz, D., Hamani, C. et al. (2005). Deep brain stimulation for treatment-resistant depression. *Neuron*, 45(5), 651–660.

McAllister, T. W. (2011). Neurobiological consequences of traumatic brain injury. *Dialogues in Clinical Neuroscience*, 13(3), 287–300.

McCloskey, H. J. (1985). Privacy and the right to privacy. In R. L. Purtill (ed.), *Moral Dilemmas: Readings in Ethics and Social Philosophy* (pp. 342–357). Belmont, CA: Wadsworth.

McCormick, M. (2001). Is it wrong to play violent video games?. *Ethics and Information Technology*, 3(4), 277–287.

McCuddy, T. & Esbensen, F. A. (2017). After the bell and into the night: The link between delinquency and traditional, cyber-, and dual-bullying victimization. *Journal of Research in Crime and Delinquency*, 54(3), 409–441.

McDonald, A. M. & Cranor, L. F. (2008). The cost of reading privacy policies. *I/S: A Journal of Law and Policy for the Information Society*, 4, 543–568.

McIntosh, E. S. (2011). Perspective on the economic evaluation of deep brain stimulation. *Frontiers in Integrative Neuroscience*, 5, 1–7.

McMahan, T., Parberry, I., & Parsons, T. D. (2015). Modality specific assessment of video game player's experience using the Emotiv. *Entertainment Computing*, 7, 1–6.

McStay, A. & Bakir, V. (2006). Privacy, online advertising and marketing techniques: The paradoxical disappearance of the user. *Ethical Space: The International Journal of Communication Ethics*, 3(1), 24–31.

Menary, R. (2007). *Cognitive Integration: Mind and Cognition Unbounded.* Basingstoke: Palgrave Macmillan.

Menary, R. (ed.). (2010). *The Extended Mind.* Cambridge, MA: MIT Press.

Merritt, M. (2013). Instituting impairment: Extended cognition and the construction of female sexual dysfunction. *Cognitive Systems Research*, 25–26, 47–53.

Meshi, D., Tamir, D. I., & Heekeren, H. R. (2015). The emerging neuroscience of social media. *Trends in Cognitive Sciences*, 19(12), 771–782.

Metzinger, T. (2003). *Being No One: The Self-Model Theory of Subjectivity.* Cambridge, MA: MIT Press.

Mihordin, R. (2012). Behavioral addiction – quo vadis?. *The Journal of Nervous and Mental Disease, 200*(6), 489–491.

Milioni, D. L., Doudaki, V., & Demertzis, N. (2014). Youth, ethnicity, and a "reverse digital divide": A study of Internet use in a divided country. Convergence: *The International Journal of Research into New Media Technologies, 20,* 316–336.

Mill, J. S. (1859/1991). *On Liberty, in On Liberty and Other Essays* (ed. J. Gray). Oxford: Oxford University Press.

Mill, J. S. (1861). *Utilitarianism.* Indianapolis. The Bobbs Merrill Company

Miller, M. & Clark, A. (2018). Happily entangled: Prediction, emotion, and the embodied mind. *Synthese, 195*(6), 2559–2575.

Miller, W. M., Jr. (1959/1997). *A Canticle for Leibowitz.* New York: Bantam.

Millikan, R. G. (1993). *White Queen Psychology and Other Essays for Alice.* Cambridge, MA: MIT Press.

Mishra, J., Anguera, J. A., & Gazzaley, A. (2016). Video games for neuro-cognitive optimization. *Neuron, 90*(2), 214–218.

Mitchell, J. P. (2008). Contributions of functional neuroimaging to the study of social cognition. *Current Directions in Psychological Science, 17*(2), 142–146.

Mitrović, D. (2017). Virtual reality and ethical neutrality of the virtual subjects of law. *Facta Universitatis, Series: Law and Politics, 15*(2), 115–125.

Mitzner, T. L., Boron, J. B., Fausset, C. B., Adams, A. E., Charness, N., Czaja, S. J., . . . & Sharit, J. (2010). Older adults talk technology: Technology usage and attitudes. *Computers in Human Behavior, 26*(6), 1710–1721.

Moghim, M., Stone, R., Rotshtein, P., & Cooke, N. (2015). Adaptive virtual environments: A physiological feedback HCI system concept. In *Computer Science and Electronic Engineering Conference (CEEC), 2015 7th* (pp. 123–128). Colchester, UK: IEEE.

Moll, J., Eslinger, P. J., & de Oliveira-Souza, R. (2001). Frontopolar and anterior temporal cortex activation in a moral judgment task: Preliminary functional MRI results in normal subjects. *Arquivos de neuro-psiquiatria, 59*(3B), 657–664.

Moll, J., de Oliviera-Souza, R., Eslinger, P. J., Bramati, I. E., Moura´o-Miranda, J., Andreiuolo, P. A., & Pessoa, L. (2002). The neural correlates of moral sensitivity: A functional magnetic resonance imaging investigation of basic and moral emotions. *Journal of Neuroscience, 22,* 2730–2736.

Moll, J., de Oliveira-Souza, R., Moll, F. T., Igna´cio, F. A., Bramati, I. E., Caparelli-Da´quer, E. M., & Eslinger, P. J. (2005). The moral affiliations of disgust: A functional MRI study. *Cognitive and Behavioral Neurology, 18,* 68–78.

Moll, J., Zahn, R., de Oliveira-Souza, R., Krueger, F., & Grafman, J. (2005). The neural basis of human moral cognition. *Nature Reviews Neuroscience, 6*(10), 799–809.

Montag, C. & Reuter, M. (eds.). (2017). *Internet Addiction: Neuroscientific Approaches and Therapeutical Implications Including Smartphone Addiction.* New York: Springer.

Montag, C., Weber, B., Trautner, P., Newport, B., Markett, S., Walter, N. T., . . . & Reuter, M. (2012). Does excessive play of violent first-person-shooter-video-games dampen brain activity in response to emotional stimuli? *Biological psychology*, 89(1), 107–111.

Moor, B. G., Crone, E. A., & van der Molen, M. W. (2010). The heartbrake of social rejection: Heart rate deceleration in response to unexpected peer rejection. *Psychological Science*, 21(9), 1326–1333.

Moor, J. H. (1991). The ethics of privacy protection. *Library Trends*, 39, 69–82.

Moor, J. H. (1997). Towards a theory of privacy in the information age. *ACM SIGCAS Computers and Society*, 27(3), 27–32.

Moor, J. H. (2000). Towards a theory of privacy for the information age. In R. M. Baird, R. Ramsower, & S. E. Rosenbaum (eds.), *Cyberethics: Moral, Social, and Legal Issues in the Computer Age* (pp. 200–212). Amherst, NY: Prometheus Books.

Moor, J. H. (2004a). *Reason, Relativity, and Responsibility in Computer Ethics. Readings in CyberEthics*, 2nd ed. (pp. 40–54). Sudbury, MA: Jones & Bartlett.

Moor J. H. (2004b). Towards a theory of privacy for the information age. In R. Spinello & H. Tavani (eds.), *Readings in CyberEthics* (pp. 407–417). Sudbury, MA: Jones & Bartlett.

Moor, J. H. (2006). Using genetic information while protecting the privacy of the soul. In H. T. Tavani (ed.), *Ethics, Computing, and Genomics* (pp.109–119). Sudbury, MA: Jones & Bartlett.

Mooradian, N. (2009). The importance of privacy revisited. Ethics and Information Technology, 11(3), 163–174.

Mori, C. K. (2011). "Digital inclusion": Are we all talking about the same thing?. In J. Steyn & G. Johanson (eds.), *ICTs and Sustainable Solutions for the Digital Divide: Theory and Perspectives* (pp. 45–64). Hershey, PA: IGI Global.

Moss, J. (2002). Power and the digital divide. Ethics and Information Technology, 4(2), 159–165.

Mossberger, K., Tolbert, C. J., & Hamilton, A. (2012). Broadband adoption: Measuring digital citizenship: Mobile access and broadband. *International Journal of Communication*, 6, 2492–2528.

Mossberger, K., Tolbert, C. J., & McNeal, R. S. (2007). Digital Citizenship: *The Internet, Society, and Participation*. Cambridge, MA: MIT Press.

Mujtaba, B. (2007). *Workforce Diversity Management: Challenges, Competencies and Strategies* (pp. 207–229). Florida: Llumina Press.

Mumford, L. (1964). Authoritarian and democratic technics. *Technology and Culture* 5(1), 1–8.

Muñoz, Y. J. & El-Hani, C. N. (2012). The student with a thousand faces: From the ethics in video games to becoming a citizen. *Cultural Studies of Science Education*, 7(4), 909–943.

Muralidharan, S., Rasmussen, L., Patterson, D., & Shin, J. H. (2011). Hope for Haiti: An analysis of Facebook and Twitter usage during the earthquake relief efforts. *Public Relations Review*, 37(2), 175–177.

Mystery at the Museum. (2003). [Computer software]. Cambridge, MA: MIT Teacher Education Program & The Education Arcade. http://education.mit.edu/ar/matm.html

Nagel, S. K., Hrincu, V., & Reiner, P. B. (2016). Algorithm anxiety: Do decision-making algorithms pose a threat to autonomy? Paper presented at the 2016 IEEE International Symposium on Ethics in Engineering, Science and Technology, May 13–14, Vancouver, BC.

Nagel, S. K. & Reiner, P. B. (2018). Skillful use of Technologies of the Extended Mind illuminate practical paths towards an ethics of consciousness. *Frontiers in Psychology*, 9, 1–2.

National Board for Certified Counselors. (1997). *Standards for the Ethical Practice of WebCounseling*. Greensboro, NC. www.nbcc.org/Assets/Ethics/NBCCPolicyRegardingPracticeofDistanceCounselingBoard.pdf.

Naqvi, N., Shiv, B., & Bechara, A. (2006). The role of emotion in decision making: A cognitive neuroscience perspective. *Current Directions in Psychological Science*, 15(5), 260–264.

Navarrete, C. D., McDonald, M. M., Mott, M. L., & Asher, B. (2012). Virtual morality: Emotion and action in a simulated three-dimensional "trolley problem". *Emotion*, 12(2), 364.

Nedelsky, J. (1989). Reconceiving autonomy: Sources, thoughts and possibilities. *Yale Journal of Law & Feminism*, 1(1), 7–36.

Nelson, J. L. (2009). Alzheimer's disease and socially extended mentation. *Metaphilosophy*, 40(3–4), 462–474.

Nelson, R. M., Beauchamp, T., Miller, V. A., Reynolds, W., Ittenbach, R. F., & Luce, M. F. (2011). The concept of voluntary consent. *The American Journal of Bioethics*, 11(8), 6–16.

Neville, H. J., Stevens, C., Pakulak, E., Bell, T. A., Fanning, J., Klein, S., & Isbell, E. (2013). Family-based training program improves brain function, cognition, and behavior in lower socioeconomic status preschoolers. *Proceedings of the National Academy of Sciences*, 110(29), 12138–12143.

Nickelson, D. W. (1998). Telehealth and the evolving health care system: Strategic opportunities for professional psychology. *Professional Psychology: Research and Practice*, 29, 527–535.

Nissenbaum, H. (2011). A contextual approach to privacy online. *Daedalus*, 140 (4), 32–48.

Norcross, J. C., Hedges, M., & Prochaska, J. O. (2002). The face of 2010: A Delphi poll on the future of psychotherapy. *Professional Psychology: Research and Practice*, 33(3), 316–322.

Norcross, J. C., Pfund, R. A., & Prochaska, J. O. (2013). Psychotherapy in 2022: A Delphi poll on its future. *Professional Psychology: Research and Practice*, 44(5), 363–370.

Norman, K. L. (2017). *Cyberpsychology: An Introduction to Human–Computer Interaction*. Cambridge: Cambridge University Press.

Norris, P. (2001). *Digital Divide: Civic Engagement, Information Poverty, and the Internet Worldwide*. Cambridge: Cambridge University Press.

Nosko, A., Wood, E., & Molema, S. (2010). All about me: Disclosure in online social networking profiles: The case of Facebook. *Computers in Human Behavior*, 26(3), 406–418.

O'Brolcháin, F., Jacquemard, T., Monaghan, D., O'Connor, N., Novitzky, P., & Gordijn, B. (2016). The convergence of virtual reality and social networks: Threats to privacy and autonomy. *Science and Engineering Ethics*, 22 (1), 1–29.

Ofcom (Office of Communications). (2013). *Disabled Consumers' Ownership of Communications Services. A Consumer Experience Report*. September 25. http://stakeholders.ofcom.org.uk/binaries/research/media-literacy/1515282/Disabled_consumers_use_of_communications_services.pdf

Oh, H., Rizo, C., Enkin, M., & Jadad, A. (2005). What is eHealth?: A systematic review of published definitions. *World Hospitals and Health Services Journal*, 41(1), 32–40.

O'Hara, K. & Stevens, D. (2006). *inequality.com: Power, Poverty and the Digital Divide*. Oxford: Oneworld Publications.

Öhman, J. & Östman, L. (2010). Clarifying the ethical tendency in education for sustainable development practice: A Wittgenstein-inspired approach. Canadian Journal of Environmental Education (CJEE), 13(1), 57–72.

OHRP (Office for Human Research Protections). (1979). *The Belmont Report: Ethical Principles and Guidelines for the Protection of Human Subjects of Research*. www.hhs.gov/ohrp/humansubjects/guidance/belmont.html

Olson, K. E., O'Brien, M. A., Rogers, W. A., & Charness, N. (2011). Diffusion of technology: Frequency of use for younger and older adults. *Ageing International*, 36(1), 123–145.

Opris, D., Pintea, S., García-Palacios, A., Botella, C., Szamosközi, S., & David, D. (2012). Virtual reality exposure therapy in anxiety disorders: A quantitative meta-analysis. *Depression and Anxiety*, 29, 85–93.

Ortega y Gasset, J. (1941). Man the technician. In C. Hanks (ed.), *Technology and Values: Essential Readings* (pp. 114–121). London: Wiley-Blackwell.

Oulasvirta, A., Rattenbury, T., Ma, L., & Raita, E. (2012). Habits make smartphone use more pervasive. *Personal and Ubiquitous Computing*, 16(1), 105–114.

Palermos, S. O. (2014). Loops, constitution, and cognitive extension. *Cognitive Systems Research*, 27, 25–41.

Pan, X., & Hamilton, A. F. D. C. (2018). Why and how to use virtual reality to study human social interaction: The challenges of exploring a new research landscape. *British Journal of Psychology*, 109(3), 395–417.

Pan, B., Hembrooke, H., Joachims, T., Lorigo, L., Gay, G., & Granka, L. (2007). In Google we trust: Users' decisions on rank, position, and relevance. Journal of Computer-Mediated Communication, 12(3), 801–823.

Panksepp, J. (1998). *Affective Neuroscience*. Oxford: Oxford University Press.

Panksepp, J. (2004). *Affective Neuroscience: The Foundations of Human and Animal Emotions*. Oxford: Oxford University Press.

Parens, E. (ed.). (2000). *Enhancing Human Traits: Ethical and Social Implications*. Washington, DC: Georgetown University Press.

Parry, M. (2011). Harvard researchers accused of breaching students' privacy: Social-network project shows promise and peril of doing social science online, *The Chronicle of Higher Education*, July 10.

Parsons, T. D. (2015a). Virtual reality for enhanced ecological validity and experimental control in the clinical, affective, and social neurosciences. *Frontiers in Human Neuroscience*, 9, 1–19.

Parsons, T. D. (2015b). Virtual reality exposure therapy for anxiety and specific phobias. In M. Khosrow-Pour (ed.), *Information Science and Technology*, 3rd ed. (pp.288–296), Hershey, PA: IGI Global.

Parsons, T. D. (2016). *Clinical Neuropsychology and Technology: What's New and How We Can Use It*. New York: Springer Press.

Parsons, T. D. (2017). *Cyberpsychology and the Brain: The Interaction of Neuroscience and Affective Computing*. Cambridge: Cambridge University Press.

Parsons, T. D. (2019). Neuroethics in educational technology: Keeping the brain in mind when developing frameworks for ethical decision making. In T. D. Parsons, L, Lin, & D. Cockerham (eds.), *Mind, Brain, and Technology: How People Learn in the Age of New Technologies* (pp. 195–210). New York: Springer-Verlag.

Parsons, T. D. & Courtney, C. (2011). Neurocognitive and psychophysiological interfaces for adaptive virtual environments. In C. Röcker & M. Ziefle (eds.), *Human Centered Design of E-Health Technologies: Concepts, Methods and Applications* (pp. 208–233). Hershey, PA: IGI Global.

Parsons, T. D., Courtney, C., & Dawson, M. (2013). Virtual Reality Stroop Task for assessment of supervisory attentional processing. *Journal of Clinical and Experimental Neuropsychology*, 35, 812–826.

Parsons, T. D., Gaggioli, A., & Riva, G. (2017). Virtual reality for research in social neuroscience. *Brain Sciences*, 7(42), 1–21.

Parsons, T. D. & Kane, R. L. (2017). Computational neuropsychology: Current and future prospects for interfacing neuropsychology and technology. In R. Kane & T. D. Parsons (eds.). *The Role of Technology in Clinical Neuropsychology* (pp.471–482). New York: Oxford University Press.

Parsons, T. D., Lin, L., & Cockerham, D. (eds.) (2019).*Mind, Brain, and Technology: Learning in the Age of Emerging Technologies*. New York: Springer Press.

Parsons, T. D., McMahan, T., & Kane, R. (2018). Practice parameters facilitating adoption of advanced technologies for enhancing neuropsychological assessment paradigms. *The Clinical Neuropsychologist*, 32(1), 16–41.

Parsons, T. D., McMahan, T., & Parberry, I. (in press). Neurogaming-based Classification of Player Experience Using Consumer-Grade Electroencephalography. IEEE Transactions on Affective Computing.

Parsons, T. D. & Phillips, A. (2016). Virtual reality for psychological assessment in clinical practice. *Practice Innovations*, 1, 197–217.

Parsons, T. D. & Reinebold, J. (2012). Adaptive virtual environments for neuropsychological assessment in serious games. *IEEE Transactions on Consumer Electronics*, 58, 197–204.

Parsons, T. D., Riva, G., Parsons, S., Mantovani, F., Newbutt, N., Lin, L., Venturini, E., & Hall, T. (2017). Virtual reality in pediatric psychology: Benefits, challenges, and future directions. *Pediatrics*, 140, 86–91.

Parsons, T. D. & Rizzo, A. A. (2008). Affective outcomes of virtual reality exposure therapy for anxiety and specific phobias: A meta-analysis. *Journal of Behavior Therapy and Experimental Psychiatry*, 39, 250–261.

Parsons, T. D., Rizzo, A. A., Rogers, S. A., & York, P. (2009). Virtual reality in pediatric rehabilitation: A review. *Developmental Neurorehabilitation*, 12, 224–238.

Parsons, T. D. & Trost, Z. (2014). Virtual reality graded exposure therapy as treatment for pain-related fear and disability in chronic pain. In M. Ma (ed.), *Virtual and Augmented Reality in Healthcare* (pp. 523–546), Berlin: Springer-Verlag.

Parvizi, J. (2009). Corticocentric myopia: Old bias in new cognitive sciences. *Trends in Cognitive Sciences*, 13(8), 354–359.

Patchin, J. W. & Hinduja, S. (2006). Bullies move beyond the schoolyard: A preliminary look at cyberbullying. *Youth Violence and Juvenile Justice*, 4(2), 148–169.

Patil, I., Cogoni, C., Zangrando, N., Chittaro, L., & Silani, G. (2014). Affective basis of judgment-behavior discrepancy in virtual experiences of moral dilemmas. *Social Neuroscience*, 9(1), 94–107.

Paulhus, D. L. & Vazire, S. (2007). The self-report method. In R. W. Robins, R. C. Fraley, & R. Krueger (eds.), *Handbook of Research Methods in Personality Psychology* (pp. 224–239). New York: Guilford Press.

Perez, B., Musolesi, M., & Stringhini, G. (2018). You are your metadata: Identification and obfuscation of social media users using metadata information. Paper presented at the Twelfth International AAAI Conference on Web and Social Media (ICWSM 2018), Palo Alto, CA, June 25–28.

Perry, J., Beyer, S. & Holm, S. (2008). Assistive technology, telecare and people with intellectual disabilities: Ethical considerations. *Journal of Medical Ethics*, 35, 81–86.

Pew Research Center. (2014). Older Adults and Technology. Washington, DC.

Pew Research Center. (2015). The Smartphone Difference. Washington, DC.

Pew Research Center. (2016). *Mobile Technology Fact Sheet*. Pew Research Center: Internet, Science & Tech. www.pewinternet.org/fact-sheets/mobile-technology-fact-sheet/

Phan, K. L., Wager, T., Taylor, S. F., & Liberzon, I. (2002). Functional neuroanatomy of emotion: A meta-analysis of emotion activation studies in PET and fMRI. Neuroimage, 16(2), 331–348.

Picard, R. W. (1997). *Affective Computing*, Vol. 252. Cambridge: MIT Press.

Plaisance, P. (2013). Virtue ethics and digital flourishing: An application of Philippa Foot to Life Online. *Journal of Mass Media Ethics*, 28(3), 91–102.

Plastow, N. A. (2006). Is big brother watching you? Responding to tagging and tracking in dementia care. British Journal of Occupational Therapy, 69(11), 525–527.

Poster, M. (2001). *What's the Matter with the Internet?*, Vol. 3. Minneapolis: University of Minnesota Press.

Poulin, C. (2001). Medical and nonmedical stimulant use among adolescents: From sanctioned to unsanctioned use. *Canadian Medical Association Journal*, 165(8), 1039–1044.

Pourmand, A., Davis, S., Marchak, A., Whiteside, T., & Sikka, N. (2018). Virtual reality as a clinical tool for pain management. *Current Pain and Headache Reports*, 22, 53–67.

Power, A. & Kirwan, G. (2013). *Cyberpsychology and New Media: A Thematic Reader*. New York: Psychology Press.

Powers, M. B. & Emmelkamp, P. M. G. (2008). Virtual reality exposure therapy for anxiety disorders: A metaanalysis. *Journal of Anxiety Disorders*, 22, 561–569.

Pöyhönen, S. (2014). Explanatory power of extended cognition. *Philosophical Psychology*, 27(5), 735–759.

Prensky, M. (2001). Digital natives, digital immigrants part 1. *On the Horizon*, 9 (5), 1–6.

Presidential Commission for the Study of Bioethical Issues. (2014). *Gray Matters: Integrative Approaches for Neuroscience, Ethics, and Society*. Vol. 1. Presidential Commission for the Study of Bioethical Issues. www.bioethics.gov/sites/defau lt/files/Gray%20Matters%20Vol%201.pdf.

President's Council on Bioethics. (2003). *Beyond Therapy*. Washington, DC: President's Council on Bioethics.

Primack, B. A., Carroll, M. V., McNamara, M., et al. (2012). Role of video games in improving health-related outcomes: A systematic review. *American Journal of Preventative Medicine*, 42, 630–638.

Puschmann, C. & Bozdag, E. (2014). Staking out the unclear ethical terrain of online social experiments. *Internet Policy Review*, 3, 1–15. https://doi.org/10 .14763/2014.4.338

Putnam, H. (1982). *Reason, Truth and History*. Cambridge: Cambridge University Press.

Quan-Haase, A. & McCay-Peet, L. (2016). Social network analysis. In K. Jensen, R. Craig, J. Pooley, & E. Rothenbuhler (eds.), *International Encyclopedia of Communication Theory and Philosophy* (pp. 123–146). Cambridge, MA: Wiley.

Quinn, M. (2009). *Ethics for the Information Age*. Boston: Pearson Education.

Quintana, D. S., Guastella, A. J., Outhred, T., Hickie, I. B., & Kemp, A. H. (2012). Heart rate variability is associated with emotion recognition: Direct evidence for a relationship between the autonomic nervous system and social cognition. *International Journal of Psychophysiology*, 86(2), 168–172.

Rachels, J. (1975). Why privacy is important. *Philosophy & Public Affairs*, 4(4), 323–333.

Rachels, J. & Rachels, S. (2015). *The Elements of Moral Philosophy*, 8th ed. Boston: McGraw Hill Education.

Racine, E. & Aspler, J. (eds.). (2017). *Debates About Neuroethics: Perspectives on Its Development, Focus, and Future.* New York: Springer.

Racine, E. & Illes, J. (2008). Neuroethics. In P. Singer & A. Viens (ed.), *Cambridge Textbook of Bioethics* (pp. 495–504). Cambridge: Cambridge University Press.

Ragnedda, M. (2017). *The Third Digital Divide: A Weberian Approach to Digital Inequalities.* New York: Routledge.

Ragusea, A. S. & VandeCreek, L. (2003). Suggestions for the ethical practice of online psychotherapy. *Psychotherapy: Theory, Research, Practice, Training,* 40, 94–102.

Ramos, K. M., Rommelfanger, K. S., Greely, H. T., & Koroshetz, W. J. (2018). Neuroethics and the NIH BRAIN Initiative. *Journal of Responsible Innovation,* 5 (1), 122–130.

Rand, A. (1964). *The Virtue of Selfishness.* New York: Penguin.

Rauhala-Hayes, M. (1997). Ethics of care work. In S. Bjorneby & A. van Berlo (eds.), *Ethical Issues in Use of Technology for Dementia Care* (pp. 73–86). Knegsel: Akontes Publishing.

Rawls, J. (1971). *A Theory of Justice.* Cambridge, MA: Harvard University Press.

Reason, J. T. (1978). Motion sickness adaptation: A neural mismatch model. *Journal of the Royal Society of Medicine,* 71(11), 819–829.

Reason, J. T. & Brand, J. J. (1975). *Motion Sickness.* Oxford: Academic Press.

Rebenitsch, L. & Owen, C. (2016). Review on cybersickness in applications and visual displays. *Virtual Reality,* 20(2), 101–125.

Reger, G. M., Koenen-Woods, P., Zetocha, K., Smolenski, D. J., Holloway, K. M., Rothbaum, B. O., et al. (2016). Randomized controlled trial of prolonged exposure using imaginal exposure vs. virtual reality exposure in active duty soldiers with deployment-related posttraumatic stress disorder (PTSD). *Journal of consulting and Clinical Psychology,* 84(11), 946–959.

Reiner, P. B. & Nagel, S. K. (2017). Technologies of the extended mind: Defining the issues. In J. Illes & S. Hossain (eds.), *Neuroethics: Anticipating the Future* (pp. 108–122). Oxford: Oxford University Press.

Reynolds, R. (2002). *Playing a "Good" Game: A Philosophical Approach to Understanding the Morality of Games.* International Game Developers Association. www-inst.cs.berkeley.edu/~cs10/fa09/dis/02/extra/reynolds_ethics .pdf

Reynolds, S. J. (2006). A neurocognitive model of the ethical decision-making process: Implications for study and practice. *Journal of Applied Psychology,* 91(4), 737–748.

Rheingold, H. (1995). *The Virtual Community: Finding Connection in a Computerized World.* London: Secker & Wargurg.

Richter, D. (2010). *Anscombe's Moral Philosophy.* Lanham, MD: Lexington Books.

Rilling, J. K., Sanfey, A. G., Aronson, J. A., Nystrom, L. E., & Cohen, J. D. (2004a). Opposing BOLD responses to reciprocated and unreciprocated altruism in putative reward pathways. *NeuroReport,* 15(16), 2539–2543.

Rilling, J. K., Sanfey, A. G., Aronson, J. A., Nystrom, L. E., & Cohen, J. D. (2004b). The neural correlates of theory of mind within interpersonal interactions. *Neuroimage*, 22(4), 1694–1703.

Riva, G. & Mantovani, F. (2012). Being there: Understanding the feeling of presence in a synthetic environment and its potential for clinical change. In C. Eichenberg (ed.), *Virtual Reality in Psychological, Medical and Pedagogical Applications*. New York: InTech.

Riva, G. & Mantovani, F. (2014). Extending the self through the tools and the others: A general framework for presence and social presence in mediated interactions. In G. Riva, J. A. Waterworth, & D. Murray (eds.), *Interacting with Presence: HCI and the Sense of Presence in Computer-Mediated Environments* (pp. 12–34). Berlin: De Gruyter.

Riva, G., Mantovani, F., Waterworth, E. L., & Waterworth, J. A. (2015). Intention, action, self and other: An evolutionary model of presence. In M. Lombard, F. Biocca, J. Freeman, W. Ijsselsteijn, & R. J. Schaevitz (eds.), *Immersed in Media* (pp. 73–100). New York: Springer.

Rizzo, A. A., Schultheis, M., & Rothbaum, B. O. (2002). Ethical issues for the use of virtual reality in the psychological sciences. In S. Bush & M. Drexler (eds.), *Ethical Issues in Clinical Neuropsychology* (pp. 243–279). Lisse: Swets & Zeitlinger.

Roberts, L. W. (2002). Informed consent and the capacity for voluntarism. *American Journal of Psychiatry*, 159(5), 705–712.

Robertson, D. C., Voegtlin, C., & Maak, T. (2017). Business ethics: The promise of neuroscience. *Journal of Business Ethics*, 144(4), 679–697.

Robillard, J. M., Johnson, T. W., Hennessey, C., Beattie, B. L., & Illes, J. (2013). Aging 2.0: Health information about dementia on Twitter. *PLoS One*, 8(7), e69861.

Robillard, J. M. & Hoey, J. (2018). Emotion and motivation in cognitive assistive technologies for dementia. *Computer*, 51(3), 24–34.

Robinson, L., Hutchings, D., Corner, L., Finch, T., Hughes, J., Brittain, K. & Bond, J. (2007). Balancing rights and risks: Conflicting perspectives in the management of wandering in dementia. *Health Risk and Society*, 9, 389–406.

Rorty, R. (1991a). *Objectivity, Relativism, and Truth: Philosophical Papers*, Vol. 1. Cambridge: Cambridge University Press.

Rorty, R. (1991b). *Essays on Heidegger and Others: Philosophical Papers*, Vol. 2. Cambridge: Cambridge University Press.

Rorty, R. M. & Rorty, R. (1998). *Truth and Progress: Philosophical Papers*, Vol. 3. Cambridge: Cambridge University Press.

Rosenbush, S. (2014). Facebook experiments tests ethics of manipulating emotion. *Wall Street Journal*, July 1. https://blogs.wsj.com/cio/2014/07/01/facebook-experiment-tests-ethics-of-manipulating-emotion/

Roskies, A. (2002). Neuroethics for the new millennium. *Neuron*, 35(1), 21–23.

Rotge, J. Y., Lemogne, C., Hinfray, S., Huguet, P., Grynszpan, O., Tartour, E., et al. (2014). A meta-analysis of the anterior cingulate contribution to social pain. *Social, Cognitive and Affective Neuroscience*, 10, 19–27.

Rudder C (2014). We experiment on human beings. *OKCupid* (*blog*), July 28. http://blog.okcupid.com/index.php/we-experiment-on-human-beings

Ruggeroni, C. (2001). Ethical education with virtual reality: Immersiveness and the knowledge transfer process. In G. Riva & F. Davide (eds.), *Communications Through Virtual Technology: Identity Community and Technology in the Internet Age* (pp. 119–133). Amsterdam: IOS Press.

Rupert, R. D. (2004). Challenges to the hypothesis of extended cognition. *The Journal of Philosophy*, 101(8), 389–428.

Ruyter, B. D. & Pelgrim, E. (2007). Ambient assisted-living research in carelab. *Interactions*, 14(4), 30–33.

Sabin, J. E. & Harland, J. C. (2017). Professional ethics for digital age psychiatry: Boundaries, privacy, and communication. *Current Psychiatry Reports*, 19(9), 55.

Salisbury, D. B., Dahdah, M., Driver, S., Parsons, T. D., & Richter, K. M. (2016). Virtual reality and brain computer interface in neurorehabilitation. *Baylor University Medical Center* Proceedings, 29(2), 124–127.

Samet, J. & Stern, Y. (2011). The neuroethics of cognitive reserve. In J. Illes & B. J. Sahakian (eds.), *Oxford Handbook of Neuroethics* (pp. 563–574). Oxford: Oxford University Press.

Sanchez-Vives, M. V. & Slater, M. (2005). From presence to consciousness through virtual reality. *Nature Reviews Neuroscience*, 6, 332–339.

Sanfey, A. G. & Chang, L. J. (2008). Multiple systems in decision making. *Annals of the New York Academy of Sciences*, 1128(1), 53–62.

Satpute, A. B. & Lieberman, M. D. (2006). Integrating automatic and controlled processes into neurocognitive models of social cognition. *Brain Research*, 1079 (1), 86–97.

Schäfer, M., Korn, S., Smith, P. K., Hunter, S. C., Mora-Merchán, J. A., Singer, M. M., & Van der Meulen, K. (2004). Lonely in the crowd: Recollections of bullying. *British Journal of Developmental Psychology*, 22, 379–394.

Schermer, M. (2011). Ethical issues in deep brain stimulation. *Frontiers in Integrative Neuroscience*, 5(17), 1–9.

Schiebener, J. & Brand, M. (2017). Decision-making and related processes in Internet gaming disorder and other types of Internet-use disorders. *Current Addiction Reports*, 4(3), 262–271.

Schneider, W. & Shiffrin, R. M. (1977). Controlled and automatic human information processing: I. Detection, search, and attention. *Psychological Review*, 84(1), 1–66.

Schubert, T., Friedmann F., & Regenbrecht H. (2001). The experience of presence: Factor analytic insights. *Presence*, 10 266–281.

Schulzke, M. (2010). Defending the morality of violent video games. Ethics and Information Technology, 12(2), 127–138.

Schultze, U. & Mason, R. O. (2012). Studying cyborgs: Re-examining Internet studies as human subjects research. *Journal of Internet Technology*, 27, 301–312.

Schwark, J. D. (2015). Toward a taxonomy of affective computing. *International Journal of Human-Computer Interaction*, 31(11), 761–768.

Scott, E., Soria, A., & Campo, M. (2017). Adaptive 3D virtual learning environments: A review of the literature. *IEEE Transactions on Learning Technologies*, 10 (3), 262–276.

Searle, J. (1980). Minds, brains, and programs. *Behavioral and Brain Sciences*, 3, 417–424.

Searle, J. (2014). What your computer can't know. *New York Review of Books*, October 9.

Seligman, M. E. P. & Csikszentmihalyi, M. (2000). Positive psychology [Special issue]. American Psychologist, 55(1).

Selinger, E. & Hartzog, W. (2016). Facebook's emotional contagion study and the ethical problem of co-opted identity in mediated environments where users lack control. *Research Ethics*, 12(1), 35–43.

Selwyn, N. (2004). Reconsidering political and popular understandings of the digital divide. *New Media & Society*, 6, 341–362.

Semetsky, I. (2009). Continuities, discontinuities, interactions: Values, education, and neuroethics. *Ethics and Education*, 4(1), 69–80.

Seth, A. K., Suzuki, K., & Critchley, H. D. (2012). An interoceptive predictive coding model of conscious presence. *Frontiers in Psychology*, 2(395), 1–7.

Sharma, S., Lomash, H., & Bawa, S. (2015). Who regulates ethics in the virtual world?. *Science and Engineering Ethics*, 21(1), 19–28.

Shennan, G. (2016). Extended mind, extended person, extended therapy?. *InterAction-The Journal of Solution Focus in Organisations*, 8(1), 7–30.

Sheridan, T. B. (1992). Musings on telepresence and virtual presence. *Presence: Teleoperators and Virtual Environments*, 1(1), 120–125.

Shiffrin, R. M. & Schneider, W. (1977). Controlled and automatic human information processing: II. Perceptual learning, automatic attending and a general theory. *Psychological Review*, 84(2), 127–190.

Short, J. A., Williams, E., & Christie, B. (1976). *The Social Psychology of Telecommunications*. London: Wiley.

Sicart, M. (2005). Game, player, ethics: A virtue ethics approach to computer games. *International Review of Information Ethics*, 4(12), 13–18.

Sicart, M. (2009). *The Ethics of Computer Games*. Cambridge, MA: MIT Press.

Sijtsema, J. J., Shoulberg, E. K., & Murray-Close, D. (2011). Physiological reactivity and different forms of aggression in girls: Moderating roles of rejection sensitivity and peer rejection. *Biological Psychology*, 86(3), 181–192.

Singer, J. & Vinson, N. G. (2002). Ethical issues in empirical studies of software engineering. *IEEE Transactions on Software Engineering*, 28(12), 1171–1180.

Singer, T., Seymour, B., O'Doherty, J., Kaube, H., Dolan, R. J., & Frith, C. D. (2004). Empathy for pain involves the affective but not sensory components of pain. *Science*, 303, 1157–1162.

Singh, I. & Kelleher, K. J. (2010). Neuroenhancement in young people: Proposal for research, policy, and clinical management. *AJOB Neuroscience*, 1(1), 3–16.

Siponen, M. & Iivari, J. (2006). Six design theories for IS security policies and guidelines. *Journal of the Association for Information Systems*, 7(7), 445–472.

Skulmowski, A., Bunge, A., Kaspar, K., & Pipa, G. (2014). Forced-choice Q19 decision-making in modified trolley dilemma situations: A virtual reality and eye tracking study. *Frontiers in Behavioral Neuroscience*, 8, 1–16.

Slagter van Tryon, P. J. & Bishop, M. J. (2012). Evaluating social connectedness online: The design and development of the Social Perceptions in Learning Contexts Instrument. *Distance Education*, 33(3), 347–364.

Slater, M. (2009). Place illusion and plausibility can lead to realistic behaviour in immersive virtual environments. *Philosophical Transactions of the Royal Society of London*, 364, 3549–3557.

Slater, M. (2018). Immersion and the illusion of presence in virtual reality. *British Journal of Psychology*, 109, 431–433.

Slater, M., Antley, A., Davison, A., Swapp, D., Guger, C., Barker, C., et al. (2006). A virtual reprise of the Stanley Milgram obedience experiments. *PLoS One*, 1(1), e39.

Slater, M. & Sanchez-Vives, M. V. (2016). Enhancing our lives with immersive virtual reality. *Frontiers in Robotics and AI*, 3(74), 1–9.

Slater, M., Spanlang, B., & Corominas, D. (2010). Simulating virtual environments within virtual environments as the basis for a psychophysics of presence. *ACM Transactions on Graphics (TOG)*, 29(4), 92.

Slater, M. & Wilbur, S. (1997). A framework for immersive virtual environments (FIVE): Speculations on the role of presence in virtual environments. *Presence: Teleoperators & Virtual Environments*, 6(6), 603–616.

Slevin, J. M. (2000). The Internet and Society. Cambridge, MA: Polity Press.

Slingerland, E. (2011). "Of what use are the Odes?" Cognitive science, virtue ethics, and early Confucian ethics. *Philosophy East and West*, 61 (1), 80–109.

Slonje, R. & Smith, P. K. (2008). Cyberbullying: Another main type of bullying?. *Scandinavian Journal of Psychology*, 49(2), 147–154.

Smart, P. R. (2012). The Web-extended mind. *Metaphilosophy*, 43(4), 446–463.

Smart, P. R. (2014). Embodiment, cognition and the World Wide Web. In L. A. Shapiro (ed.), *The Routledge Handbook of Embodied Cognition*. New York: Routledge.

Smart, P. R. (2018). Emerging digital technologies: Implications for extended conceptions of cognition and knowledge. In A. J. Carter, A Clark, J. Kallestrup, O. S. Palermos, & D. Pritchard (eds.), *Extended Epistemology*. Oxford: Oxford University Press.

Smart, P., Clowes, R., & Heersmink, R. (2017). Minds online: The interface between web science, cognitive science and the philosophy of mind. *Foundations and Trends in Web Science*, 6(1–2), 1–232.

Smart, P., Heersmink, R., & Clowes, R. W. (2017). The cognitive ecology of the Internet. In S. J. Cowley & F. Vallée-Tourangeau (eds.), *Cognition Beyond the Brain*, 2nd ed. (pp. 251–282). Cham: Springer.

Smart, P. & Shadbolt, N. (2018). The World Wide Web. In J. Chase & D. Coady (eds.), *Routledge Handbook of Applied Epistemology* (pp. 16–27). New York: Routledge.

Smids, J. (2012). The voluntariness of persuasive technology. In M. Bang & E. L. Ragnemalm (eds.), International Conference on Persuasive Technology (pp. 123–132). Berlin: Springer.

Smith, A. (1776). *An Inquiry into the Wealth of Nations*. London: Strahan and Cadell.

Smith, A. W. & Duggan, M. (2013). *Online Dating & Relationships*. Washington, DC: Pew Research Center.

Smith, P. K., Mahdavi, J., Carvalho, M., Fisher, S., Russell, S., & Tippett, N. (2008). Cyberbullying: Its nature and impact in secondary school pupils. *Journal of Child Psychology and Psychiatry*, 49, 376–385.

Smith, S., Ferguson, C., & Beaver, K. (2018). A longitudinal analysis of shooter games and their relationship with conduct disorder and self-reported delinquency. *International Journal of Law and Psychiatry*, 58, 48–53.

Sneddon, A. (2002). Towards externalist psychopathology. *Philosophical Psychology*, 15, 297–316.

Solberg, L. (2010). Data mining on Facebook: A free space for researchers or an IRB nightmare?. *University of Illinois Journal of Law, Technology & Policy*, 2, 311.

Southgate, E., Smith, S. P., & Scevak, J. (2017). Asking ethical questions in research using immersive virtual and augmented reality technologies with children and youth. In *2017 IEEE Virtual Reality (VR)* (pp. 12–18). Los Angeles: IEEE.

Spector, J. M. (2005). Innovations in instructional technology: An introduction to this volume. In J. M. Spector, C. Ohrazda, A. Van Schaack, & D. A. Wiley (eds.), *Innovations in Instructional Technology: Essays in Honor of M. David Merrill* (pp. xxxi–xxxvi). Mahwah, NJ: Lawrence Erlbaum Associates.

Spector, J. M. (2015). *Foundations of Educational Technology: Integrative Approaches and Interdisciplinary Perspectives*, 2nd ed. New York: Routledge.

Spector, J. M. (2016). Ethics in educational technology: Towards a framework for ethical decision making in and for the discipline. *Educational Technology Research and Development*, 64(5), 1003–1011.

Spector, J. M., Merrill, M. D., Elen, J., & Bishop, M. J. (eds.). (2013). *Handbook of Research on Educational Communications and Technology*, 4th ed. New York: Springer.

Spiegel, J. S. (2018). The ethics of virtual reality technology: Social hazards and public policy recommendations. Science and Engineering Ethics, 24(5), 1537–1550.

Spunt, R. P. & Lieberman, M. D. (2014). Automaticity, control, and the social brain. In J. Sherman, B. Gawronski, & Y. Trope (eds.), *Dual Process Theories of the Social Mind* (pp. 279–298). New York: Guildford Press.

Squire, K. (2006). From content to context: Videogames as designed experience. *Educational Researcher*, 35(8), 19–29.

Stallman, R. M. (1990). The GNU manifesto. In M. D. Ermann & M. S. Shauf (eds.), Computers, Ethics, & Society (pp. 153–162). New York: New York University Press.

Stamatellos, G. (2011a). Computer ethics and neoplatonic virtue: A reconsideration of cyberethics in the light of Plotinus' ethical theory. *International Journal of Cyber Ethics in Education*, 1(1), 1–11.

Stamatellos, G. (2011b). Virtue, privacy and self-determination: A Plotinian approach to the problem of information privacy. *International Journal of Cyber Ethics in Education*, 1(4), 35–41. https://doi.org/10.4018/ijcee.2011100104

Stanovich, K. E. (2009a). Distinguishing the reflective, algorithmic, and autonomous minds: Is it time for a tri-process theory. In J. Evans & K. Frankish (eds.), *Two Minds: Dual Processes and Beyond* (pp. 55–88). Oxford: Oxford University Press.

Stanovich, K. E. (2009b). *What Intelligence Tests Miss: The Psychology of Rational Thought*. New Haven, CT: Yale University Press.

Stanovich, K. E. (2010). *Rationality and the Reflective Mind*. Oxford: Oxford University Press.

Stanovich, K. E., West, R. F., & Toplak, M. E. (2011). The complexity of developmental predictions from dual process models. *Developmental Review*, 31(2–3), 103–118.

Starcevic, V., & Billieux, J. (2017). Does the construct of Internet addiction reflect a single entity or a spectrum of disorders?. *Clinical Neuropsychiatry*, 14(1), 5–10.

Statista. (2017a). *Number of Smartphone Users Worldwide from 2014 to 2020*. www.statista.com/statistics/330695/number-of-smartphone-users-worldwide/

Statista. (2017b). *Unit Sales of the Apple iPhone Worldwide from 2007 to 2017 (in millions)*. www.statista.com/statistics/276306/global-apple-iphone-sales-since-fiscal-year-2007/

Stauffer, S., Heath, M., Coyne, S., & Ferrin, S. (2012). High school teachers' perceptions of cyberbullying prevention and intervention strategies. *Psychology in the Schools*, 49, 352–367.

Stein, Z. & Fischer, K. W. (2011). Directions for mind, brain, and education: Methods, models, and morality. *Educational Philosophy & Theory*, 43(1), 56–66.

Sterelny, K. (2010). Minds: Extended or scaffolded?. *Phenomenology and the Cognitive Sciences*, 9(4), 465–481.

Stevenson, N. (2003). Cultural citizenship in the "cultural" society: A cosmopolitan approach. *Citizenship Studies*, 7, 331–348.

Stevenson, N. (2007). Cultural citizenship: Questions of consumerism, consumption and policy. In T. Edwards (ed.), *Cultural Theory: Classical and Contemporary Positions* (pp. 255–273). London: Sage.

Stewart, B. (2017). Twitter as method: Using Twitter as a tool to conduct research. In L. Sloan & A. Quan-Hasse (eds.), *The SAGE Handbook of Social Media Research Methods* (pp.251–265). London: Sage.

Strittmatter, E., Kaess, M., Parzer, P., Fischer, G., Carli, V., Hoven, C. W., et al. (2015). Pathological Internet use among adolescents: Comparing gamers and non-gamers. *Psychiatry Research*, 228(1), 128–135.

Stump, R. L., Gong, W., & Li, Z. (2008). Exploring the digital divide in mobile-phone adoption levels across countries: Do population socioeconomic traits operate in the same manner as their individual-level demographic counterparts?. *Journal of Macromarketing*, 28(4), 397–412.

Sudai, G. S. & Blumberg, D. J. (1999). U.S. Patent No. 5,950,200. Washington, DC: U.S. Patent and Trademark Office.

Suddath, C. (2014). The science behind the perfect dating profile. *Bloomberg BusinessWeek*, September 4. www.businessweek.com/articles/2014–09-04/mining-okcupids-data-reveals-how-we-date-now.

Suh, A. & Prophet, J. (2018). The state of immersive technology research: A literature analysis. *Computers in Human Behavior*, 86, 77–90.

Sum, S., Mathews, R. M., Hughes, I., & Campbell, A. (2008). Internet use and loneliness in older adults. *Cyberpsychology & Behavior*, 11(2), 208–211.

Sun, F. T., Kuo, C., Cheng, H. T., Buthpitiya, S., Collins, P., & Griss, M. (2010). Activity-aware mental stress detection using physiological sensors. In *International Conference on Mobile Computing, Applications, and Services* (pp. 282–301). Berlin: Springer.

Sutton, J. (2010). Exograms and interdisciplinarity: History, the extended mind, and the civilizing process. In R. Menary (ed.), *The Extended Mind* (pp. 189–225). Cambridge, MA: MIT Press.

Synofzik, M., Schatton, C., Giese, M., Wolf, J., Schöls, L., & Ilg, W. (2013). Videogame-based coordinative training can improve advanced, multisystemic early-onset ataxia. *Journal of Neurology*, 260(10), 2656–2658.

Tabibnia, G. & Lieberman, M. D. (2007). Fairness and cooperation are rewarding. *Annals of the New York Academy of Sciences*, 1118(1), 90–101.

Taddeo, M. & Floridi, L. (2016). The debate on the moral responsibilities of online service providers. *Science and Engineering Ethics*, 22(6), 1575–1603.

Taddeo, M. & Floridi, L. (2017). The moral responsibilities of online service providers. In M. Taddeo & L. Floridi (eds.), *The Responsibilities of Online Service Providers: Law, Governance and Technology Series*, vol. 31 (pp. 13–42). Cham: Springer.

Tavani, H. (2000). *Privacy and Security:* Internet Ethics. London: Macmillan.

Tavani, H. T. (2007). Philosophical theories of privacy: Implications for an adequate online privacy policy. *Metaphilosophy*, 38(1), 1–22.

Tavani, H. T. (2008a). Informational privacy: Concepts, theories, and controversies. In K. E. Himma & H. T. Tavani (eds.), *The Handbook of Information and Computer Ethics* (pp. 131–164). London: John Wiley & Sons.

Tavani, H. T. (2008b). Floridi's ontological theory of informational privacy: Some implications and challenges. *Ethics and Information Technology*, 10(2–3), 155–166.

Tavani, H. T. (2011). *Ethics and Technology: Controversies, Questions, and Strategies for Ethical Computing*. London: John Wiley & Sons.

Tavani, H. T. & Moor, J. H. (2001). Privacy protection, control of information, and privacy-enhancing technologies. *ACM SIGCAS Computers and Society*, 31 (1), 6–11.

Tavinor, G. (2007). Towards an ethics of video gaming. Paper presented at the 2007 Conference on Future Play, Toronto, Canada, November 15–17.

Tavinor, G. (2009). BioShock and the art of rapture. *Philosophy and Literature*, 33 (1), 91–106.

Thege, B. K., Woodin, E. M., Hodgins, D. C., & Williams, R. J. (2015). Natural course of behavioral addictions: A 5-year longitudinal study. *BMC psychiatry*, 15 (1), 1–14.

Thomson, J. J. (1985). The Trolley Problem. The Yale Law Journal, 94(6), 1395–1415.

Tieri, G., Morone, G., Paolucci, S., & Iosa, M. (2018). Virtual reality in cognitive and motor rehabilitation: Facts, fiction and fallacies. *Expert Review of Medical Devices*, 15(2), 107–117.

Tokunaga, R. S. (2010). Following you home from school: A critical review and synthesis of research on cyberbullying victimization. *Computers in Human Behavior*, 26(3), 277–287.

Tononi, G. (2008). Consciousness as integrated information: A provisional Manifesto. *Biological Bulletin*, 215, 216–242.

Tononi, G. & Koch, C. (2008). The neural correlate of consciousness: An update. *Annals of the New York Academy of Sciences*, 1124, 239–261.

Torous, J. & Roberts, L. W. (2017). The ethical use of mobile health technology in clinical psychiatry. *The Journal of Nervous and Mental Disease*, 205(1), 4–8.

Townsend, L., & Wallace, C. (2016). *Social Media Research: A Guide to Ethics.* www.dotrural.ac.uk/socialmediaresearchethics.pdf

Tranel, D. & Damasio, A. R. (1985). Knowledge without awareness: An autonomic index of facial recognition by prosopagnosics. *Science*, 228(4706), 1453–1454.

Trost, Z. & Parsons, T. D. (2014). Beyond distraction: Virtual reality graded exposure therapy as treatment for pain-related fear and disability in chronic pain. *Journal of Applied Biobehavioral Research*, 19, 106–126.

Tufekci, Z. (2015). Algorithmic harms beyond Facebook and Google: Emergent challenges of computational agency. *Journal on Telecommunications & High Technology Law*, 13, 203–217.

Turkle, S. (2011). *Life on the Screen.* New York: Simon and Schuster.

Turner, B. S. (2001). Outline of a general theory of cultural citizenship. In N. Stevenson (ed.), *Culture and Citizenship* (pp. 11–32). London: Sage.

Turner, D. C. & Sahakian, B. J. (2006). Neuroethics of cognitive enhancements. *BioSocieties*, 1(1), 113–123.

Uddin, L. Q., Iacoboni, M., Lange, C., & Keenan, J. P. (2007). The self and social cognition: The role of cortical midline structures and mirror neurons. *Trends in Cognitive Sciences*, 11(4), 153–157.

Valentine, A. & Kurczek, J. (2016). "Social" neuroscience: Leveraging social media to increase student engagement and public understanding of neuroscience. *Journal of Undergraduate Neuroscience Education*, 15(1), A94.

Vallor, S. (2010). Social networking technology and the virtues. *Ethics and Information Technology*, 12(2), 157–170.

Van Berlo, A. (2002). Smart home technology: Have older people paved the way. *Gerontechnology*, 2(1), 77–87.

van Deursen, A. J. & van Dijk, J. A. (2014). The digital divide shifts to differences in usage. *New Media & Society*, 16(3), 507e526.

Van Dyk, L. (2014). A review of telehealth service implementation frameworks. *International Journal of Environmental Research and Public Health*, *11*(2), 1279–1298.

Van Hoof, J., Demiris, G., & Wouters, E. J. (eds.). (2017). *Handbook of Smart Homes, Health Care and Well-Being*. Springer.

Van Horn, J. D., Irimia, A., Torgerson, C. M., Chambers, M. C., Kikinis, R., & Toga, A. W. (2012). Mapping connectivity damage in the case of Phineas Gage. *PLoS One*, *7*(5), e37454.

Van Norden, B. W. (2003). Virtue ethics and Confucianism. Comparative Approaches to Chinese Philosophy, 23, 99–121.

Ventriglio, A. & Bhugra, D. (2015). Descartes' dogma and damage to Western psychiatry. *Epidemiology and Psychiatric Sciences*, *24*(5), 368–370.

Venturini, E. & Parsons, T. D. (2018). Virtual environments for assessment of social exclusion in autism: A systematic review. *Journal of Autism and Developmental Disorders*, *5*(4), 408–421.

Venturini, E., Riva, P., Serpetti, F., Romero, L., Pallavincini, F., Mantovani, F., . . . Parsons, T. D. (2016). A comparison of 3D versus 2D virtual environments on the feelings of social exclusion, inclusion and over-inclusion. *Annual Review of CyberTherapy and Telemedicine*, 14, 89–94.

Verbeek, P.-P. (2005). *What Things Do: Philosophical Reflections on Technology, Agency, and Design* (trans. R.P. Crease). University Park: Pennsylvania State University Press.

Verbeek, P.-P. (2006). Persuasive technology and moral responsibility toward an ethical framework for persuasive technologies. *Persuasive*, 6, 1–15.

Verbeek, P.-P. (2009). Ambient intelligence and persuasive technology: The blurring boundaries between human and technology. NanoEthics, *3*(3), 231–242.

Verbeek, P.-P. (2011). *Moralizing Technology: Understanding and Designing the Morality of Things*. Chicago: University of Chicago Press.

Verbeek, P.-P. (2012). Expanding mediation theory. *Foundations of Science*, *17*(4), 391–395.

Vicente, M. R. & Lopez, A. J. (2010). A multidimensional analysis of the disability digital divide: Some evidence for Internet use. *The Information Society*, *26*(1), 48–64.

Vines, J., McNaney, R., Holden, A., Poliakov, I., Wright, P., & Olivier, P. (2016). Our year with the glass: Expectations, letdowns and ethical dilemmas of technology trials with vulnerable people. *Interacting with Computers*, *29*(1), 27–44.

Vingilis, E., Seeley, J., Wiesenthal, D. L., Wickens, C. M., Fischer, P., & Mann, R. E. (2013). Street racing video games and risk-taking driving: An Internet survey of automobile enthusiasts. *Accident Analysis & Prevention*, 50, 1–7.

Vitak, J. (2017). Facebook as a research tool in the social and computer sciences. In L. Sloan & A. Quan-Hasse (eds.), *The SAGE Handbook of Social Media Research Methods* (pp. 627–644). London: Sage.

Von Schomberg, R. (2014). The quest for the "right" impacts of science and technology: A framework for responsible research and innovation. In L. van den Hoven, N. Doorn, T. Swierstra, B. J. Koops, & H. Romijn (eds.), *Responsible Innovation 1: Innovative Solutions for Global Issues* (pp. 33–50). Dordrecht: Springer.

Vroman, K. G., Arthanat, S., & Lysack, C. (2015). "Who over 65 is online?" Older adults' dispositions toward information communication technology. *Computers in Human Behavior*, 43, 156–166.

Waddington, D. (2007). Locating the wrongness in ultra-violent video games. *Ethics and Information Technology*, 9, 121–128.

Wagner, N., Hassanein, K., & Head, M. (2010). Computer use by older adults: A multi-disciplinary review. *Computers in Human Behavior*, 26(5), 870–882.

Wai-Ying, W. (2001). Confucian ethics and virtue ethics. *Journal of Chinese philosophy*, 28(3), 285–300.

Walaszek, A. (2009). Clinical ethics issues in geriatric psychiatry. *Psychiatric Clinics*, 32(2), 343–359.

Wang, Y., Mathews, V. P., Kalnin, A. J., Mosier, K. M., Dunn, D. W., Saykin, A. J., & Kronenberger, W. G. (2009). Short term exposure to a violent video game induces changes in frontolimbic circuitry in adolescents. *Brain Imaging and Behavior*, 3(1), 38–50.

Ward, T. (2009). The extended mind theory of cognitive distortions in sex offenders. *Journal of Sexual Aggression*, 15(3), 247–259.

Ward, T. & Casey, A. (2010). Extending the mind into the world: A new theory of cognitive distortions in sex offenders. *Aggression and Violent Behavior*, 15(1), 49–58.

Waskul, D. (1996). Considering the electronic participant: Some polemical observations on the ethics of on-line research. *The Information Society*, 12 (2), 129–140.

Waskul, D. & Douglass, M. (1996). Considering the electronic participant: Some polemical observations on the ethics of online research. *The Information Society: An International Journal*, 12(2), 129–139.

Waterworth, J. A. & Riva, G. (2014). *Feeling Present in the Physical World and in Computer-Mediated Environments*. Basingstoke: Palgrave Macmillan.

Weber, M. (1903/1958). *The Protestant Work Ethic and the Spirit of Capitalism* (trans. T. Parsons). New York: Scribner.

Weber, R., Ritterfeld, U., & Mathiak, K. (2006). Does playing violent video games induce aggression? Empirical evidence of a functional magnetic resonance imaging study. *Media Psychology*, 8(1), 39–60.

Wesselmann, E. D., Wirth, J. H., Mroczek, D. K., & Williams, K. D. (2012). Dial a feeling: Detecting moderation of affect decline during ostracism. *Personality and Individual Differences*, 53, 580–586.

Westerman, D., Spence, P. R., & Van Der Heide, B. (2014). Social media as information source: Recency of updates and credibility of information. *Journal of Computer-Mediated Communication*, 19(2), 171–183.

Westin, A. F. & Ruebhausen, O. M. (1967). Privacy and Freedom, Vol. 1. New York: Atheneum.

Whalley, L. J. (1995). Ethical issues in the application of virtual reality to medicine. *Computers in Biology and Medicine*, 25(2), 107–114.

Wheeler, M. (2011). Thinking beyond the brain: Educating and building, from the standpoint of extended cognition. Computational Culture, 1. http://computa tionalculture.net/beyond-the-brain/

Widdershoven, G. A. (1998). Ethics and gerontechnology: A plea for integration. *Studies in Health Technology and Informatics*, 74, 105–114.

Wilens, T. E., Adler, L. A., Adams, J., Sgambati, S., Rotrosen, J., Sawtelle, R., et al. (2008). Misuse and diversion of stimulants prescribed for ADHD: A systematic review of the literature. *Journal of the American Academy of Child & Adolescent Psychiatry*, 47(1), 21–31.

Williams, B. (1985). *Ethics and the Limits of Philosophy*. London: Routledge.

Williams, K. D. (2007). Ostracism. *Annual Review of Psychology*, 58, 425–452.

Wilson, C. & Dunn, A. (2011). Digital media in the Egyptian revolution: Descriptive analysis from the Tahrir Data sets. *International Journal of Communication*, 5, 1248–1272.

Wilson, F. (2003). Can compute, won't compute: Women's participation in the culture of computing. *New Technology, Work and Employment*, 18(2), 127–142.

Wilson, R. & Clark, A. (2009). How to situate cognition: Letting nature take its course. In P. Robbins & M. Aydede (eds.), *The Cambridge Handbook of Situated Cognition* (pp.55–77). Cambridge: Cambridge University Press.

Wilson, R. E., Gosling, S. D., & Graham, L. T. (2012). A review of Facebook research in the social sciences. *Perspectives on Psychological Science*, 7, 203–220.

Wilson, R. & Lenart, B. (2015). Extended mind and identity. In J. Clausen & N. Levy (eds.), *Handbook of Neuroethics* (pp. 423–439). New York: Springer.

Wirth, J. H., Sacco, D. F., Hugenberg, K., & Williams, K. D. (2010). Eye Q20 gaze as relational evaluation: Averted eye gaze leads to feelings of ostracism and relational devaluation. *Personality and Social Psychology Bulletin*, 36, 869–882.

Witmer, B. G. & Singer, M. J. (1998). Measuring presence in virtual environments: A presence questionnaire. *Presence*, 7(3), 225–240.

Wood, M. (2014). OKCupid plays with love in user experiments, *New York Times*, July 28. www.nytimes.com/2014/07/29/technology/okcupid-publishes-findings -of-user-experiments.html.

Woodhead, M. & Faulkner, D. (2000). Subjects, objects or participants? Dilemmas of psychological research with children. In P. Christensen & A. James (eds.), *Research with Children: Perspectives and Practices* (pp.10–39). London: Falmer Press.

World Bank. (2016). World Development Report 2016: Digital Dividends. World Bank, Washington, DC.

World Health Organization. (2008). *Towards the development of an mHealth strategy: A literature review*. Geneva: World Health Organization.

World Health Organization. (2015). *Public Health Implications of Excessive Use of the Internet, Computers, Smartphones and Similar Electronic Devices: Meeting Report*, Main Meeting Hall, Foundation for Promotion of Cancer Research, National Cancer Research Centre, Tokyo, Japan, August 27–29, 2014.

World Medical Association. (1964). World Medical Association Declaration of Helsinki – Ethical principles for medical research involving human subjects. World Medical Association, Ferney-Voltaire, France.

Wortham, J. (2009). Mobile Internet use shrinks digital divide. *New York Times*, 22 July, www.bits.blogs.nytimes.com.

Wiederhold, B. K. (2015). Brain interventions and neuroethics must coexist peacefully. *Cyberpsychology, Behavior, and Social Networking*, 18, 57–58.

Williams, B. (2011). *Ethics and the Limits of Philosophy*. Taylor & Francis.

Windmann, S., Kirsch, P., Mier, D., Stark, R., Walter, B., Güntürkün, O., et al. (2006). On framing effects in decision making: Linking lateral versus medial orbitofrontal cortex activation to choice outcome processing. *Journal of Cognitive Neuroscience*, 18, 1198–1211.

Winston, M. & Edelbach, R. (2011). *Society, Ethics, and Technology*. Belmont, CA: Wadsworth Publishing.

Wise, K., Alhabash, S., & Park, H. (2010). Emotional responses during social information seeking on Facebook. *Cyberpsychology, Behavior, and Social Networking*, 13(5), 555–562.

Wittgenstein, L. (1947/1980a). *Remarks on the Philosophy of Psychology*. Vol. 1 (ed. G. E. M. Anscombe & G. H. von Wright, trans. G. E. M. Anscombe). Oxford: Blackwell.

Wittgenstein, L. (1947/1980b). *Remarks on the Philosophy of Psychology*. Vol. 2. (ed. G. H. von Wright & H. Nyma, trans. C. G. Luckhardt & M. A. E. Aeu). Oxford: Blackwell.

Wittgenstein, L. (1953/2009). *Philosophical Investigations*, rev. 4th ed. (trans. G. E. M. Anscombe, P. M. S. Hacker, & J. Schulte). Malden, MA: Wiley.

Wittgenstein, L. (1958). *Blue and Brown Books*. New York: Harper & Row.

Wittgenstein, L. (1969). *On Certainty* (trans. D. Paul & G. E. M. Anscombe). Oxford: Basil Blackwell.

Wittgenstein, L. (1977/1998). *Culture and Value* (ed. Georg Henrik von Wright), rev. ed. London: Wiley-Blackwell.

World Medical Association. (1964). World Medical Association Declaration of Helsinki – Ethical principles for medical research involving human subjects. World Medical Association, Ferney-Voltaire, France.

Wu, D., Parsons, T. D., Mower, E., & Narayanan, S. (2010). Speech emotion estimation in 3D space. In *2010 IEEE International Conference on Multimedia and Expo (ICME)* (pp. 737–742). Singapore: IEEE.

Wu, D., Parsons, T. D., & Narayanan, S. S. (2010). Acoustic Feature Analysis in Speech Emotion Primitives Estimation. Paper presented at the Proceedings of InterSpeech, Makuhari, Japan, September 26–30.

Xu, X., Venkatesh, V., Tam, K. Y., & Hong, S. J. (2010). Model of migration and use of platforms: Role of hierarchy, current generation, and complementarities in consumer settings. *Management Science*, 56(8), 1304–1323.

Ybarra, M. L., Huesmann, L. R., Korchmaros, J. D., & Reisner, S. L. (2014). Cross-sectional associations between violent video and computer game playing and weapon carrying in a national cohort of children. *Aggressive Behavior*, 40(4), 345–358.

Ybarra, M. L. & Mitchell, K. J. (2004). Youth engaging in online harassment: Associations with caregiver–child relationships, Internet use, and personal characteristics. *Journal of Adolescence*, 27, 319–336.

Ybarra, M. L., Mitchell, K. J., Wolak, J., & Finkelhor, D. (2006). Examining characteristics and associated distress related to Internet harassment: Findings from the Second Youth Internet Safety Survey. *Pediatrics*, 118(4), e1169–e1177.

Yeaman, A. R. J. (2016). Competence and circumstance. *TechTrends*, 60, 195–196.

Yellowlees, P. M., Holloway, K. M., & Parish, M. B. (2012). Therapy in virtual environments: Clinical and ethical issues. *Telemedicine and e-Health*, 18(7), 558–564.

Yen, J. Y., Ko, C. H., Yen, C. F., Wu, H. Y., & Yang, M. J. (2007). The comorbid psychiatric symptoms of Internet addiction: Attention deficit and hyperactivity disorder (ADHD), depression, social phobia, and hostility. *Journal of Adolescent Health*, 41(1), 93–98.

Yoder, K. & Decety, J. (2014). The good, the bad, and the just: Justice sensitivity predicts neural response during moral evaluation of actions performed by others. *Journal of Neuroscience*, 34(12), 4161–4166.

Yoder, K. J. & Decety, J. (2018). The neuroscience of morality and social decision-making. *Psychology, Crime & Law*, 24(3), 279–295.

Young, K. (2010). Policies and procedures to manage employee Internet abuse. *Computers in Human Behavior*, 26, 1467–1471.

Young, L., Cushman, F., Hauser, M., & Sax, R. (2007). The neural basis of the interaction between theory of mind and moral judgment. *Proceedings of the National Academy of Sciences of the United States of America*, 104(20), 8235–8240.

Yu, J. (2013). *The Ethics of Confucius and Aristotle: Mirrors of Virtue*, Vol. 7. New York: Routledge.

Zadro, L., Williams, K. D., & Richardson, R. (2004). How low can you go? Ostracism by a computer lowers belonging, control, self-esteem and meaningful existence. *Journal of Experimental Social Psychology*, 40, 560–567.

Zauchner, S., Korunka, C., Weiss, A., & Kafka-Lützow, A. (2000). Gender-related effects of information technology implementation. *Gender, Work & Organization*, 7(2), 119–132.

Zeki, S. (2002). Neural concept formation and art: Dante, Michelangelo, Wagner. *Journal of Consciousness Studies*, 9, 53–76.

Zeller, F. (2017). Analyzing social media data and other data sources: A methodological overview. In L. Sloan & A. Quan-Hasse (eds.), *The SAGE Handbook of Social Media Research Methods* (pp.386–404). London: Sage.

Zeng, Z., Pantic, M., Roisman, G. I., & Huang, T. S. (2009). A survey of affect recognition methods: Audio, visual, and spontaneous expressions. *IEEE Transactions on Pattern Analysis and Machine Intelligence*, 31(1), 39–58.

Zhao, D. & Rosson, M. B. (2009). How and why people Twitter: The role that micro-blogging plays in informal communication at work. In *Proceedings of the*

ACM 2009 International Conference on Supporting Group Work (pp.243–252). Florida: ACM.

Zhang, M. (2015). Internet use that reproduces educational inequalities: Evidence from big data. *Computers & Education*, 86, 212–223.

Zillien, N. & Hargittai, E. (2009). Digital distinction: Status-specific types of internet usage. *Social Science Quarterly*, 90(2), 274–291.

Zimmer, M. (2010). "But the data is already public": On the ethics of research in Facebook. *Ethics and Information Technology*, 12(4), 313–325.

Zur, O. (2008). The Google factor: Therapists' self-disclosure in the age of the Internet. *Independent Practitioner*, 28(2), 83–85.

Zwijsen, S. A., Niemeijer, A. R., & Hertogh, C. M. (2011). Ethics of using assistive technology in the care for community-dwelling elderly people: An overview of the literature. *Aging & Mental Health*, 15(4), 419–427.

Zwilling, M. (2013). How many more online dating sites do we need? *Forbes*, March 1.

Zwolinski, J. (2012). Psychological and neuroendocrine reactivity to ostracism. *Aggressive Behavior*, 38, 108–125.

Author Index

Subject Index